1866-1991

125th

ANNIVERSARY

OTHER BOOKS BY JAY CONRAD LEVINSON

*The Most Important $1.00 Book Ever Written*

*Secrets of Successful Free-Lancing*

*San Francisco: An Unusual Guide to Unusual Shopping*
  (with John Bear and Pat Levinson)

*Earning Money Without a Job* (Revised for the '90s)

*Small Business Savvy*

*An Earthling's Guide to Satellite TV*

*Guerrilla Marketing*

*150 Secrets of Successful Weight Loss*
  (with Michael Lavin and Michael Rokeach, M.D.)

*Quit Your Job!*

*Guerrilla Marketing Attack*

*The Ninety-Minute Hour*

*Guerrilla Marketing Weapons*

*Guerrilla Financing* (with Bruce Blechman)

*Guerrilla Selling* (with Bill Gallagher
  and Orvel Ray Wilson)

# 555

## *ways to earn*

## *extra money*

### *Revised for the '90s*

## Jay Conrad Levinson

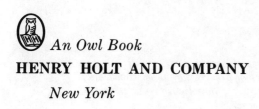

*An Owl Book*
**HENRY HOLT AND COMPANY**
*New York*

Published by Henry Holt and Company, Inc.,
115 West 18th Street, New York, New York 10011.
Published in Canada by Fitzhenry & Whiteside Limited,
195 Allstate Parkway, Markham, Ontario L3R 4T8.

Library of Congress Cataloging-in-Publication Data
Levinson, Jay Conrad.
555 ways to earn extra money : revised for the '90s / Jay Conrad
Levinson. — Rev. ed.
    p.  cm.
"An Owl book."
Includes bibliographical references and index.
1. Part-time employment.    2. Supplementary employment.
3. Self-employed.    I. Title.    II. Title: Five hundred and
fifty-five ways to earn extra money.
HD5110.L48    1991                                    90-29063
658.02'2—dc20                                              CIP

ISBN 0–8050–1459–4

Henry Holt books are available at special discounts
for bulk purchases for sales promotions, premiums,
fund-raising, or educational use. Special editions
or book excerpts can also be created to specification.
For details contact:
Special Sales Director, Henry Holt and Company, Inc.,
115 West 18th Street, New York, New York 10011.

Revised Edition—1991

Designed by Robert Bull

Printed in the United States of America
Recognizing the importance of preserving the written word,
Henry Holt and Company, Inc., by policy, prints all of its
first editions on acid-free paper. ∞

10  9  8  7  6  5  4  3  2

# CONTENTS

# ACKNOWLEDGMENTS

Many people are responsible for the creation of a book, although only the author is singled out for mention on the cover. Donald Hutter, my original editor at Holt, also belongs in the spotlight, for he helped share the book and he masterminded the flow, the content, and the soul of the ideas within. David Stanford also deserves a pat on the back, a medal on the chest, and a compliment on this page for his combination of brilliant, painstaking, and witty editing. Michael Larsen and Elizabeth Pomada, my high-determination, high-imagination literary agents, suggested the book to me in the first place, then coddled and coaxed it into your hands. Bill Shear has worked his tail off to make my name and my books a household name in at least my own household. Myrette Macpherson helped me with the complex mechanical task of updating and pasting the updates in the right place on the right pages. Thank heavens Myrette did that and not me. My mother, Sadelle Kovoloff, sent me article after article as fodder for this book (Mom, you can stop now). My kid, Amy, has lived by the principles in this book and can probably afford to buy her own Jeep next time. I thank my beautiful, sexy, and talented wife, Patsy, for more than the usual amount of encouragement, suggestions, patience, inspiration, hugging, and faith. And finally, I thank the brave, brave people who are blazing trails into the new economic system of which I write, giving wings to my words. Without them, there would be no such book, no such earning ideas, no such insight into the freedom we all possess to shape our own destinies and bloom into our own flowers.

J. C. L.
Marin County, California

# 555

*ways to earn
extra money*

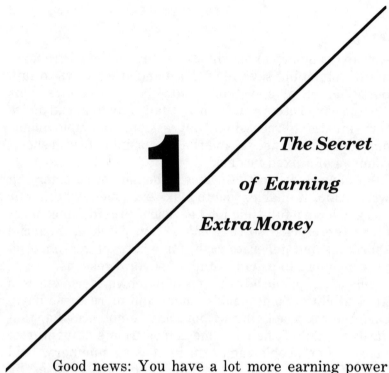

# 1 The Secret of Earning Extra Money

Good news: You have a lot more earning power than you think.

You have the basic human ability to earn money by using any of a number of skills. But the chances are, you're using only one of those skills, exercising a mere fraction of your earning power.

This book has been written to activate all of your earning power. By tapping more of your skills and talents, you can earn more money—lots and lots of it. Along with that money, you'll gain a new sense of self-worth, a new way of perceiving the concept of work, and a more enlightened view of economic survival in today's world, not to mention tomorrow's world.

You're about to learn of 555 ways to earn extra money: ingenious ways, obvious ways, new ways, proven ways, surefire ways, outrageous ways to put your earning power into high gear.

But these pages offer you far more than 555 ways to

earn extra money. You will also be presented with a manner of combining several of those and other ways to support yourself by a system of _patchwork economics_. This system can protect you from virtually any financial disaster: inflation, recession, depression, unemployment, emergency cash needs, and the increasingly brutal shortcomings of a fixed income.

Patchwork economics seems to be part of an emerging work ethic. It enables you to make ends meet whether or not you have a full-time job because it provides income to fill in the cracks, so to speak ... to patch up financial shortages and generate cash, for whatever reason. And most people can usually think of several reasons.

One of the prime advantages of patchwork economics is its flexibility. Some people, more and more these days, earn their entire living without any semblance of a standard job. All of their income comes from side ventures. Many other people, again in increasing numbers, hold down full-time jobs but supplement their salaries by moonlighting or having additional sources of income. That's what I mean by the flexibility of patchwork economics: it can serve as the basis for all of your income or part of your income. You choose.

If you now have a full-time job, you'll be pleased to learn that patchwork economics can easily be tailored to fit your exact work and life situation. It allows you to take on an earning endeavor (or endeavors) that can easily be accomplished in your spare time, making little if any demands upon your work time. It can also provide income without diverting much of the energy you devote toward fulfilling your family and social responsibilities.

That's what I mean about filling in the cracks. Instead of requiring you to work set hours and set days, patchwork economics allows you to work only when it is convenient and reasonable for you to work. Instead of providing you with a set income, patchwork economics offers you the benefit of an adaptable income. In fact, patchwork economics might be termed adaptable economics, for it suggests that you adapt your work time to your life situation. The established system of economics suggests the exact opposite.

Another characteristic of patchwork economics is that it enables you to fit into your community more fully and directly. As you look over the 555 methods of earning extra money you'll sense a need for many of them right where you live. You'll also begin to recognize the opportunities that exist in your community. Wonderful. That's probably how patchwork economics came about in the first place.

Even as we build more freeways and send more probes into space, we seem to be getting more community oriented. Perhaps that's because of better communications within the community in the form of neighborhood papers and cable TV. Maybe it's because of the energy crisis. And possibly it's merely a return to the community spirit that was part of early America. In all likelihood, it is a combination of these factors.

And now that you are aware of this, you can begin to adjust your earning antennae to the needs and opportunities of your community. Do earning opportunities exist in your community, your neighborhood, your area? Are they being met? Ask these questions silently to yourself as you read through the 555 earning ideas in this book.

At this point, I want to insert a thought into your mind. I do not expect you to embrace this thought immediately, for it is probably at odds with the teachings directed at you since birth.

The thought that I now direct to your deeper, inner mind, your unconscious mind, is that *it is possible to earn money without a job.*

I hope you understand that I am talking about earning

money without a *job*, and not earning money without *working*. You will have to work, but you need not work within the usual structure of a job. Instead, I want to suggest to your unconscious mind that you can work and earn money for that work without regular employment, and gain a vast amount of freedom while you're at it.

Jobless earning provides you with the freedom to set your own income, your own responsibilities, your own hours, the days you work, the clothes you wear, and your working conditions.

I have been without a job for twenty years now, yet I earn considerably more than I did with a job, and I do it working only three days a week. I take at least four vacations a year. I work from my own home. I love every aspect of my work. Yet, from a technical standpoint, I have no job.

Because I appreciate the fringe benefits of a job—that is, of full-time employment—I have given myself those very same fringe benefits: health insurance, life insurance, disability insurance, paid vacations, Christmas bonus, profit sharing, pension plan, the works. Of course those goodies don't come free; I have to set aside a portion of my income to pay for them.

The new work ethic that will become the norm of the future, replacing the Puritan work ethic practiced by our parents and grandparents (and properly so), will offer lifetimes tempered by a balance of work and leisure. Emphasis will be on personal fulfillment and freedom.

Right now, we believe that slavery no longer exists. But many people are wage slaves, shackled by employers into five-day-a-week, nine-to-five jobs. This book offers you a way out of that condition of servitude. This book provides you with the information necessary to fill your life with freedom. Prior to writing this book, I wrote one called *Earning Money Without a Job.* In that volume, I plumped for a life of freedom without suggesting income supplementation to those with full-time jobs.

Now I wish to point out that there is a difference between patchwork economics as discussed in this book, and *modular economics* as discussed in *Earning Money Without a Job.*

Patchwork economics suggests that you develop income sources to fill the gaps in your own income, in your own free time, in your own community.

Modular economics suggests that you become a part of a larger system. If you are a carpenter, modular economics would urge you to connect up in a loose alliance with an electrician, a mason, a house painter, a plumber, an architect, a gardener, a roofer, a paper hanger, a glazier. By connecting up with these related independent contractors, you can not only offer a far wider range of services yourself, but you also gain the benefit of far more referral business. By becoming part of a modular system, you can offer all the services of a giant contracting firm, but maintain your independence at the same time. To be sure, more people will be attracted to you if you offer a range of services than if you offer carpentry and nothing else. And it's a wonderful feeling when you obtain business because it was referred to you by a fellow modular economist. And far less expensive than advertising, I can assure you.

*This* book is directed to people who are employed full-time, part-time, and no time. Although I believe it is possible to maintain a full-time job and earn extra money, my heart is in the kind of life in which I call all the shots, a life of jobless earning.

I do it. I love it. I recommend it. But I understand that such a life is not for everyone. Therefore, in addition to the economics of freedom to which I am fervently devoted, I recognize the need for full-time employment, supplemented by extra income.

It's not all that easy to earn extra money. But it can be done. You can do it as thousands before you have done it. Every day, more and more people are finding it absolutely necessary to earn extra money, then surprising themselves with their innate ability to earn it without taking on a second job.

Is there a secret to earning extra money? You bet your bankbook there is. The secret: Develop multiple sources of income. Don't lose sight of that secret or you'll lose your ability to succeed at patchwork economics.

If you're like most people, you have one source of income—your paycheck. Well, now you can keep that source, and add four more sources of income to it. Or, you could even give up your paycheck and replace it with ten different sources of income. I haven't received a paycheck in two decades, yet I support a lofty life-style. How do I do it? With nine separate sources of income. Sometimes it's five sources, other times it's twelve sources. But right now—today—it's nine sources.

I earn money as an advertising consultant, as a lecturer and seminar leader, as an author, as a syndicated columnist, as a TV producer, as the owner of a mail-order business, as a publisher, and as a counselor to budding entrepreneurs. None of these endeavors could individually handle the tab for my living expenses. But together they do a very nice job of it, thank you.

Now I ought to warn you that your conscious mind may not be ready to assimilate all of the information it will be receiving as you read this book. But your unconscious mind will assimilate, understand, and take great comfort in the concept of patchwork economics. And before too long, your unconscious will motivate your conscious to put some extra joy into your bank account. Better, your conscious mind will know exactly how to go about it.

Starting right now, you'd be doing your potential income a good turn if you began to engage in survival thinking—an awareness of the ways people are earning money these days other than by standard jobs. By developing this survival thinking, you'll be able to spot 555 *more* ways to earn extra money, beyond those listed in this book.

You've got to be on the active lookout for these ways. Many of them probably don't even exist right now. But new ways of earning money are being developed all the time. You can discover them by scouring newspapers and opportunity magazines, especially the advertisements, including the classifieds. Read the Yellow Pages, actually read them cover to cover. You'll hardly find the plot for a movie, but you will find a wealth of earning ideas.

Be clear on this: You'll need to breathe life into some of these ideas. To take advantage of the evolutionary splendors of patchwork economics, you've got to have your own earning endeavor or endeavors, aside from your salaried job.

With such endeavors, you will not only have more money, you'll also have more freedom. And freedom is a lot more elusive than the mighty dollar bill. If you are willing to face the economic facts, you and your family can have several independent sources of income. Don't forget, I'm not talking about thousands and thousands of dollars. I mean a few sources of a few hundred extra dollars per month.

A few sources of a few hundred extra dollars per month seem to have an enchanting way of becoming thousands and thousands. But your aim needn't be all that high. Rather than a high aim, you merely need several targets.

This book offers you 555 targets. I've divided these 555 earning endeavors into four major categories, but actually many of the ideas fit into more than one category.

The first category, earning extra money because you're artistic, has five subcategories. The second category, earning extra money because you're oriented to people, has its own three subcategories. The third category, earning extra money because you're oriented to things, is divided into seven distinct sections. And the fourth category, earning extra money because you're oriented to ideas, has four subcategories (and overlaps some of the other categories, particularly people and things).

Understand, too, that some of the earning endeavors I've explored will provide you with money only while you do the actual work, and will cease bringing in the dollars when you stop doing the work. Other earning endeavors not only provide you with money while you're working at them, but also have the wondrous ability to be sold at a later date, just as you'd sell a business.

With many of the earning opportunities, which from here on we'll call *earnways*, you can get the work going, keep it going, and keep everything you make—except for taxes. And you'll have a strong say in how much you make, based upon your ability to line up new customers and devote your time to the work.

Many other earnways enable you to delegate the work to others. You get to keep a fair-sized piece of the action, but you'll have to relinquish a good-sized piece to someone else, or to several other people. That's only fair.

Still other earnways require a lot of work out front, then virtually no work later. Finally, some sources of income are so easy to develop and get going, they become almost automatic. These include certain mail-order businesses, proven earning winners from the past, and other easily systematized earning endeavors.

You can judge the relationship you will have with each earnway by recognizing the degree of skill involved. If the endeavor requires a difficult skill, you'll probably have to do the work yourself. If the endeavor calls for some skill, it may in time be simple to line up others to do it for you. If the earnway requires hardly any special skill but a whole lot of work in the very beginning, consider doing it yourself at first, then delegating it.

When I consider the last type of situation, I summon to mind the woman who arranged for sandwich delivery to office workers in her building. At first, she worked at a frantic pace, arranging with a cafeteria to make the sandwiches and give her a volume discount. Then, she posted bulletins in all the offices of her building, announcing the availability of sandwiches, listing their prices, and mentioning the fact that they could be delivered right to the desk of the worker. Then, she searched until she finally contracted with a person to pick up the sandwiches from the cafeteria and deliver them to the workers, collecting the money and giving it (the meatier share) to her.

All that took about two weeks of hard work. But for the seven years since she started the business, she's done virtually nothing to keep it going, and she's been pocketing about $25 per day in profits. Hard work first; hard cash later. Hope you can work out something as glorious.

The way you consider the 555 earning endeavors in this book should be influenced by whether or not you currently have a job. If you don't have a job, seriously consider doing a lot of the work yourself and keeping all the marbles. If you are already employed on a full-time basis, then think about delegating the work to others once you've got the thing going.

But whatever you do, don't pick out the endeavor that feels best to you and do *only* that. The secret to earning extra money and feeling secure about it is to develop *multiple* sources of income. So pick out the twenty earnways that feel right to you, then do the ten that feel most right.

Even if half of the ten fail, which is highly unlikely if you go about them in the right way, you'll still be left with five new sources of income. And five sources of income are better than money in the bank.

Better than money in the bank? Well, more inflation-

proof. Longer-lasting. More capable of growing. Easier
to sell at an attractive profit. More self-regenerating.
And a lot more fun.

You see, patchwork economics is a very sensible way of
living. And not only is it sensible, it is also necessary
now. It's compatible with employment or unemployment.
It's available to everyone, and I do mean everyone—
young, old, educated, uneducated, male, female, healthy,
unhealthy, even lazy. And patchwork economics is a
hedge against any economic ugliness that may be around
the corner.

Before I go any further, I must admit that I am relatively uninterested in money. I have never had a lot of it
and I doubt if I ever will (though I wouldn't mind seeing
what it's like to have too much of it). I fervently believe
that there are many things on this planet that are far
more important than money.

Health is more crucial than money. Love certainly is.
Faith and hope surpass money any day. And freedom is
more precious than money, too. Friendship and good
times and nature and honor are also more important than
money. But don't get the idea that I'm bad-mouthing
money. To the contrary, I intend to good-mouth money
for the next seven chapters.

It's just that I want to place money in its proper perspective. Our lives, even our work lives, ought to be
devoted to a higher, a more noble purpose than the mere
accumulation of capital.

Current scientific theory holds that we are almost certainly the only form of life in the observable universe.
Although there are trillions and trillions of potential solar
systems amongst the stars, the odds against life occur-
ring are trillions and trillions and trillions to one. From a
mathematical standpoint, the chances are overwhelming
that life exists only on earth.

This being the case, we seem to have an obligation to

devote our rare and fleeting lives to more than money.

Now, in one breath I have told you to start an earning endeavor, then build the business with imagination and determination for a fat profit. In the next breath I have told you that you might consider that we all have an obligation to make some contribution to the good of humanity.

Is money truly compatible with higher purpose? Of course it is! Many people equate money with evil, but that is an unnecessary equation. George Bernard Shaw never said that money is the root of all evil. He said that *lack* of money is the root of all evil. And the Bible says that the *love* of money is the root of all evil. Money itself is innocent.

John Lester, a contemporary financial guru, says that money is "something." He discusses the power of money, the energy of money, and the idea of money. But he settles on the irrefutable definition that money is something. And then he goes on to explain that one property of money is that it flows. It flows into your life and out of your life. You control the flow. And the bottom line is that it is within your power to make the flowing-in more powerful than the flowing-out.

One thing is for sure: Money causes behavioral changes. I've seen perfectly normal people behave abnormally and irrationally when dealing with money. I've seen otherwise honest humans act like dishonest subhumans in their relationships with money.

Researchers from Columbia University tell us even more. Over a period of several weeks these researchers observed behavior patterns of people as they entered banks in New York City. They were led to conclude that people, in general, become extremely tense and alert immediately upon entering a bank. Focusing on people's eye movements, body language, and general behavior, the Columbia researchers noticed that people become exceptionally quiet and serious in a bank. Reverence, respect, and attentiveness were more pronounced among people in banks than people in other settings. People in a bank seemed even more solemn than people in church.

It is important that you recognize this human quirk when it comes to money, especially if your only source of money has been a paycheck. And your knowledge of it will help you immensely now that you may be seeking money from other sources. People can act just plain weird when it comes to money. Either at the prospect of parting with it, or on the chance of making it. Don't say I didn't warn you.

Last month I went on a twenty-day river trip. It cost me $1,500, including round-trip transportation from my home to Utah's Green River. Knowing that, a couple of months ago I went out and gave myself a $1,500 raise for the month. I didn't have a spare $1,500, so I did the next best thing. I earned it as extra income. I can't tell you how much satisfaction that gives me.

Gas prices are going up. So I earn a bit more extra money to keep up with the oil companies' greed. No big problem. This freedom afforded me by the ability to earn extra money is a sheer delight. Its protection from sky-rocketing prices and unforeseen expenses is warm and comforting. There are a myriad of reasons to earn extra money. I have a feeling you don't need too much convincing.

Of the 555 ways to earn extra money listed in this book, you could probably do about 333 of them, if you had to (though not all at once). More likely, you might consider doing as many as 55 of them. You certainly have the basic ability to earn money along that many avenues.

After considering so broad a field, I recommend that you zero in on ten ways. I further recommend that you try all ten. Don't put all your eggs in one earnway. Don't attempt to make a killing in any one of the ten (although there is no law against that kind of killing). Instead, aim low and often. For purposes of overall emotional and financial security, I have found it far healthier to get ten checks for $500 per month than one check for $5,000. Having had it both ways, I speak with wisdom based on vivid memories of the pain of losing the source of that $5,000 check.

To take greatest advantage of this book, commit this single secret of chapter 1 to memory. Then select your potential earnways from chapters 2, 3, 4, and 5. For each of the 555 earnways listed, I have also suggested a name for the business, along with recommendations for advertising and marketing it. Feel free to use the name and/or recommendations, as you choose.

Read, then reread, then reread once more chapter 6, for it is the ability to market your earning endeavors that will make the difference between failure and success. If there is any other secret as significant as that of developing multiple sources of income, it is that you must promote and market your earning endeavors in order to bring them to fruition. So chapter 6 is going to be key.

Chapter 7 is the only magical chapter in the book, indeed the only magical chapter I have ever written. By assiduously following the suggestions for access to power that are given you in chapter 7, your selected earning endeavors will sprout wings and fly. I do believe you can succeed without chapter 7, but then I also believe you can walk across the continent. The point is—there are better ways. And chapter 7 will provide you with the best ways I know of to earn exactly as much as you wish to earn . . . with certainty.

Chapter 8 will bring everything together for you into a neat, handy bundle, and will help start you on your way to earning extra money. The appendix can prove to be of enormous benefit to you, depending upon your needs and aspirations. Check it over carefully, and let yourself be attracted to those publications that exert a natural attraction to you.

While reading this book, in fact starting right now, begin tuning in to the needs of the times, of your community, of the world. The time-honored advice for budding money-earners has been to find a need and fill it. More and more, it has been proved possible to fill that need in many ways.

Just how many ways? Let's examine the need of a person who wishes to quit smoking. That particular need may be met by a *product* such as a lozenge that negates the desire for a cigarette. It may also be filled by a *book* on quitting smoking. Certainly, the need is met by a stop-smoking *course*. There are *institutes* dedicated to helping people to stop smoking. *Seminars* help other people end the habit. Then there are stop-smoking *cassettes*, and also people who act as *consultants* to people who wish to quit. Are there any other ways? Sure. There can be a magazine *article* on quitting smoking, even a *film* or *videotape*. And in time, there will most likely be a drug found effective in combating the smoking habit.

So while you're ascertaining the needs of society, open your mind to the plethora of methods to fill those needs.

Earning extra money is an inherent human ability, a relatively simple task, and a goal that provides you with a wide selection of choices as to how you will attain it. Still, you will notice that I never said earning extra money does not require work. It requires quite a bit of work—hard work, smart work, effective work.

Here's what else is required of you if you wish to earn extra money:

### Commitment
If you seriously commit yourself to making each selected earning endeavor really happen, each will happen. And if they don't happen, it won't be because you failed, but

because you quit trying. And if you have a firm enough commitment to succeed, you won't quit trying. Recognize that obstacles will confront you, that things will get fouled up in spite of your good efforts, that success will not come instantly, that unforeseen barriers will appear from nowhere, and that you may be tempted to drop the whole thing. If you're truly committed to succeeding, you will find ways to surmount all of these problems. Commitment is an attribute you need constantly: before you begin an earning endeavor as well as throughout the life of the endeavor.

### *Determination*

Determination is a by-product of commitment. It is built from it as from a cornerstone. Determination means that you must be willing to wade through an ocean of negativity before you reach an island of positivity. It means staying with your commitment no matter what. Determination does not require intensity of effort so much as consistency of effort. The world is loaded with frustrated geniuses who had all it takes to succeed except for determination. The same world is peopled with successful non-geniuses who achieved their success primarily by brute force of determination.

### *Organization*

You've got to take over control of your time in order to be organized. You've got to make lists, decide priorities, keep calendars, put things in writing—especially notes to yourself. You need to maintain a degree of order. I find that organization almost automatically happens with the help of my daily calendar. Each page is devoted to one day. When tasks must be accomplished, I write them down on the day on which I intend to accomplish them. This simple tool, my calendar, helps keep me organized even though I am juggling nine balls in the air at the same time. My particular calendar, called "Day at a Glance," is put out by Sheaffer Eaton division of Textron. It ought to be available in any stationery store. And it will help keep you well organized.

### *Discipline*
As commitment is the cornerstone for determination, organization is the cornerstone for discipline. When I have eleven tasks written down on a page of my calendar, I consider that to be eleven promises I have made to myself. By breaking or not keeping these promises, I realize I am deluding myself. So I keep all eleven promises, even though a friend beckons me to join him for a sail on the bay, or a sunny day invites me into its warmth and beauty, or a phone call tempts me to join an impromptu party. Keeping all my promises keeps me disciplined. Maintaining discipline enables me to earn a lot of extra money.

### *Effectiveness*
If you've got commitment, determination, organization, and discipline, there is still room for failure if you are not good at what you plan to do to earn extra money. You've got to be good at the work that requires your commitment, determination, organization, and discipline. And, never forget, you've got to be very effective in the marketing of your earning endeavor.

If you do 90 percent of your earning endeavor properly, you won't be nearly as successful as if you did 100 percent of it properly. And make no mistake: Doing absolutely everything right is challenging. It means not only doing the work well, but also having the right tools, the correct training, the proper attitude. It means having a dynamic ad in the Yellow Pages, a high degree of professionalism in your business cards, stationery, and invoice forms. Doing everything right means that you've got to market your products or services in the right places with the right words and pictures, or the right letters to the right people. It means you've got to be good at superb customer service, accurate record-keeping, intelligent financial management. Doing absolutely everything right is not easy, because several minute details are involved: a clear filing system, a backup in case you're going to be unavailable, follow-through notes or phone calls expressing gratitude for work already accomplished, dressing properly, and especially being a pleasant person with whom to do business.

These days, a new work ethic is replacing our old, Puritan work ethic. The old work ethic was the right one for our parents and grandparents, but the present and the future call for a totally new ethic—one based upon individual enterprise balanced with the pursuit of joy.

The new work ethic places more responsibility upon you and less upon your employer. It makes demands upon your imagination, your sense of enterprise, your wits. The new work ethic offers you far greater control over your destiny than the old Puritan work ethic. More enticing leisure-time activities require that we earn more money and have the time to avail ourselves of those activities. Our forefathers were not tempted by many of today's leisure lures: gondolas to whisk them to the top of a magnificently skiable mountain, inflatable rafts to provide them with an exciting white-water experience on a wilderness river, hang gliders to enable them to sense the flight of eagles. Today we have a fantastic selection of national parks and national monuments, jet ski boats, wind-surfing equipment, low-cost charters to Europe, and many other trappings of a fun-loving, enlightened society.

The availability of these delightful pursuits gently nudges us into becoming more enterprising, into developing the ability to enjoy them, into earning the extra money necessary to take advantage of them.

This new age has been characterized by some as the Age of the Entrepreneur. This should come as good news since almost anyone can become an entrepreneur. You can be a steady employee part of the time and a dynamite entrepreneur another part of the time. You can even arrange your life so that you are a full-time employee with a standard job, while enjoying the fruits of your entrepreneurial efforts of a year ago.

Many people have created a sideline venture for themselves while holding down a full-time job, then experienced the thrill of watching that sideline venture eventually exceed the income derived from their full-time job. Best of all, the sideline venture made few demands upon their time after the outset. A glorious situation, and I wish it upon you.

Once again, please understand that I am not bad-mouthing work. Work is wonderful. It's the idea of a full-time job that seems so depressing for a full-fledged human being. Work is so dandy that retired people by the droves are wishing they were working again. Nearly two million retired Americans say they want to be working. The labor pool of older people is far larger, more qualified, more flexible, and more committed than was previously believed.

The Department of Labor tells us that 40 percent of all employed people are dissatisfied with their employment. Psychologists tell us that number is more like 80 percent. The new work ethic will change that. It will bring more emotional rewards to employment while stimulating more people to experiment with self-employment. An increase in paycheck money is not enough to end employee dissatisfaction. Gaining more control over one's destiny is required. Enjoying respect for oneself as an individual is required. These are all difficult for multinational corporations and conglomerates to provide. Yet they are wonderful side effects of earning extra money.

Our parents' work ethic demanded that we dedicate our lives to a single career. The new work ethic says that not only may we pursue several careers, but we may pursue many of them at the same time. Such an attitude breeds more individualism, more job satisfaction, and certainly more money.

Up till now, most such single-minded careers were dictated by a combination of luck, contacts, chance exposure to the work of others, parental expectation, and peer-group pressure. But now, people are also seeking self-fulfillment. They are becoming increasingly aware that they are what they do, and if they do the work of a drone, they become drones.

In the course of lining up earning endeavors to reflect your own personality, you will be setting your sights on more than the financial rewards. They'll be yours, all right, but along with them will come other rewards, too, such as the fulfillment of dreams, the utilization of your real potential, and pure and simple fun.

Up there at the top of the ladder of success you'll find *yourself*, not merely a pot of gold or a fancy corner office.

It's sad to realize that the new work ethic was revealed to the public well over a century ago. In 1851, English social critic John Ruskin wrote: "In order that people may be happy in their work, these three things are needed: They must be fit for it. They must not do too much of it. And they must have a sense of success in it." Perhaps our grandparents missed out on reading those words as they settled instead for work that offered them security, an opportunity to climb the ladder, and a modicum of prestige and financial reward.

To help avoid falling into the same employment trap as your ancestors, read this book with a pencil nearby. Check the earning endeavors that feel best to you, being rather indiscriminate at first. Or else, jot down earning ideas that deserve more thought. Take an active part in the earning process, beginning with the next chapter.

All 555 earning endeavors coming up are based upon real, potential, budding, new, old, possible, probable, realistic, proven, or current earning ideas. Hardly any are a piece of cake. All will require commitment, determination, organization, discipline, and effectiveness. Almost all will require intelligent marketing.

There is going to be a direct correlation between how actively you participate in the reading of this book and how much extra money you will earn. If you can visualize yourself succeeding at each endeavor as you read about it, you will end up with a far longer list of potential earning endeavors than if you merely read of each endeavor from the standpoint of a spectator or skeptic.

You may feel a bit heady at being presented with 555 potential earning endeavors in just one book. In that case, recognize that this is but a first-grade primer when compared with the 35,000 earning endeavors listed in the *Dictionary of Occupational Titles* published by the U.S. Department of Labor. To get a copy (a good idea after you've completed this book), send $12 to the Superintendent of Documents, U.S. Government Printing Office, Washington, DC 20402. After you've read all 1,371 pages in the *Dictionary*, you'll realize that I'm just a piker when it comes to listing earnways.

Many people who read my book, *Earning Money Without a Job*, tried their hand at jobless earning, which is a rather comprehensive manner of maintaining several earning endeavors and eliminating entirely the necessity for a job.

Of those people who made the attempt, several wrote to me detailing their experiences. The one common denominator in virtually all of the letters was that success came more quickly and more easily than the people expected. Now, I figure that some people tried to earn money without a job, but couldn't pull it off. And I suspect that those people never wrote to me. Why would they? Nobody likes to chronicle an unsuccessful endeavor. But enough people stated in writing that earning money was a fast and simple task to encourage me no end. I hope it will be the same for you. It certainly can be, if you'll let it.

You are about to become involved not with a get-rich-quick book, but with a get-fulfilled-quick book. You will gain the fulfillment of having enough money, enough independence, enough self-esteem, enough control, and enough freedom to provide you with more true wealth than any get-rich-quick book could provide.

The moment you embark upon your first earning endeavor you will be taking a giant step into the new age of individual enterprise. Keep with you forever the basic secret of supporting yourself with several sources of income. Take comfort in the knowledge that you now have the opportunity to protect yourself from inflation, layoffs, strikes, job insecurity, and draconian company policies.

In the coming pages, you will not be asked to make any major investment. You will be provided with a manner of unleashing all of your earning power—and that's a considerable amount of power. The economic condition that necessitated your reading of this book in the first place could prove a disguised blessing, for thereby you may learn for the very first time what an effective earning machine you are.

Although I provide you with information for starting 555 different businesses, I hope you do not confuse this with the standard concept of going into business for yourself. For although that is what you will be doing, you won't be going about it the way your forefathers did. You will not be placing all the emphasis upon work and money.

Instead, freedom and efficiency will be more important to you.

In California, where there are over 2.6 small businesses (under fifty employees), more than half of them have no employees other than the owner. In fact, one in every ten California residents is self-employed.

More about the Golden State: Almost one in every seven small businesses in America is located in California; almost three-fourths of the state's small businesses are sole proprietorships; more than one million full-time California businesses are conducted from the home, and at least 216,000 part-time, one-person businesses are run from home. I'm self-employed, working part-time from home because of the natural diversions offered by California: mountains, rivers, redwood forests, waterfalls, an ocean, deserts, vast stretches of wilderness, and the city of San Francisco. I'm not sure about the other patchwork economists in the state, but I know I wasn't beckoned by such splendors while living in Illinois or Maryland.

In the United States, 26.8 million people work from home. Most do it on a moonlighting or part-time basis, but they've figured a way to escape from the evil Commute. The number of home workers will rise to 38.8 million by 1993, and more rapid escalation will be the byword after that.

Right now, half of all U.S. businesses are less than twelve years old. To put that into perspective, consider that most European firms are over 100 years old. And to gain an even deeper insight, recognize that business ownership by women is increasing twice as fast as male-owned businesses. Best of all, the latest figures show that 40 percent of new firms survive six or more years. That's twice as high as previous figures. Still, this book does not ever suggest that you actually go into business as that was meant in the old days—back before the sixties.

In fact, this entire book does not deal with the going-into-business concept as much as it deals with the idea of free-lancing. A free-lancer is a person who sells his or her services to various employers without a long-term commitment to any one of them. In other words, a person who proceeds as an independent.

Now, my old dictionary suggests that free-lancing pertains especially to writers and artists. No longer true. These days, as products of the new work ethic, there are many types of free-lancing. We see free-lance accountants, free-lance typists, free-lance bakers, free-lance moviemakers, free-lance gardeners, in fact free-lance almost anything. For just about anything that can be done on a full-time basis can be done on a free-lance basis, too.

Right now, many services are being performed on an independent basis that never before fell under the free-lance aegis. People and companies that never hired free-lancers are discovering them to be highly desirable because they require no overhead, no office, no secretary, no fringe benefits, no large salary, no usual employer-employee hassles.

Word of warning: The earning endeavors listed on the pages coming up might appear deceptively simple because they are covered with a minimum of verbiage. But while it is true that I use few words to describe an earn-way, don't be misled by my brevity. It is never, alas, quite as simple as it may seem on these pages. Each endeavor requires some attention to detail. Let me illustrate my point with the details of what is required to succeed just as a window washer. A similar amount of detail will be necessary for most other endeavors. Although the nature of the particulars will vary, the attention to detail remains the same.

A successful window-washing endeavor requires that the window washer solicit business from stores in a commercial area during the morning. During the afternoon, the window washer will be washing windows. While soliciting new business, the window washer with success on his or her mind wears clean, plain clothes, carries an order book, and has a clean rag hanging from a rear pocket.

Each storekeeper should be asked, "May I give you an estimate for washing your windows?" It's an easy question to answer with a yes.

The estimate should be of the double-barreled variety: one price to wash the outside windows plus the outside and inside front door; another price to wash both the outside and inside of all windows plus the front door.

After completing the job with excellence, the successful earner-of-extra-money-by-washing-windows hands the storekeeper a bill, collects the amount due, and asks, "Would you like this service weekly? Biweekly? Monthly?" By doing this, each visit to the same commercial area will add new names to the list of regular customers. Each visit completed in this manner is both a marketing effort and a work effort.

Once the business takes off, a listing in the Yellow Pages is recommended, and to go along with that listing, a phone must be manned: by a human, an answering service, or an answering machine. And if you want to really make a hit of your window-washing business, print up business cards at the outset, presenting one each time you canvass a store. The business cards add a wee bit more professionalism. And professionalism breeds trust, which in turn nets new business.

A very successful window-washing operation in the Southwest was opened with an $8 investment, and sold three years later for $25,000. These days, you can figure on a $25 investment: for bucket, window-washing brush, pole, razor scraper and spare blades, two sizes of squeegees with rubbers, one dozen clean, white Turkish towel rags, and the smallest possible container of general purpose liquid detergent—to be used one drop per bucket. All of these supplies may be obtained from a janitorial supply house.

Now, here comes the more winning side of window washing: How much money do you wish to earn on an hourly basis? Since you'll be making your estimates by time, how much you want to make should be a known quantity at the outset.

Perhaps you'll tell the shopkeeper it will cost $25 to wash his windows. Since the job will take fifteen minutes of your time, you'd be making $100 per hour. You'll probably get a lot more business if you estimate your cost at $5, earning you $20 per hour and a far longer list of regular customers. The point is, the amount you earn is now up to you. You can give yourself raises by raising your rates—a legitimate move in times of rising costs.

You've got to be able to handle rejection in order to make it in the window-washing biz. You've got to be psychologically prepared to handle about twenty rejections of your window-washing offers for every one acceptance. Such understanding may be your single most important attribute if you want to earn extra money along this line.

The name you select for your window-washing venture is important. It should inspire confidence or good feelings while describing the nature of the business.

By far the most important marketing you can do for this particular business is store-by-store canvassing. You might consider direct mail if you wish to appeal to home owners as well as store owners. And by all means explore the idea of telephone canvassing.

You can get a whole lot more information on starting this business by writing to the International Entrepreneurs Association, 2392 Morse Ave., P.O. Box 19787, Irvine, CA 92713. Their catalog of start-up manuals will prove very helpful to you if you're serious about getting into the business of achieving financial independence.

Now the window-washing business seems the essence of simplicity . . . until you examine it. I did in the past few pages, and I ended up recommending a more copious source of information. So it will be for virtually every earning idea suggested in these next chapters. The more you know about each earnway, the better armed you will be to succeed. And yet, innocence can also stand you in good stead, as it enables you to operate unconstrained by the foolishly held traditions of the industry.

While you select a headful of methods by which you can earn extra money, it's a good idea to have your radar tuned to the ways you might market these methods, even before you get to chapter 6.

I've identified a full one hundred marketing weapons in my books *Guerrilla Marketing*, *Guerrilla Marketing Attack*, and *Guerrilla Marketing Weapons*. Almost any business requires about twenty of these weapons in order to succeed, so here are twenty-one.

### Canvassing
You can call on prospects yourself, or you can have someone do it for you. It's effective, time-consuming, and inexpensive, unless you do it yourself and figure your hourly rate. Canvassing should be considered if your target audience can be found running stores, working in offices, or living in residential neighborhoods.

### Personal Letters
Again, not expensive, quite effective, and a very direct way of saying all that you have to say to the exact people to whom you ought to be saying it. With the new word processing machines, personal letters enable you to add your personal touch to electronically typed letters. This has been my prime method of attracting new clients to my own advertising consultancy. Out of every ten letters I

send, as many as eight may be ignored, one results in a form-letter rejection, and one results in a new client.

### Telephone Calls

You can make them yourself, saying approximately what you'd say in canvassing. Or, you can delegate the phoning task to others. Telephone marketing is growing in direct proportion to the resentment against it. Still, for those people with a winning telephone manner, this low-cost method of marketing should be given serious consideration.

### Distributing Circulars

Printed circulars cost a mere few cents each, and they may be distributed in specially targeted areas: wealthy neighborhoods, hardware store parking lots, areas with large concentrations of white-collar workers, flea markets, and a whole lot more. Your circular can be as brief as eight well-chosen words, or as lengthy as eight well-worded pages—making your circular a brochure.

### Posting Bulletins

You can pin up your circular in a high-traffic location or locations. Where I live, there are companies that offer to post your bulletin in twenty locales, each with a well-read bulletin board. This is another unique, low-cost method of marketing your product or service. Post either your circular or your specially designed bulletin or poster.

### Classified Ads

Still another of the low-cost marketing methods. You can home in on your target audience with low-cost classified ads run in newspapers and magazines throughout the United States. I have conducted a relatively profitable mail-order business by means of classified ads only. For a minor hassle, it means a major return to me. But the audience size for classified ads is limited. Still, classified ads can be a prime marketing method for practitioners of patchwork economics.

### Signs
These are usually less wordy than circulars but considerably larger. Signs are excellent for certain businesses such as flea markets, garage sales, knife-sharpening services, fruit stands, and the like. Low-cost, they are worth considering if at all feasible for your earning endeavors.

### Yellow Pages Advertising
Almost any business can benefit from Yellow Pages exposure. Though I have never used Yellow Pages ads for five of my enterprises—my mail-order business, smoked salmon importing company, seminar company, authoring endeavors, and column-writing firm—my other four income producers have benefited from Yellow Pages listings in their names. And I've seen the Yellow Pages work wonders for some of my clients. The Yellow Pages enable you to run an ad as big as your biggest competitor. To do the same with consistent newspaper ads would be very costly.

### Newspaper Advertising
Now, we're getting to where marketing costs can add up. However, newspaper advertising does not have to be costly. Small ads in local papers cost very little. For newspaper ads to be an effective marketing method, you have to run your ads consistently. So even a small cost becomes a big cost when you multiply an inexpensive weekly ad by the fifty-two times you ought to be running it. Consistent exposure tells your message to a whale of a lot of people and breeds confidence at the same time. The higher the level of confidence, the greater the level of sales.

### Direct Mail

This is similar to writing personal letters. Only instead of mailing 5 letters, you mail 5,000, or 25,000, or more. Direct mail has been the most productive marketing method for one of my businesses, and the least productive for another. It proves what the direct-mail experts tell us: test, test, test. Direct mail ordinarily means that your message gets sent, in your words, to a list of people purchased from a direct mail company. It enables you to zero in on a clearly targeted group of people and is the keystone to many a success story.

### Radio Advertising

Although each radio commercial is not expensive, the number of commercials required to adequately advertise a product or service usually necessitates a rather large sum of money. Still, with a few hundred dollars, radio enables you to make a widely heard splash in a selected area. Your local radio station can help immensely in selecting schedules and producing the finished commercial. For some businesses, radio is amazingly effective.

### Television Advertising

I doubt if you need me to tell you that TV is both the most costly and the most effective advertising medium ever devised. It allows you to reach a gigantic number of people—to demonstrate your product or service, to use both audio and video techniques to put your point across, to gain the credibility that comes with TV advertising, and to add touches of glamour and pizzazz to your message. Be careful, though: TV is a complex medium, and its misuse is as common as its use. If you can possibly see your way toward using it, talk to an expert first. If you use TV carefully, you'll love it. If you misuse it, you'll spend a bundle and waste most of it.

### Billboard Advertising

Basically, this is a reminder medium, best used when combined with other marketing tools. Nevertheless, some businesses thrive on billboard advertising. If you think yours could be one of them, look into the medium. The best billboard phrase is "Next Exit." Maybe your business can make use of a billboard carrying those words.

### Public Relations

This marketing tool works best when combined with advertising. Public relations basically means "planting" stories about your business in newspapers, magazines, TV, or radio. The story appears not as an ad, but as a legitimate article. Although PR will give you credibility, you have little control and no possibilities of repetition. Since repetition is so important, reliance solely upon public relations is rarely a good idea.

### Advertising Specialties

Ballpoint pens with store names, calendars with company names, and doodads of almost any kind featuring the name of a business—that's what I mean by advertising specialties. Right now, my desk has a paper clip holder from radio station K101, a ruler with the Coca-Cola imprint, and a key ring from Peppers Water Beds—making me a typical member of the audience for advertising specialties. How effective are they? Beats me. Though I do listen to K101 a lot while sipping a Coke and thinking comfortable thoughts about my water bed.

### Events

This can easily be put under the heading of public relations, but it can also stand by itself. A turkey race is an event. So is an auto race, especially if one of the cars has your business name on it. Street parties qualify as events, as do contests, sweepstakes, and hot dog eating parties. For some money-earning endeavors, events are just the ticket.

### Free Seminars and Demonstrations

I have, more than once, been transfixed by a dexterous and facile in-store demonstrator. And my wife was once persuaded to write a $400 check after attending a free seminar. If, by giving a seminar, lecture, or demonstration of your service, you can raise a healthy crop of customers, by all means add this method to your marketing arsenal. (I must also admit that my unfree seminars on jobless earning have been a boon to the sale of my books, though I'm sure that if the seminars had been free, even more books would have been sold.)

### Sampling

This is somewhat akin to free demonstrations, but different enough to deserve a paragraph of its own. Sampling is very expensive, and unless you have a product or service so good that a single use will result in repeat business, you should steer clear of sampling. On the other hand, there is no better way to truly market your offering if one exposure is likely to lead to continuous purchase. A few products in my house would never have found their way there if they hadn't first made an appearance as a free sample. Sampling is not done by many businesses, so if you can employ it you will be assailed by little competition.

### Trade Shows, Exhibits, and Fairs

A good number of firms use impressive display booths at shows and fairs as their primary marketing tool. Some businesses inherently lend themselves to such methods of propaganda. If yours is one, be sure to check out the possibilities of exhibiting your product or service to the semiattentive throngs who will visit the show, exhibit, or fair at which your product or service will be displayed. It's almost always a good idea to disseminate circulars/brochures at your show booth.

### *Magazine Advertising*
Surprise! It costs less than $800 to run a full-page ad in *Time* magazine. Of course, that's a full-page ad only in the Indianapolis edition of *Time*. The point is that many magazines publish regional editions, and the cost to get in those is far less than you might imagine. With a one-half column ad, the cost drops dramatically. So even a part-time, run-from-home earning endeavor might benefit from magazine advertising. Many national magazines have classified sections, and these particularly are worth looking into as a potential ad medium. Magazines make it easy to target an audience, and lend prestige to your offering. All that plus reprints you can mail or display years after the original ad ran.

### *Unique and New Marketing Tools*
Since new methods of getting the word out are constantly being developed, I include them here. Among such methods: paid word-of-mouth advertising, searchlights, parade advertising, skywriting, dirigible advertising, bus and taxi signs, people wearing sandwich ad boards, ads on benches, T-shirt advertising, ads on shopping bags, bowling and Little League team sponsorships, and many more. Once you begin to promote your business, you may well be contacted by representatives of these off-the-wall media. My suggestion is to listen carefully to the reps, then decide how fitting the marketing method will be. Just because it's new doesn't mean it's not great.

One final thought before getting down to actual earn-ways . . . about money.

The amount of money that you earn along most any earning avenue is very dependent upon the time you devote, the brainpower you apply, and the energy you will dedicate to earning extra money. However, some of the earnways, even with maximum time, brains, and energy, will earn no more than $100 per month at best. I mean, if you decide to be a notary, no matter how much effort you put forth, you're just not going to strike it rich. Same thing with serving a summons or painting rusty TV antennas. For many earnways, the upper limit of earning isn't very high, and they should be considered just for filling in the gaps, so to speak.

On the other hand, a menial task such as window washing can earn $100 monthly or $3,000 monthly for you. Depends how you go about obtaining customers, how many window washers you have to whom you can delegate routes, how many communities you decide to serve.

As a general rule, you'll be able to increase your income dramatically if you promote properly, delegate properly, and make yourself into as efficient an earning machine as possible.

Okay, now that your mind is open to the many methods of marketing and the range of income you can expect to receive, it's time to take brief looks at the earning endeavors that just might spark your imagination.

It's time to pick up that pencil now. Be prepared to use it to make a check mark next to any earning endeavor that has even the slightest appeal to you. You can winnow down the list later.

However, the more checks you make now, the more checks you'll receive later. (Pun cheerily intended.)

Happy earning!

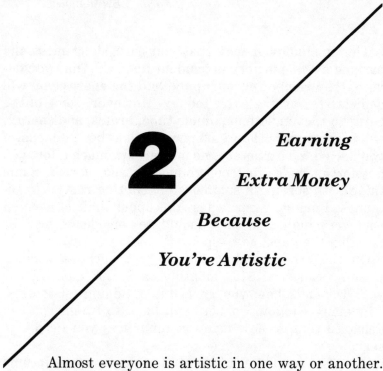

# 2 *Earning Extra Money Because You're Artistic*

Almost everyone is artistic in one way or another. This chapter will show you how to turn your artistic talents into profitable earning endeavors.

When I talk about artistic talents, I'm referring to your writing ability, your drawing or painting or illustrating ability, your skill with crafts and creations, your penchant for photography or moviemaking or videotaping, and your talent as a performer.

The more of these skills you have, the more you can put to use earning money for you. Most of these endeavors are difficult to delegate because they require talent. On the other hand, it is possible to find people with talent—if you know where to look. I've located many a budding artist at an art school. I've found writers among business people who had never written anything professionally, but nursed a secret passion for the pen.

So remember that although you will absolutely require talent to get your earnway going, it just may be possible to find someone to fill your shoes once you have the momentum on your side. Just be sure you do not delegate anything to anyone who will not do the work as well as you.

When you are studying the upcoming earnways, it will be relatively simple to determine whether or not you're the right person for the work. If you're not too adept with grammar, you'd better leave the writing earnways for others. If you freeze up under the gaze of a crowd, you may as well not put any check marks by any of the earnways in the performing section of this chapter. Still, keep your mind open to trying some of the earnways that really tempt you. Even if you've never crafted a lamp from an old statue, consider giving it a try if you think you can do it. This chapter may reveal some latent talents you possess but have never exploited. Certainly, it will show you how to utilize your acknowledged talents.

Each earnway listed in this book is listed first by a possible name for your endeavor, then by a more explanatory title for the actual earnway. Enough explanation. Now it's time to earn some money.

## WRITING

## 1  MEMORY LANE MEMOIRS

(Writing memoirs for others)    Writing the memoirs of others can prove to be fulfilling for them, profitable for you. All that's required is a taped or well-noted interview with the interviewee, plus a modicum of writing ability on your part. You can probably attract people who desire to read their own memoirs by advertising in the classified section of local papers or carefully selected magazines. Display ads in those same magazines might garner customers for you, too. You can charge your customers by the hour or by the memoir. I certainly would never charge less than $100 per memoir, and because I'm a professional writer I might charge up to $1,000, even more for a known personality. By reading the memoirs of others (you can find them in any library or bookstore), you'll know what style of writing is called for. This business probably won't make you rich, but it might make you (and your customers) famous. Or infamous.

## 2   THE COMEDY SUPERMARKET

(Writing comedy material for professionals) Quite a few smiling free-lance writers got those smiles from the checks they received for writing comedy material for others. Sometimes those others are professional comedians. Sometimes they are politicians. Sometimes they are publications. If you can write funny stuff, you can make serious money. I'm told comedians pay handsomely. Advertise your offerings in show business publications and with mailings to selected comedians, publications, and politicians. A publicity story on your craft wouldn't hurt. Neither would your appearance on a radio talk show. Demonstrate your wit at trade shows or fairs. And write to literary agents who are ordinarily in touch with the people who need your funny material. You've got to be able to write comedy rather than merely write the English language. Woody Allen, for one, got his start writing rather than performing comedy. Mel Brooks, too.

## 3   FOREVER AFTER

(Writing eulogies) This type of business falls into a rather macabre area. But if you're a good writer—sensitive and able to compose inspirational pieces—this might be right up your earning alley. You obtain customers with classified ads in regional and national newspapers. The facts of the person's life are furnished to you, then you compose a warmly and sincerely worded eulogy. You might even do a direct mailing to ministers. Another earning outlet for Forever After would be to write histories of local grave-yards, then sell the histories to local newspapers. Not a lot of competition in this area. By attending a few funerals, you'll understand what is required to write a eulogy. Charge by the time spent or on a per eulogy basis. You're not going to earn your entire living in this manner, thank heavens, but you can earn, say, $250 per eulogy. Inciden-tally, my dictionary defines eulogy as a speech or writing in praise of a person or thing, especially one in honor of a deceased person. So you've got to be a positive perceiver. Even when you're writing about a negative person.

## 4  LOVE AND HATE LIMITED

(Writing reviews for publications)   It's wonderful indeed to be paid for your opinions. And newspapers happily pay their book and movie critics. If you have strong opinions on books, movies, restaurants, hotels, plays, or even auto-mobiles, offer to write reviews for publications. Although many publications already have reviewers, many more do not, and they might be happy to sign you on, provided your opinions are sound, your writing is fluent, and your rates are reasonable. My wife and I use our local movie critic to guide our lives. We see everything he hates and miss everything he loves. Guess our critic has an uncanny way of coming up with opinions that are reliably 100 per-cent contrary to ours. Direct mailings to publishers (con-taining sample reviews) is how you land the job of loving and hating professionally. Small papers will pay around $10 for a review. Larger publications will pay consider-ably more—I once received $100 for a book review. A friend of mine was recently named movie critic for a ma-jor newspaper. She makes enough money that way to require no other income. You should have a strong knowledge of the field you will review, and of course, you need a literate writing style. Start reading reviews in magazines and newspapers to see how the reviewers write. If you don't like what they write, perhaps you'll feel impelled to write reviews of their reviews.

## 5 CREATIVE REALTY

(Writing real estate ads)  Reading through the ads in the real estate section of your newspaper, you will be appalled first at the sameness of the ads, and then at their lack of creativity. You can make real estate ads stand out from the ordinary if you write them with the same care you might apply to writing advertising for many mass-marketed products. If you have this ability, for heaven's sake offer it to real estate companies and to house sellers. You can charge a fee for your writing ability, and once your ads start selling houses, you'll find a lot of business heading your way. Anywhere from $10 to $100 seems a fair price to charge for a great classified ad. Just read the ads in this Sunday's paper and you'll see the dire need for your originality. Attract business by advertising in real estate trade publications (find them in your *Standard Rate and Data Business Publication Rates and Data* at your library), and by running classified ads in the real estate section, claiming that you can write better ads than those all around you. If you really can, you can prosper.

## 6 TATTLETALE

(Writing a syndicated newspaper column)  Buy or borrow a copy of *Writer's Market* (check the appendix of this book to get details about this book) and turn to the section on syndicates. Read it carefully, then focus on newspaper syndicates and mull over the possibility of doing a syndicated newspaper column. Others are doing it. Maybe you've got as much ability. Getting your column published is something you can do through an agent, or by writing directly to the syndicates. Don't forget to enclose six sample columns. It helps if you have them designed and typeset. If self-syndication is the avenue you select, classified or display ads in *Editor and Publisher* magazine (see appendix) can bring newspapers to you. If you work with an existing syndicate, they'll probably want to split everything with you on a fifty-fifty basis. If you handle the syndication yourself, figure on earning about $7.50 per column. Not much, but when you multiply that by the two hundred newspapers in which your daily column appears, it comes to $1,500 per day. Of course, you can also write a weekly column, though you won't get as rich. This is a long-shot earnway. The odds are overwhelmingly against anyone syndicating a column. But the rewards are worth it. Just ask Dear Abby.

# 7  SOAP DOPE

(Writing a newsletter about soap operas)   If you tune in to all the soap operas, you can put out a newsletter for those who don't or can't. Some people are so hooked on the soaps that if they miss just one episode, they're all ruffled inside. So they'll be very grateful for your writings. Fill them in on all the gory details and don't let them miss out on even one perversion, one clandestine affair. This business becomes a whole lot easier if you have a videotape cassette recorder and can record the shows to view at the time of your own choosing. You can handle the writing of the newsletter. Your local instant printer can print it instantly. And you can draw subscribers with newspaper display ads, classified ads, or ads in your local issue of *TV Guide*. It would be pretty marvelous if you could afford to advertise your newsletter on TV during the soaps themselves—if you live in a small town and have access to an inexpensive cable station, you should consider doing just that. You can charge from $15 to $50 for an annual subscription to your monthly report, more if it's weekly. A California woman who started the first such newsletter (there are now several) supposedly got many subscribers right off the bat.

# 8 A POEM FOR YOU

(Writing personalized poems)   With classified ads in newspapers throughout the country, you can announce that you write personalized poetry. The ads should request that the customer write to you with details about the poem (enclosing a check). Then, you send back a professional, sensitive, beautiful, soul-stroking poem. You can offer the same service with a song instead of a poem. But you'd be tempted to charge more. I guess a poem is worth about $50, and a song about $100. You can even make out well charging half that amount. Be sure you know how to write a proper poem or song before offering your services. I once saw a truck in San Francisco with a sign on it: Fresh Poems $1.00. Charge more than that.

# 9 RIGHTEOUS RÉSUMÉS

(Writing résumés for people) The inability to write a proper résumé keeps otherwise qualified people from landing jobs. It's not all that easy to write a good résumé, one that will result in a job interview. Once you've learned how to do it (and it takes more than mere writing talent), offer to write the résumés of others. You can secure customers with classified ads, a listing in the Yellow Pages, posting signs on bulletin boards, or running small display ads in the business section of the daily paper. This seems to be a growing service. When I was applying for my first job, I sent out twenty résumés and received only two replies and zero interviews. Then I read a few books on résumé writing (I call your attention to *What Color Is*

*Your Parachute?* by Richard Nelson Bolles; see the appendix). Next time, I sent out twenty résumés and received fourteen interviews and four job offers. That's why you can charge up to $100 per résumé and still be within the bounds of reason.

## 10 THE GHOST

(Writing term papers for students) Specialize in (shhh!) ghostwriting term papers for students. Oh, I know it's no way for a student to learn, but how much do you remember from your term papers you wrote as a student? Well, here's your chance to make up for all that lost learning. Discreet ads in student newspapers plus an active word-of-mouth advertising campaign will get this business going. Letters to fraternity and sorority houses wouldn't hurt. And signs on dorm bulletin boards. In-person calls to students can help, too. To do this earnway, you've got to be good at writing, researching, and meeting deadlines. You'll probably make more money offering this service to college students than high school students, because the former probably have more money to spend . . . and harder term papers to write. I figure you can charge around $25 per term paper, depending upon the length. Or you can charge $10 per hour. I know of someone who once paid $150 for someone to write his twenty-page term paper. Unfortunately, this service is already offered at many schools. As with every other one of the 555 earning ideas in this book, don't offer this service unless you can do an A+ job. And make sure it's legal in your state.

## 11 THE SUMMARIZER

(Writing summaries of lectures) Attend important classes, speeches, lectures, even seminars. Then sell summaries of the talks to registered students. You may even end up being retained to attend those events for others who are unable to make them. They'll learn of you from classified ads, signs on bulletin boards, and in a free publicity story about your service. Others can find out about you when they receive your circular, handed to them as they leave a class, speech, lecture, or seminar. Because of the varying amounts of time necessary to attend the event and write the summary, a flat hourly charge seems best for this endeavor. To succeed, you need patience, and the ability to take good notes and to write clearly. Oh yes, about that hourly rate—$10 seems about right. You say $15? Okay, $15.

## ART

## 12    PLATE PAINTING WHILE-U-WAIT

(Painting commemorative plates)   There's a man in Florida who hangs out in maternity ward waiting rooms. He offers to paint commemorative plates for brand-new fathers. Paints the name of the baby, the birthdate, and the birth weight. Think those new fathers buy his plates? You bet your bootees they do. All that he can paint. Next to stamps and coins, plates are the most collected objects in America. You can get your artistic jollies, add to the joy of parenthood, and enrich your coffers by painting commemorative plates. And don't limit your commemorations to births. People also wish to remember marriages, graduations, confirmations, pennants, Super Bowl victories, raises, promotions, and more. You barely need to market this endeavor. But you can attract customers with classified ads and small newspaper display cards. Charge from $25 to $100 per plate, depending upon your painting ability. Of course, that charge should also cover the plate itself. You can learn more about commemorative plates by checking out *The Bradford Book of Collector's Plates* (see the appendix). You need a deft touch and a serious dollop of illustrative and artistic talent to do as well as the Florida plate painter.

# 13 ILLUSTRIOUS ILLUSTRATIONS

(Sketching storefronts)   You can make extra money and exercise your artistic skills if you offer to sketch storefronts for store owners, then sell the sketches to them for publicity purposes. The store owners can display the sketches in their windows, frame them for use on their walls, offer them for publicity purposes, or use them in their advertising. You can be sure (or you can hint) that an enterprising store owner can make superb use of your illustration, providing it has enough inherent excellence of its own. The storefront itself need not be gorgeous in order for you to sketch it. A creative artist can pick up the charm and beauty in any storefront. And don't limit your offerings to store owners. There are also home owners, car owners, and office owners. It's easy to publicize your business. You can run pictures that you have sketched as ads in your local paper, or distribute circulars featuring your art to store owners. And don't underestimate the power of in-person calls, during which time you show off your illustrations. If you have the ability to do accurate illustrations with a touch of style, and if you can do them rather rapidly, you will probably find this earning endeavor easy to advertise and a cinch for success. Having purchased the services of such a person (for $150) for a restaurant in which I had an interest, I know what I'm talking about. In fact, I was able to locate three people who wanted the job. The highest bid was $500. The lowest was $50. I selected the mid-range artist and was not at all disappointed. That reminds me, don't forget to offer your sketching service to restaurants.

# 14 PET PORTRAITS

(Drawing pictures of peoples' pets) Around Christmas each year, some artist out here places classified ads offering to paint dogs' and cats' pictures to be used as Christmas gifts, even as the basis for Christmas cards. I have not yet availed myself of this artistic offer, but I've been tempted, and someday I'll probably succumb to the charm of it all. Painting doggies and kitties is an artistic outlet at worst, and an interesting manner of earning money at best. Of course, you need artistic talent (in virtually any media—tempera, oil, acrylic, chalk, charcoal, pen, pencil) and some experience drawing animals. But if you have these abilities, you can use them to paint pets from life or from a photo. Just be sure you show the pet in a good light, one that captures the essence of the beastie. You can probably get all the business you want with bulletins in pet stores and at vets, and with display or classified newspaper ads. You can even advertise in national magazines—classified sections—with an offer to accomplish your portraiture from photographs. Charge anywhere from $25 to $150. And you'll see—a doggie Dali can earn a decent dollar.

# 15 THE MAGIC MURALIST

(Painting murals) Design and paint murals both indoors and out and you will make the world (and your bank statement) more beautiful. Just because you are good at making small sketches does not mean you can accomplish the same on a large scale. So practice on your own wall before designing walls for others. Gain business by posting bulletins, running small display newspaper ads, and distributing circulars. Small sketches (along with photos of completed murals) will get you started. Make personal calls and show your work to prospective customers. A good publicity story in the newspaper and/or on television will help. You might even paint a free mural in a high traffic area, thereby attracting attention and dollars. Some cities—San Francisco, for instance—award grants for murals that beautify the city. One friend painted a 40-square-foot mural in Chicago for which she charged $750. Another was paid $3,600 for a larger mural (600 square feet) in San Francisco. The better you are, the more you can charge. The $3,600 mural was gigantic. So I suggest that your price increase with the size of the mural.

## 16  THE U.S. POSTER OFFICE

(Painting posters)  Use your artistic ability to paint posters for businesses, churches, or clubs. Offer large, full-color posters as well as small black-and-white or two-color posters at lower prices. Naturally, you should develop a portfolio of posters you have created to use in wooing prospective employers. Market your poster prowess with a brochure mailed to potential customers, with small display ads in the newspaper, a Yellow Pages listing, and posters. A Missouri doctor once turned a photo he had taken into a full-color poster and sold over 100,000 of them at $2.50 to $5.00 each. You can charge $25 to $100 for your posters depending upon the work involved. And if you believe any should be reproduced, remember the Missouri doctor. And Farrah Fawcett . . .

## 17  MENUSCRIPT

(Lettering Menus)  There is a woman on the West Coast who specializes in lettering menus. If that doesn't impress you, consider that in one year she made $100,000 writing menus in her Old English script . . . working only on the West Coast. She had twelve people helping her. If you have an appetizing manner of printing, you can attract business to your menu lettering firm merely by mailing a brochure that includes samples of your work, preferably as it appears on menus (real or imaginary). Naturally, your brochure should be sent to restaurateurs. Expert calligraphy will be the main attribute for success in this endeavor. (But don't try to build your empire on the West Coast—the competition's too stiff.)

# 18 PAINT-A-POOL

(Painting designs in swimming pools)  Earn a hefty sum painting gorgeous designs in swimming pools. The pools must be drained before you begin. Your design must be approved by the pool owner. You've got to use special paint, and you need special fixatives. Worse yet, you've got to tell the pool owner that the design won't last many years. And you need a ton of talent to paint large, large surfaces such as the bottom of a pool. Okay. Having surmounted these obstacles, you're ready to begin. Direct mail to pool owners is the best way to attract business. Mailings to pool maintenance firms and pool contractors will also serve as conduits to customers. Consider posting bulletins in pool shops if they'll let you. As with so many other money earning measures, be prepared for prospects asking to see photos of work you've already accomplished ... or even to see the pools. Try to arrange a pool party at a pool you've painted. You can ask for around $1,000 a pool if you're good ... maybe even more. When my pool was being replastered, I paid a few hundred dollars extra to have it plastered in black. For a few hundred more, I could have hired you to make a painting in it. But you hadn't contacted me. Maybe next time.

# 19 OUT OF THE BLUE

(Doing paintings based on blueprints)  You can show people visions of the future and earn a tidy sum at the same time if you can turn blueprints of buildings into paintings of the same buildings. You need illustrating skill, drafting talent, and more than a nodding acquaintance with architectural renderings to do this work. But if you are armed with the appropriate talent, try mailings (indicating locations of your work) to architects and building contractors. They (or the company retaining them) will pay you handsomely for your visionary and artistic talents. By handsomely, I mean anywhere from $250 to $1,500.

## 20 DREAMS COME TRUE

(Painting portraits with imaginary backgrounds) If you're a pretty fair portrait artist you can make more than a pretty fair income if you paint peoples' portraits while portraying their "dreams come true." My buddy Howard used to dream of having been a New York Yankee, playing alongside Babe Ruth, Lou Gehrig, and the other Yankee stalwarts of the past. No problem to my other friend Norman, a portrait artist acquaintance. Norman painted Howard, picturing him in the Yankee dugout, wearing the famed pin-striped uniform, flanked by Ruth and Gehrig. Howard now has that expensively framed portrait hanging proudly in his office. It was worth the $2,500 he paid for it. Offer to paint others accepting Academy Awards, Nobel prizes, checks from Rockefeller, even in the Oval Office. Paint fat people thin, old people young, sad people happy. If you can make their dreams come true on canvas, they can help you make your financial dreams come true. Market your portraiture with classified ads, with an exhibit of your work, and with mailings to galleries where your circular, and maybe even a painting, may be posted—and the gallery owner given a cut of the purchase price. You can do the whole painting working from photos. If you gain a reputation for this work, you will get a lot of commissions. Norman now charges $5,000 for such portraiture. Not bad for patchwork economics.

# 21   GREETINGS FRIEND

(Designing greeting cards and stationery)   Got a good idea for a unique line of greeting cards or stationery? Then design several prototypes, go to the annual Stationery Show (held at various places around the country; ask your local greeting card store owner when and where the next one is), and set up a booth. Or, offer your cards and letters to a company with an existing booth. The idea is to display to and capture the fancy of the first-rate distributors—the people who can sell your creations throughout America. If you can manufacture all that your distributors order, you can receive a lot of mail with checks inside while flexing your artistic muscles. To get a line on the type of art needed, check a copy of *Greetings Magazine* (please see the appendix under periodicals). Gather even more data by reading *Writer's Market*—in the greeting card publishers section. Good luck! Love and kisses, Jay.

# 22   CARICATURES WITH CARE

(Doing caricatures)   If you can do caricatures with class, do them professionally in public places. Position yourself in some high-traffic area, put up a sign describing your services, display a couple of your masterpieces, and go to work—capturing the essence of your customers on good quality, framable art paper. Arrange for comfortable seating for your models and for those waiting to be your models. You must be a very good caricature artist, and be able to work and think fast, to succeed at this endeavor. Mere artistic or cartooning ability just won't do it. You might run a classified ad under "entertainment" or do a mailing to party-planners. You can charge from $5 to $15 per caricature. I guess that explains why speed is so important. You also don't want interested impulse purchasers to have to wait so long they lose interest. The caricature artist near Fisherman's Wharf seems always to have a line of potential models. To you, I wish the same.

## 23 WORDSMITH

(Doing calligraphy) Take advantage of your spectacular handwriting to be a professional calligrapher. Offer your calligraphy services to advertising agencies, graphics studios, party-planners, and mailing houses. Do it with mailings to these organizations. Offer your handwriting services to the general public, too. For them, you can embellish their party invitations with your calligraphic class. Market your services with beautifully lettered signs on bulletin boards and a display ad that demonstrates your lettering style or styles. Ads in *Advertising Age* (see appendix) will enable you to practice your craft long-distance. A fair price is $25 per hour, though I paid $50 per hour when I was working at an ad agency.

## 24 FANCY ADDRESS

(Painting addresses on curbs and mailboxes) Anyone can have a fancy address, regardless of where they live. How? You can paint their addresses on their curbs. Or their mailboxes. Or their fences. You can hand letter the numerals, making sure they are clear and readable, even at night. Don't you wish all addresses were clear and readable? Marketing is best done with door-to-door solicitations, supplemented with classified ads, distributed circulars, and telephone canvassing. If you lack true artistic ability, consider working with a stencil. Just be sure your numerals are legible. If you work with a stencil, you'll have to charge less—maybe from $10 to $25. But if you really want to live up to your fancy name, hand lettering may be more in order—and you can charge from $25 to $50. Use long-lasting weatherproof paint. This business can be built into a regular producer of income if you expand area by area, suburb by suburb, neighborhood by neighborhood. Want a good, long list of prospects? Read the white pages of your telephone directory.

# 25 THE WEEKEND GALLERY

(Turning your home into a weekend art gallery)  Turn your home or apartment into a weekend art gallery. Contact several good artists, sculptors, and craftspeople, and display their works in your home. Enjoy the work by yourself during the week. On the weekends, try to sell as much of it as you can. A friend of mine earns her entire income this way. Perhaps you can, too. She charges each artist 33 percent of the purchase price paid for the painting. Advertise by having your gallery listed in the Sunday newspapers where galleries receive free listings. Also place small display ads in the art section of the Sunday paper. Do mailings to your own customers, to art critics, clubs, and known art buyers. Distribute circulars at art fairs and exhibits. Put up signs in your community. Generate publicity by encouraging media stories about your artists. You might hold free seminars on art in your home. If you have good taste in art, if you understand and can talk art, if you are a warm and sincere salesperson, this can be both an enjoyable and profitable way to earn money. If your gallery becomes a big success, you can hire someone to handle the weekend shows and you can go off on weekend holidays. You don't even need artistic talent to succeed here, just artistic judgment. You also need a whole lot of wall space, good lighting, and an interest in developing warm relationships with lots and lots of talented artists.

## CRAFTS AND CREATIONS

## 26  THE LIGHT FANTASTIC LAMP SHADE COMPANY

(Making custom lamp shades)   Making custom lamp shades can make quite a bit of money for you. You can use unusual materials, such as photos, newspapers, special clothing (T-shirts, for example), and other types of objects not ordinarily associated with your run-of-the-mill lamp shade. By incorporating special fabrics that match or complement your customers' draperies or upholstery you can design lamps that will add unique style to a home or office. Not a lot of people are making custom lamp shades, so the competition probably won't be stiff. The best way to get the word out is by exhibiting your talents. Show completed lamp shades at fairs and exhibits; post bulletins in fabric stores; use classified ads; distribute circulars; and make free, customized sample shades for high visibility locations such as restaurants, cocktail lounges, libraries, and anywhere else the manager will let you have some free display space in return for a free lamp. You just have to be an able and careful craftsperson to make a lamp shade. If you've got the talent, you can charge up to $100 per shade, and ever more for complex assignments.

## 27  ALBUMS UNLIMITED

(Compiling photo albums)   Money can be earned, along with love and gratitude, if you can creatively organize and put photos, cards, invitations, letters, newspaper clippings, menus, and other memorabilia of weddings, parties, anniversaries, and notable achievements into albums. Most people seem to have the components for an album stashed in a drawer or box, but never get around to putting it all together. Some people think an album is just a collection of pictures glued into a scrapbook, but a good album-maker (you) mixes pictures with change-of-pace items to make a more fascinating volume. Classified ads, along with a couple of nifty albums to show off, ought to get your business going. To succeed, you should have a flair for design, and patience. Show your completed albums to professional photographers—they may recommend your services to their clients. You can charge a rather hefty price ($100 to $250) for your labors and talents because it's difficult to put a price tag on priceless memories.

# 28 THE CHRISTMAS COMPANY

(Making unique Christmas ornaments) Make unusual Christmas ornaments and sell them at Christmas fairs, to retail stores, and even door-to-door at Christmas time. You can market your unusual ornaments (which can be made out of virtually *any* materials—natural, artificial, old, new, baked . . . ) with classified ads (start early in the season), and with publicity stories written by the reporters to whom you sent sample ornaments (clever you). Give some to the people who put up the community tree so that everyone can see how talented the president of the Christmas Company is. If there's a flea market in your area, that's also a fine place to show and sell your creations. Selling them at Christmas tree lots would also be effective. Your simplest ornaments could sell for $1, with your fanciest going for as much as $25. One person I know turned this part-time earning endeavor into a gigantic company. Careful you don't fall into the same trap or you'll find yourself in a life with too much money and not enough free time. A good aspect of this business is that it can apply to many crafts—so be crafty and see if you can turn your talent into an ornament for Christmas.

## 29 THE FRONT DOOR

(Doing carved relief on front doors)   If you happen to be a near-master at wood carving, you can specialize in doing carved relief work for front doors. With so many tract homes and town houses looking alike, your offer of a distinctive carving ought to be appreciated by home-owning individualists. Bring a few photographs (or better yet an entire carved front door) to the front door of your prospective customers. Market your service with direct mailing to contractors, architects, and door sellers, with Sunday display ads in the real estate section of your newspaper (showing off a home embellished with one of your works), and with circulars distributed to homes with blah front doors. Oh yes, you can charge from $50 to $150 for your services depending on the level of your talent and the difficulty of the design. I know a person who paid $250 for his front-door carving, but it was a very large carving. If you carve large, charge large. This is the ultimate door-to-door business.

## 30 THE END

(Making bookends)   Make ends meet by making bookends. There's not a big selection of these items, if you've looked lately. I have, and I hope you create a line of bookends that are distributed here so I can buy some. You can make them out of just about anything that will hold books up— out of existing objects (such as an old iron affixed to a marble base) or out of objects created by you (such as bricks arranged as a sculpture). Not much marketing is needed, just imagination. You can sell them at fairs, to retailers, and wherever craftspeople offer their wares. If you can line up a distributor at a trade fair, you might find yourself booking a lot of sales from your bookends. Charge at least $10 for Plain Jane bookends. And be sure your charges include your materials, your time, and your talent. There. That's The End.

# 31 JACK BE NIMBLE

(Making customized candles)  Truly, the craft of candle making is also an art form. Having paid $15 for one candle, I know it is art. Why else would I shell out $15 for a candle? Believe me, there's money in wax. It's not too hard to learn how to make candles; you can even purchase kits. You can look around your local gift or crafts store to get a line on the types of candles available these days; you can also borrow some ideas from work on display at flea markets and craft fairs. Once you get going you might even invent a new type of candle. Custom candles, just as custom bookends, can be sold to retailers for resale, or can be sold directly to the public wherever crafts are sold. Normal media advertising is not warranted, but exposure at flea markets, fairs, swap meets, and open air markets is highly encouraged. Prices you can charge will vary, depending upon materials and time.

# 32 WINDOW DRESSING

(Design window displays)  Become a professional designer of window displays. If you walk down commercial streets, you'll see a whole lot of dismally designed windows. Great! These stores are your prime customers. Show them your brochure, pictures of windows you've designed, accounts of the glorious sales that resulted from your appealing displays. A listing in the Yellow Pages along with a direct-mail campaign can get you started in this artistic, yet commercially-oriented business. To be good, you need an excellent design sense, a sense of business realism, a knowledge of lighting, a feeling for color and spatial relations, and a flair for the unique. If you're good, you'll probably be paid on a regular basis (amount to be determined by the size of the store), and best of all, your work will constantly be on display.

## 33 SHOPPING CENTER CREATIONS

(Decorating shopping centers) Specialize in decorating shopping centers for Christmas, Easter, and any other festive time. You don't have to decorate many centers to make a bundle of extra money, and if you do a good job you'll get lots of repeat business. I'd obtain customers by mailing brochures to shopping center owners throughout your area. My brochure would feature photos of decorations I'd designed and constructed. How would I get my first display to photograph? Same way as you—sheer determination. In order to create a shopping center display you've got to know how to get or make the display items you'll need. You should understand how to work in a large space. And you need a basic knowledge of lighting and color. Imagination will be your main ally. Successful shopping center decorators earn $1,000 (plus material costs) for their efforts. This I learned from a person who runs a shopping center. And he's a penny pincher. So maybe you can earn even more.

## 34 PATCHWORK

(Making custom sew-on patches) You can succeed at patchwork economics if part of your patchwork is patches. You can design and make custom sew-on patches. You must be able to dream up and design patch ideas and to sew them if you're to flourish in this endeavor. Small mailings with photos (even samples) of your custom patches will attract retailers. You can also sell to crafts distributors, or to the public at street fairs or flea markets. Signs advertising that you make customized patches will be very much in

order at public gatherings. Keep your material costs down
because you shouldn't ask more than, say, $2 a patch. If
you get an order for five thousand patches from an organization, that price can drop considerably just as your
overall income from the endeavor will rise considerably.

## 35 THE METALARTIST
(Doing ornamental metal work) The Metalartist. That's
you—if you can do ornamental metal work or welding repairs. The Metalartist makes steel garden gates, window
grilles, sculptures, lamps, candelabra, and a whole lot
more. The Metalartist markets his or her wares with ads
in the newspaper, exhibits at fairs and shows, leads seminars on metalworking, and has an ad in the Yellow Pages.
You'll need metalworking equipment and skill to succeed
at this endeavor. I met a midwestern metal artist (he sold
me a metal candelabrum for $60) who was a blacksmith-
turned-artist. His handworked iron fencing was a great
testament to his talent.

## 36 RECYCLED FRAMES
(Making picture frames from scrap material) Some folks are
busy making money by turning scrap material into picture frames. Care to join them? Scrap material may be
found just about anywhere. And you can market your
frames by means of displays at fairs and shows, circulars
distributed to the right people, and in-person calls at retail outlets that may sell your merchandise. If you design
a real winner, some store might just order five hundred of
them, or more. That happened to my wife. Might happen
to you. My wife, who ordinarily charged $15 per frame,
charged $8 when she got the volume order, and still made
a lot of money. Again, the skills of working with almost
any craft can be applied to this product. And you can
scour even the Library of Congress without finding any

books on making picture frames from recycled scrap. That means two things: (1) you have only your imagination to lean on, and (2) you ought to write a book about it.

## 37 LAMP CHAMP

(Making personalized lamps) Personalized lamps are unique and rather wonderful. They can be made (by you, of course) from old toys, tennis rackets, golf clubs, ski boots, telephones, antique anythings—and there's just no limit to the number of things that you can use for the bases. If you know how to electrify your lamp, all the better, but if you can't, lamp stores can. And will. Classified ads in your own newspaper—even display ads—will get you business. Classified ads in national magazines will get you more business. I'd display some lamps at shows, stores, fairs, and any other exhibits (besides, you're not only displaying art—you can also provide illumination). You might even splurge for a direct mailing to people who order custom-crafted furnishings by mail. There don't seem to be many Lamp Champs around, so you will be most welcome. Right now, people are making lamps (and money) from parking meters, gumball machines, and bowling balls. So let your imagination run rampant. Oh, one more thing—you should consider making oil lamps as well as electrical lamps. It's hard to put a price on your work without having seen it, but I doubt if you'll want to sell a lamp for under $35.

## 38 MY TIME IS YOUR TIME

(Customizing clocks)  Not only can you make lamps from just about anything (as long as you can get them wired) but you can also make clocks from just about anything (as long as you can make them tick, or hum, or talk). Please understand that I am not talking about your making a clock itself. I am talking about your taking a clock and

making a base or stand or box or housing for it. You can
leave the clock's face as is, or you can creatively adapt
that, too. Advertise your prowess with classified ads
(newspapers and decorator-oriented magazines), and with
showings of your timeless timepieces at shows and fairs.
Naturally, the prices you charge will depend upon the
time you put into this venture and the clocks and other
materials you use. If you can accomplish clock making,
you can accomplish money-making.

# 39 SUPERIOR INTERIORS

(Doing interior decorating)   Many a housewife, contemplat-
ing reentry into the work market, might realize that one
of her greatest talents was developed in decorating her
own home. In fact many ex-housewives have achieved reentry in style by becoming interior decorators. If you
have flair in that direction and know your way around the
furnishings industry, you can earn money decorating
other people's homes. Advertise your skills in the Yellow
Pages, with small display ads in home-oriented sections of
the newspaper, and even with direct mailings to furniture
stores, offering your services as a part-time interior deco-
rator. Interior decorators normally get paid a percentage
of the money spent on furnishings, but that is not a firm,
fast rule. You can charge by the hour, by the project, or
any other way you'd like. A woman from Los Angeles,
who thought she had absolutely no earning talent, earned
over $10,000 the first year she tried her hand at interior
decorating. So don't underestimate your earning talent if
you've got decorating talent in your interior.

# 40 THE VILLAGE TAXIDERMIST

(Stuffing animals)   As long as there are hunters who hunt
for sport (not recommended by me or by the game itself),
there will be the need for taxidermists to stuff and mount

the animals in a lifelike state. My accountant, normal in most respects, is abnormal in my eyes because of the three giant stuffed fish hanging in his living room. Of course, his taxidermist loves him. You can learn this craft by reading a book, taking a course, practicing, or even doing an informal apprenticeship. And you can earn pretty good money at it. Post bulletins and do a direct mailing to hunting and fishing services and clubs. Put up signs in sporting supply shops, too. Sometimes science teachers are interested in obtaining stuffed specimens, so you might try them once you get going. Small display ads in hunting magazines will bring in even more business. If you live in a big city you are less likely to make out well at taxidermy than if you live in or near a hunting community. You charge by the creature being stuffed—more for a deer than a mouse. I remember a fishing guide told me it would cost $200 to stuff a sport fish I had just caught. I also remember the look he gave me as I set the fish free. It was a lucky fish—lots of people would have gone fishing for a taxidermist.

## 41 REGAL RUGS

(Making rugs)   Are you one of those people with a talent for making rugs? Have you ever tried? If you can learn to make rugs by hand, then you can make custom designed rugs for companies (featuring the company logo or trademark), for stores (featuring their name or logo), and for families (featuring any design or crest they want). It takes very little capital to get started. You just need to make a couple of practice rugs both to learn how and to get samples. Then make in-person calls and show your wares, and also list your business in the Yellow Pages. Newspaper display ads in the decorating section might be good, too, and a booth at an art fair might attract customers. I'd also try to arrange a display at an office furniture show and a home furniture show. Since rugs sell for more than $10,000 if they're special enough, make yours very special.

# 42 THE VOLGA BOOTMAN

(Making custom boots and sandals)   It's not all that easy to be a custom boot and sandal maker. You've got to be trained, and you've got to practice. But once you master the craft, you can earn money with style. Attract your first customers with phone calls or personal letters, and arrange for appointments. When making your first call, take measurements of people's feet and collect 50 percent of the purchase price. On your next visit, fit the boots, collect your other 50 percent, and collect the names of new prospects. You might want to give your friends special deals at first to get the shoes, sandals, or boots on their feet and on the street. Once you get going you'll have people all over town asking their friends "Say, those are nice. Where did you get them?" The key to this business is having your old customers' friends become your new customers. You can hold your current job for your main money using your added shoe income (booty?) to supplement your salary. Or you eventually can become a full-time shoemaker and live wherever you want. Then you can either make boots and relax, or make more boots and make more money. I know a person who has earned all the money he's needed during the past seven years just by making custom boots. He charges exactly the same as the boots would cost had you purchased them at a store. So by offering custom boots at noncustom prices, he gets quite a bit of business. He claims there are no shortcuts to acquiring the skill. According to him apprenticeship is the only way. He gets to live like a hermit in the mountains. Boot making made his dream come true. Yours, too, I hope.

# 43   WINNING WINDOWS

(Making stained glass windows)   Boy, is it hard to make a really good stained glass window. But boy, is it profitable. And once you get the hang of it, it's fun. You'll have to take some classes in the art, but with some training and practice, you'll be billing yourself as a stained glass pro in no time. Once your dues are paid, and you're good, customers will pay you plenty for your customized functional art. To market your windows, direct mailings to likely houses, condos, and stores are recommended, as are Yellow Pages advertising, bulletins in fancy shopping centers, newspaper display ads, and exhibits (with brochures) at local crafts fairs. It will also help your Winning Windows biz if you do a mailing to local contractors, decorators, and architects. The best way to demonstrate your prowess to them is with color pictures in your brochure. Sell your windows for as little as $100 for a small one. Large ones should cost a lot. And once you have mastered the art of stained glass windows consider making stained glass lamp shades, too. Mr. Tiffany did well with them.

# 44   MIRROR IMAGE

(Making customized pub mirrors)   Interest in pub mirrors is growing and will probably never disappear. It's one thing to walk into Vicki's Hot-Time Lounge and see a pub mirror heralding beer. It's something else to see a pub mirror heralding Vicki's Hot-Time Lounge. You can be sure that Vicki will agree. As soon as you have the craft down pat, direct mailings to pubs and restaurants ought to net you quite a bit of business. An exhibit of your mirrors at a restaurant/cocktail lounge supply show won't hurt either. Be sure your brochure features pictures of your mirrors. You might even consider mass production and contact large companies that might order large quantities. Breweries seem an especially good prospect. I own three pub mirrors. One was a gift; one cost $75, and one cost $25. Luckily, the most expensive one was the gift.

## 45 TINY TABLES

(Making miniature furniture for dollhouses)   You don't need a large workshop to make furniture if you make miniature furniture for dollhouses and collections. The market for teeny tables, chairs, beds, dressers, and the rest is surprisingly unteeny, so if you're good you'll be able to sell all you make. Find customers by displaying at toy shows, by making presentations at retail outlets that carry this kind of Lilliputian merchandise, and by selling directly to the public at exhibits and fairs. To succeed will take painstaking craftsmanship, good eyesight, and the ability to think small. Some people spend several thousand dollars furnishing a dollhouse. Luckily, our dollhouse only cost several hundred dollars to furnish. Check the dollhouse furniture at your local toy store to see what items you might make for them.

## 46 PLAY WITH ME

(Creating games)   My wife and I have created four board games. One of those games made us some money ($500). We sold it to a game company. The other three times we had a ball working on the games and didn't even care (much) that we made nary a cent. You don't come up with a Scrabble or Monopoly every day, but it is possible to earn money creating games. Producing most board games costs a fortune, so you will probably have to sell your game to existing manufacturers. But you might be able to develop an inexpensive board game and make and distribute it yourself. That's the most certain way of making money, but it won't be the big money that a nationally distributed game can make. With the mail-order industry growing, I notice more and more ads for games. You might leaf through some special interest magazines (try *Psychology Today*) to see the kinds of games being offered. You might notice the absence of games in your particular area of special interest. And you might be able to come up with a winner.

## 47 DOLLY DOCTOR

(Making and repairing dolls)   You probably knew from the name that Dolly Doctor repairs broken dolls. But did you realize that the good doctor also makes dolls, too? It's true if you want it to be. Dolls may be made with many types of materials. If you're good at making and/or fixing dollies, then hang out your shingle with classified ads, signs in toy stores (with the owner's permission), circulars distributed to doll-owning-age-kids' parents (find them in the park near the swings, teeter-totters, monkey bars, and slides), and with dolls for sale at fairs and crafts shows. Charge as little as $5 for a simple rag doll. Charge as much as $100 for a complex art-type doll. Want to learn more? I call to your attention the appendix: read *The Doll*.

## 48 SCENTS OF BEAUTY

(Making decorative air fresheners)   Here's a relatively new one for you: make and sell decorative air fresheners. You've probably seen lots of crafts exhibits where you are tempted by displays of necklaces, earrings, T-shirts, rings, and paintings. But how many decorative air fresheners have you seen? It is a way to combine art with function, to appeal to special interest groups, and to single-handedly fight air pollution. Market your scents with classified ads, even display ads in the low-cost newspapers called "shoppers," and with in-person calls to retail stores that may serve as outlets for you. You can use many different forms and materials for your air fresheners. And you can price them depending upon the quality of your work. Make scents to you?

## 49 SHADOW BOXER

(Making shadow boxes) Every Christmas, my wife and daughter make a Christmas-oriented shadow box. They fill the compartments in the unfinished-wood shadow box with Santas, angels, yarns, popcorn, ornaments, elves, and all sorts of festive doodads. Then they paint the wood, or stain it, and we display it on a bookshelf or table, along with our shadow boxes from Christmases past. You can do the same. You need not even limit your themes to Christmas. And you need not keep your boxes. You can sell them. But not to my wife and daughter, please. Sell them at fairs and shows, to retailers, with classified ads, and with ads in the special Christmas section (there really is one in December in most metropolitan dailies). Maybe you'll want to display your shadow boxes in restaurants, along with a notice that you make these lovely boxes (or even personalized boxes—you'll get more orders if you offer personalized *anything*) for a price. I've seen shadow boxes priced up to $100. Use your own judgment, based upon your investment of time and materials.

## 50 DOLLY CREATIONS

(Creating doll clothing) Let your creative spirits soar and come up with exciting new fashions—so exciting that toy-store owners want them, doll owners want them, and even *Vogue* secretly longs to run a feature on them. You'll turn up customers if you exhibit your creations at fairs, if you put up signs and distribute circulars, and if you can find a true believer (in your fashions) to run a magazine or newspaper story (pictorial, of course) about Dolly Creations. Once you have customers and designs, you can try to develop an entire line of doll clothes. You've got to be a talented clothes designer (or clothes copier) to make money with this idea, but if you are, make tiny rather than life-sized clothes. Chances are you'll make more than tiny money.

## 51 DRY IS BEAUTIFUL

(Making dried flower arrangements)   Dried flower arrangements are not hard to make. Materials don't cost much (they're free if you know where to look), and the finished product is beautiful. You just need a knowledge of where to find (or buy) dried flowers and weeds, a sense of color design, and an appreciation for the unique beauty of flowers. Make several arrangements of dried flowers, put them into suitable containers (be creative), then take them in person to plant stores, gift stores, department stores, and anywhere else (flea market stalls, fairs, variety stores) they may be sold. Once you've lined up some customers, make a careful plan for delivering, collecting, bookkeeping, and expanding, and you'll have a small (but going and growing) business. Your dried flower arrangements can also be sold directly to the public at crafts shows—even from pushcarts. In fact, we purchased our last such arrangement at a fair from a pushcart. (Cost us $5 and that was about two years ago; and the arrangement still looks beautiful.) Sell your arrangements for as low as $3 for a tiny one all the way up to $25 for a large one. Once you're involved in this business, you'll begin to see weeds in a new way.

## 52 EGGSCELLENT EGGS

(Decorating eggs as gifts)   I was dazzled, amazed, impressed, and charmed by some gift eggs decorated by the wife of a friend. I mean those eggs were works of art, worthy of a place in a major museum. As an art lover, I do not relegate items to museums lightly. This woman sells her eggs mainly at Easter and primarily to fancy stores, but she also sells them at other times of the year—as objets d'art, pendants, and pins—to stores and to private individuals. Her marketing is by personal visits to the stores, which often purchase the eggs as soon as they see them. Circulars are left behind after the sales calls. She not only earns a good income decorating and selling eggs, but is now also in the process of teaching others to do the work for her. To succeed at this endeavor you must have artistic talent, patience, a steady hand, and a whole lot of eggs. If you're as good as Mrs. Nelson from San Diego, you can sell your eggs at prices ranging from $12.50 to $250.00. And you thought the price of the eggs *you* buy was high?

## 53 YOUR GOOD NAME

(Carving wooden nameplates)  You can earn extra money by carving wooden nameplates for people to hang on their houses. Somebody gave us one for our house, but I prefer to remain incognito, so I enjoy having the wooden nameplate in the hallway to remind me who I am. Other people, however, want to tell the world, or at least their neighbors, who they are. They'd be pleased to adorn their homes with your nameplates. How will they find out about you? With a circular delivered to their mailboxes. By reading about your business in the classified ad section of the newspaper. By seeing signs on their local bulletin boards. By seeing sample nameplates in hardware stores. You've got to know about wood carving and have work space and the proper carving tools to pursue this spare time earning activity. I know a man who earns his entire living carving wooden nameplates. He charges $25 for a simple residential nameplate, and $300 for a larger commercial wooden nameplate. And he gets loads of business, mainly by word-of-mouth now. Best of all, he absolutely enjoys his work and tells me feels as though he is getting paid to enjoy his hobby.

## 54 JACK O. LANTERN

(Carving jack-o'-lanterns) Here's one of your more seasonal earnways: buy pumpkins, carve them into jack-o'-lanterns, and sell them. Sell to the public or to stores. Sell from carts or from pumpkin sales lots. As a professional carver, you can ask a pretty penny for your pretty pumpkins ($10 to $25). Your best marketing tools will be your jack-o'-lanterns, plus your signs. Once you get a feel for the business, try to sell your works at as many outlets as possible, getting other people to do the actual selling in all the locations except the one that you man/woman. You won't earn enough to keep going all year, but you might earn a lot in a little time. A very little time.

## 55 STITCHES IN TIME

(Repairing the needlework of others) Be the person who repairs the needlework of others. Be it embroidery, knitting, needlepoint, or crewel, if you're handy with a needle, you can make a few extra dollars. It seems that the people who make these items find it difficult to repair them. That's why you're needed. Advertise your expertise with display ads in women's publications, even national magazine classified sections. Put up signs in needlework stores. Mail circulars to women's clubs. Charge on an hourly basis (perhaps $7.50 to $10.00 per hour), or by the project. It's work you can do at home, and work that requires few tools. In Chicago, I know a person who charged $50.00 to fix a fancy needlepoint pillow. Who would ever pay that much? A sentimental needlepointer, I guess.

# 56   CANDID BUTTONS

(Affixing photos to pins or buttons) You've seen the buttons that say "Vote for Whoever." Well, by investing in a simple machine you can make buttons yourself, but instead of a politician's name you put photographs of your customers on each pin. All it takes is a camera (Polaroid) and the aforementioned machine. The only marketing you need is to display attractive signs near your machine at fairs, street markets, shows, flea markets, and any other high-traffic places. This is a relatively simple business, and the only skills you require are competency with a simple camera, competency with a simple button machine, and the ability to make your models smile. A few years ago, we paid $2.50 for such a button. You won't be able to retire on your earnings, but you'll find that this business is easy to do and to delegate. Hope you get it clicking.

# 57   ALLURING LURES

(Making fishing lures) Make money by making lures that fish will love. Sell them to fishing shops, bait shops. Advertise them in the classified section of national fishing magazines. Display your Alluring Lures at fishing and sports shows. Sell your lures in person at popular fishing spots. Post bulletins in all places that fishermen visit. You've got to know about fish, and about the existing lure market. You can learn about them by going fishing, by visiting fishing stores, and by reading the *Field and Stream Fishing Annual, Fins and Feathers, Fishing Facts, Fishing World,* and *Fly Fisherman Magazine.* Maybe you'll come up with the most lovable lure fish have seen in years. That will make Alluring Lures very alluring to you, I can assure you.

# 58   THE SLEEP SCENE

(Making scenic pillows and quilts) Encourage others to have pleasant dreams with the beautiful scenic pillows and quilts that you make. You can make any scene you want, but your work will sell at a brisker pace if you can depict the same scenes that tourists to your area gawk over. The creation of scenic bedding is quite an art, and quite a few people practice it with skill and aplomb. If you are one of them, or can learn to be one (with skills at either quilt making or pillow making), you can earn quite a bit of money. Quilts sell for several hundred dollars. If you don't know the craft, and don't want to learn, you may be able to set up a business and delegate the actual quilting/pillowing to others. Market your scenic bedding at quilt stores, tourist stores (if any are near you), with display ads (showing your work), at shows and fairs, and even with signs on bulletin boards. It's a business that lets you sleep at night.

## 59  KUSTOM KEY

(Making custom key chains) Kustom Keys would be a pretty corny name for a service that makes key chains out of just about anything small. To practice this trade, you need a device that can puncture a hole in nearly any material, strands of good, strong, nonbreakable key chain, and decent marketing. A good imagination will also stand you in good stead. Decent marketing would consist of signs at crafts fairs, displays of some of your custom chains, classified ads in national newspapers, and signs at auto parts stores (they may wish, and will deserve, a cut of your action). My current key chain was made by my daughter out of leather. Though she gave it to me free (thanks again, Amy), I've seen similar key chains selling for $3.95. A local jeweler sells a jewel-encrusted key chain for $500.00. There's your price range, Once you've got your business going, relax and read your copy of *Phunny Phacts*.

## 60  DINING FASHIONS

(Creating wardrobes for waiters and waitresses) There are people who earn extra money designing wardrobes for waiters and waitresses. Sometimes they create entire ensembles. Other times just special hats, vests, aprons, or pinnable hankies. If you can design restaurant attire and create the finished product (or cause it to be created), you can get in on some tasty profits. Of course, you've got to be good at making patterns, sewing, and creating clothes of many different styles and themes. Advertise your service in restaurant trade publications and do special mailings to restaurants. You might write just a few letters at first to just a few of your local eateries. Once you have outfitted them, then spread the word to the rest of the world, using samples of the attire you created for them to demonstrate your flair. This business, which can be a sideline for you if you delegate the actual wardrobe making, can pull in a five-figure annual income.

# 61  CUSTOM COSTUMES

(Creating costumes)  If you are mildly interested in the prospect of creating restaurant attire, you'll be wildly interested at the prospect of creating costumes for gorillas, chambermaids, ghosts, angels, skeletons, musketeers, kings, and outer-space folk. The idea is to create custom costumes for anyone to wear anywhere. You'll most likely be busiest at (or just before) Halloween. Market your Custom Costumes directly to costume shops. Do your own Yellow Pages advertising, run display ads in October, use classified advertising, exhibit at trade shows, and make a few free costumes for a local acting troupe (in exchange for being named and credited in their programs). If you are handy with a needle, know about making patterns, and have a kooky imagination, you might be the ideal costumer. If you know good seamstresses, let them follow your designs so that you can sit back and do what wealthy people do—figure out ways to accumulate more wealth.

# 62 MR. MONOGRAM (OR MS. MONOGRAM)

(Monogramming anything)   Yep, you can earn money monogramming absolutely anything. If you have a modest amount of requisite artistic talent, you can run classified or display ads and offer to monogram clothing, sports equipment, kitchen equipment, towels, linen, quilts, cars, toys, and office machines—anything but people (unless you're also a tattooist). You can satisfy one of the most significant human needs—the need for identity. Use a paintbrush, an engraving machine, or a welding machine. Use embroidery, needlepoint, or pen and ink. Offer your services to clothing and sporting goods stores by means of a mailing. They could increase their sales by using your skills. Be imaginative. All you need is a knowledge of the alphabet and crafts abilities. With them, you can help a lot of identities identify themselves.

# 63 THE PUZZLE PLACE

(Making jigsaw puzzles)   You can make money with both customized jigsaw puzzles and noncustomized jigsaw puzzles. The customized kind should net you more money—offer to make jigsaw puzzles out of people's photographs. (Charge anywhere from $50 to $100 for this service.) You must blow up the photo, mount it onto cardboard, and create a jigsaw puzzle out of it. You can obtain business for your photographic jigsaw puzzles with classified ads in national magazines. The noncustomized jigsaw puzzles (retailing for about $10) would have either an original design or a photo or something that customers might love—a picture of a tourist attraction or a national landmark (Grand Canyon). Your puzzles can be marketed with mailings and follow-up visits to "puzzle outlets" (toy stores, variety stores, bookstores, gift stores—with supporting point-of-purchase displays), and with signs at fairs and exhibits. I think the customized puzzles would be more fun, more profitable, and more work, but the choice is up to you. Don't puzzle over it too long. You can run this kind of business on a mail-order, straight retail, or wholesale basis. And you can be involved in either the craftsmanship (puzzle making) and/or the selling and distributing end. These days, puzzles are more creative than ever, and if you're creative, you'll flourish. You need cardboard-cutting ability and a love and understanding of jigsaw puzzles.

# 64   REBORN BOOKS

(Repairing old books) Repair, recover, and rebind old books. Offer your service by mailing a letter and brochure to libraries and known book collectors, and purveyors of old books. Also, run classified ads and put up signs on bulletin boards announcing that you can give new life to old books. Exhibit some of your reborn books at shows or fairs. And see if your local bookstores will let you place piles of brochures on their counters, thus offering the service to their customers. Of course, you've got to learn the craft of bookbinding to succeed at this endeavor. It's not a task for everyone, but if it is a task you enjoy, you can also enjoy newborn profits. Then you can settle back and read a good book.

# 65   OPEN WIDE

(Making teeth for dentists)   This earnway may sound a little strange, but it is a perfectly legitimate and not uncommon method of bringing in dollars. Make teeth for dentists. That's right—take the training (call your dentist to ask where) to learn how to craft realistic false teeth. Someone has to make them. Why not you? Once you know how to do it, tell the world with mailings to dentists and dental supply houses. Arrange for exhibits at dental supply shows, and soon you can have a substantial and delegable business. You've got to be good at handcrafting, naturally, and you must be able to work to exacting standards. You can earn over $100 per set of teeth. So go to it. Got all that? Okay. Rinse and spit.

# 66  A TOUCH OF CLASS

(Embroidering cloth napkins)   Restaurants can offer a touch of class if their tables are adorned with custom-embroidered cloth napkins created by your company. Personal letters and direct mailings to restaurants, and ads in national restaurant trade publications can result in lots of business—possibly more than you can handle. Your ability to embroider with grace and style, combined with your ample supply of needles, thread, and thimbles, will help restaurants to be unique and classy. And restaurants constantly wear out and lose napkins, so your business should thrive for a long time. Are you genuinely creative, with a good sense of color? Good. Now get out there and thrive.

# 67  FRAME GAME

(Framing pictures)   Go into the picture-framing business—and do it with flair. Offer pickup and delivery, one-day service, and competitive pricing. I'm not talking about using unique materials for framing. Nope. That's a whole different earnway—number 36. I'm talking about unique services using standard materials. For instance you might experiment with a framing-while-you-wait booth at a flea market. Classified ads, circulars, an ad in the Yellow Pages, and a display of your frames at a show or art exhibit should net you new customers. Mailings to art galleries should provide you with even more business. Another suggestion: offer your service with brochures at a photography store. Not enough photos are framed, and more should be. Certainly the photo store would agree. Once you've got your frame business going, you'll agree, too. How much to charge? Ask your local frame store what they charge. You charge less. That's not unethical—that's the frame game.

## 68 REWARDING REWEAVING

(Reweaving anything)   Extra money is yours if you become accomplished (or are accomplished) at the skill of reweaving fabric. It takes training and practice. And you must be a perfectionist. But if you're good at it, you can market your services with mailings to cleaning stores along with classified ads and a listing in the Yellow Pages. Your services will be in demand if you're really skillful. You can end up making very good money by rescuing really expensive fabric items from disaster. (A local reweaver quoted me $35 as the cost to reweave a hole in the sleeve of a sport jacket for which I paid $75.) It makes sense to train a backup weaver should you be offered an excess of business or wish to depart for a vacation. There will always be a need for reweaving, so you can see that it makes sense to position yourself to satisfy this constant need. What happens when a person with a $5,000 oriental rug finds a hole in it? The person calls in a reweaver. How much does that reweaver charge? If he (or she) charged $500, the rug owner might gladly pay it. Moral: Don't get a hole in your oriental rug *whatever* you do.

## 69 TRUE BLUEPRINTS

(Obtaining, framing, and selling blueprints)   If you can obtain blueprints of famous structures (not difficult), you can earn money by framing and selling them. Sell them at fairs, flea markets, and art exhibits. Sell them to retailers, too. Some of my friends have framed blueprints of the

Golden Gate Bridge ($50). Great looking, I might add. Since people already know what the famous structure looks like and know what a blueprint looks like, you can sell framed blueprints with classified and small display ads. You can also sell them directly to retailers (tourist shops, gift stores, department stores, unserious art galleries). You don't really require a lot of craft or artistic ability in this endeavor. But you do need a good eye, artistic and architectural judgment, and access to some blueprints.

# 70  THE BRONZE AGE

(Bronzing anything)  Offer to bronze just about anything: baby shoes (five million new babies per year), beloved old pipes, baseballs, leaves, insects, fruit, shells, pottery, driftwood, tools, antiques—almost everything except your mother-in-law. In addition to bronzing, you can offer to cover items with silver or gold. You can also electroplate or porcelainize items. Small classified or display ads in national magazines and newspapers should bring in a raft of business. You can get the real lowdown on this business by writing to the Warner Electric Company, 1512 West Jarvis Avenue, Chicago, Illinois 60626. Now I agree that bronzing baby's bootees will not test the far reaches of your creative abilities. But bronzing is an enduring art form (sort of). Anyhow, I still have the baby shoes my parents bronzed for me. See? Aren't they cute?

## AUDIO/VIDEO/FILM/PHOTOGRAPHY

# 71  LIVING HISTORY TAPES

(Audiotaping or videotaping events)  There's more money to be made by recording events on audiotape or (better still) on videotape than most people yet realize. By recording events—municipal, social, personal, sports, educational, religious, current—you can provide your community with accurate records while providing your bank account with welcome deposits. Market your service with display ads in local publications, letters to appropriate dignitaries and officials, and demonstrations of your taping abilities. A presentation of your tapes ought to convince people of the value of this work. Charge your customers the cost of the tape plus, say, $25 per hour for your time. If you're going to give this business a good start, you've got to know your equipment, tape and recorder, and you should be experienced in operating it. It requires a combination of technical skill and artistic talent, with an emphasis on the former. It sure won't hurt to take a video course in your local community college or the brief workshops provided by many video/audio equipment retailers.

# 72 ROCK BOTTOM PRODUCTIONS

(Producing low-budget movies or videotapes)  Produce low-budget movies and/or videotapes and you have the chance to make a high-budget income. With figures such as $25 and $40 million being bandied about by big-time movie producers, your ability to produce watchable productions for a fraction of those costs—usually from $500 to $5,000—will make you attractive to your potential customers. They might be companies desiring sales or training films, or service companies that wish to have a demonstration film or videotape of their service. They might be families wanting a good family movie, or just some people who want a movie for some old reason of their own. Actually, you can probably convince just about any company or anybody that they can really use a movie or tape. Some large firms might be able to use several different kinds of films—for advertising, for training, for recruiting. Since you will have low overhead, and since you may be using rented equipment and will be performing most of the labor yourself (lighting, props, cameraperson, editor), you will be able to charge rock-bottom prices for high quality films and videotapes. Market your services with the Yellow Pages, with direct mailings to likely prospects, with consistent newspaper advertising, and with a sample film you can take around or even show at a local theater. Trade magazine ads won't hurt, either. And you might as well look into the use of local cable TV. There are new books on filming and videotaping coming out every month. To get a line on the best ones, ask for a catalog from Crain Books, 740 N. Rush Street, Chicago, Illinois 60611. I know a person who earned over $250,000 in 1989 merely by producing low-budget movies and tapes. Your company may be Rock Bottom, but your income can be rock top.

# 73 ACTION STUDIOS

(Producing films and tapes of people in action sports) As long as we're on the subject of film and tape, let me tell you what happened to me while skiing at Vail, Colorado, during the winter of 1980. A skier, carrying his camera, schussed up to me and asked if I wanted a film made of me skiing. "Me? Skiing on film?" I asked, dreaming that it might lead to my discovery by the U.S. Olympic Ski Team, or at least Hollywood. "How much?" I asked, disguising my excitement. I was told that for a mere $10 per minute, I could have a full-color, completely edited film of any length. Better yet, the cinematographer offered special effects. He said he could speed me up when I skied too slowly, or slow me down when I was doing everything right so that I could enjoy the sight of myself being perfect in super-slow motion. From my point of view $50 for a five-minute film of me skiing like a superstar (with the help of special effects) sounded reasonable. Now this guy told me that his two main interests are skiing and making movies. He said he makes enough money filming in the morning that he can just ski all afternoon. His happiness indicated that this man had indeed found his niche in life. Come to think of it, he may have found my niche, too. I love skiing and moviemaking. The basic idea is to film people doing exciting, action-packed activities: skiing, kayaking, wind surfing, hang gliding, rock climbing, motorcycle racing, playing baseball, tennis, volleyball, football, racquetball, or Ping-Pong. No, not backgammon. No, not jogging. Ads in local papers seem to be a sensible marketing approach. Those ads plus a few cleverly posted bulletins and some free screenings of your films ought to get you your customers. The personal approach, right on the slopes, worked for the Vail filmmaker. Combine your moviemaking talent with your favorite action activity and you might be as happy as he is. Carry lots of business cards, and give them away generously. You've got to be good at the sport (my filmer skied as he filmed), and at filming or taping. You should have a good knowledge of editing and special effects. And you should be prepared to live in Nirvana, wherever yours is.

# 74 THE TAPEWORM

(Videotaping for businesses) The Tapeworm videotapes important business events, including meetings, conferences, lectures, parades, and other gatherings. Businesses and institutions, rather than individuals, are the target of your business. Direct mail to schools, lecturers, parade coordinators, sports teams, city officials, conference centers, and business marketing departments should net you enough business. A brochure describing your services, along with a demonstration videotape, should do the trick. Videotape is much cheaper than film. There is no cost for processing because there is no processing. Since videotape is still a relatively new technology, the sooner you get into the field the better. If no videotape companies are listed in your Yellow Pages, you know you're in the right place at the right time. Again, charge for the materials plus your time. If you want, specialize in something such as lectures or conferences. But whatever you do, explore this avenue of extra earning. Lights . . . camera . . . earning!

# 75 PHOTOPET

(Photographing pets) If an artist can earn an extra buck painting pooches, a photographer should make money by aiming a camera at them. A number of photographers are already hauling in good money photographing dogs, cats, fish (yes, fish!), birds, horses, and whatever other critters people keep as pets. In rural areas, this includes most of the barnyard beasts: any cow, bull, steer, heifer, hog, goat, rooster, hen, or sheep worthy of being entered in a fair is worthy of a full-color photo. You can secure business the same way the pet portrait painters do—post bulletins, place display and classified ads in newspapers, and distribute circulars at dog, cat, horse, and livestock shows. You can also go to all the state and county fairs and make a whole lot of money photographing the animal entrants, alone or along with their owners. Charge $5 to $25 per photo (or do a set of six). If you're a good photographer (skilled in composition, lighting, cameras, film) and can keep a fidgety puppy in focus, you'll do well.

# 76 CANDID KEY CHAIN

(Photographing people for display in key chains) Smile! You're on Candid Key chain! You might find yourself saying that if you have a basic knowledge of photography and a $265 instrument. You take color action photos of tennis players, joggers, golfers, and other sportsfolk, even nonsportsfolk, then offer them key-chain slide viewers with their photos inside. No marketing is necessary other than your presence, camera in hand, where the sportsfolk and nonsportsfolk congregate. Each key chain will cost you about $.15, and you can sell them for at least $2.95. Thank heaven people enjoy looking at themselves.

# 77 GROWING GROWING GROWN

(Videotaping the growth of children)   By now you may have recognized that videotape is a versatile earning tool. More and more people are earning money with it. With a videotape camera (less than $1,000 brand new; far less if used) you can offer to film people's kids. You can come on each birthday (and half-birthday) and shoot about five or ten minutes of videotape. Each segment captures an episode in a child's growth. When all are put together, the parents and the child have a super record of the child's growth. I know. I have my daughter's first twelve years on videotape, and my wife and I frequently view the tape, never complaining that it's a rerun. Recruit customers with a free showing of a tape you've done, or by mailings to new parents (get 'em while they're hot). Small classified ads will net more business for you. Charge about $5 per minute of taping plus the cost of tape and materials. If you think this earning endeavor is fun and rewarding, you're right.

# 78 RECORD OF THE YEAR

(Making custom phonograph records and audiotapes)   Making custom phonograph records and tapes can make you money. Record a family putting on a talent show or a play; record a child as the child grows up—from baby talk to perfect enunciation; make a commemorative record or tape for a party or birthday gift. Using your imagination, you'll see there are many applications of this earning idea.

Be sure you have the equipment or use o.
you can produce first-class finished records .
may also need to assemble outside talent to p.
of your sounds. You can market your service w
the entertainment section of the classified ads, ʏ          ʋ
stories in the paper, mailings to party planners, anₑ  ₐdio
commercials on local stations. If you use special sound effects (available at record stores) and background music,
your homemade job might come out sounding very professional. As with videotape, charge for materials plus your
hourly charge—anywhere from $10 to $20 per hour.

# 79 SHOOTER

(Photographing houses and cars) Shooter takes magnifi-
cent photographs of peoples' houses and cars, enlarges
and frames them, and sells them for anywhere from $25
to $100. Shooter probably distributes circulars to owners
of photogenic homes, also to owners of star quality automobiles. By offering such a rare service, Shooter's bank
account is really clicking. Of course, Shooter is a very good
photographer. A person in my area offers this service and
calls his company Hot Shots. All I know is that it provides
him with all the income he needs to cover his living expenses. Never underestimate your ability to earn money
by massaging people's egos.

# 80 INSURAVISION

(Videotaping possessions for insurance purposes) When
people take out home-owners' insurance, it's a good idea
for them to make a very accurate record of their possessions. Many insurance companies require such a record.
These days, the technology exists to make more accurate
records than ever before: videotape. Buy or rent a videotape camera (black and white is okay, but color is better),

then run ads in local newspapers offering to videotape possessions for insurance purposes. Do a mailing to all the insurance agents in town, letting them know of your service. Give a copy of the finished videotape to the insured who will keep it in a safe place (like a bank vault). One hopes it will never be needed. But if it is, insurance companies will respect its accuracy. Now, aiming a camera and keeping things in focus isn't all that difficult, so you don't need all that much videotaping skill. But you should know how to light and how to shoot an object so that it is easily and clearly identifiable. Once again, charge per hour. A company like this is already flourishing in my community. Get a company flourishing in yours.

# 81   INSTANT NOSTALGIA

(Photographing people and then antiquing the photos)   As one pundit puts it, "Nostalgia isn't what it used to be." But nostalgia can be exactly what it used to be, or even better than it ever was, if you specialize in taking antique photos. You use modern equipment to take photos, then process, print, and frame the photos so they come out looking like old tintypes. You might even costume your subjects so that they look antiquey, too. Antique photography is earning bundles for not-all-that-talented photographers in malls, tourist traps, fairs, and other high-traffic locations. They charge $10 for a tintype-type photo. Not bad. The equipment doesn't cost all that much, and the marketing can be as simple as classified ads and signs at your place of photography. And you really don't require a whole lot of photographic talent. But you should be able to establish proper lighting, compose your photos properly, and capture a mood. A good basic photography book will teach you these things. A course in photography at a local community college will also help, especially if it includes both shooting and processing. I mentioned that the antique photographer in this area charges $10 for a photo. But did I tell you that on the weekends people are usually lined up to get their pictures taken? And that it takes ten minutes to shoot the photo? When you do the proper arithmetic, you will see that just working weekends will make these the good old days for you.

# 82  THE HIDDEN CAMERA

(Videotaping market research interviews)  You've seen those commercials in which an unsuspecting shopper is interviewed by a grinning announcer, and then the hidden camera is revealed. You can earn extra money operating that hidden camera. Offer to videotape market research interviews. These interviews are conducted frequently, and many are videotaped. After you contact the American Marketing Association at 420 Lexington Avenue, Suite 1733, New York, New York 10070, they'll send you a list of companies that conduct market surveys. Write to these companies offering to videotape their interviews in your area. As I continue to mention throughout this chapter, a videotape camera is a multifaceted earning tool. Many companies, stores, and individuals will be pleased to help you earn extra money if you help them earn extra money with your videotape camera. You need a basic knowledge of how to operate a videotape camera (very, very, very simple), and you should quote an hourly rate.

# 83  PHOTO REBIRTH

(Restoring old photos)  In the living room of my house is an old picture in a gold frame with a red velvet mat. Looks very antiquey, as well it should. It's very meaningful to my family because the people in the photo are all members of my wife's family—dating way, way back. I think it was shot in 1910. Well, if the photo is so old, how come it looks so new? Because we brought it to a photo restoration shop. If you have the training and the equipment, you can offer photographic restoration, too. It doesn't work as well with color as it does with black and white, but even color photos can be tinted and improved. Market your services with classified ads in the photography section of your newspaper, with classified ads in national photo magazines, and certainly with displays of your restoration work. Go to a camera shop and ask if they know anyone who restores old photos. If not, tell them that you're in the business now. See if they will let you put up your display and also place a pile of brochures in the store. We paid $45 for the restoration, frame, and mat. It was easily worth it. Photo restoration is something you can read about in the library. It's not hard, but it's not easy either. That's why it's a good way to earn extra money.

# 84  PRETTY AS A PICTURE

(Photographing products)   Specialize in the photography of products. Many people make a fair amount of money shooting still photos of soup, wine, cars, wristwatches, shirts, tea, ketchup, tables, and a whole lot more. Correct lighting is essential, as is a good camera. Business can be secured with mailings to manufacturers, advertising agencies, graphics houses, and with small ads in business publications. A portfolio of photos you have taken will help secure business. To break in, you might do sample photographs of products on your own, and show them to the producers of those products. There is a wide range of prices for this work: one of my advertising clients paid a photographer $25 to shoot his product, while another paid a different photographer $5,000. Naturally, you'll find a whole lot more $25 clients than $5,000 clients. And you better know a whale of a lot about lighting, film, cameras, and beauty.

# 85 THE REAL PICTURE

(Photographing real estate)   Take pictures of properties for real estate salespeople. Mailings to them will tell them of your service, and with the photos you take (color will be best), you make their jobs a whole lot easier. When you see homes listed "for sale by owner," write to the owner offering to take a photo of the home so that prospective buyers can have the picture for reference purposes. A good photo might help close a sale, so your work can be of real importance. Charge $10 to $25 per picture, plus materials and processing. And you really don't need a whole lot of photographic talent to succeed in this endeavor.

# 86 PHOTOCRAFT

(Photographing crafts and artwork)   With your trusty camera (and color film), visit crafts fairs and offer your service to the creators of crafts and artwork. Just like you, they're trying to earn extra money. And just like you, they can earn more if they can show great color pictures of their creations. Market your service with circulars and cards handed to these creative types. There are enough art and crafts fairs to make this a busy business. And a lucrative one. Even if you charge only $10 per shot (including processing and materials), the total will really mount up—you'll find hundreds of craftspeople at large fairs. You must be a good photographer, but you need not be a great photographer.

# 87 AUTOTOUR AUTOTAPES

(Making audiotapes of auto tours)   If you can't get a personal guide for a vacation, the next best thing may be an Autotour Autotape. By making these ninety-minute tapes, you can allow vacationers and visitors to enjoy your city, state, region, park, seashore, forest, desert, or county just as if a personal guide was sitting right next to them. Your narrative might include music and sound effects. Cassettes are ideal for use in many cars. These tapes should be fun (if challenging) to make, and once made, can earn money for you for years to come. Market them with ads in tourist publications, mailings to travel agents, and with small display ads in travel magazines and local entertainment guides. You've got to have an intimate knowledge of the area for which you are preparing the tape, you've got to describe visitor attractions clearly and interestingly, and you've got to be able to direct a smooth production—including narrative and any background sounds and/or music. If you want to you can have an audio production company handle the duplication of the tape for you. Right now, a company is offering tapes such as these, with a listing of more than fifty different tapes. Figure on charging about $10 to $15 per tape. If your tape is good and people hear about it, you'll probably have no trouble selling a hundred tapes during the tourist season, wherever you live, which comes to at least $1,000 in sales. So you can understand why you, too, would do well with fifty different tapes. Get moving!

# 88 MY MOVIEHOUSE

(Showing movies in your own moviehouse)   If you leave it up to the big movie theaters, all you can see is first-run or second-run movies. So don't leave it up to the biggies. Establish your own moviehouse. Show the kind of movies *you* (and your public) want to see. Show them when you want to show them. Weekends seem best, or maybe just summers would be best in your area. You can rent both the moviehouse and the movies, and you can arrange the schedule to suit your needs. Instead of Junior Mints, you might sell yogurt (but I'll take the Junior Mints, please). You can even serve dinner if you want. Point is, it is not hard to make a moviehouse sufficiently different from the others to attract regular crowds and give you a steady source of income. You need a good knowledge of movies, and you need to be keenly attuned to the people in your area so that you can court their favor. Some people in my part of the world are doing this and making big bucks by showing only cult movies or movies featuring cult heroes. They always seem to have a Bogart Festival or Busby Berkeley Festival or some such event. You can, too. Hell, you can even put your own name on the marquee.

# 89 THE VIDEO FESTIVAL

(Holding a festival for homemade videotapes)   Lots of people have home videotape outfits these days. Many have developed quite a talent putting together videotapes of their families, holidays, pets, almost anything. Just look at the success of top TV shows that feature homemade videotapes. So? So have a home videotape festival. It is just like the Cannes Film Festival, only the women wear tops, and instead of movies, you show videotapes. Although you'd be exhibiting material created by amateurs, don't be surprised if it surpasses much of the material put together by pros. Market your festival with mailings to videotape camera owners (not difficult to find them; consult a list broker, listed under "Mailing Lists" in your Yellow Pages). Run small ads in the movie section of the newspaper, and talk to a PR person to secure free publicity stories (this idea is a natural for free publicity). Put up signs, and even run late night TV spots if you can get them inexpensively enough—maybe on cable TV. Make money by charging each entrant a fee. Also charge each person who attends ($5 to $10, depending upon the length of the festival). Give trophies or plaques to the winners and be sure the newspaper gives them a write-up. To succeed you need the ability to organize an event, a good knowledge of what makes a good videotape, and the ability to attract publicity. Once you get such a festival going it ought to be a continuing event each year. To get a better line on this earnway (and on other earnways dealing with film and video), look over a few recent issues of *American Film*. This publication reports on films, videotapes, film festivals, and books on film and home video.

# 90  YOU WERE THERE!

(Photographing people at events)   Many people attend special events, but do not bring their cameras. I, for one, dislike taking my camera *anywhere*. So if you get into this business, be sure to look for me. What business? The business of photographing people at events. Sell people pictures of themselves. Charge them the moment you take the picture, but offer a full refund if the picture is not first-class. You should be able to market this service with no more than a ten-second sales pitch. You could also put up signs that announce your service. It shouldn't be hard to find plenty of people out for a good time at a fair, picnic, racetrack, or concert, who want to immortalize their pleasure or their partner's on film. And all you need is a basic knowledge of photography and a pleasant manner. Willing subjects will abound, as well as events suitable for your efforts.

# 91  THE DETROIT FILM FESTIVAL

(Holding a film festival in your own community)   People seem to enjoy film festivals because the films are better (usually) than standard theater fare. Take advantage of this by establishing a film festival for your own community. I named this imaginary festival after the city of my birth, but I suggest you name yours after the place in which it

will be held. Attract filmmakers (all of whom get charged
an entry fee) with mailings to production houses, to entrants in other festivals, and to producers. Look beyond
the United States for your mailings; many films are made
in Europe. Attract an audience with the oodles of free
publicity such an event can generate, and with newspaper
display ads. Rent a moviehouse and show the films over a
period of a week. If you go about this project properly,
you might find that it becomes an annual event, bringing
fame, glory, and extra money. Naturally, it will help immensely if you go to a film festival yourself before trying
to hold one of your own. Again, you need a knowledge of
organization, publicity, and films. And again, the publication *American Film* will direct you to helpful people and
books. The San Francisco Film Festival, which could serve
as the ideal model for your festival, has been an artistic
and financial success since it started less than ten years
ago. If San Francisco can have a festival, your town
can, too.

# 92  THE GAME'S ON TV

(Videotaping local sporting events) Videotape the local
baseball game, then show the tape that night at the local
tavern. I'm not talking about major or minor league baseball. I'm talking about the factory league, about the city-
wide intramural league. Those players would love to see
themselves in action, and without you, where else would
they get the opportunity? Charge a fee to the ball club
*and* to the tavern where the tape will be shown. After all,
both the club and the bar will benefit from your videotaping. Mailings to industrial league baseball (football and
basketball, too) clubs should bring in the original business.
Mailings to taverns will bring in some more. Right now,
several bars are jammed with locals watching themselves
round the bases. In one instance, I heard that the bar

owner paid $100 to the videotaper for his time, plus $25 for his tape. That's not bad, but I'll bet the bar owner made much more than the $125 he paid for the full house of drinking sportsmen. You should know how to handle a videotape camera for this one, and also have a working knowledge of the sporting event you are taping. In addition to action shots, close-ups of the players seem to go over quite well.

## PERFORMING

# 93  STRINGFELLOW PUPPETS

(Putting on puppet shows)   Be a puppeteer and earn extra money merely by pulling a few strings. Puppets or marionettes can make lovely contributions to your bank balance if your brilliant marketing efforts result in your giving puppet shows at parties, fairs, schools, shopping centers, stores, restaurants, or (good old show biz) on television. You may find there aren't as many puppeteers as you think, and if you market your puppetry properly you can make a place for yourself. You need to create a message conveying the charm, attraction, and benefits of a puppet show, and then disseminate that message via bulletin boards, in classified ads, in the omnipresent Yellow Pages, in the Sunday entertainment section (with display ads), and with a few well-placed publicity stories or some TV coverage. Of course, those free stories are a big help with virtually any earning endeavor, but puppetry seems to be especially publicizable. You've got to be good at handling puppets, capable of writing and/or staging a show, and you've got to be a good actor or actress. Knowledge of stage and set design helps, too. If you're really good, maybe you can earn $100,000 yearly with your own TV puppet show. If you're not that good, you can still charge $100 for your half-hour presentation.

## 94  COUNTRY DANCIN'

(Calling square dances)  If you've ever square danced, you appreciate the talents of the people who call the dances. Maybe you have the talent to call square dances. If so (and don't forget there are lots of calls to commit to memory), you can earn good pocket money calling dances professionally. To bring in the business post bulletins where dances are held, mail your flyer to organizations that hold dances, call people who arrange square dances, or just organize a square dance yourself and show off your calling skill. Requirements for success: a feel for and love of music and dancing, a strong voice, a square dancin' soul, and a peek at the appendix of this book. (Look under Books About Earning Endeavors.) Earn from $25 on up (way up) per evening.

## 95  WISH YOU WERE HERE

(Delivering a travelogue)  You can obtain bookings and pretty decent speaking fees ($100 to $5,000) from clubs, schools, libraries, churches, trade organizations, and show producers if you have a traveling travelogue. Go to incredible places. Take lots of photographs or shoot lots of movie footage or videotape. Then come home and edit, add a sound track and music (live or taped), and prepare to travel the lecture circuit. You can make a new travelogue every year or every few years. If your show is professional enough, you can obtain regular bookings. You'll get your dates by writing and sending brochures to your potential customers. This can be a real money-maker if you have the time to travel, an enthusiasm for it, and the ability to communicate your enthusiasm.

## 96  PRESENTING CHUCKY

(Being a professional toastmaster or MC)  Introducing that famous earning method—star of stage, banquet, and

meeting: you. Be a professional toastmaster, MC, or parli-
amentarian. These three people are constantly in demand.
If you've got stage presence and are a ham at heart, write
letters, enclosing a brochure about yourself, to all the
clubs and organizations in your area. Better yet, try to get
an agent to secure bookings for you—you can concentrate
on titillating the audiences. Of course, you've got to feel
very much at home in front of large groups. You've got to
have a headful of one-liners, a mouthful of gleaming
teeth, and a good smile (it helps if you really like people),
and a total knowledge of *Robert's Rules of Order.*

# 97   THE AMELIA RADIO SHOW

(Producing a radio show) If you've got a good idea for a
very short radio show (I'm talking about a maximum of
five minutes), you might be able to syndicate it. Tape six
episodes of your show—of finished quality, as you'd do it
on the air—and send the tape (along with a letter about it,
about you, and about why the show is great) to radio show
syndicators, one at a time. Along with the tape's six episodes should come a description of what you intend further episodes to contain. If you can't get a syndicator or
an agent interested, send the tape directly to radio stations in various market areas. If one station uses it, others
are more likely to do the same. In time, if your show is
good enough, perhaps it can be picked up by a large syndicate, or possibly syndicated by you. The current edition of
*Writer's Market* can give you the names and addresses of
the syndicates to contact. According to the pros, what's
needed to make it with a syndicated show is a winning
personality. Most shows are two minutes or less, so you
don't need endurance, just sparkle. You've got to be able
to write, talk, and produce audio (or find people to do these
things for you). How much money you earn is based upon
the size of the market in which your show airs. A mid-

sized city pays about $10 per show, but when you multiply that by twenty-five cities, times fifty-two weeks, and then five times more if you're putting together a daily show, the earnings are impressive. They become awesome if you can create a syndicated TV show, two minutes long. Those "inserts" pay $40 per episode.

## 98 BUSKER BROWN

(Entertaining people waiting in line)   In England, while people wait in line for anything (and the English seem to love to wait in line), they get entertained by jugglers, magicians, dancers, mimes, sword swallowers, singers, musicians, and other entertainers. These show biz types are called buskers, and they get paid by the people in the line (called the queue). Busking queues is a time-honored way of earning extra money in England. Well, we have almost as many queues as the British, so if you can busk, you can earn. No marketing needed. Just guts and talent. Word is you can earn the British equivalent of $25 per evening in London. I wonder what you could earn busking in New York?

## 99 LIFE OF THE PARTY

(Entertaining at parties)   Be a party entertainer. You can entertain at children's parties or adults' parties. And you can be almost anything you want: a singer, magician, fire-eater, puppeteer, comic, gorilla, impersonator, storyteller, or tap dancer. You can give speeches or be an alien from a distant planet. You can get into this line of work with classified ads, by listing yourself with a local talent agent, by appearing for free on local TV or radio, by posting bulletins, and by appearing at public events and handing out your cards. (When you're entertaining at any benefit, be sure someone hands out your cards.) If you're good,

word-of-mouth advertising will take care of the rest of
your marketing. One mime in this area marketed his services by performing often, for free, to crowds in down-
town San Francisco. I don't think he handed out cards, but
he did end up a national TV star. I bet in his earlier days
Robert Shields was the life of a few parties. Although
Robert earns more, you can ask $50 for an evening of
entertainment.

# 100 ONCE-UPON-A-PHONE

(Telling bedtime stories by phone) Naturally, Once-
Upon-A-Phone is the name of a service that tells bedtime
stories to kids by telephone. Once-Upon-A-Phone charges
monthly fees, and for those fees, tells wonderfully-spun
yarns that transfix kids and peacefully put them to sleep.
How many yarns per month? Depends upon the fee. You
can do the storytelling live or on tape . . . or with a mixture of both. You should be able to offer your services successfully with classified ads in the newspaper, bulletins in
toy stores, and circulars mailed or distributed to parents.
Mailings to schools won't hurt either. Charge to attain the
hourly earnings you desire. If you spend fifteen minutes
telling a story, and you're aiming for $20 per hour, charge
$5. That means you'd charge the family $40 a month for
two stories a week. Get eight families signed up, and by
working two hours a night, two nights a week, you'll earn
$320 extra each month, just by telling stories. For more
information, consult *Fables* by Aesop, or *Fairy Tales* by
the Brothers Grimm.

# 101 THE HIGHEST BIDDER

(Conducting auctions)  In your Sunday newspaper, you'll
usually find ads for auctions that are being held. Attend
several before you even dream of trying this earnway.
Watching and hearing an auction pro go through his paces
(I've never seen or heard a female auctioneer, but I don't

see why females can't auction with the b
you'll realize that you really earn your m
It takes salesmanship, alertness, fast-talking
and authority. If you've got them, give this earn
look-see. You've really got to be able to talk fast—even
faster than the dudes who do those high-pressure stereo
commercials on the radio. But if you can, you can earn lots
of money as an auctioneer. There are lots of professional
auction houses that might sign you on, and you can do
mailings to clubs and organizations suggesting an auction
as a fund-raising idea, offering yourself as auctioneer.
Auctioneers earn either a flat fee (around $100 and up) or
a slice of the action.

# 102 CLOWNING AROUND

(Being a clown) Be a clown. Be a clown. All the world
loves to earn money, and you can earn it clowning around.
Clown around at childrens' parties, at fairs and festivals,
at stores and shopping centers, at circuses and parades.
Market your services through a booking agent. Also market them with Yellow Pages advertising, mailings to clubs
and organizations, and classified ads in the entertainment
section. If you do use an agent, your agent will take care
of all the marketing for you. Probably. But if not, use as
many marketing tools as you can—especially free sampling of your talents. Free publicity photos in the newspaper won't hurt your cause either, Funnyface. If you
want to be a clown, but don't quite know how, take a few
drama or improvisation classes at your community college, or consider attending Ringling Brothers' Clown
School in Sarasota, Florida.

# 103 THE AVAILABLE EXTRA

(Acting as a movie or TV extra) Sign up with a talent
agency in the nearest city where movies and/or TV shows
are made. If you live in Omaha, you won't get much work.

ut if you're near New York, San Francisco, Los Angeles, or Chicago, you may get quite a bit of work as an extra. The work is irregular and infrequent, but the pay is darned good. You may or may not have to join a union, depending on where you'll be working. Work as an extra is not nearly so intense as work as a featured player, but it is interesting just to be part of a movie or television show. A friend of mine lived for several months in relatively high style, all from the money he earned as a movie and TV extra. As you'll note from the name of this imaginary earnway, my friend was always available when they needed him. You require absolutely no talent or experience to be an extra. Zero training is needed. Just be available when they need you.

# 104 WATCH AS I DEMONSTRATE

(Demonstrating products in stores) You can earn extra money performing on the fringes of show biz as an in-store demonstrator. Such people are gifted, for they are able to talk and demonstrate complex gadgetry at the same time. Mailings to stores will get you some business, mailings to manufacturers of demonstrable products will get you even more. Actually, this earnway calls more for performing skills than selling skills, so the hammier you are, the more you'll earn. You'll be paid either an hourly fee ($10 and up) or with a piece of the sales action. To succeed, acting experience and public speaking experience are important. I think belief in the product is also essential. As a teenager, I was paid $75 per day to demonstrate that Formica is fireproof. I would stand in a store window, pour lighter fluid onto a Formica-topped table, ignite the fluid, then rub away the fluid and flame, and tip the table-top to show the captivated audience that the table suffered no damage: the miracle of Formica. All the while, I was explaining the nature of Formica into a microphone. For some reason, I never listed that work on my résumé.

# 105 RENT-A-NUDE

(Posing nude)   A number of people have learn|
can earn extra money merely by taking off t
and relaxing. They just sit there being naked, while others paint or draw or photograph them. Sometimes those
others are professionals, but usually they are amateurs
trying to become as good as professionals. If you have the
ability to cast modesty (and clothing) aside, you can earn
around $25 for a two- to three-hour session in the buff.
Market your body with a mailing to art and photography
schools, to artists and photographers, and to art and photo
supply stores. You might also post bulletins in the schools
and stores. The good news is that you can secure work as a
nude model whether you're skinny or fat, black or white,
tall or short, male or female. As long as you're naked,
you're okay. The only experience required is birth.

# 106 TONS OF TALENT

(Booking talent)   Become the booking switchboard for local
talent. With mailings to the right schools, with classified
ads and signs in places where performers meet, you can
attract a sizable stable of talented people. Then do mailings to the types of places that hire people: nightclubs,
party planners, private clubs, and local TV shows. In time,
your roster of talented people will grow. And so will your
reputation as a booker of talent. And so will your bank
balance. You collect a percentage (10 percent to 33 percent) of the fee paid to each performer. Some part-time
talent bookers are millionaires. Maybe you'll discover the
next Streisand or Beatle. You should be a good judge of
talent and a good salesperson, and a background in show
business sure won't hurt your earning cause.

# 107  TELECROON

(Delivering singing telegrams)  One of the best days in history for independent money-makers was the day that Western Union stopped delivering singing telegrams. That opened the door for other companies to deliver them, and these days, they're delivering them with more style and verve than Western Union ever mustered. The current telegram singers wear outlandish outfits, sing greetings in praise of birthdays, anniversaries, promotions, bar mitzvahs, graduations, confirmations, and more. You can do the same. And you can be sure that if you advertise your service with classified ads along with a Yellow Pages listing, you will have a chance to sing your little heart out. You do have to possess real talent. I haven't seen a faker in this business yet. A person I know started a company like this and charged $25 per message. Some nights she delivered eight messages. Nice work if you're comfortable in the role of laughingstock.

# 108  CROWD-PLEASING PRODUCTIONS

(Producing and promoting productions)  You can earn a hefty income if you get into the part-time business of producing and promoting. The main thing to remember is that you don't necessarily have to try for a sell-out crowd with a headline act in a major auditorium. Instead, aim for a sell-out crowd at a small performance hall with proven talent. You might produce plays. Or concerts. Or lectures. Obtain business primarily with free publicity in newspapers, radio, and television. Put up posters in key locations—lots of locations. And try to tune in to the needs and tastes of your community. Your sense of realistic expectations will have a direct effect on your income. You make whatever is left over after paying for advertising, for the performers, for the performance hall, and for miscellaneous expenses. That amount "left over" can be either a $5,000 profit or a $5,000 debt. Whichever one, it's yours. So be careful! Again, experience with show business will help, as will a strong sense of organization, an ability to negotiate and do business, and the ability to judge talent by the standards of your own community.

# 109 SANTA BUNNY

(Being Santa Claus and the Easter Bunny)  Some of the earnways in this book can earn a whole lot of money for you. As an earnway in point, I cite number 108. Other earnways will never earn a whole lot of money for you. Earnway in point: number 109. Be a Santa every Christmas. Be the Bunny every Easter. If you want to be a jack-o'-lantern every Halloween, that's up to you. But with letters to large stores and shopping centers, you can be fairly certain of two gigs per year. You'd better enjoy being with kids if you take on this earnway. Expect to be paid anywhere from $50 to $100 per day for your work. And other than being born fat, with big ears, you really don't need that much experience.

You certainly shouldn't get all excited about earning money with your artistic talents if you know plain and simple that you have no such talents. If you have a hidden talent, you can make it very visible. You can fulfill your secret longing with public performances. You can use your natural or learned talents to earn extra money—a talent in itself.

Do understand that all of the 109 earnways mentioned so far are businesses. You must promote them, keep accurate records, and be totally professional while you are doing the actual work. Also, you must work hard at turning your raw talent into an earnway.

It may be obvious by now that you can do more than 1

of these 109 earnways. Being a normal person, you're probably attracted strongly to some, repelled by others, neutral on the rest. I hope you put check marks next to the ones that sparked your imagination. Perhaps you realized that you could begin some immediately, and add others later. You probably figured that with some training and practice, there are many money-earning avenues that would be open to you.

Right now, America is undergoing a renaissance of economic freedom. A whole new system of alternative economics is developing. You now have 109 examples of how you can fit into that system. Remember, you do not have to hit it big in any one of these undertakings. Hitting it mediocre in several will net you a good income, and most will be compatible with your current job, if you have one.

Don't forget—you yourself do not necessarily have to be the person performing the work in many of these earnways. Frequently it will be possible to delegate the work and earn your share of income as instigator, ramrod, promoter, and manager.

In time, it may be that some of these earning endeavors will bring in enough money that you will think about letting go of your full-time job.

There is absolutely no way that any of these earning methods can bring dollar one into your life if you don't get started on them. Almost without exception, the hardest part of these endeavors will be starting them up.

You can make all the check marks and all the plans in the world. But if you don't actually get started, the check marks will fade and the plans will dissipate like mist. So treat this book as the beginning of a beginning. As you read later chapters you'll be moving closer and closer to the actual earning.

For those of you who have absolutely no special talents there are still 446 earnways open to you. Your reaction to these earnways, in the next three chapters, will depend upon whether you are more interested in working with people, things, or ideas.

You just might be the kind of person who enjoys work best, and achieves the greatest success, if the work is centered around people. If that's the case, you're going to find some mighty enticing earning ideas in the next chapter.

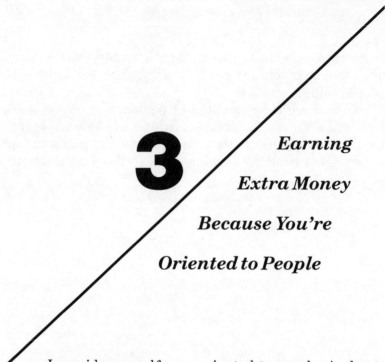

# 3 Earning Extra Money Because You're Oriented to People

I consider myself very oriented to people. And yet, for the most part, I work alone from my home. I have a friend in lines of work that are similar to mine. But unlike me, he just cannot bear to work alone. He has to be among people, or at least with another person. For that reason, he has rented office space in someone else's office.

I've worked with individuals who maintained a quiet, unassuming attitude while in their offices. But when confronted with an audience—be it four people or forty-four—they came alive with a spark and vigor that dazzled me. Apparently, these folks were very oriented to people.

If that describes you, I say welcome to chapter three—no chapter for hermits, but a delightful array of pages if you are hooked on the human race. I fully realize that the vast majority of the 555 earnways in this book require that you have at least *some* interfacing with people. This chapter focuses on the earnways that are *primarily* oriented to people.

Perhaps you've always known that you're a people kind of person, but have been kept from them due to the nature of your work. Well, after reading the upcoming earning endeavors, you may consider selling or teaching or performing services for people. You can practice these earnways while maintaining your current job. And it just may be that you become so enthralled at the success you achieve and the joy you experience that you will chuck the monastic life for a more gregarious mode of work.

Keep an open mind while perusing the following earnways, especially when they suggest the concept of you selling. If you're selling something in which you fervently believe, and if you're truly happy dealing with people, you'll find that selling is more fun than work. And it is extremely–and I do mean *extremely*–rewarding financially. In many companies, the salespeople earn more than the president. And they deserve those earnings.

After you've read this chapter, check the appendix. There, among other books on selling, you'll find *Selling Is Simple . . . If You Don't Make It Complicated* by Karl Bach and *Guerrilla Selling* by Bill Gallagher, Orvel Ray Wilson, and Jay Conrad Levinson. Just the tickets for a people person such as yourself.

## SELLING

# 110 THE DIAMOND DOORWAY
(Selling almost anything door to door)   Earn extra money by getting into door-to-door sales. You'll find it a lot easier if you're truly interested in the product being sold. I know a couple who were put off at the very thought of door-to-door sales. But after they grossed $150,000 their *first year* going from door to door, they were less put off. In fact, the only reason they entered the sales field was

because they sincerely believed in the world of the encyclopedia they were selling. Products that are successfully sold door to door include cosmetics, vitamins, vacuum cleaners, portrait photography, brushes, and encyclopedias. Lots of people who want to earn extra money are earning more than they dreamed possible by working for such door-to-door stalwarts as Avon, Amway, Shaklee, Mary Kay, and many more. I was once a Fuller Brush salesman. It helped pay for part of my college tuition. Perhaps it wasn't one of the high points in my life, but it wasn't all that bad. As I've mentioned, if your heart is really in it, this kind of selling can give you an ideal balance of income and freedom. Selling is simple if you don't make it complicated. For one thing, you don't have to advertise. But you do have to enjoy dealing with human beings. And you do have to feel comfortable enthusing about your product. And you have to possess a relatively thick skin–since you'll have to deal with a lot of rejections. Of the many earnways in this book, those that deal with selling are among the most lucrative. Look through some of the selling books in the appendix. Consider mailing letters to the door-to-door sales companies I've just listed–letters in which you ask them to describe their operations to you. And keep in mind that you don't have to spend any of your own money promoting for this earnway. The people who make the things you'll be selling will take care of the marketing and promotion for you. Nice of them, wouldn't you say?

# 111 PARTY PERSON

(Selling at parties)   You've probably heard about people who make scads of money holding parties at which they sell cookware, plants, art, and the like. Well, why not become one of those people? The work is part-time, very profitable, and it's supposed to be fun–though I've been to a lot of parties that were fun without someone hawking saucepans. Contact party-plan companies to see how you can throw parties for them. The first party-plan company I think of is Tupperware. Happily, they'll handle the marketing for you and show you how to go about setting up and selling at your parties. Just check the white pages of your telephone directory under "Tupperware Home Parties Corp." They have offices throughout the United States. You might even suggest this idea to certain kinds of neighborhood stores, such as plant stores. To succeed in party-plan selling, a love of people and your products are the main requirements. Enthusiasm helps, as does the ability to address groups of people clearly, sincerely, and cogently. Your earnings will vary, but some women who give such parties (and they're not always women) report an average of $35 and up per party. Figure on such a party lasting from one and a half to two hours.

# 112 ART MART

(Selling the works of artists and craftspeople)   Be a representative of artists and/or craftspeople. Sell their works at fairs, to graphics houses, galleries, stores, flea market stall-holders, and even at flea markets with you doing the selling. Because most artists spend a great deal of their work time creating, and haven't a clue as to how to market their creations, you will find many of them welcoming your offer to represent them. The more exceptional the artists you represent, the more exceptional money you'll make. You can charge from 10 percent to 33 percent of the purchase price as your commission. One weekend, working at 25 percent, my wife and I made $500 standing in front of paintings created by an artist who was too person-shy to represent his own works. An acquaintance of ours earns her entire living by repping artists. I'd put her income at $25,000, and I figure she puts in no more than a good twenty-hour week. Market your artistic offerings with in-person calls and with as frequent exhibits as possible.

# 113 CONVALESCENT CRAFTS

(Selling crafts supplies to convalescent homes)   There's a California woman who has found a way to enrich the lives of people who are convalescing . . . while she enriches her own bank account. What she does is sell crafts supplies (all kinds) to nursing and convalescent homes. Naturally, the shut-ins appreciate the opportunity to engage in a craft, and the entrepreneuring crafts supplies saleswoman pockets $600 per week. Servicing her regular route takes no more than a few days a week (and that route isn't even concentrated in a big city). As a way of figuring how much you can make at this venture, consider that the star of this earnway services only ten nursing homes. Does that indicate that if you service twenty nursing homes you'll make $1,200 a week? Looks that way to me. The marketing of your service is simple. Do a mailing, describing all the crafts supplies you can sell (and there ought to be no limit) to the nursing and convalescent homes in your area. Of course, many such homes may have their own crafts supplies, though hardly as wide a range as you can offer. You ought to know about crafts if you're to do well in this venture. If you don't, the potential of this earnway may make it worth your while to study up on crafts. I think the California woman who makes so much with so little effort would agree.

# 114 REAL ESTATE GENIUS

(Selling real estate part-time)   Several years ago, my friend Jane professed to be frustrated with her life. Her real desire, she realized, was to travel like mad and see as much of the world as possible. But how could she do this with her full-time job as a laboratory assistant? Here's how Jane did it. She took a real estate course and made the decision to be the best real estate salesperson around. With this kind of determination, plus her own innate brains (and zero selling or real estate experience), she became so good at locating houses, locating buyers, and putting the two together that she was able to quit her full-time job to sell real estate six months a year, and travel the world the other six months. Now the selling of real estate may not seem like a part-time job. But it can be. And if you have Jane's commitment, you can sell real estate part of the time and do absolutely anything else you want the rest of the time. Market your services just as Jane did. She joined a realty firm on a six-months-a-year basis and let them put forth all the marketing effort. Because she's so good at selling and so oriented to people (why she was a lab assistant is still a mystery to me), that same real estate firm has now been her sometime employer for over ten years. And then there's all that traveling Jane does.

# 115  I'VE GOT YOU COVERED

(Selling insurance part-time)   Now, I'm not suggesting here that you become a full-time insurance salesperson, but rather that you become a part-time insurance salesperson. It takes as much work and training to do it part-time as full-time, so there are no shortcuts to success. But once you've done the preparation, you can go to work for an insurance company or insurance broker—on a part-time basis. Soon you'll be able to function as your own independent broker—selling all types of insurance or specializing in any one. I've always heard that insurance salespeople close one out of nine sales. So think in terms of nine sales calls and earn a not unimpressive income as a not full-time insurance rep. You should be good with figures (at least own and know how to operate a pocket calculator) and come across as a person sincerely interested in people. A Chicago man did so well selling insurance on a part-time basis that he took his savings and bought himself a *bank*. Even if you do one-fifth as well you'll be smiling as you go to *your* bank.

# 116 OPEN-AIR ENTERPRISES

(Vending from a pushcart)  Remember the good old days when people vended from pushcarts? Well, they still do. At flea markets. At tourist attractions. On weekends in parks, ski areas, beaches, almost anywhere they can find a lot of people. And just what is it they vend? Anything. Apples and wristwatches. Pretzels and ties. Records and doughnuts. You get the idea. And once you also get the pushcart, you can market your wares with a clear and lovely sign right on your pushcart. Of course it wouldn't hurt to have a few signs pointing the way to your cart. As you have probably figured, this earnway requires a love of people more than a love of selling. You don't even have to have an iota of selling skills at this baby. A pushcart pretzel pusher at a Colorado ski resort claims to earn $100 daily, working weekends only. Not terribly shabby, I'd say. Incidentally, if you decide to vend those fat, hot, salted pretzels, save a couple for me.

# 117 SATSUN STORE

(Selling from a store that's open weekends only)  There's no law that says stores must be open six or seven days a week. You can rent space with retail sales potential and sell from there on Saturdays and Sundays only . . . unless your state has blue laws that say you can't. (Better check with your lawyer.) Advertise your wares, whatever they be (lawn furniture, clothing, records, plants, almost anything), on radio, television, and newspapers. But be open solely on weekends. By avoiding the overhead of your own permanent space, and renting for weekends only (not even every weekend), you stand to do quite well, especially if you charge lower prices than your high-overhead competition. With the right merchandise, this can be a real money-maker. In my neck of the world, one company rented the Cow Palace (our large indoor stadium) to sell leather jackets on weekends. The grapevine leaked word that the leather jacket operation made a fortune for its operators. What's a fortune? Try $15,000 per day in gross sales. You've got to know about retailing for this sales venture. But if you can combine retailing, selling, and a love of people, maybe you can make a fortune on Sats. and Suns.

# 118 THE SPECIALTY SPECIALIST

(Selling advertising specialties) My brother-in-law Marvin retired at a young age. How? By successfully selling advertising specialties—ball-point pens, calendars, matches, loads of imprintable items. Better still, *he* didn't even sell them. Instead, he delegated the selling to others. Good thinking, Marvin. You can copy Marvin's thinking if you gain access to a large selection of advertising specialties (not hard; catalogs of them are available), then recruit salespeople to sell them for you (not hard; advertise in the opportunity magazines listed in the appendix). As I learned by watching Marvin (who seemed to spend an inordinate amount of time on his big boat), this business is just made for delegating. Selling is usually by in-person calls, phone calls, and mailings to stores and businesses that use these specialties. One marketing tool that you might consider is your own advertising specialty. You should be good at either selling or organization, depend-

ing upon whether you do it yourself or delegate the selling. You earn a commission, usually 50 percent or more of
the selling price. Frequently, the selling price is only $1.
But just as frequently, the order is for a thousand units.
That's why Marvin retired so early.

# 119 SUNGLASS SALON

(Selling sunglasses on weekends)  Sell sunglasses in malls
on weekends. Sell them at the beach or at a ski resort. Sell
them almost anywhere the sun gets in people's eyes. You
sure don't need an expensive inventory. One woman with
$400 in inventory earns $125 daily at a flea market. The
product is so small and light you can carry around (or
store) a large selection . . . and you have the option of
working only on sunny days. You can even delegate the
selling to someone who will work sunny days outdoors or
cloudy days indoors in malls. Because of the unusually
high markup (300 percent to 500 percent), you can expect
a bright future. Not much knowledge of selling is needed.
In fact, you don't even have to be people-oriented, just
profit-oriented. To learn more about this, request the
proper manual from the *Entrepreneur Business Manual
Catalog* listed in the appendix.

# 120 TELEVISION STARS UNLIMITED

(Selling advertising time on cable TV stations)  Solicit advertising time on cable TV stations. Offer to make a store the
star of a TV commercial—that is, if the store signs up for
TV advertising on the station you represent. Naturally,
all good TV commercials make a star of the product, service, or store they feature. You can and should promise the
same. Local cable companies cannot afford to hire enough
sales talent to call on all potential local advertisers. That's
why your offer of doing it for them will be heard by grate-

ful ears. Just be sure those same ears hear that you understand the power and benefits of TV advertising, and be sure your mouth is telling the truth when it makes this claim. That understanding, coupled with your enthusiasm and people orientation, will make you a financial star while you make each individual client a TV star. You can earn anywhere from $150 to $10,000 per month selling TV time, depending upon your own star quality and the time you are willing to commit. The publications offered by *Advertising Age* (see the appendix) will provide you with more information about this earning endeavor. Meanwhile, welcome to show biz!

# 121  SNACKTOWN

(Selling inexpensive food items) There are many lovely tales of people who have earned up to $40,000 a year part-time selling popcorn, caramel corn, cotton candy, and/or sno-cones. How can they earn so much money with such cheap items? Markup. A high markup is equal to high profits in many cases. And probably the highest margin of profit is made in the sale of inexpensive snack food. As little as 10 percent of the retail price goes into the product, so the profits are juicy indeed. Marketing is almost free: catchy signs and a wonderfully decorated food stand. You might even delegate your selling to several people— one for your popcorn, one for your caramel corn, one for your cotton candy, and one more for your sno-cones. I hope you send the cotton candy person to my house.

# 122  PASS THE WORD

(Being a professional word-of-mouth specialist) Of the twenty-one marketing tools I introduced in chapter 1, the twenty-first was "unique and new marketing methods." Among the newest is that of a professional word-of-mouth specialist. Such a person spreads the word about places like restaurants, boutiques, resorts, cruises, masseuses, and more. Such a person could be you. Offer, through mailings to advertisers, to talk up their businesses at gatherings such as parties, conventions, events, and the like. Just briefly tell as many people as possible of your client's offerings. For verification for the advertisers who pay you, you might record your good words on a cassette recorder. Word-of-mouth advertising is very credible, but until you came along it was difficult to generate. Now, you can cause it to happen, using your love of people, your natural enthusiasm, and your honest belief in the place, product, or service you're recommending to earn $10 per hour (or more) as a person who is known to talk up a storm. Such a person occasionally advertises in the classified section out here. One would think he'd talk merrily about his service to any advertiser who will listen. There are absolutely *no* books on this earnway, so you get to make up all the rules yourself.

# 123 LIVING SECURE

(Selling security devices)  Living secure means having the proper security devices in the home: fire alarms, smoke alarms, burglar alarms, fire extinguishers, and switches that turn lights on and off automatically. Secure people may even own a phonograph record of a fiercely growling dog. By offering to sell and install these security items, you will be providing a valuable service to your community, and you deserve to be well compensated for your efforts. You've got to select the right devices, know the statistics that make such devices necessary (consult the *World Almanac and Book of Facts*), find someone (yourself?) who can do a good job of installing them, and then market them with mailings to home-owners, phone calls to these same security-minded people, listings in the Yellow Pages, and Sunday display ads in the newspaper. You will probably attract quite a bit more business by also offering free one-hour seminars on home security (you may even be able to get your local fire and police officials to speak at your seminars). Be sure you are armed with enough information to go along with your enthusiasm. Then, if you're determined and community-minded, you'll find that in truth, crime *does* pay. Fire, too.

## 124 THE FLEA FLOATER

(Operating a consignment booth at a flea market)  Have a continuing booth at your local flea market or swap meet. But instead of rounding up the merchandise you sell, accept goods on consignment from the local citizens. That requires hardly any investment. You pay the people who give you goods only if you sell the goods. Otherwise, you return them. Attract customers, both for consignment and for sales, with classified ads and circulars at the flea market. Attract more with your very attractive flea market sign. Your ever-changing offerings should make your stall a popular and profitable one. You need a talent for knowing what to accept and what to reject for consignment. Once you've got this talent down pat, you can earn $100 per day. Some flea stall-holders claim you can earn considerably more, but $100 per day should do. In the meantime, we've got this broken gum-ball machine that may interest you, and . . .

## 125 GARAGE SALE GURU

(Holding garage sales for others)  Hold garage sales for others, keeping a slice of the sales volume for yourself. Attract people to your service by distributing circulars at flea markets and other garage sales, by posting notices on bulletin boards, and with classified advertisements. The idea is to do the *whole* job on the items you merchandise. You've got to clean them, price them, display them, and then advertise them, especially the big items, with signs and classified ads. Most people haven't a clue as to how to proceed with these tasks. That's why they'll gladly let you take your 10 percent to 33 percent right off the top. In other words, if you run a garage sale at which $2,500 is earned, you are entitled to anywhere from $250 to $833, depending upon your initial arrangements. Let's face it: holding a garage sale isn't all that hard. Once you know how to do it, you can begin delegating and holding as many as five or six garage sales (or others) per week—just as a Chicago garage saler does. (She earns around $1,000 every weekend this way, and has for years.) That's how other peoples' junk can add up to your fortune. You should have a working knowledge of garage sale and flea market prices (easy; just attend a few yourself). And have a garage sale of your own just for practice. We made $650 at ours.

# 126 RECYCLED FINERY
(Selling used clothing)   Open a recycled clothing store and operate it on a part-time basis. Take clothing on consignment (or buy it dirt cheap), then sell it to the public, keeping a fair share—actually the lion's share—for yourself. Everybody has clothing to recycle. Everybody wants a good deal on clothing he or she buys. The two can be combined to make this business a hit. Operate your operation out of a low-overhead space, and keep the personnel to a minimum. You will draw crowds if you place ads in the newspaper, put up signs on bulletin boards, advertise on the radio the day before you are open, and do mailings to regular customers (let them sign up for your mailing list on their first visit to your store). Watch out, or this earnway will become a full-time business. Instead, allow it to earn extra money for you, maybe even a lifetime of extra money. You should know the rag trade, be up-to-date on the styles your customers appreciate, enjoy being with

clothes-conscious (and money-conscious) people, and have a feel for retailing.

# 127 THE PLANT FEEDER

(Selling plant food) If you're thinking that The Plant Feeder markets sandwiches to factories, your mind is on the wrong kind of plant. The Plant Feeder sells plant food to gardeners, plant stores, hardware stores, nurseries, variety stores, wholesalers, jobbers, and any other reachable place where it may be sold. What makes this possible? The fact that plant food that used to be available only to farmers in large volume is now available to anyone in any volume. With the right kind of plant food for the right kind of people, you can do as well as the Iowa man who earned $240 the first afternoon he tried this earnway. (He received his merchandise at noon and sold forty cases before 6:00 P.M.) If you know about plants, live in an area where plant food can attract many customers, enjoy selling, and believe in the product, you can do quite well, maybe even better than the Iowa man. For more information about this business, write for the free sales packet to Pure Plant Food International, Ltd., P.O. Box 483, Sioux Falls, Iowa 57101. Market your (or their) products with in-person calls, telephone marketing, direct mail, and possibly some classified or display ads in your local paper. A wonderful side benefit to this selling business—as well as to so many selling endeavors—is that once you get your first order, you may make much more money with reorders.

## TEACHING

# 128 TIMELY TUTORING

(Tutoring in any subject) If you know a subject well, but don't feel inclined to write about it, then consider tutoring. Almost any topic has both experts and people who wish to become experts. If you're in the former category, you can tutor people in the latter category. Find them with bulletin postings, classified ads, circulars, even ads in the Yellow Pages. You'll gain more students if you tutor common topics such as English, math, cooking, auto repair, art, piano, guitar, French, Spanish, basic computers, and home repairs. But you can also tutor uncommon topics if you're an expert and others covet your expertise. Naturally, you must know your subject inside and out (though not necessarily with any special degrees). You should be a good explainer and enjoy explaining things to people. It also helps (your students) if you are patient and conscientious. Charge an hourly rate per student. The going rate these days in my part of the planet seems to be $15 per hour. Tutoring is the only source of income for one of our friends in Denver, but most people use it simply as an extra income producer.

# **129** TRAINING UNLIMITED

(Training company employees)   Offer to train company employees in skills for which the company does not already offer training or where the company cannot afford an internal training department. I know many people who are succeeding in this extra money-earning endeavor, and no two train in the same skill. One offers sales training. One offers training in clarity of corporate communications. Still others engage in assertiveness training, in telephone marketing, even in teaching speed-reading to businesses. Companies are usually a better target than individuals since companies have more money. A direct-mail campaign to prospective companies will be your best marketing tool, especially if your letter is accompanied by an attractive brochure. Follow up each mailing with telephone calls. Gain further business by distributing circulars at business trade shows and by making phone calls to personnel directors. Offer in-person meetings to discuss your training and to outline the benefits to any company that puts its employees through that training. Consider hooking up with those who offer other types of training to make yourself part of a loose-knit, modular training organization. Earnings vary. One person charges $1,500 for a two-day training session. Another charges by the employee: $75 per employee per day. And still another spreads his training over five afternoon sessions at $500 per afternoon and no limit to the number of people who can attend. It goes without saying that you should be worth more than you charge. If you are, and if you are good at teaching and enjoy dealing with people, your earnings can be as unlimited as the training you do.

# 130 MOTIVATION

(Engaging in sales training)   If you're good at firing people up, or merely at locating tapes and records that fire people up (get them from Success Motivation Cassette Tapes, P.O. Box 7614, Waco, Texas 76710), you can be a professional motivator. To accomplish such motivation, also called sales training, you've got to know about selling, people, psychology, and hypnosis. (I enthusiastically call your attention to *Hypnotic Realities* by Milton Erickson.) If you do know about these things, you can make a not-so-small fortune helping others to make not-so-small fortunes through your motivating talks, tapes, and meetings. Direct mailings to businesses, along with an occasional display ad in a business section or even regional business magazine, should net you enough customers—if your message is motivating enough. Sales trainers usually charge by the day, and $500 to $1,000 per day is not uncommon. Be sure you make the distinction between *training* employees and *motivating* them. There's a huge difference.

It's a lot easier to train than to fire folks up. Got that?
Okay. Now let's put it all together and earn, earn, earn!

# 131 THE TEST COACH

(Teaching people how to pass tests)   Many people begin to
come apart at the seams when confronted with the prospect of taking a test. Others sail through with flying (and
passing) colors. If you can train people to prepare properly for a test, intellectually and emotionally, you can
make money doing it. My wife, who holds a black belt in
test-passing, created a whole college course entitled "How
to Pass The Big Exam." Books on the topic are in most
libraries. By showing people exactly *how* to study, how to
learn *what* to study, how to *time the studying* with the
test, and how to *relax* while taking the test, you have
earned your salt and their dollars. Advertise your coaching ability with bulletins in schools, ads in school papers,
even ads in professional journals read by people who are
about to take tests. Charge your students $15 to $25 per
hour for your coaching. If you can prepare people to pass
specific tests (bar exam, SATs, CPA exam, citizenship test,
and so on), all the better. The more you teach, the more
you can charge. Got that, Coach?

# 132 CARE TO SHARE

(Teaching job-sharing to employers)   These days, you hear
more and more about job-sharing. That refers to two or
more part-timers sharing one full-time job. Good idea
since it increases free time and decreases unemployment.
Most people don't know much about the concept, so you
can cash in by delivering seminars on job-sharing to employers (and their employees). Direct mail to employers
will get you some business, as will ads in the business
section of local papers. Naturally, you've got to know what

you're talking about when you're advising companies and human beings on the subject of job-sharing. And you've got to be able to communicate what you know. But all the people who hear you will appreciate your knowledge. And you'll appreciate their seminar fees. Companies will pay up to $500 for a day's worth of your smarts.

# 133    IMPRESSIVE INTERVIEWS

(Teaching people to have successful interviews)    Many people have what it takes to succeed at certain jobs, but never get hired for these jobs because they flunk the interviews. With your help, they won't flunk those interviews. You'll train them in how to dress, talk, sit, relate, describe their history and goals, and impress any interviewer. Better still, you will set up job interview role-playing so that your clients can play the parts of both interviewer and interviewee–all so that they can develop insights into the hiring process. Attract customers with classified ads, display ads in the business section of a newspaper, even bulletins in unemployment offices. To get a better line on what you'll be teaching, read: *The Ultimate Interview: How to Get It, Get Ready, and Get the Job You Want* by John Caple, and the extremely valuable *What Color Is Your Parachute? A Practical Manual for Job-Hunters and Career Changers* by Richard Nelson Bolles. It helps if you have a background in personnel, or at least in being interviewed successfully. Charge from $10 to $25 per hour for your service. There's an interview coach in New York who charges even more.

# 134    LEARN MY CRAFT

(Teaching a craft or skill via the apprentice method)    If you are truly expert at a particular craft or skill that others might want to learn, teach them what they must know while they serve you as apprentices. To gain such knowledge, they pay you tuition. Perhaps you can have several apprentices at the same time. A local art therapist (who happens also to be my wife) has four apprentices, all paying her a stiff fee per hour. She teaches them how to use art as a psychotherapeutic tool, and thereby secure employment. As long as you can honestly teach your apprentices how to succeed in your endeavor, you'll earn the tuition you charge. Apprenticing beats the dickens out of straight book-learning because it is so reality-based. Attract apprentices with classified ads, bulletins in unemployment offices, even seminars in your craft. This is one of those wonderful "everybody wins" situations.

# 135 REALITY COLLEGE

(Teaching specific subjects in specific stores)   Teach classes in a specific topic in a store devoted to that topic. That means teaching cooking in a kitchen supply store, teaching carpentry in a hardware store, teaching auto repairs in a garage, teaching computer programming in a computer store. Charge both a fee to your students and a commission to your cooperative store owner based upon items sold. Said store owner will appreciate both the exposure and the sales. And the students will receive a firm grounding in the real thing. Attention to your offering may be drawn by classified ads, signs in the store's windows, bulletins in likely locations (schools), and circulars distributed to the proper age groups at open events where they may congregate. You should be good at teaching and comfortable with people, and you must be familiar with both the subject you are teaching and the equipment in the store. You can charge as low as $10 per hour per student because you'll be making a commission, probably around 10 percent, on the items your students purchase. If you're already thinking about giving music lessons in a music store, you've got the idea.

# 136 TALK TALK TALK

(Being a professional lecturer)  I know what I'm talking about when I tell you that there's good money in being a professional lecturer. It's also lots of fun, with a great feeling if your topic contributes to the well-being of even a small portion of mankind. I market my own lecturing services through a speaking agent. She mails brochures to colleges, along with covering letters. Then she follows through with phone calls. My brochures are disseminated at shows that attract speaker-bookers, resulting in even more engagements. I speak only twice a month or so, but the pay is more than I used to earn in two months. Not bad for two hours of talk talk talk. Yet I'm just small potatoes when I hear of lecturers being paid $10,000 for a two-hour talk. Admittedly, you require great fame for that. Lacking the fame, and as general requirements, you need good stage presence, a joyful feeling at the chance to lecture, conscientiousness in being sure that your audience is understanding your ideas, and a touch of ham.

# 137 THE PROFESSIONAL PROFESSOR

(Teaching a course at a local college)  My wife, Pat, an art therapist, doesn't lecture on her field; it's too complex to be reduced down to a few hours. Instead, she teaches a course in the subject at a local college. You might be able to do the same. If you can teach a class in a subject with which you are extremely well acquainted, you will find, as did Pat, that it is difficult, fun, rewarding, and keeps you on your toes. You can write to the institutions in your area that offer educational courses. Or you can place ads in your local newspaper and teach at a noninstitution, such as your home. Or in the park. Don't underestimate your knowledge. Many people might sign up for a course in what you know. My wife got paid $600 for a six-week course, three hours per night, once a week. She is, as you must be, a good explainer, and she armed herself with a very comprehensive outline. Plus, having a master's degree didn't hurt her case. The Yellow Pages will point you to the educational institutions in your area, or you might check the current edition of *Lovejoy's College Guide* (see the appendix or your library).

# 138  HAVE TEACHING CERTIFICATE; WILL TRAVEL

(Doing substitute teaching) A very popular method of earning extra money is substitute teaching. It can be hard to get yourself a regular teaching job, but not so for a sub job. Of course, you need the proper education and credentials for this earnway, but they're not all that hard to obtain. The right education is a college degree, and the right credentials consist of your certification as a teacher. Occasionally, a state will experience an emergency teacher situation and will allow you to teach without the degree or certification. You can substitute teach almost anywhere anytime. Not that it's easy, just that it's available. Letters to school districts and boards of education will be all the marketing you'll need, though in-person visits may be required too. If you like, you can even become a permanent substitute available, say, on Fridays only. The situation for subs differs from school district to school district . . . worth looking into if you're an ex-teacher, or want to be an ex-teacher. Pay is pretty good— as high as $75 per day in certain areas. A Chicago buddy of mine, a tall, strong lad, quit his sub job because he said the kids were too tough. That, unfortunately, is a common complaint among subs.

# 139  THE SEWING PRO

(Giving sewing lessons) Things you take for granted may be things for which others long. Sewing and clothes-making talent, for instance. If you're dexterous with needle and thread, or needle and yarn, consider giving sewing lessons. Give them to one person at a time, or give classes to groups. The more you know about sewing, the more students you can enroll with your classified ads, mailings and signs for women's clubs, bulletins posted in Laundromats, Yellow Pages ads, display ads in church publications, and at sewing seminars. (The latter are events at which you show all that a person can accomplish with a knowledge of sewing.) I single sewing out as a subject to teach because so many people know how to do it well, and so many others want to know how to do it well. Charge $10 per student per hour. At least that's what local sewing experts charge.

# 140  WATCH YOUR LANGUAGE

(Teaching a second language to people who speak English) If you speak some other language in addition to English, give language lessons. Give them privately or to groups, personally or by tape, at a public school or for a language school. You can gain new customers by placing classified ads, putting up signs in clubs, or distributing circulars to likely prospects. And let's not forget the omnipresent Yellow Pages listing. If you speak an unusual language, you have a better chance to sell your services to schools and institutions. And consider being an interpreter while you're considering being a teacher. As with sewing lessons, the going rate seems to be in the area of $10 per student per hour, though one woman out here is charging $15 and getting it.

# 141  SPEAK UP

(Instructing others in public speaking)  Of the many fears we humble mortals suffer, the fear of public speaking ranks close to the top of the list. It is a fear that often separates effective people from the success they otherwise deserve. During my corporate life, I've seen associates passed over for promotion because of an inability (prompted by fear) to present their work in meetings. By coaching people with lessons or group classes (far better than individual lessons) in the art of speaking before an audience, and instilling in them the confidence, courage, and delight at the opportunity to speak in the first place, you will have earned the tuition you charge ($5 to $15 per student per hour). Because public speaking is a reality-based subject, be sure you graduate no one until that student has successfully spoken before a good-sized group. I realized, after having taken such a course in college, that one of the keys to success in public speaking is practice, practice, practice. So I suggest that you teach a long rather than a short course.

# 142 ALL-STAR COACH

(Coaching a sport professionally)   If you excel or did excel at a sport, you may be able to coach that sport. Almost any sport can attract youngsters who lack the knowledge of how to be proficient at it. If you can impart that knowledge, your coaching will be much appreciated—by your student athlete as well as his (or her) more proficient teammates. Market your coaching with signs on school and club bulletin boards, with ads in school papers, classified ads under announcements, cards handed out on playing fields to likely prospects, and mailings to companies that make team uniforms. You can put up signs in golf and tennis clubs if you want to coach adults in those sports. Same for racquetball, squash, handball, bowling, Ping-Pong, and pool. A Detroit acquaintance earns $250 for a season of coaching a youth-league softball team; a San Francisco ex-jock earned $1,000 plus a free trip to

Germany coaching an all-kid basketball team. Naturally, you require more than athletic skill to coach; you also need an understanding of the teamwork necessary to win in that sport.

## 143  SAFETY FIRST DRIVING SCHOOL

(Teaching driving)  I wouldn't teach driving professionally for $500 an hour. But if you'd do it for less, can get the proper licensing, are patient and fearless enough to teach driving to neophyte motorists, and are willing to market your driving school, you can earn a steady trickle of income. With enough students—and you should be able to handle as many as five a day—that trickle can become a flow. Get enough students with savvy marketing: Yellow Pages ads (big ones), classified ads under announcements, ads in school newspapers, bulletins posted in high-traffic areas (people traffic, that is, not vehicular traffic), and a tasteful, but very readable sign atop your vehicle. A substantial amount of automobile insurance is also recommended. The usual rate charged is $18 an hour. The extras that seem to attract students are dual-controlled cars, unmarked cars, pickup service, plus experience in instructing "nervous" students. I guess it's those "nervous" types that keep me from earning money teaching driving.

## 144  SURF THE WIND

(Teaching windsurfing)  To teach the sport of windsurfing requires a sailboard (like a surfboard with a mast and sail), water, and wind. It also requires that you know how to perform and teach the sport. And it requires a willing student. You can provide both the boardsailing equipment and the instruction, and then you can prosper as the sport continues its phenomenal growth in popularity (in case you haven't noticed, windsurfing is today where skiing and waterskiing were twenty-five years ago). Set up your operation in an area frequented by tourists or water-sports lovers. Find them near bays, oceans, sounds, river mouths, and lakes. Signs can herald your offerings, as can Yellow Pages ads, classified ads, display ads in tourist magazines, and publicity stories in the sports section. Try to work out a deal with a manufacturer. The idea is to furnish a demonstration, lessons, and sales of windsurfing equipment in one operation. The charge is usually from $15 to $25 per hour for instruction.

# 145 SHAPE UP

(Holding exercise classes) Be an exercise instructor to earn extra money. It shouldn't be hard to get a number of people to sign up for exercise groups since the cost is so low compared with skiing, golf, even jogging (in designer jogging clothes). Get your customers with posted signs, circulars, and big signs near your exercise class. You'll need to learn the latest effective exercises (so many different books and so much new technology—you should carefully check your bookstore or library) and arm yourself with good information on nutrition; it seems that exercise falls by the wayside when the exerciser fails to practice proper nutrition. You've got to be in good physical shape to do this, you've got to be able to lead people, and you've got to know all the latest data on physical fitness at all times. Some people I know pay $60 per month to belong to their exercise club. They tell me the instructors earn a piece of that action rather than an hourly wage; I guess the size of the piece is up to you. Maybe you can arrange to keep it all if you provide the equipment and space. As long as America is on a fitness kick, you ought to earn a consistent income working part-time as an exercise instructor. Learn a lot more about this business from the International Entrepreneur's Association, listed conveniently in the appendix under Books About Earning Endeavors. (Ask for their manual number 172, *Physical Fitness Center*.)

# 146 THE UNIVERSITY OF WORK

(Starting a trade school)  If you know a particular trade very well, and know other people who are equally well-versed in the field, you might do well establishing a trade school. Trade schools of all varieties are booming—the number of graduates from trade schools has tripled in the last ten years. Who makes up the bulk of the market? Disillusioned college graduates. Once again, the International Entrepreneur's Association rushes to your side with a manual dealing with starting and running a trade school. That manual, which you'll have to order through their *Business Manual Catalog* (see the appendix), specializes in showing how a successful bartender's school can make a go of it. But its concepts apply to virtually any kind of trade school. They claim that if you have four students per day, you'll net $1,000 per week. They also point out, happily, that start-up costs are low. Your only expenses are materials, space, and marketing. Pay your teachers a percentage of your net. If you're oriented to people and know how to teach, maybe you ought to start a trade school.

# 147 CORRESPONDENCE COLLEGE

(Starting a correspondence course)  What can you teach? Set up a correspondence course on the topic. What can members of your family teach? Set up correspondence courses on the topics. How about your friends? Business associates? Because of the regular time demands of standard educational institutions, many people favor learning by correspondence. So if you can establish several correspondence courses, you stand to make money for a long time. Naturally, you've got to keep your subject matter updated. And you've got to market your courses in the appropriate publications (mostly national special interest magazines) on a consistent basis. But once you've got your system going, it should keep going without too many demands on your time and energy. It goes without saying that the more courses you offer, the more money you'll make (if you don't know that, you might consider taking a correspondence course in basic economics). How much you charge for your course can range from $25 up to $1,000, depending upon the length of time and materials required. In this endeavor, you should be people-oriented to succeed even though you'll have very little to do with people in person. You must be skilled not only in the topic of your course, but also in the art of putting it all in writing, making lesson plans, creating tests, and suggesting support literature.

# 148 BAD BACK/GOOD BACK

(Conducting classes for people with bad backs) You'd be amazed at how many people suffer from back problems. You'd be equally amazed at how many methods there are of avoiding bad backs. Get in on the pain by organizing classes for people who suffer from bad backs. You've got to know what you're doing, what you can accomplish with your classes, what you cannot accomplish with your classes, and when to send people straight to the orthopedist. But many proven back exercises do exist. Trouble is, many people lack the discipline to exercise alone. That's why they'll be attracted to your group exercises. Catch them with classified ads, mailings to clubs, and free seminars on back exercises and back maintenance. People with bad backs will gladly pay $10 per hour if you can relieve their pains. And with so many people aching, you've just got to be careful you don't hurt your own back carrying their cash to the bank. Wouldn't you love that problem? There's a local back school here that charges $250 for a twelve-week back course. That should give you some idea of how much you can earn.

# 149  YOU CAN DO IT

(Starting a do-it-yourself school)  Almost everyone has a number of skills that may be taught to others. By rounding up several such people, you can start an earning endeavor devoted to teaching others to do-it-themselves. Do what? Repair a car, paint a house, put up wallpaper, build a bookshelf, bake a cake, plant a vegetable garden . . . almost anything. The idea is to make people self-sufficient. And today, many people need a little self-sufficiency just to make ends meet. In fact, making ends meet is another course that may be offered by your earnway. Attract teachers by means of phone calls to practitioners of the skills. Attract students with classified ads, signs on bulletin boards, circulars, and occasional newspaper display ads. The effort required to get a do-it-yourself school going is substantial. But so are the possibilities of long-term profit. If you take only 15 percent of what your teachers charge, you'll have quite a bit for yourself. A teacher may charge $10 per student per hour. With ten students, that teacher earns $200 per 2-hour class. If the teacher has two classes per week, that's $400 per week per teacher, or $60 per week for you. If you have ten teachers going at it, you've got $600 per week coming in. And you don't have to do the work once you've got the school all set up.

# 150  YUM-YUM UNIVERSITY

(Teaching cooking)  If you're a good cook and have a fair-sized kitchen, you can earn extra money teaching cooking. It seems that there are always people around who need to learn how to cook, so if you can teach them, do it. You can teach large classes or small classes, or you can tutor individual would-be cooks. Classified ads plus signs on bulletin boards will keep your marketing costs down but your marketing energy up. Samples of your fare at fairs will net you more business. To make your college unique, offer specialized courses: baking, casseroles, quick dishes, Mexican cookery, magic with chicken, dessert cookery, French cooking. Oh well, you get the idea. Of course you'll need a good supply of cookbooks. It might take a year or so, but once you become known as a good teacher of good cooking, you'll find that your income will equal your reputation. One more time, about $10 per student per hour is the going fee.

## SERVICES FOR PEOPLE

# 151  THE INTRODUCTION INSTITUTE

(Introducing people to each other)   Earn money and love by introducing people to each other. Introduce men to women, men to men, women to women, tennis player to tennis player, mime to mime, couple to couple, skier to skier, entrepreneur to entrepreneur. By putting together people of similar interests, you are performing a valuable public service that is not ordinarily available—except through lewd-sounding classified ads. Market your institute with wholesome classified ads, radio spots, signs on bulletin boards, and free publicity stories and talk show appearances. Such free publicity is a natural for so unique a business. Write a news story about it and send your story to the local newspapers and radio and TV stations. By keeping the business free of scandal, it can result in income that keeps on coming. Charge a flat fee to each person who registers with you. This kind of service, already existing in Miami, includes parties in which attendees are charged $10 at the door if not a member, $4 if they are a member. Attendance runs as high as seven hundred, so you can see how the dollars mount up as the introductions mount up. You'll need a keen sensitivity to people, a sense of organization, and a knowledge of psychology—not formalized as with a degree, but informalized as with a multitude of friends and acquaintances. The Miami firm gets people together in one-on-one sessions, dances, discussion sessions, or house parties.

# 152   THE CHILDREN'S CENTER

(Setting up a day-care center for children)   Set up a day-care center. Be sure you comply with all the rules in your area (check with your county's children's services division). Be sure you provide the kids with proper supervision, fresh air and exercise, hard-to-break toys and games, wholesome food, and conscientious leaders. Then advertise your service with signs on bulletin boards, mailings to schools, a listing in the Yellow Pages, and circulars distributed to parents of young children. Don't engage in this earnway unless you have a genuine love for children; it takes more than a profit motive to succeed with kids. You can establish your center at your home or in a rented space. Wherever, there is always a need for good day-care centers, and if yours falls into the category of good, it will provide you with income. A Connecticut woman started up such a service as an extra-money earning endeavor and it turned into a sole source of income. Quite a good income at that. Better yet—she delegated much of the work. She says she got all of her business by talking to parents at a PTA-type meeting, then calling them later. Figure on $5 to $10 per child per day. With enough kids, that's income enough.

# 153 RENT-A-GRANNY

(Doing household tasks)   What do grannies do? Well, they help around the house, do some cooking, love to be with kids, keep a house neat as a pin, lend moral support, plant-sit, pet-sit, handle food shopping, tell stories, and a whole lot more. If you're a closet granny, this is a wonderful opportunity for you to earn extra money while getting all of your granny jollies. Market your granniness with classified ads, signs on bulletin boards, and a free publicity story. Soon, you might enlist the aid of other would-be grannies (even real-life grannies are okay) and leave most of the granny work to them while you profit from dreaming up such a lovable if outlandish idea. There's a Rent-A-Wife operation in California. Now there can be a Rent-A-Granny operation in your state. Charge by the hour: $10 to $20 depending on the work and number of hours. The only qualifications you need are those possessed by world-class grannies like your own.

# 154 SALON ON WHEELS

(Being a traveling hairstylist)   Anyone who has hairstyling ability plus a car can combine the two into a profitable earnway. Become a traveling stylist. Make house calls to cut, style, shampoo, color, perm, or otherwise treat hair. First you've got to have the ability to work in a great salon in order to operate this traveling business, and the right equipment. If you do, you can offer your customers the convenience of home styling, along with a lower price than the salons charge, with their overhead habit to support. You can gain more than enough business with display ads in the womens' section of your newspaper, with circulars distributed in the right places, with bulletins posted in Laundromats and supermarkets, and even with an occasional publicity story. Charge a wee bit less than the prevailing rates in your town, but earn consistently more than the salon stylist. If you're good enough, word-of-mouth advertising will soon have you in everyone's hair.

# 155 NAILBIRD

(Being a traveling manicurist)  If there can be a traveling hairstylist, there can be a traveling manicurist. In fact, there already is. In Las Vegas, one woman reportedly pulled in $5,000 in one year just doing nails on a part-time portable basis. As with the hairstylist, the manicurist has to be good at her work, have the right equipment, and be able to get around. The same kind of marketing tactics will help: display ads, circulars, bulletins, publicity stories, and even handing a bunch of your business cards to the traveling hairstylist.

# 156 THE PUBLIC SERVANT

(Getting elected or appointed to a community post)  Pay close attention here. This is a different type of earning endeavor. Instead of earning via a business, you earn extra money by getting elected or appointed to a community post. Are you qualified? Interested? If you answered yes to both questions, consider earning money as a part-time public official. Personal letters and personal phone calls are about the only way to set sail into the world of politics. If you're an ex-general, that helps, too. I know one person who earns a paltry $250 monthly serving as mayor of a small town in Colorado. His prime credential for the job is that he was an ex-high school football hero in the town. When I lived in Chicago, I knew many people who held appointed city jobs. They just knocked themselves out trying to get Mayor Daley elected, and as a gift of gratitude they received juicy appointments. It's a shame, but the system does work that way. It even enabled President Nixon to appoint a man to a $40,000-plus post as liaison to former presidents. Not bad, considering that at the time there were no living former presidents. For more insight, check into *The Plum Book: The Official United States Guide to Leading Positions in the Government, Presidential and Executive Appointments, Salaries, Requirements, and Other Vital Statistics for Job Seekers.* There really is such a book. Find out more in the appendix.

## 157 DEFENDER OF THE FLAG

(Joining the reserves or National Guard)   As long as we're on the subject of earning money outside standard earning channels, joining the military reserves or National Guard is well outside my standard channels, though I must admit to having been a member of the reserves—only because it was mandatory. It's not mandatory at the moment, and it is a method by which you may bring extra bucks (amount is dependent upon your rank) into your life. No experience is needed. No marketing is required to put a few hundred dollars per month into your pocket that way. Just sign on the dotted line and raise your right hand. Get a lot more information by checking the white pages in your directory under "United States of America, U.S. Army Reserve Recruiting."

## 158 FATHER-FIGURE/MOTHER-FIGURE

(Serving as a house-parent)   Earn extra money making kids happy by serving as a house-parent or resident adviser. Many residential homes for juveniles are in need of father- and mother-figures. These people earn room, board, plus a monthly stipend—several hundred dollars per month. In return, they must offer love, patience, understanding, flexibility, and most of the other human virtues.

Of course, in addition to money, you earn love and respect and undying gratitude—assuming you're dynamite at being a parental figure or adviser. Letters to residential treatment homes, which are usually under city or county auspices, will put you on the right trail. If I were you, I'd start with a call to your city hall or county hall.

# 159  HAIR TODAY, GONE TOMORROW

(Removing unwanted hair)   With the proper equipment and training, you can use electrolysis to remove unwanted hair for people. Many stunning women used electrolysis to remove hair from their faces; the gay population (not every member) uses it to remove bodily hair. Electrolysis success will come to you with classified ads, a Yellow Pages listing, small display ads in the women's section of the Sunday paper, and with bulletins in beauty salons. And at gathering spots for gays. You can earn $25 per hour and up if you're good at the work.

# 160  PLAY BALL

(Umpiring or refereeing sporting events)   You can be sure to make both enemies and money (probably more enemies than money) if you become a sports umpire or referee. There's a whole lot of baseball, basketball, hockey, soccer, football, and other competitive sports activity going on. They all need umping and refing. If you know the sport, the rules, the psychology, and the strategy, and have a sense of sports justice, you might be just the person for one of these many part-time jobs available throughout the year. Letters to parks and recreation departments, to city and county parks, to schools, and to league officers will get you on the field, court, or rink in a hurry. Expect $10 to $25 per game for your efforts. I know a Chicago man who gave vent to his sports love via this method. At first, he pocketed a few extra dollars refereeing amateur football games. Today, he pockets a few extra thousand dollars refereeing pro football games in the NFL. The job is still a part-time endeavor. He still maintains his regular job. But now he gets to be booed by tens of thousands of fans.

# 161 SHOW GROUPIE

(Working at trade shows)  If you live in or near a city in which conventions and trade shows are held, work is available to you on a part-time basis. It's work for people who enjoy earning extra money doing some of the plethora of jobs that arise in connection with these trade shows. You might be called upon to take names, put up signs, hand out circulars, tack up bunting, demonstrate an appliance, greet customers, take tickets, or open refrigerator doors. You can offer your services by contacting your city's visitor and convention bureau, learning which shows and conventions are coming, along with the names of their honchos, then writing said honchos stating your availability. Letters to convention and show halls are also in order. A phone call to your local chamber of commerce will also put you on the right track. As with all the other endeavors in this chapter, you must enjoy dealing with people. You can earn from $25 to $250 per day at this work. Depends whether or not your remuneration is based on a commission system. Example: A company may pay you a base fee of $50 per day plus $1 per name you obtain for a list, or $10 per sale you make. The work is sporadic, but many say it's fun.

# 162 AT YOUR SERVICE

(Serving summonses as a process-server)  Be a process-server. Secure your credentials by applying at your city or county hall, then list yourself in the Yellow Pages as one who will serve a summons for the going rate—about $35 and going up, up, up. The work is not steady, not fun, and not hard. I don't think much other marketing (maybe a bulletin posted at your city or county hall) is necessary. No prior experience of any kind is necessary. Funny, the other day, I noticed that a professional process-server had filed to become a corporation. Maybe there's more money in this gig than meets the eye. Whatever happens, I wish you well in this endeavor, and may our paths never cross.

## 163  BOOKS THAT TALK

(Reading to vision-impaired people)   You'll never be a millionaire, except perhaps in terms of emotional rewards, if you earn money reading to the elderly or vision-impaired. Although this is often a volunteer effort, it is also a money-earner. Just ask the many people who earn $5 to $10 hourly reading aloud. You can get going with mailings to senior citizens' homes, nursing homes, hospitals, and senior citizen groups. Once you have a steady and growing clientele, you can enjoy your favorite books while getting paid to share their contents with others. Some people are even selling their voices on recorded tapes of books. The only requirement for success at this earnway is that you be able to read clearly and be sensitive to the needs of vision-impaired people.

## 164  FRIEND IN NEED

(Being a professional companion)   Friend in Need is exactly what you figure it to be—a service that provides companions to the sick, elderly, or handicapped. Friend in Need places signs on bulletin boards, does mailings to senior citizens homes, places classified ads under announcements, and is probably the subject of a newspaper story extolling the virtues of the service. Friend in Need pro-

vides loving care, honest companionship with warm conversation, occasional joking, complete sincerity, and true
friendship. It is hardly possible to put a price tag on these
factors. Suffice it to say that your rewards will be more
than monetary. And the person who pays you will feel
that you're worth far more than you're being paid—anywhere from $5 per hour to $50 per day. People who participate in this line of work are expected to do so on a
relatively consistent basis. One woman I know works as a
Friend in Need from after work (5:30 P.M.) until after dinner (7:30 P.M.). For her companionship, she earns $25 per
day (not too bad for a two-hour day).

# 165 THE CONSTANT COMPANION

(Serving as a companion for out-of-home activities)  Friend
in Need provides companionship to people who spend a
great deal of time indoors. The Constant Companion has a
different *mise-en-scène*. Let's face it—it's not a whole lot
of fun going to restaurants alone. Or movies alone. Or the
theater or ball games alone. Okay, solve that problem for
others by offering to go with them to restaurants, movies,
theaters, ball games, and other events. Find such people
with classified ads and signs on bulletin boards. It's pretty
brazen, but you might also consider handing circulars to
people who are alone at such events. Along with the nominal hourly fee you'll receive ($5 to $10 per hour, from what
I have learned), you'll benefit from free meals, movies,
plays, and ball games. No experience is needed. But you
should be a compassionate person and a good conversa-
tionalist.

# 166 BABYLOVE BABY-SITTING

(Baby-sitting and delegating baby-sitting)  Possibly the least
imaginative method of earning extra money is baby-sit-

ting. But no list of 555 ways to earn extra money would be complete without it. So here it is. The rate for sitters is constantly climbing, now at $1.50 per hour in my neighborhood. Secure customers with signs, classified ads in local papers, notices on bulletin boards, and circulars handed out to homes or inserted in mailboxes in a neighborhood where babies are present or expected. Contact your local high school or college to find good people to whom the baby-sitting may be delegated. Then, sit out while others sit in and give you a share of their sitting money. A woman I know who runs a baby-sitting service has a stable of ten sitters. She charges $2.00 per hour, paying her sitters $1.50. She gets $.50 just for arranging the service. On a busy weekend that means she's earning $5.00 per hour for doing nothing. Of course, she probably has to shell out some of that for her own baby-sitter. Probably the only qualifications you need to be a good baby-sitter are an ability never to panic, a warm feeling toward kids, a conscientious attitude about the property of others, and punctuality.

## 167 RACER PACER

(Serving as the pace car for races)   Use your car, van, truck, station wagon, bus, or tank to serve as a pace car for the many road-running races that are held these days. You won't make much money on the starts, but you will make quite a bit offering return rides to the racers. After all, they must get back to the starting point one way or another. By charging nominal fees to runners ($2 per ride is what local runners pay) you can pack your car with pooped racers, and make several trips after each race. That car will add up to a wonderful service for the runners and a source of income for you. Market your service with mailings to race promoters, then with signs at the sites of the races—start and finish. A sign on your car will help, too.

You'll probably require a chauffeur's license to do this, but that's not hard to get. With so many racers and so many races, it is my fond hope that you stay the only Racer Pacer in your area.

# 168 PAID PARENTHOOD

(Taking kids to events)   Take kids on trips to museums, circuses, sporting events, zoos, and other such attractions. Provide the transportation, the overseeing, the love, and the care. In return, receive money from each parent—based upon the amount of time you spend with the kids. The current rate is $1.50 per hour, just as with baby-sitting, but with six kids in tow, it comes to $9.00 hourly for you. At a three-hour circus with a one-hour round-trip ride, that amounts to $36.00 for your efforts. But make no mistake—taking kids to the circus is not a small effort. Attract parents who can use your services with circulars distributed where parents gather, with classified ads, with mailings to nursery schools, and with the inevitable signs on bulletin boards. Ads in local church publications will also help. You will require a chauffeur's license if much driving is involved, and an ability to get along with a gang of kids. (Gangs of kids are far more unruly than individual kids.) Once a business such as this gets established, it can be part of your community for a long time. And as it prospers, you prosper.

# 169 MIDNIGHT TRANSIT

(Driving folks home at night)   You will be very much appreciated if you meet workers who toil till late at night, then drive them home. Unfortunately, there is an ever-more-powerful need for such a service because of the rising crime rate. So, fortunately, you stand to earn quite a bit of extra money with this type of earnway—one California person charges $5 per rider. Mailings to factories, hospitals, hotels, and other places with late-night employees should net you enough business in a short time. Then you can concentrate on expanding your business through delegating. Some enlightened employers are actually footing half the bill for their employees. That's why I suggested that you write to factories in the first place. Yup, you'll probably need a chauffeur's license. Also a city map.

## **170** THE COMMUTER CONNECTION
(Taking commuters to and from their public transportation)
It's all well and good for commuters to save time, effort, and energy by taking public transportation. But how, pray tell, are they going to get home from the bus or train station? Glad you asked. If they lack a station car, or station parking facilities are too much of a hassle, too expensive, or nonexistent, your service transports them from home to the station in the morning, then from the station back home in the afternoon. You'll attract commuters with circulars distributed to their homes, with classified ads, and with signs on local bulletin boards. And don't forget to put a sign on the van, station wagon, or car that does the transporting. It won't take you long to sign up a bunch of eager commuters. And you can probably arrange two or three runs per morning and the same two or three runs per evening. Charge a weekly $10 to $25, depending upon the size of your vehicle (bigger vehicle, smaller fee) and the distance to the public transit. A chauffeur's license and a painstaking attentiveness to punctuality are necessities. You should possess a good working knowledge of psychology, too. After all, many of your best customers will be ogres in the morning.

## **171** ESCORTS ANONYMOUS
(Providing an escort service)  Very frequently a person is invited to an event and hates to go alone. Or someone

visits a city and doesn't want to hit the high (or low) spots alone. What to do? Hire an escort from an escort service. If you're considering starting such a service, what can you expect of the escorts you hire for it? Will they be on the up and up? The answer is up to you. You'll need both male and female escorts, and you'll have to be careful about selecting them. They'll have to know your area, the restaurants, the nightspots, and the other places worth visiting. Naturally, the question of sex has to be considered. If your eye is on long-term success and community acceptance, you'll be better off running a totally nonsexual service. You should make that very clear to your escorts. Since you can recruit professional escorts with classified ads, you can offer professional escorts the same way, and by means of the Yellow Pages. An escort can charge from $25 to $100 per six-hour engagement, so if you operate as a one-person service, that's what you can charge and keep. If you set up the service to use other escorts, you get to keep only 25 percent to 50 percent of that amount. Once your service does have a good reputation, you can relax and know that other peoples' loneliness will mean business for you.

# 172 JOBS GALORE

(Offering a job-finding service)   Most jobs are not offered through classified ads or by employment agencies. In fact, in the San Francisco Bay Area in 1989, over 80 percent of the open jobs were never advertised or listed. Instead, their availability traveled along certain grapevines. By becoming a party to such grapevines, you can offer a job-finding service to people who either wish to have a job or to earn a bit of extra money. Once you have really begun to concentrate on finding jobs, you'll be surprised at how many you'll find. A mailing to the companies that hire the most people in your community should get you started.

Classified ads directed to job seekers will constitute the rest of the marketing for you. Supplement that with a Yellow Pages listing and signs on bulletin boards. Incidentally, you can make money at this endeavor in several ways—by charging the employer, the employee, or both. Whichever you do, the amount charged is commonly a percentage of the salary, varying from 10 percent to 50 percent over a period extending from one to three months. Learn more by perusing *What Color Is Your Parachute?*

# **173**  CAMP RUNAMOK

(Running a children's summer camp)  Being a kid lolling around at home during the summer isn't all it's cracked up to be. Oh, there's lots of free time, but there's lots of boredom, too. That's why summer camps seem to do so well. You can enter this lucrative business. You'll need cabins, a bucolic setting, counselors, a program, good food, recreational activities and equipment, a camp nurse, and a whole bunch of youngsters. The youngsters may be attracted with in-person calls to parents, direct mailings to the same parents, a classy brochure, even slides, film, or videotape to show to prospective parents. By charging competitive rates (not hard; most camps charge a fortune—we paid $1,000 per summer while our Amy went to an eight-week camp, and costs have gone up since), you can make a name for your camp. If you are conscientious about the details of your camp, it can become a summertime institution (I mean the word *institution* in its most favorable sense). Mind you, this is a difficult and sometimes debilitating way to earn money. But if you have an understanding of kids, a keen sense of organization, and are considered an unflappable individual, it's a most rewarding way (I mean rewarding to include emotions, finances, intellect, and love). Get lots more information by writing to camps selected from *Guide to Summer*

*Camps and Summer Schools.* It's in the appendix and your library.

# 174 SANCTUARY

(Providing nursing care in your home)  Find out the local rules, then if you're able to comply you can use that spare room or rooms in your home to provide nursing care. Perhaps one of the rooms may be given for free to a person who will do all the work for your residents: meal preparation, room cleaning, shopping, companionship. Yellow Pages listings, signs on bulletin boards, mailings to certain organizations, and yes, classified ads will get you the residents you need. Following a couple months of preparation (including personal observation of several successful homes along with interviews with the staff and the residents), your nursing care (not necessarily a full-time, live-in offering) should provide you with the extra money you seek. You must be people-oriented to succeed, and you'll need quick access to medical help, should your residents ever require it. Earnings can range from $250 to $500 per month per resident (but for that money, meals should be served). I figure that for most budding earners one resident will do, maybe two. A fancy local home I know of charges $1,500 monthly, but what they offer cannot be accomplished by anyone on a part-time basis.

# 175 MOUNTAIN GUIDE

(Guiding skiers at ski areas)  I'm an avid skier, yet I have trouble figuring out the lay of the slopes at most any ski area I visit for the first time. Even with the full-color ski maps provided, I can easily get lost. So if a hard-core skier such as I am has trouble, you can imagine the problem for novices. That's why a ski guide service should (and does) prosper. A few strategically located signs, along with small display ads in local ski bulletins or sports sections of local newspapers, should be all the marketing you will need. You can set up guides at several areas once you get into a position to delegate, thereby multiplying your earning possibilities. There is no question of the opportunities for this service: skiers are usually well-off financially, and the popularity of the sport continues to grow. I've met ski instructors who charge as much as (ready?) $250 per day to guide small groups of skiers. All of which can add up to profits that, for you, will go uphill as your customers go downhill.

# 176 MAGIC FINGERS

(Giving massages) There are as many types of massages as there are places on the body that feel absolutely marvelous while being massaged. By becoming a master of any one of these massage techniques, you can become both beloved and well paid. Of course, if you train others in your technique, you will be even better paid. Obtain customers with classified ads, circulars, a Yellow Pages listing, and brief, free sample massages at fairs. You might even have a seminar, free of course, on massaging. These days, a nonsexual massage (yes folks, those still do exist) runs $20 to $25 per hour. If you do a good job learning massage and training others to massage for you, you'll have enough repeat business to make you feel as good all over as your customers. Two classic books on the topic are *The Massage Book* and *The Art of Sensual Massage*. (See the appendix.)

# 177 CHAMPIONS OF THE WORLD

(Organizing tournaments) You can earn extra money (and maybe even win a trophy) if you organize tournaments. Offer your tournaments in one or more of several highly popular activities: Frisbee throwing, backgammon, dominoes, gin rummy, poker, general knowledge quizzes, cribbage, Monopoly, Scrabble . . . the opportunities are endless. Charge entry fees ($10 to $125 are the fees I've encountered) to the entrants, and admission fees ($5 or less) to the spectators. Advertise your tourney with newspaper display ads, maybe even magazine ads in special interest magazines. Try for free publicity in newspapers and magazines, on radio and TV. And try mailings to likely organizations. If you offer trophies to the winners, you can make a lot of money. If you offer money to the winners, you make considerably less money. If the tournament is smoothly run, it can become an annual event. And an annual source of income. Just remember to watch out for cheaters.

## 178 VITAL VISITS

(Visiting shut-ins)  By establishing a visiting service for shut-ins, you will earn extra money along with extra soul-satisfaction. Such a service requires that you be able to make conversation, become a true companion, exhibit empathy, be reliable, and usually be of good cheer. Market your service with mailings to social workers, nursing homes, hospitals, and known shut-ins, along with classified ads. You'll be able to schedule your visits on a regular basis, and in all likelihood you'll end up looking forward to the visits, for they'll seem more like a pleasure than an earning endeavor (actually, they'll be both). That's why so many people do this on a volunteer basis. Still, a lot of others charge from $5 to $10 for the service. So can you.

## 179 TRIP PERSON

(Caring for kids while parents are away on a trip)  Care for kids while their parents go away on a trip. I remember paying top dollar ($200 per week) for this service while my kid was still a kid . . . and I recall being glad just to be able to find such a person. You can be that person with classified ads, signs on bulletin boards, and circulars handed to parents in playgrounds. Actually, your best marketing method will be to offer so much quality that you generate word-of-mouth advertising. You'll probably have to stay in the kid's home, not yours. And if you're good, you will find that you are always in demand. And you can charge stiff fees for your services. Just be careful you don't get booked fifty-two weeks a year. Leave some time to take a trip yourself.

# 180 THE COMMUNITY CABBIE
(Offering part-time community taxi service)   Once you've obtained the proper license (chauffeur's) and insurance, you can offer a part-time community taxi service. Circulars delivered to the homes in your community will bring in the business, especially if you back them with a Yellow Pages listing, a sign on your cab, and a display ad in a local paper. This business will really take off when you start to make regular runs such as picking up kids at school, commuters at buses, nurses at hospitals. By limiting your service to one community you will soon become a familiar service, and in marketing familiarity breeds success. To maintain enough freedom, know out front the days and hours you wish to work, for I am talking about a part-time service and not a full-time job. Once you are established, you can earn $25 to $50 daily.

# 181 TIME WELL SPENT
(Providing programs for convention spouses)   Very often a husband will take his wife along to an out-of-town business meeting or convention. While he is attending confer-

ences, seminars, luncheons, and presentations, what's the poor woman to do? Aha! You say you've got a service that creates innovative programs for convention spouses? Perfect! The wife (or company) will gladly pay your steep fee ($50 per day is not uncommon) for the marvelous tour, show, and shopping program you have planned for her. To establish such a service, first figure out how you will entertain convention spouses, then mail your descriptive brochure to convention planners or to corporations scheduled to meet in your city. Your city's tourist bureau will have their names, addresses, and the dates of their conventions, and the big hotels can tell you about smaller meetings. You might also mail to organizations that hold conventions because your service might be enough to justify a convention in or expand one to your town. Really. Once you get this convention service going, you might even sit back and turn it over to someone else. Such businesses are already flourishing in San Francisco and Las Vegas. They offer group discounts, but the owners say they really clean up whether their programs are for individuals or groups.

# 182 UNITED WE STAND

(Forming merchants' associations)  You can make quite a bit of extra money if you form merchants' associations. To do this, you canvass the actual merchants, paying in-person calls and explaining that if they join your association, they can benefit from low rates for group advertising, group promotions, group merchandising. Because you bring these merchants together and find the right ad agency for them, the right promotion company, and the right source of merchandising displays, you are entitled to a fee from each participating merchant. You can set up associations among merchants situated on a commercial street, in a shopping center, in a small town, or even among merchants of similar merchandise. I remember seeing a group of TV commercials for a small town. These spots suggested that the auto dealers in the town offered such low, small-town prices that it was worth the drive. Whoever dreamed up that one certainly deserved the fee he or she charged. If you can do the same, you can charge from $25 to $100 monthly per merchant for your expertise. And that expertise should be in the areas of marketing, merchandising, promoting, retailing, and organizing. But don't even dream of doing this unless you are oriented to people.

With many earnways throughout this book, I bring up the possibility of delegating the work. Your long-range interests and chance for sizable earnings will improve if you succeed with an earnway first, then delegate it to another. Those others will be motivated by the success you have achieved. And you will have gained enough insights to understand the business better.

Since you will be playing an ever-decreasing role in those earnways you decide to delegate, and assuming you manage to turn up consistent profits, you'll be able to sell the business at a later date. After all, you will have started it, you will have created the original momentum, and you will have masterminded the marketing. And because you have *not* made yourself indispensable, you will have created a continuing source of income.

Patchwork economics suggests that you do some work for yourself, delegate other work, and sell other businesses you have created. Always remember that the world has many talented people who lack the talent to create and organize a business. These are the people to whom you might delegate, and they are also the people who might want to purchase your business. They are smart, energetic, willing, able, reliable, and hardworking. All they lack is the ability to create a business from scratch.

Because you do have that ability, it is only reasonable that you profit from it. Those profits can come in the form of a monthly or weekly stream of income, or from one enormous glob of income as a result of selling your delegable business.

I have a good friend whose life goals are to create businesses and then sell them for ridiculously high sums—well in excess of one million dollars. He didn't even realize his talent at this until he first got the idea in his mid-forties. Now, a scant ten years after that first realization, he is a millionaire many times over.

If you, too, happen to be over forty, take heart in the fact that more than half the people listed in *Who's Who* didn't even start their climb to fame and fortune until they were forty. So there.

Now, a word for you people who would just as soon not work with other people. In fact, more than a word—here comes an entire chapter. Of course, it will deal with work that involves people. But it will not be about work that is dependent upon them. It will deal more with *things*.

One can do many things when one is working with things. What kinds of things? Read on.

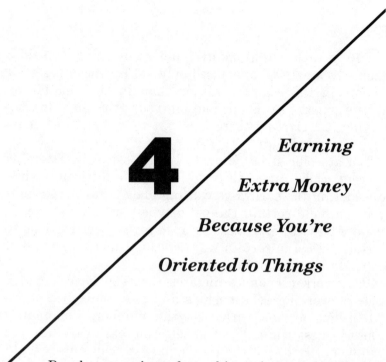

# 4 / Earning Extra Money Because You're Oriented to Things

People are oriented to things in many different ways. People can (and do) earn extra money building things, repairing things, cleaning things, maintaining things, delivering things, operating things, renting things, finding things, and cooking things. Other people earn money by applying an affinity for particular things—like food or nature or animals. The more ways you relate to things, the more avenues you have to explore in your quest for extra money.

If some of the upcoming earnways intrigue you, but you're one course or two books or three months of apprenticing away from being able to do them well, you should seriously consider undertaking this training. It would be in keeping with the spirit of patchwork economics—and you'll be able to earn more money because you'll be able to tap more of your skills. So as you read continue making check marks by the earnways that interest you, and remember that you need not mark only skills you already possess. Skills you might want to learn count, too.

I fully realize that many builders of things consider themselves artists, and justifiably so. By including your talents in this chapter rather than in the chapter on things artistic, I was not judging your work, merely classifying it. Certainly there is an art to cooking, and cooking is included here.

You are officially invited to think positively, laterally, concentrically, imaginatively, and egocentrically while considering the earnways waiting ahead. For instance, if you can build certain things, maybe you can also repair them. And vice versa. Just because you've been relating to certain things in certain ways does not mean you cannot expand that relationship.

Patchwork economics dictates that you have a multitude of working relationships and that the types of relationships are as varied as the number. Community consciousness will aid you in selecting earnways, for you will be quick to spot the needs you can help satisfy right on your own home turf. You know what they say about finding a need and filling it.

Ideally, many of these earning endeavors will be so enjoyable for you that you will joyfully engage in them, hardly ever considering your activities as "work." Only about 20 percent of all working people feel that way, according to figures from the experts. I suspect the world would be much better off if that number were closer to 100 percent. Well, here's your chance to up the averages. Here's a bright green opportunity to earn money in ways that fascinate, titillate, and captivate you.

Anyone can earn money doing something that makes him/her miserable. It takes a truly evolved individual to earn money while having fun.

## BUILDING AND REPAIRING

# 183 TUNED IN INSTRUMENT REPAIRS

(Repairing musical instruments)   You can earn extra money if you can repair or restore musical instruments. By specializing in pianos, in guitars and other stringed instruments, in woodwinds, in brass instruments, or in percussion instruments, you can pick up a pretty penny from many a musician. They can learn of your services by means of bulletins posted in musical instrument stores, and at studios by circulars distributed to musicians, and by classified ads in the musical instrument section of a local paper. Best of all, see if a retail store will let you be their repair department. If so, your financial life may become quite harmonious. It will help if you're musically inclined, but musical talent is not a requirement for financial success. Unless you are an accomplished specialist and can charge by the project, you'll be best off charging by the hour. The going rate is $15 per hour—and, of course, add to that the charge for materials. If you get this earnway down pat, you'll pick up broken instruments at a local musical instrument store on Friday, and return fixed instruments on the following Friday—earning your money during your free time throughout the week. You might talk to the people at your local music shops to learn more about this business. If you can work on electric guitars and accessories you could do especially well these days. Your old-world craftsmanship on advanced instruments will strike a happy note with many a music-maker.

# 184 THE MOBILE MECHANIC

(Making house calls to repair cars)   It's an honest-to-goodness inconvenience getting a car serviced. You've got to arrange your own transportation from the garage, back to the garage, and if your car isn't ready when promised, you've got even more transportation hassles. No wonder you'd be glad to call The Mobile Mechanic—if there was one in your community. There is one in my community. Probably more than one. These mechanics come right to your home and service your car at an hour when you're not using it. No transportation hassles for you, and if the work isn't finished in time, so what? The garage won't close. The work will be finished later. No inconvenience. If you're mechanically inclined, and can get all the tools together, you can earn a lot of extra money and a lot of gratitude from grateful motorists. Get your customers with a listing in the Yellow Pages, with display ads in the local paper, and with radio advertising, broadcast during drive time—morning and evening rush hours. Such advertising is costly, but it reaches a whole lot of prospects. In the long run, that makes it turn out to be very uncostly. A mechanic in my area uses radio spots to herald his house calls. It goes without saying that you've got to be a super-competent and versatile mechanic to earn money this way. You also need a vehicle to transport you and your tools. Because most vehicles are at home only after working hours, being a Mobile Mechanic is ideally suited to after-hours earning. Since a Mobile Mechanic doesn't have a high overhead as does a standard garage, he or she can charge a fiercely competitive price . . . and gain quite a bit of business. Even if you charge less than the local garage, you can earn more than the mechanics who work there.

# 185 I WANT YOUR BODY

(Doing auto body work on the owner's premises) The neat but naughty name of this earnway might be useful to you if you can do auto body work right on the car owner's premises . . . or anywhere else other than a garage that would require overhead to maintain. My father was driving in Florida once, and a fellow hailed him from another car at a red light. The guy said he could remove the dents from my father's car right then and there. When my dad heard how little it would cost, he couldn't refuse the offer. He pulled over to the curb and the bodywork man parked behind him, took his tools from his trunk, and proceeded to get all the dents out of dad's car—for a fraction of what a body shop would have charged. Both sides were happy. This bodywork expert used a marketing tool I hadn't even considered: car-to-car sales calls. You can also use more conventional methods like classified ads, Yellow Pages advertising, and posted bulletins. It will be easiest for you if you've done this kind of work in a garage already and have a good line on your skills and tools. I don't know how much you can earn with this method, but my father said those repairs would have cost him $300 in a garage, cost only $75 from the mobile mechanic, and took less than thirty minutes. Hmmm, that comes to $150 per hour. Sound good?

# 186 SECOND TIME AROUND

(Rebuilding auto parts at home)   Rebuilding auto parts at home is a better way than you might think of earning extra money. If you have the tools, talent, and work space, rebuilding can be fun and profitable at the same time. The prime customers for your rebuilt parts will be garages and auto parts stores, so your marketing can be directed to them. Try direct mail or deliver circulars in person and give a sales pitch. Try running a few classified ads to see if you can sell directly to the public. Second Time Around is a relatively recession-proof business since cars will continue to be necessary and will need parts whatever happens. Some in this field charge by the part but you'll be best off charging by the hour. The going rate range is $7.50 to $15.00 per hour.

# 187 THE CONVERTIBLE MAN (OR WOMAN)

(Converting structures) The Convertible Man converts sheds into guest houses, closets into bathrooms, attics into nurseries, and basements into dens. The Convertible Man can convert any room in your house into another form. It's a lot easier and cheaper to convert a house than to move altogether. As one who paid to have a shed converted into a guest room, I can heartily recommend this concept from both sides. It's a good way to earn money, and it's a good way to improve your home. By specializing in conversions you can convert your skill into a large bankroll. Market your converting abilities with classified ads, circulars distributed to home owners, and Yellow Pages advertising. If you really want to go for it, run a series of newspaper display ads in a local paper. Better yet, join up with a contractor as a conversion specialist. Of course, your best advertising will be an impressive display of before-and-after photos and the free publicity your work will generate as proud and happy home owners show off their "new" houses to their friends. To make it at this endeavor, you'll have to know your stuff—this is serious biz. And you can earn serious bucks—about $20 per hour after materials costs. More if you're very good.

# 188 INSPECTOR RESKIN

(Inspecting houses)   The house inspector I know is Inspector Reskin. But you can be Inspector Jones or Inspector Gomez. Whoever you are, you'll do a first-class job of inspecting buildings for drainage, foundation condition, roof and exterior siding, heating, electrical system, plumbing system, floors, walls, doors, windows, and ter-

mites—and earn a first-class living doing it. Charge about
$100 per inspection (cheap when compared to the price of
a house or the cost of a major defect), and market your
inspection services with Yellow Pages ads and direct mailings to real estate brokers. It will also help to have your
ad in the classified section near the real estate section.
And it will be of enormous aid to read *How to Inspect a
House* by George Hoffman. Right, Inspector?

## 189  DO-IT-YOURSELF WITH ME

(Designing plans for do-it-yourselfers)   Create, design, draw
up, and sell do-it-yourself plans for any of many items:
houses, barbecue pits, hot tubs, outdoor decks, patios,
guest rooms, furniture, electric bicycles, automobile conversions (like changing a mild-mannered economy car to a
souped-up monster), boats, and a raft of other things (like
rafts). If you're good at designing and are able to put
ideas down on paper as building plans, there are a lot of
talented do-it-yourselfers who lack your particular talent
and will be glad to pay for your plans. They'll pay $10 for
simple plans and $500 and up (way up—ask any architect)
for complex plans. Let them find out about you from
ads in do-it-yourselfer magazines, bulletins in hardware
stores, and from direct mailings to known do-it-yourselfers. You can get a lead on new publications in this field
by checking on a recent edition of *Popular Mechanics* or
*Popular Science*. (Truth is that both publications can help
you with many of the earnways listed in this chapter since
both are very thing-oriented.)

## 190  THE CAMERA HOSPITAL

(Repairing cameras)   I'm amazed at the high prices I pay
the man who repairs my camera. I'd be glad to let you
handle any future repairs (hope I never need them again)

if you could do such good work for a more reasonable price. If you're gifted at photographic fixing, you can really earn money with your gift. Find customers with Yellow Pages ads, with mailings to known photographers in your area, and with bulletins posted in camera stores (the ones that do not offer repairs). Write personal letters to camera stores offering to be their outside repair department. Classified ads in the photography section of the newspaper will help too, I'll bet. You'd better know your way around the inside of a camera, and have the proper tools and a deft touch to practice this earnway. I'm not sure how much you should charge per hour, but I know I paid $75 to have my camera fixed the first time, and $135 the second time. Of that, about 10 percent went for parts. The rest was strictly labor. Learn about camera repairing by leafing through the many photography magazines (I can find nine) in search of the latest literature on the topic.

# 191  PICTURE PERFECT PAINTINGS

(Cleaning paintings)   The art of painting is nearly matched in difficulty by the art of cleaning paintings. If you can master how to clean art, you can earn extra money (up to $100 per hour) from private collectors, museums, and businesses or institutions that display artwork. Don't limit your cleaning abilities to paintings. The cleaning of any delicate artwork is a necessary skill worth quite a bit of money. Even $100 per hour is beneath the usual cost for the most accomplished people in this field. Direct mail seems the most likely marketing tool, but you might also consider ads in art-oriented publications and even a short listing in the Yellow Pages. Giving your brochure to galleries won't hurt, since they'll be able to serve their public better by being able to recommend your picture perfect services. This is not a job for an amateur, and it can be a very profitable endeavor. The best way to learn it is by apprenticing. You'll find plenty of places at which this may be done if you check under "Art Restoration & Conservation" in a metropolitan Yellow Pages. Since you'll be doing this as a part-time endeavor, you'll probably get to clean only a very small number of paintings per month . . . one to four, I figure. But that will earn you a classic extra income.

# 192 PEDALPOWER

(Building pedal-powered machines)   As long as the nation is energy conscious, and that will probably be for another half-century at least, many people will see the common sense in pedal-powered machines. If you can build such machines, or convert other machines to pedal power, you can get free publicity and save the nation's energy resources at the same time. Naturally, skill and inventiveness are required. Display ads in the main news section of the newspaper seem sensible, as do mailings to people with convertible machines. A traveling exhibit of one or two of your pedal-powered machines will net quite a bit of exposure and new business for you. These days, energy fairs are held in numerous cities. I'd sure recommend that you attend and exhibit at some of those. One that I've attended on several occasions is the New Earth Expo. Until that fair reaches your city (or until you start one in your area), leaf through current issues of *Popular Mechanics*, *Popular Science*, and the latest *Whole Earth Catalog*.

# 193 DOCTOR LOCK

(Being a part-time locksmith)   Once you've taken the appropriate training and become a first-class locksmith, you'll have the key to earning money forever, wherever. You need not do it on a full-time basis. With listings in the Yellow Pages, classified ads, and posted bulletins, you can make your locksmithing part of a successful patchwork economics plan. If you can locate your business (you) in an area with few locksmiths, you'll probably make more than a few dollars. Our local person charges $30 per hour. These days, locksmiths offer lock repairs, lock opening, lock replacement, lock installation, key fabrication, vault installation, lock and vault sales, combination changing, key systems for industry, and security service. And, naturally, they offer home service. After all, you can't expect a person to bring his front door to you for repairs. Want more information? Check your omnipresent Yellow Pages under "Locksmiths' Equip. & Supls." and look for schools of locksmithing. They'll have plenty of information.

# 194 KNOCK-KNOCK
(Creating knockdown furniture)  People move much more often these days than they ever did before. That's why there has been such healthy growth in the knockdown furniture industry. Such furniture comes apart easily for no-hassle moving. If you can design and create this KD furniture, you can make a healthy living. Sell it through stores, classified ads, flea markets, fairs, bulletins in neighborhoods with apartment buildings, and bulletins right in apartment buildings themselves. You need to know the art of furniture making before you can succeed at knockdown furniture making. Charge your customers for your materials and your labor ($5 to $25 per hour, your choice . . . depending upon your ability).

# 195 GUN FIXER
(Repairing guns)  Repair pistols and rifles to earn extra money. Do a mailing to gun stores to see if you can be their part-time repair department. Run a classified ad in the guns section of the paper, and consider a small display ad in the sports section. Post bulletins at gun and hunting

clubs. It would also be advisable to list your service in the Yellow Pages. I'm assuming you know how to repair weapons if you plan to do it professionally. Gunsmiths charge $50 per hour, and the honest ones will admit that many repairs take only fifteen minutes. These will charge only $8.75 to make those guns go bang again.

## 196 KITCHEN FACE-LIFTS

(Replacing kitchen cabinet doors) You can make a dramatic difference in the appearance of a kitchen by replacing all the cabinet doors. This is the basis for a lucrative business. And many home owners, not to mention apartment dwellers, will know that they need you when they see your display ads in the newspaper, your mailings to their homes and apartments, and your TV commercials on that inexpensive local cable channel. (This is an instance when TV advertising can be utilized to its greatest effect.) It goes without saying (but I'd better say it) that advertising to high-income families will net you a higher income without increasing your work time. A local company advertises in the newspaper every Sunday, with the headline: "Don't Replace it! Reface it!" A basic (very basic) knowledge of carpentry is required, along with familiarity with woods, hinges, colors, and cabinet accessories such as handles. I know a person who does this work. He charges a 100 percent markup (double the price) of the cabinet doors he installs, along with $15 per hour for his time. If you saw one of the kitchens he's refaced, you'd think he should raise his fee. And he can usually get to two kitchens per day, working alone.

## 197 THE INVENTOR'S INVENTOR

(Building prototypes of inventions) Many brilliant inventors conceive a breakthrough product, but just cannot figure out how to build the prototype. They need your help. Building prototypes of other people's inventions can make you rich and them rich and famous. You can attract their attention with ads in scientific magazines, with classified or display ads, and with attentive attendance at science fairs. A California outfit doing this work gets its business with mailings to companies—offering to build their prototypes. They have charged as much as $5,000 to build one, but usually their charge is less than $1,000. Some people just have the knack of putting things together, but aren't inventive. If that's you, your opposite number will be delighted to meet you.

# 198 PETE THE BLACKSMITH
(Blacksmithing)　You don't become a professional blacksmith by reading a book or two. But you can take the right course, or apprentice to the right person, and learn enough to set up shop and earn money at this basic, necessary, and sensible trade. You can make a lot of your own tools. You can repair the tools of people in your town. You can repair or make many metal items, and you can get the word out with Yellow Pages ads, small newspaper display ads (telling exactly what you can do), and with signs posted on well-read bulletin boards. Shop time at a blacksmith's runs around $30 per hour. If you decide to set up a shop, try to locate it under a spreading chestnut tree.

# 199 HANDY AND DANDY
(Building, repairing, operating, and installing a variety of things)　If you are good at building, repairing, operating, and installing lots of things, you have the ability to earn lots of money. Offer your services to the types of service companies that might occasionally require extra help. That means you've got to know how to professionally perform the services you offer: carpentry, appliance installation, plumbing, masonry, auto repair, and the rest. If you

can do the work, you can be sure that your phone will ring often with an offer of work for a day or two, even a few hours. Although you won't always be able to plan your time well, you'll have far more control over your life than if you were a full-time employee of these service companies. Tell them why they should hire Handy and Dandy with a direct mailing to them, enclosing a circular or brochure describing your capabilities. You might even offer your services to the public with a clever ad in the service section of the classifieds. Stick with a basic hourly charge—whatever you want to earn ($5 to $50)—for whatever you're hired to do. To earn the maximum, make that a flexible hourly rate, depending upon the specific skill required.

## 200 THE RESTORATION ORGANIZATION

(Restoring church statuary)   With such a highfalutin name, you probably do something like restore religious statues for churches. Sounds like a good idea. They certainly have the money. They're inclined to keep their statuary in good shape. And it is true that many of their statues require your time and attention. If you know the art of restoring statues (get it from a school or a professional, not from any book), a direct mailing to churches and museums will probably go a long way toward putting you in business. You might also include art galleries in your mailing; their statues need The Restoration Organization too, at times. Because of the painstaking nature of this work, you might not get to restore more than one or two statues a month. On the other hand, at $100 to $500 per statue, that's not too shabby an earnway.

## 201 THE VENDER MENDER

(Repairing vending machines)   The Vender Mender earns money two ways—repairing and servicing vending machines for their owners, and rescuing and restoring old, unused vending machines. The Vender Mender knows where to buy these old machines, how to fix them, and where to sell them. New customers for repaired vending machines may be found with mailings to establishments that are likely prospects. If the machines are old enough, this includes antique and collectibles stores. Even classified ads under miscellaneous might turn up customers for The Vender Mender. In time, you might be able to expand this service to other areas. If you're willing to do a bit of traveling you'll earn more. Repairing broken machines can earn you $5 to $10 per hour. Repairing and selling classic vending machines can bring in ten times that amount for you. To gain more data about this field, check in your library for a copy of *Vending Times*. It's only one of several trade publications in this growing industry.

# 202 THE WORD PROCESSORS CLINIC

(Maintaining and repairing word processors)   Be the person responsible for keeping word processors in good shape and restoring their health when they become ill. These tasks are usually performed by in-store service departments, but you can probably do the job for less money. The going rate is $40 per hour plus parts. Gain customers with small display or classified ads in the local business newspaper, any local computer magazine, and the business section of your daily newspaper. Do a postcard mailing to small businesses in your locale. Offer to be the part-time maintenance department for existing stores. Many schools now teach the skills. Acquire these skills; you shouldn't try this unless you're willing to take some courses and get down to some intensive learning. In addition to businesses, increasing numbers of private citizens are switching from typewriters to word processors. Business looks good.

# 203 GREENHOUSE CITY

(Selling and assembling prefabricated greenhouses) This is a real growth industry, and in time you may well sell and assemble a city's worth of prefabricated greenhouses, so go ahead and bill yourself as Greenhouse City. As Greenhouse City, you've got to know a whole lot about greenhouses: their materials, construction, the best manufacturers, and the types of growing things that thrive best in greenhouses. Then you can become a full-fledged greenhouse broker, selling and assembling greenhouses. Greenhouses do come with directions for assembly, but, as with most directions, part B doesn't always connect up that easily with part F. Hence, the need for a pro. And of all the greenhouses from which one may select, which is best? Hence, the need for Greenhouse City. Bulletins in plant stores, classified ads in the paper, exhibits at plant-oriented shows, circulars distributed to likely greenhouse buyers, and direct mailings to gardening-oriented house owners ought to make Greenhouse City a thriving metropolis. If it does get growing, you just might have to delegate some of the greenhouses and some of the green. Charge a markup on the greenhouse (50 percent to 100 percent) plus an hourly fee for assembly ($10 to $25).

# 204 GARDENS TO GO

(Making movable containers for plants) Gardens to Go are gardens in movable containers. If you've ever tried to move a large, healthy plant you'll quickly understand why such a business can catch on. Just tell plant lovers about it with signs on bulletin boards, classified ads, circulars distributed to plant owners, and exhibits at shows and fairs. The best way to make your movable containers is probably to add wheels to regular containers. You can then sell the container either empty or with a plant in it. The choice is up to you. What to charge? Charge for the container and for your time and ingenuity. I know of an office that paid $20 per container . . . and *they* supplied the containers. So the $20 went for wheels and labor. You can probably make more if you sell them *with* plants.

# 205 FURNITURE STRIPPING EXTRAORDINAIRE

(Stripping furniture)   The antique craze has made furniture stripping a lively and money-making business. Few people know how to do this work properly without training. So get trained, and then be prepared for a lot of extra work and money. The demand is so great for furniture strippers that you have to delegate some of the work. Obtain business with posted signs, Yellow Pages ads, bulletins in equipment rental shops, classified ads (under antiques), and mailings to antique-store owners. Distribute circulars to flea marketers. In this earnway, although you can charge up to $25 per hour, you can't cut corners with time since furniture stripping is by its nature time-consuming. On the other hand, maybe you'll enjoy doing it.

# 206 GOOD BUDDY MOBILE RADIO SERVICE

(Selling, installing, repairing two-way mobile radios)   Many truck, van, and auto owners would benefit from having two-way mobile radios. Fine. So can you. By selling, installing, and/or repairing these radios, you can earn money from other people's need to communicate. Classified ads or small display ads, along with signs on bulletin boards and in parking lots, and circulars under auto windshields can net you a supply of customers. Mailings to auto repair shops can lead to more business. You can decrease your initial overhead by limiting your offerings to installation and repairs only. If you do, try a special mailing to outlets where these two-way radios are sold, offer-

ing your services as a good buddy who installs and repairs. Charge $10 to $25 per hour of your time.

# 207 REMBRANDT AUTO PAINTING

(Painting automobiles)  Bill yourself as an auto painting artist, then live up to your billing. Offer superb painting jobs
(using superb paint–probably acrylic lacquer) from a
rented space in which you have the latest painting equipment. Market your painting with newspaper display ads,
signs on bulletin boards motorists are likely to see, and a
listing in the Yellow Pages. You will need a special space
with special ventilation for this undertaking. Still, your
overhead will be less than that of the large companies
that paint cars, so you will be able to charge competitive
prices. Keep in mind that many owners of $10,000-plus
cars don't want to save money on their paint jobs. So you
might do well to offer three types of paint jobs: great,
greater, and greatest. You might charge $100, $300, and
$500. A friend of mine paid $500 to have his Volkswagen
painted. Why so much? Because he had pictures of clouds
painted all over it.

# 208 BORN-AGAIN BATTERIES

(Reconditioning old batteries)  Reconditioning old batteries
for resale is not a glamorous business, but it is a practical
business. And you can make money doing it–about $10
per battery. Write to places where old batteries are left
(garages, repair shops, dealerships, junkyards) to get the
old batteries, and do mailings to auto parts stores to net
you your customers for the reconditioned batteries. You
can learn more about this business by discussing it with
one of the companies listed in your Yellow Pages under
"Batteries–Storage–Retail." But don't even consider it if
you hate to get your hands dirty.

# 209 CUSTOMIZED CONVEYANCES

(Customizing vans and campers) You can really make a truckload of money if you have the talent to customize vans and campers. You could specialize in interiors or exteriors, but most customers will want both. By offering unique and handsome designs you can make large sums in this growing business. The cost of customizing runs from about $350 to $2,500, according to my sources, and they tell me that is only for the Plain Jane jobs. Furry interiors with leather benches and quadrophonic sound cost real money. Get a bit of this real money yourself when you attract customizing customers with classified ads, a Yellow Pages listing, a display ad showing a photo of your work, and signs in prominent places. Post more signs in garages. Place circulars under the windshield wipers of likely customers. It's important to have the right talent, tools, and work space.

# 210 WALLY THE WALLPAPER HANGER

(Hanging wallpaper) If your name is not Wally but Sally, you can be Sally the Wallpaper Hanger. The idea of your service comes through clearly: you hang wallpaper. You do it quickly and perfectly. You make certain that your paper is always straight; you never leave a mess; your overlapping seams always face away from the door to the room in which the paper is hung. You market your service with mailings to wallpaper stores, signs on bulletin boards, and classified ads in the newspaper. Charge anywhere from $7.50 to $15.00 per hour, depending upon the difficulty of the job. Or, charge for the overall project, regardless of time. If you do that you should use an hourly fee to estimate the price you quote your customer. There are lots of details to get straight with this work, so be sure you learn from a master before striking out on your own. This business isn't as simple as it seems . . . or should I say not as simple as it seams?

## 211  THE INSULATION ORGANIZATION

(Installing insulation) It probably didn't take you more than a moment to figure out that The Insulation Organization sells and installs insulation. That puts the company in the business of energy conservation—a promising industry for the future. A good way to market your service is with mailings to home owners expounding the benefits of proper insulation. I'd back that with small display ads in the newspaper offering your free brochure. And I'd have a listing in the Yellow Pages. The technology involved in insulation and insulation installation is changing rapidly, so try to keep up with the field as your business grows. It's another one of those wondrous earnways in which you have the option of selling, installing, or both. If you don't want to get involved in sales, offer your installation services to existing insulation sellers. Charge a minimum of $10 per hour for your services. You can learn quite a bit about modern insulation by contacting your local utility company—the gas and electric people.

## 212  THE GREAT OUTDOORS FURNITURE COMPANY

(Making outdoor furniture) You can make a good deal of extra money if you can make outdoor furniture. If you have the talent, you can handcraft wooden lawn, porch, balcony, and patio tables, chairs, and chaises. Sell them with display ads in your Sunday newspaper, at fairs and shows, or to outdoor-furniture retailers. With interesting designs, you can build a prosperous company (selling items at an average cost of $100 to $200 per piece). It's a good way to put your building, carpentry, and design skills to work for you. And think of the gorgeous suntans your customers will get. In Tucson, a man turns out one piece of outdoor furniture per week in his spare time, and sells it for $75 to $350 ($200 on the average). His materials cost is $50 average, and it takes him about four hours to complete each piece. That means he's earning a bit under $40 per hour for work he enjoys so much he'd do it for free. Where did he learn his skills? Practice, practice, practice.

# 213 SECOND WIND

(Refinishing furniture)  Be a furniture refinisher. Specialize in it. Announce your specialization with signs on bulletin boards, circulars handed out at flea markets, mailings to antique stores, even classified ads. You can either refinish for others, or you can buy, refinish, then sell. There's more money and more risk in the latter course. Refinishing is not all that easy, and if you decide to go into this particular earning endeavor, read the latest books on the topic. Your library or bookstore will probably be excellent sources. You can earn quite a bit, perhaps around $25 per hour, if you're good at refinishing. Old furniture will look better than new when you get finished with it.

# 214 VITAL VINYL REPAIR

(Repairing vinyl)  It may sound pedestrian to go into the vinyl repair business, but according to those already in the business, it's pretty darned profitable. Seems that more things are made of vinyl these days than ever before, so there's more vinyl that needs repairing than ever before. If you can repair it, at your home or the vinyl's home, you can earn extra money. You might earn lots of it—many people report earnings of $20 per hour and more. Types of vinyl items that often need repairing include upholstery for theater seats, restaurant booths, and bar stools. As you can imagine, these can mean a high volume of work along with a high volume of money. Other things needing vinyl repair are home furnishings and automobile interiors. Market your services with letters and brochures aimed at the high-volume customers, with classified ads luring the rest. And consider a listing in the Yellow Pages under "Vinyl Repair Svce." By the way, the repairing of vinyl requires training. Some companies claim they can teach you what you need to know in a matter of days. Learn more about the training and the opportunities by dropping a line requesting free facts to Vinyl Industrial Products, 2021 Montrose Avenue, Chicago, Illinois 60618. You can even call them toll-free at 800-621-5809.

# 215  INTO THE CLOSET

(Expanding closets)   In these times when everyone and his brother (and sister) are coming out of the closet, I suggest you make extra money by going *into* the closet. Do it by offering to triple the capacity of other people's closets. This can be done with relatively simple technology. Just figure out how to include shelving, racks, and drawers (actually someone else figured it out; all you have to do is copy). You'll help people solve the problem of not enough space by giving them big closets, yawning with space. An ad run by a local company in our local newspaper shows a before-and-after illustration. The before illustration indicates a messy, crowded closet. The after illustration shows the same items in a neat, uncrowded closet. The ad solicits appointments to talk about custom design. A similar ad in your own community newspaper will be effective. You might also do mailings to contractors, home owners, and decorators. Because no major structural changes are required to restructure a closet, this endeavor does not require a whole lot of training. For your information, should you pursue this earnway in the future, the local company advertising this service claims: (1) to be able to show how to make the most of every closet inch; (2) that all pieces are factory manufactured; and (3) that their designs fit standard or walk-in closets. If you'd like to make money exploring inner space (about $200 to $500 per closet), this might be your perfect opportunity.

# 216 BIKE DOC

(Repairing bicycles)   Repair bicycles for extra money. Offer your services to bike shops, post signs on bulletin boards and along bike paths, distribute circulars to bicyclists, and even run small classified ads in local papers. By offering to repair bikes with house calls to customers' homes you will become very popular. Many bike shops charge only by the project (i.e., $6.50 to adjust brakes) and not by the hour. But those who should know tell me it comes to about $20 to $30 an hour to repair a bike. Not bad. Of course, you've got to know your stuff when it comes to repairing both new-fangled and old-fangled bikes. Catch up on the latest bike repair books by looking through a recent copy of *Bicycling* magazine. This earn-way can really boom with the energy crisis.

# 217 CASE IN POINT

(Making custom cases)   You can earn a caseload of extra money making custom cases for salespeople. There is a machine that enables you to make these cases, and with mailings to manufacturing firms, you ought to net quite a few customers for your custom cases. Ads in business publications will garner even more. Some people claim to earn $500 weekly at home making custom cases for salesmen's samples, sound equipment, photo equipment, musical instruments, guns, tools, jewelry, and anything else that's portable. Want to learn more? Write to Custom Case Supply Company, 6061 DeSoto Avenue, Woodland Hills, California 91364. You don't need any experience to succeed, but you do need to learn how to make cases. There. I have stated my case.

# 218 AUTOMOTIVE ENCORE

(Restoring old automobiles)   You can make a whole lot of money if you can buy old clunkers and restore them. If you can get these cars to showroom condition, you'll make even more. Such a business would be ideal for an imaginative and comprehensive mechanic, especially one who knows bodywork or can connect up with someone who does. You'll need to be able to make an entire car—inside, outside, and powerside—as good as new. Market your finished products with classified ads and with mailings to used (or classic) car dealers. I know a person who purchased a beat-up Aston Martin for $500 and sold it for $5,000 one month later. He invested $1,000 in parts, and worked on it part-time—you can see his profit for the month was not too bad. As I said, you can make a whole lot of money in this business. Start your clunker hunt.

# 219 INSTALLATION CONTRACTOR

(Installing things)   An installation contractor is a person who specializes in installing things. I know such a person. He makes out just fine financially by installing skylights, sun decks, and tree houses. He markets his business with small display ads in local papers, with classified ads, with brochures distributed over a small geographic area, with signs on bulletin boards, and with a sampling of his work—he built a deck for free in a hot tub showroom. All of this marketing attracts new customers to my friend. This allows him to install large sums of money in his savings account—from his charges of $12.50 to $25.00 per hour, depending upon the difficulty of the installation. You don't have to limit your installations to skylights, sun decks, and tree houses. Loads of other things require installation, too. Like what? Like French doors, hot tubs, swimming pools, trees, fences, doggie doors, washing machines, dishwashers, videotape recorders, water beds, stereo systems, satellite reception dishes, bookshelves . . . I have a feeling I've convinced you that a bunch of uninstalled items require installation. Hope you use that to earn money.

# 220 THE SUNSHINE BOYS

(Putting sunroofs into cars)   Because I drive a convertible, on warm and clear days my heart is filled with pity for you folks in sunless cars. It may be some time before America starts making convertibles again. In the meantime, you can contribute to the sunning of America by installing sunroofs. This is not a difficult chore, and is quite lucrative. At this writing, a sunroof installation runs from $425 to $525, including the cost of the sunroof itself. What is involved is cutting open the roof of a car and then replacing the hole with a sliding sunroof. The technology is already developed, so all you've got to do is learn it from a pro. Again, this kind of skill is better learned by apprenticing than from a book. And you'll need the proper space, tools, and promotion. Attract customers with small display ads in the newspaper, signs on bulletin boards, brochures placed under the windshield wipers of parked cars (not convertibles or cars with sunroofs . . . and be sure you place your brochures on sunny days), and with radio commercials . . . also played on sunny days. With consistent marketing, you can realize profits from this business for years and years . . . perhaps for as long as there is a sun.

# 221 CREATIVE RENOVATIONS

(Buying then renovating houses)  A man I know moved to northern California where he made an unbelievably small down payment ($2,500) for an unbelievably cheap house ($25,000). He spent the next three months working hard and smart, and sold the house for a then unbelievably high price ($80,000). With that money, he purchased two cheap houses, renovated them, then sold one and rented out the other. As you might guess, the man has since entered into a state of semiretirement, still in his early thirties, aboard a houseboat (which he purchased for a song, then renovated to its current magnificence). If you can get involved in the finding, buying, renovating, then selling or renting of houses, you can end up with either a lot of money, which can then bring in investment income, or a lot of houses, which can bring in rental income. Both sound pretty good to me. If you want to keep all the money yourself, you need to be skilled at contracting, designing, carpentry, painting, masonry, plumbing, electronics, estimating costs, and coordinating the activities of people who will help you. But if you've got the ability to put these skills together–either by yourself or with a few modular earners–you've got the ability to make a lot of money.

# 222 THE RENOVATOR

(Renovating houses)  The Renovator is different from Creative Renovations in that The Renovator never buys any property. The Renovator renovates the property of others. That means he or she invests less (zero) to begin and makes less afterwards. An interesting aspect of The Renovator's business is that this clever person charges in one of three ways: a flat project fee, a slice of the final sale price, or a slice of the rental income. By renovating many properties over the course of, say, two years, The Renovator can have an engaging combination of project money, sales price money, and rental money. With all that money, The Renovator might seriously consider becoming Creative Renovations. The Renovator secures initial business with mailings to prospective house owners (determined by walking or driving around) and with classified ads, signs on bulletin boards, and free seminars on home remodeling and restoration. Once The Renovator gets into high gear, he or she will find that this part-time business can provide a full-time income. A Chicago man worked as The Renovator on weekends for five years of his life while working full-time at an ad agency. He earned and saved enough from the renovating to quit the ad agency job and spend the majority of his time fishing. To you, I wish the same.

# 223 THE CANVAS CLINIC

(Repairing canvas)  To get involved in this earning endeavor, first purchase (or borrow or rent or lease) a used industrial sewing machine. Okay, now take walks along commercial streets, noting each store that needs repair work on its awning. Now, write to each store, describing how you repair canvas awnings. Do another mailing to places that have canvas-upholstered outdoor furniture, and to any other prospects who may have need of your canvas repair services. List your business in the Yellow Pages under "Canvas Repairs." Finally, be sure you save some time to stretch out on your canvas hammock, knowing you've developed a steady earnway that can bring in about $15 per hour for you. And all you have to know is how to operate your industrial sewing machine.

# 224 RIGHT ON ROOFING

(Sealing and insulating roofs)  If you can help other people save energy, you can help yourself make money by covering roofs with a spray that repairs leaks, insulates, renews, and waterproofs. The types of edifices that will want what you spray should include schools, shopping centers, factories, hospitals, and apartment complexes. So a mailing to the managers of these buildings will be your primary marketing effort. The average order is $1,000 worth of work—so this might be the amount of your very first order. Such are the joys of dealing with big businesses. (The average school sale is in excess of $1,000; the average shopping center sale is in excess of $2,500.) Many people offering this service spend no more than eight hours a week at it. And it doesn't require any experience at all. Learn more about how to put yourself on the roof by writing for a brochure to Pace Products, Inc., 81st and Indiana, Kansas City, Missouri 64132. You can prosper as our energy dwindles. Poor us. Lucky you.

## CLEANING / MAINTENANCE / DELIVERY

# 225 TUNE IN

(Tuning pianos and organs)   Listen carefully: you can put the jingle jangle of extra money into your pocket by tuning pianos and organs. It takes training and a good ear. To get customers takes a listing in the Yellow Pages, signs on bulletin boards that music lovers read, classified ads in the musical instrument section, and letters (enclosing your card) to known piano/organ owners. Then, do follow-up mailings to existing customers, reminding them that the time for their annual tuning has come. This will net you regular repeat business. You can specialize in pianos, organs, Moog synthesizers, or tune them all. Hear? Right now, it costs around $35 to have a piano tuned by a well-trained tuner who takes one and a half to two hours to do the work. So if you tune only one piano per day, working weekdays only, you'll make $700 per month. And you'll be paid to play piano even if you play poorly.

# 226 SKY-HIGH DELIVERY SERVICE

(Contracting with small airplanes to deliver packages) Contract with small airplane fliers to deliver packages for you. Many fliers cover thousands of miles weekly with loads of empty cargo space. By arranging an informal network of fliers, you can offer airborne delivery service. You don't need a pilot's license, it's all right if you suffer from extreme acrophobia, and you can even succeed if you're prone to airsickness. The more fliers you have connected up with, the bolder your ads can be (place them in the business section of newspapers, the business segment of radio news shows, and the Yellow Pages). Try direct mail marketing. You can take in sky-high profits without ever leaving the ground. Each pilot, of course, gets a per parcel delivery fee—usually 50 percent. It's almost like found money for him or her. You get what's left over from the delivery fee you charge. An Arizona man engaged in this pursuit says his average charge is $50, and he'll sometimes arrange for ten deliveries in one week. That adds up to a $250 profit for him, and fills the sky with grateful pilots.

# 227 I-HAUL-IT

(Moving or delivering things) I-Haul-It is the entrepreneur's version of U-Haul-It. It means that you use your own or a rented truck or hauling conveyance to move or deliver things for others. Advertise in the Yellow Pages, with classified ads, with display ads in local shopper-type newspapers, with posted signs on bulletin boards, and even with signs on your rented (or owned) vehicle. You'll probably need to obtain the services of a helper for those heavy and awkward items. But you'll make the most if you operate alone. (Some people actually delegate all the work, and still make out fairly well.) Have all bills paid by check or money order made out to the company. That may present one kind of hassle (bad checks), but eliminates another (embezzlement by your employees). Charge a flat rate for your moving, based upon the number and size of items to be moved and the distance you'll be moving them. A local person, working a few evenings and a few weekends per month, clears around $500 per month . . . and he uses a rented truck. So he gets to keep $500, minus Uncle Sam's share. Oh yes, the requirements for success: brawn, knowledge of spatial relations, patience, conscientiousness about the belongings of others, sense of humor.

## 228 PLANTMOVERS

(Moving plants)   Just in case a person, office, or store does not have the movable gardens discussed elsewhere in this tome (earnway number 204), offer to move gardens and hanging plants for them. Do it in rented moving equipment, unless of course you own your own. Secure customers with mailings directed at movers and building superintendents, with classified ads, and by distributing circulars to likely prospects. It's not easy to move plants (especially hanging plants) so be sure you can do the job right. Charge $10 per hour to be competitive (with the cost of living). And consider delegating the work once you've put out the word that you're a plantmover.

## 229 AQUARIUM SPARKLING

(Cleaning aquariums)   The people who work at stores where aquariums are sold do not relish the task of keeping the aquariums sparkling clean. So they'll appreciate it if you tell them that keeping aquariums sparkling clean just happens to be your specialty. With in-person calls to aquarium stores, or with mailings and follow-up phone calls, you should develop an aquarium-cleaning route, and a slew of appreciative store owners (or ex-aquarium cleaners). It should be fairly easy to develop a customer list and the work will be regular—if you're good. Charge a flat weekly fee, based upon your estimate of the time you'll spend, or go with a reasonable $10.00 per hour. Nothing fishy about that.

## 230  BRIGHT AND SHINY AUTO DETAILING

(Detailing automobiles)  Detailing automobiles means attending to the tiny touches: perfecting paint jobs with careful touch-ups, polishing chrome, making all the glass gleam, making the interior immaculate. Car owners will pay you handsomely ($75 to $150) for this service. Even car dealers require detailing. Circulars distributed to car owners and mailings directed to dealers (and garages) should bring in quite a bit of business. This is a little known but highly lucrative part of the auto industry. Cosmetics ordinarily means a lot to the owner of a luxury car, and since you are really a car cosmetician (hey, not a bad name for your company), you stand to make out well . . . even if you delegate some of the detail work. Classified ads should prove to be a source of business. You should be a good auto body person (or auto interior expert) to make a go of this endeavor. It also will help if you love cars and are a true perfectionist.

## 231  RELAXING WAXING

(Waxing cars)  This earning method enables car owners to relax while you wax. You will come to the car owner's place of business or residence. There, you will wash and wax his or her car or cars. You'll attract motorists with classified ads, display ads, posted signs, even circulars handed directly to motorists. You've got to do a spectacular job at a reasonable price. (These days, a reasonable price for waxing runs from $30 to $75, depending upon the wax used, time spent, and greed of the waxer.) Encourage word-of-mouth advertising by handing satisfied owners your card or circular. Write to or phone them every year for follow-up waxing. And tell them how waxing prolongs the life of the auto finish, not to mention bolstering the ego of the owner. You must have strong arms to be a good waxer, or have good waxing equipment. Look for this business to improve as the economy worsens and people hang on to their cars longer.

## 232  GOOD AS NEW

(Beautifying cars on used-car lots)  With all this talk about auto waxing and detailing, you should look into offering your services to used-car lots. What kind of services? Auto detailing, auto polishing and waxing. Interior cleaning. Engine cleaning. Get business with a mailing of brochures to all the used-car lots around. Then, be prepared for quite a bit of business and repeat business. A used-car lot owner will realize that even by paying you $50 for your services, he can raise the price of the car by $150. So you'll pocket $50 per beautified car. You'll be able to do about six cars per weekend (more if you delegate intelligently). And you'll become an appreciated member of the automotive industry, not to mention a familiar face at the bank.

## 233  CLEAN SCREEN

(Cleaning screens)  Clean screens for money. Screen cleaning is not all that hard, but few people want to do it themselves. Drives them buggy. That's why they'll happily hire you. They'll find out about you because of your classified ads and the circulars you send to the houses with lots of screens. You might consider mailing to screen companies so that they can recommend you to their customers. If you promise them a commission for each sale they get for you, I'll bet they recommend you more often and more enthusiastically. Mailings to window washers might also result in business for you. Since the cleaning job isn't hard, you should be able to delegate this job if you want to. Hourly charges prevail in this business (with $7.50 the most commonly levied charge), although some firms charge by the screen. Now if you could charge by the number of teensy holes in the screen, you'd really be talking big bucks.

# 234  SQUEEGEE-CLEAN WINDOWS

(Washing windows)  Window washing is a very available method of earning extra money in virtually any populated area in the United States. Although I have detailed the components necessary to succeed in this endeavor in chapter 1, I feel impelled to mention this earnway once again since it is so profitable, so necessary, so available, so delegable, and so simple. For marketing details, along with many other window-washing details you might want to know, please refer to chapter 1. For information that just might result in your earning $70,000 per year washing windows (true!), ask for manual number 12, *Window Cleaning Business*, from the International Entrepreneurs Association. See the appendix for their address, or call them toll-free (if you want to charge it to your credit card) at 800-421-2300; California, in 800-352-4449.

# 235  TIDY BLINDS

(Cleaning Venetian blinds)  Some businesses can make a lot of money for you. Some can make a little. By specializing in the cleaning of Venetian blinds you will probably be somewhere in the middle. Classified ads and posted bulletins can herald your unique service. Mailings to building maintenance companies, window cleaners, building supervisors, and Venetian blind sellers will attract even more business. You can charge $10 per hour and won't have to worry about being besieged by competition. It will help immensely if you were taught how to clean Venetian blinds by my mother. A real stickler for clean blinds, that wonderful lady.

## 236 BATHS FOR BARBECUES

(Cleaning barbecue grills)   When I think about barbecuing, I think "yum." But when I look at my barbecue, I think "yuk." It's not easy to clean a barbecue. At least that's what I tell my wife. I think lots of barbecuers already know that. All the more reason for you to start up a barbecue cleaning service. Market it with signs where barbecue equipment is sold, with classified ads, notices on bulletin boards in suburban communities, and circulars delivered to home owners. You can charge $10 to $25 per barbecue, and although this may be a gooey way to earn money, it is effective. Almost anyone would rather think "yum" than "yuk."

## 237 HOUSEFRAU

(Cleaning houses)   This is unquestionably one of America's most common earnways. Housecleaners earn from $5 to $10 per hour, and they get to pick the hours and days they work. So it's no wonder a whole lot of people are cleaning up cleaning up. Starting a maid service is a low-overhead, simple-to-operate business that can earn for you a lot more than the hourly rate I just quoted. An Atlanta housewife started with $5 worth of supplies and made $45,000 her first year. Today, thanks to bright delegating and incredible ambition, she's grossing over $1,000,000 per year. As a housecleaner? You got it. Not surprisingly, the enterprising International Entrepreneurs Association offers their Manual Number 160, *Maid Service*, to help you on your way. Good luck. And keep it clean.

# 238 THE IMMACULATE FIREPLACE

(Cleaning fireplaces)   Is it really possible to have an immaculate fireplace? After you've finished cleaning a fireplace professionally, it sure better be immaculate. Our fireplace needs cleaning about once a month during the cold season (though there never really is a cold season in the San Francisco Bay Area, except possibly in summer), and nobody really feels sootable for the job. That's why we have it done by a pro. All that's required is an emptying of the ashes, a brushing out, and a checking of the upward passageway. If you can multiply our aversion to fireplace cleaning by the number of fireplace owners, you can readily see how your cleaning service will be welcomed. People will pay you $10 to $25 to make their fireplace a showplace. Let them know of your ability with classified ads, circulars delivered to homes with fireplaces, and posted bulletins. You should take great pains to keep the soot off everything near the fireplace. And you ideally should have a real attraction to ashes, and a fetish for cleanliness to succeed.

# 239 SANTA'S CHIMNEY-SWEEPING SERVICE

(Chimney sweeping)   As energy consciousness is raised and people try to cut down on oil and electricity consumption, the need for chimney sweeping will increase. You can get in on this profitable business with the right training, equipment, and marketing. You'll have to read a few books, take a course, or attend a seminar to learn the skill. You'll have to invest a few hundred in equipment. And you can figure on getting around $75 per chimney. For marketing, consider classified ads, mailings to homes with chimneys, display ads in local shops, signs on bulletin boards, and phone calls to homes with chimneys. ("Hello, this is Santa, and I wish you'd do something about the inside of your chimney.") With ongoing marketing (any time of year but best during winter) you can be doing the right thing at the right time all the time. Remember, you cannot do a good job at this unless you have been trained. To learn more about this earnway, maybe you ought to contact the National Chimney Sweep Guild. There are members in most cities, so your Yellow Pages might be the place to begin. If you make it in this business, you'll appreciate the income and the real Santa will appreciate the cleanliness.

# 240   SUNSHINE PATIO FURNITURE CLEANING

(Cleaning patio furniture)   Because it's such a drag to clean patio furniture, you ought to be able to do fairly well with a service that both cleans and refurbishes it. You might offer, in addition to cleaning, recanvasing, rewebbing, and restoring. Even if you charge a lot, people will prefer your reworking prices to the cost of replacement. It's a well-known fact that weather is an enemy of patio furniture. Which makes weather a friend of your service. Whether or not you succeed depends on your marketing skills. Advertise with circulars, signs, and classified ads. Give your satisfied customers a few circulars and cards to pass out to friends. If you understand how to make old patio furniture look like new again, you can earn enough to sit back and relax on your own patio furniture.

# 241   HOT TUB HOTSHOT

(Maintaining hot tubs)   It seems that people who succeed most wildly at earning extra money are those who are aware of or anticipate new trends. An alert lad in my area noticed the rapidly increasing sales of hot tubs. He realized that if he billed himself as one who maintains hot tubs he'd be the only person offering such a service. He was right. He ran a few display ads and soon had a good-sized customer list. These people needed regular servicing of their heated havens (cleaning, filter treating, component flushing, water analyzing). Now, he no longer needs to advertise. You can charge in the area of $30 monthly for four weekly hot tub calls (each taking about fifteen minutes). So if you have ten customers, you'll be pulling in $300 of extra income. And if you have a hundred customers, you'll earn $3,000 monthly, though much of that will go to the person to whom you delegate the lion's share of the work. Hit it big by marketing your service with display ads and mailings to hot tub owners as well as hot tub sales outlets, and continue until you have as many customers as you want. If you know about swimming pool maintenance (or even aquarium maintenance) you'll have a head start on the expertise for this field. Hope you earn enough to buy your own hot tub. It's a high joy activity, hot tubbing, I assure you.

## 242 WALLPAPER AWAY

(Stripping away wallpaper) Remember Wally the Wallpaper Hanger (earnway number 210)? Well, this business does the exact opposite work of Wally's. Here, you strip away old wallpaper, or clean it to make it look like it was just hung. A machine helps with the stripping. Proper cleaning equipment helps with the cosmetics. Business can be obtained with good old classified ads, signs on bulletin boards, and circulars distributed at remodeling shows. Friends of ours paid $7.50 an hour to a person who stripped their wallpaper. That ought to give you some idea of your potential earnings. Don't forget—those earnings can multiply if you delegate.

# 243 PAINSTAKING PAINTING COMPANY

(Painting buildings, inside and/or out)  If I hired someone to do some painting for me (I did), I'd hope they'd do a careful job of it (they didn't). If you can do a good job, you might offer to paint insides and outsides of residences or offices or stores—or just about any edifice. I know you can attract customers with mailings to paint stores (they might put up your poster or hand out your circular), posting of signs, running of display or classified ads, and mailings to contractors and remodelers. A Yellow Pages ad will also be necessary. You'll need the right equipment: ladders, scaffolding, brushes, rollers, drop cloths, the works. Figure to earn $12 per hour ... $15 if you're truly painstaking. Consider rounding up some experienced painters to whom you can delegate the painstaking, leaving you to concentrate on the profit-taking.

# 244 NEATNIK

(Cleaning anything)  Jay Conrad Levinson's book, *555 Ways to Earn Extra Money*, defines a neatnik as: "one who cleans the hell out of basements, attics, sheds, closets, spare rooms, storage spaces, lockers, yards, garages, crawl spaces, offices, and other messy spaces, leaving the areas neat and tidy . . ." A proper neatnik would market all those neat services with classified ads, signs on bulletin boards, and circulars distributed to residents of houses and apartments. That same neatnik would charge from $5 to $10 per hour, and would earn every dime of it. Now does a neatnik truly deserve all that neat wealth and glory? You betcha. At least that's what it says in Levinson's book.

# 245  TV OR NOT TV?

(Painting rusty TV antennas)   Shame on me. Here I tell you to name your earnway in a way that inspires confidence, and then I suggest a wishy-washy name like TV or Not TV. On the other hand, I said it was okay to use a name that makes people feel good about you. This name might do that. It will certainly call attention to your service, which paints rusty TV antennas so that they shine like new. It's an odd business, but if you'll check out antennas during the next week or so, you'll see that TV or Not TV solves an existing problem. Marketing? Classified ads, mailings to homes with repulsive antennas, signs on bulletin boards, even a little display ad in your local edition of *TV Guide*. (Though it's America's most widely circulated magazine, local rates are reasonable.) To make this business a reality, you should not be acrophobic, and you should be handy with a paintbrush. Charge $10 to $15 per antenna, and figure on spending no more than fifteen minutes earning your money. That's a potential of $60 per hour. Not bad for a company with such a cockamamie name.

# 246  CARPET CARE

(Cleaning carpets)   Lots of people earn extra money cleaning carpets. The equipment you need may be purchased, leased, or rented. The marketing is straightforward: Yellow Pages ads, classified ads, inexpensive circulars mailed to likely customers, even display ads in local shoppers. Telephone marketing really helps around Christmas time . . . starting in mid-November. Maybe a local carpet store will sign you on as a modular carpet cleaner. You do the cleaning in the homes of your customers, so you won't need work space. Many carpet cleaning machines also clean upholstery and walls. Some carpet cleaners report earnings of $500 weekly, working part-time. You can get a free booklet on the biz by writing to Von Schrader Company, 2291 Place, Racine, Wisconsin 53403. They'll appreciate your toll-free call, too. The number is (800) 558-2484.

# 247 THE FINISHING TOUCH

(Refinishing floors) It's a shame how many handsome wood floors have been covered with tacky linoleum or tackier paint. Too bad those floors weren't refinished. But hold on—I've got good news! Those floors *can* be refinished. And *you* can refinish them. Find customers for your refinishing services with mailings to owners of older homes, with classified ads, signs on bulletin boards, even small displays at remodeling shows. Do a mailing to contractors and professional home remodelers. Then, you might teach your finishing craft to others, allowing them to keep the lion's share of the proceeds. Be sure you keep the lamb's share—you'll be earning it with your continuing marketing efforts. Although you should bid on floor refinishing jobs with an overall price, figure your bid so that you're earning around $15 an hour.

# 248 FARFETCHED DELIVERY SERVICE

(Delivering items on a regular basis) People who run stores and offices often find that it is difficult and time-consuming to pick up needed supplies. That's great—for you. Offer to pick up and deliver supplies for them on a regular basis. The key phrase is "on a regular basis." This is not a standard delivery service, but a specialized one. You specialize in working with businesses, not individuals. And you specialize in regular pickups and deliveries, not occasional ones. That means you can target your mailings to stores and offices in your region, many of which will be thrilled at your offer. You will need wheels, dependability, and time to devote to your regular runs in order to succeed at this endeavor. The $10 to $15 that you earn hourly should also cover your fuel costs. If not, raise your fee. That's not too farfetched, is it?

# 249 AFTERGLOW

(Cleaning premises for rental agencies)   Make money by offering cleaning services to rental agencies. Tell them that you'll clean the premises after the old tenants move out so that the rental agencies can attract new tenants. That ought to make sense to any rental agency. A simple mailing to all the sizable apartment buildings in your area, along with a mailing to rental agencies, should get you all set. You'll have to be a good cleaner with the right equipment to earn the $7.50 or so you'll be charging for your service. And either you or your clean-minded delegate will have to be available when needed.

# 250 THE STRIPE TYPE

(Painting stripes in parking lots)   Who do you suppose paints all those stripes in parking lots? Forget who painted them in the past. *You* can paint them now. An inexpensive machine makes it possible. And mailings to owners of parking lots (indoors and outdoors, and let's not forget shopping centers and arenas, for goodness sake) should bring in the business. Although this is a fairly lucrative business (charge by the project, which will come to about $15 to $25 per hour of your painting time), it's kind of boring. But you will succeed in this not-very-artistic endeavor if you have the right machine (some people "invent" their own machines) and can paint a straight line.

# 251 SNOW GO

(Removing snow)   Look out there—it's not snowing snow—it's snowing money. *If* you're in the snow removal business. Remove that snow by shovel or by machine. Make an attempt to get regular routes: streets not serviced by the town or county, along with driveways and sidewalks. Obtain snow removal customers by delivering circulars to their residences or stores—all concentrated in a reasonably sized region. Then, be sure that you've got a warm coat, hat, muffler, and gloves. These days, people will pay a flat rate of $25 to $50 monthly for guaranteed snow removal. Multiply this monthly rate by, say, a hundred subscribers, and you can see how a snowy winter can be green for you. I remember all too well living in a place where I had to do all the snow removal myself. Where were you? In case you have visions of earning $5,000 per month year-round, remember that this is a November to April job . . . unless you spend your summers in New Zealand.

## 252   THE FISHERMEN'S FRIEND

(Cleaning fish for fishermen)   The Fishermen's Friend obviously cleans fish for fishermen. The Fishermen's Friend waits at the wharf or riverbank with his brightly colored sign offering fish-cleaning services. This is The Fishermen's Friend's only marketing tool. The Fishermen's Friend charges $1.50 to $2.50 per fish cleaned, but supplements that with occasional sales of bait, lures, equipment . . . and even fish. Now that's a friend.

## 253   HOME JAMES

(Being a part-time chauffeur)   Earn some extra money as a part-time chauffeur. Offer your services to limo rental firms via letter. Advertising in the classified section won't hurt you either. You might decide to do your chauffeuring at night or on weekends, so that the rest of your time is free for you to play or earn money on other avenues. To be a pro chauffeur, even part-time, you'll probably need a chauffeur's license—just a bit more difficult to obtain than a normal driver's license. You'll also need a working knowledge of the area in which you'll drive (or at least a good map). Figure on earning from $5 to $10 per hour—more if you supply the car along with the driving. A person I know of gets all the chauffeur's business he wants and needs through a local service broker. And his name isn't even James.

# 254 LEMME LAUNDER

(Doing laundry and ironing)  Nobody really likes to do the laundry and ironing. That's why you can make money doing it for others. Consider this endeavor a free-lance activity—you don't have to open your own laundry facility. Offer to launder on the premises of your customer or at your own place. Or even at a Laundromat. By putting up signs in Laundromats, on bulletin boards, and even in apartment building laundry rooms, you could be doing one hell of a lot of laundry. With classified ads, you might be up to your ears in suds. And cash. Although the charges vary throughout the United States, my experts report that $5 per hour seems to be the most commonly charged rate these days. To succeed, all you need is experience in keeping clothes clean. And ironed.

# 255 SAMPLE DELIVERY

(Delivering samples)  Sampling is an effective marketing tool because it offers a consumer the opportunity to test a product without risking any money. It's a good investment for the producer of the sample product, but it is expensive. Delivery is especially costly, so if you can offer reliable, inexpensive delivery service you'll be cashing in on a solid opportunity. Write to companies that offer samples and make your services known. Write also to large local distributors. Once you are known in the industry

(once they've had a sample of your service) you'll have
plenty of business. Sample deliverers now earn $10 per
hour. To that, add the cost of gasoline. You'll have to have
your own vehicle.

# 256  FLIER EXPRESS

(Delivering circulars) Often I have suggested that you
market your services with circulars or fliers. Who delivers
and distributes them? People like you—people who want
to earn extra money disseminating fliers. Sound like a
business worthy of your interest and time? If so, write to
distributing companies, delivery companies, and even
printers—offering to deliver or hand out circulars, brochures, fliers—anything. You can expect to earn $5 per
hour, and zero experience is required. If you happen to
delegate this task to a person who will distribute for $3
per hour, then you're earning $2 just for setting up the
service and getting the jobs. Sounds pretty good that
way, huh?

# 257  PREHEATED POTS

(Buying, cleaning, then selling pots and pans) Preheated
Pots buys old pots and pans, cleans them, then sells them
at high profits. The resale is accomplished at flea markets,
swap meets, garage sales, and secondhand stores. You'd
be surprised if you saw how new old pots and pans can be
made to look. Many people buy an old pot for $1, spend ten
minutes cleaning it, and sell it for $5. That comes to . . .
let's see . . . $24 an hour! Don't figure on working forty-
hour weeks, but do figure on earning a bit of extra money.

# 258  SPOTLESS SHELTER

(Cleaning and mending tents and sleeping bags) This earning endeavor involves cleaning and mending tents and

sleeping bags. As one who takes long, long, sandy, sandy river trips, I need my sleeping bag de-sanded at the conclusion of each river. Sure I can do it myself . . . and often do. But sometimes, folks, it just gets too grungy. Where to take it, other than a cleaner? If you were around, I'd give you my business. I'd probably find out about you from a sign in a sporting goods shop, an ad in the classified section, a recommendation from a river-running firm that received your mailing, or you might have found my name on some hiking club list and sent me a flier directly. You should also distribute circulars at sporting goods shows. A San Francisco company that specializes in this cleaning business usually charges $8.50 to clean a down sleeping bag. Tent mending is more, depending upon the size of the rip. As more and more people get involved in outdoor activities, this earnway ought to flourish. Hope it leaves you holding the bag.

# 259 FIRST MATE

(Cleaning and repairing boats)  Put up signs in all the boat clubs and docking facilities in your area. On each sign (designed in a nautical motif) tell boat owners that you are a specialist in the cleaning and repairing of boats. List your phone number, then go home and expect to hear it ringing. And ringing and ringing. Almost any boat owner could use help in cleaning and/or repairing. Almost any boat owner has trouble finding this help. That's why your sign will be so welcome, and that's why you'll need no other marketing tools. Figure to earn $5 to $10 per hour for your efforts. Watch out or you'll find yourself going around the world with some appreciative customer. A surprising number of people earn their keep as boat cleaners and repairers. If you like boats, why not you?

# 260 MESSAGE RECEIVED

(Being a messenger)  Be a courier or messenger to earn extra money. Obtain business with an ad in the Yellow

Pages, signs on bulletin boards, even with classified ads—
though the first two seem best. Deliver your messages by
any conveyance you like . . . but be sure they are delivered
reliably and on time. Find several people to whom you can
delegate deliveries so that you will always be able to accept message delivery assignments. And don't be surprised if one day you are asked to go across town and the
next day you are asked to go to Australia. Such are the
vagaries of the message and courier game. The most successful such service in these parts charges (at this writing) $.82 per mile, $9.39 for weight from 0 to 25 pounds, on
up to $36.00 for 500 pounds, and $5.80 per fifteen minutes
of waiting time. Complex charges, but you can be sure
Aero Delivery figured it all out very carefully. By the way,
those charges triple during holiday times, so if you specialize in holiday delivery, you'll be making a hefty wage.
Naturally, you will need an appropriate vehicle for your
deliveries, and you've got to know your way around—
literally.

## 261  TELEPHONE BOOKS TO GO

(Delivering phone books)  Once a year, all over America,
the new telephone books must be delivered. Who does all
that delivering? Well, you can if you'd like. You'll make $6
per hour. Many people earn extra dollars delivering these
boring but indispensable tomes. Letters or calls to the
phone companies will let them know of your availability,
and should result in a letter back to you giving all the
answers to the questions you might have. Phone book delivering requires a car, truck, or van plus a good bit of
muscle power. If you don't have those attributes, find
someone else who does.

## 262  ETERNAL MAINTENANCE

(Maintaining cemetery plots)  Earn money by maintaining cemetery plots. That means keeping the plots well
planted, free from weeds, and in generally good order.

You can obtain business with signs at cemeteries and with mailings to cemeteries. These mailings can list your service as being available to individuals directly, or you can offer to work through the cemetery itself on a modular basis. I've heard $250 quoted as the annual rate per customer for this work, so you can see this won't make you a millionaire (unless you have four thousand customers). But it will assure you of a regular source of supplemental income. And all you've got to be good at is gardening.

## 263 OH WHAT A BEAUTIFUL TIRE

(Beautifying tires) Millions and millions of automobile tires have been damaged—especially whitewalls. You can make a good amount of money beautifying these poor tires. Even if you charge only $5 for each whitewall you work on, you'll get $20 a car—$25 if the owner wants the spare to be beautiful, too. Because it takes only twenty minutes to make four tires gorgeous, you can handle up to twenty cars on a good (really a *great*) day. That comes to $400 per day. Even cut in half, that's a good income. Actually, people in the business report you'll probably average only $100 per day. (Gee, is that all?) Market your tire beautification business with circulars slipped under the windshields of prospective autos, with classified ads, with signs near parking lots, with in-person inquiries at places where you are likely to find many motorists (like car washes), and with the inevitable signs on bulletin boards. You might also do a mailing to used-car lots. Perhaps you'll want to expand this money-earning endeavor and also repair curb damage, match up unmatched tires, make blackwalls white, enlarge whitewalls, paint color racing stripes, and maybe even hand-letter or decorate a tire for an owner seeking real individuality. To learn more about this business, including how to get the equipment and training you'll need, you might want to get in touch with

Tire Cosmetology, Inc., 2862 Nagle, Dallas, Texas 75220. In a hurry? Call them toll-free at (800) 527-5039. They'll convince you that tire beautifying and customizing can make your financial wheels go round.

# 264 MILES OF MEALS

(Delivering meals for restaurants) Sometimes it's just too much hassle to go to a restaurant. Even though you're hungry right now, you've got to get dressed, drive to the eatery, find a parking place, order, wait for the food, wait for the bill, then drive home again. All that for a hot meal. Wouldn't it be great if all restaurants offered delivery service? Wouldn't it be wonderful to call a fine dining establishment, order your food, then have it delivered, piping hot, to your front door? Of course it would be wonderful. But is it possible? Aha, I thought you'd never ask. *You* can make it possible. You can offer a delivery service for a restaurant that does not yet offer a delivery service. All you've got to do is contact enough restaurants (just stop by, after you've called them up or written a letter requesting an appointment) until you find the right one. Or two. Then, get them to market their delivery service with a line or two in their Yellow Pages or newspaper ads, with signs prominently displayed within the restaurant, even with a couple of lines of copy on their menus. You might even spring for a weekly display ad in the newspaper yourself . . . if the restaurant approves. And they'll probably approve so much, they'll split the ad cost with you. Occasional radio commercials for the restaurant (and its delivery service) might be run—with the cost to be shared by both you and the restaurant. This business requires a reliable delivery person, a delivery van equipped to keep meals hot, and a restaurant that agrees to pay you a share of the total delivery tabs in return for this glorious new delivery service. If you put enough effort into really getting this business going, you should profit for a long time. And you'll make the restaurant owner quite happy—not to mention those hungry people who don't want the hassle of going out to the restaurant. Several years ago, a friend in London earned the equivalent of $200 weekly making such deliveries. He worked five nights a week, from 6:00 P.M. till 10:00 P.M. Many people do even better these days.

# 265 HOME-COOKED DELIVERIES

(Delivering hot meals to offices)   It is no joy to work late at the office. It's even worse when you have to sustain yourself on some mediocre sandwich. Late-working executives and secretaries alike are entitled to a home-cooked meal, delivered right to the desk. And that is precisely what you'll give them. Market this business with mailings to office managers, signs in office buildings, classified ads, and with brochures distributed at lunchtime in the business district of your town. Once you get the business going, you might let someone else earn extra money doing the cooking and delivering while you just sit back and take it easy, smug in the knowledge that your brilliant business concept has allowed you to indulge in the good life. Where will the recipes come from? The recipes, the dishes—those are minor details, easily dealt with. The big thing is the idea itself, and now you've got it.

# 266 AUTO TRANSPORT OF AMERICA

(Transporting cars)   It sounds like a really big outfit. It sounds like they move cars from point to point. It sounds as though individuals can call the company and get their cars transported. It also sounds as though other individuals can call the company and drive the cars. Such a business would probably advertise in the Sunday classifieds in the newspaper—in the transportation section. I'm sure the hardest part is setting it up. Keeping it going should be much simpler. Too bad you've got to do the hard part. But then it'll be nice during the easy part, when you get to sit back and watch your profits roll in. To get an idea of how much money you can earn, call a few of the companies listed in your Sunday paper and ask their rates.

# 267 ONLY OIL

(Changing oil)   Establish a weekend (or evening) business that specializes in changing oil for motorists. This would be a real convenience to motorists, a real profit-maker for you, and a source of work and money for the people to whom you ultimately delegate some (or all) of the work. You profit both from the sale of the oil and from the service itself. Not much space is required. Big signs where you do the oil changing, along with newspaper display ads (in the sports sections), should be all the marketing you need. This business won't make you an oil baron, but it will do a pretty good job of lubricating your personal money machine. Actually, several franchises are already offered in this field. Learn about the field and the franchises by visiting your library and consulting the *Franchise Opportunity Handbook*.

# 268 ERRAND RUNNER

(Running errands)   Set up a service running errands. Run almost any kind of errand for almost any kind of person. Pick up the kids. Drop off the laundry. Do the shopping. Pick up the family from the airport. Go to the hardware store. I don't have to tell you how many different types of errands there are and how many people don't have time to run them. It's important to have several people with vehicles available to do the errands; you can recruit these people with a classified ad in the help wanted section. You can attract the ones who need their errands run with classified ads too, and also with display ads, signs on bulletin boards, circulars, and even radio commercials (in a small test market first). Charge from $5 to $10 per hour, along with a mileage charge. By saving time for other people you should make money for yourself.

# 269 SKIBUS

(Transporting skiers)   Charter a bus and driver and drive skiers to ski areas. Lord knows they'll be grateful for the freedom from putting on chains, paying for gas, carrying their skis from distant parking lots, and putting up with frozen fuel lines. You can easily find the passengers. Put up signs at ski resorts, bulletins at ski shops, ads in the sports section of the newspaper, and classified ads. The year I ran such a service, it hardly even snowed in Colorado. My bad luck. I can guarantee that it will snow in Colorado every winter from now on, and if you have a skibus business, you'll make out well. If you pay $200 for the bus and driver, and charge your fifty passengers a mere $20 each, you make $800 (less gasoline costs) per round trip. In addition to a skibus you can have a beach-bus, a fisherbus, a boatbus, and a ballgamebus. Get the picture?

# 270 SPECIAL DELIVERY

(Delivering for grocery stores)   Although this may actually apply to other types of businesses, let's limit the discussion here to grocery stores. Not supermarkets. Grocery stores. Many of them would love to deliver, but don't have the ability. Many of their customers would appreciate home delivery, but it's just not available. Beginning to sense my plan? Offer your delivery service to groceries, enabling them to offer it to their customers. They will market your services with signs in their windows, more signs at their checkout counters, and mentions in their newspaper ads. You charge a per-delivery fee to the grocer ($1?) *and* to the customer ($2?). Both will benefit from your service. All you need is a vehicle (probably a van) and a driver (either you or some other eager earner). You might be able to use a bicycle—lots of cities still have custom bikes with a big box mounted in front, to hold lots of goods. If you do it this way, you can earn your money, save on expenses, and get some exercise all at the same time. Not to mention saving gas for its own sake. There. Now that you can see how it can work for a grocer, you can see how it can work for a cleaner, plant store, hardware store, pharmacy, and more.

## 271 MOBILE CLEANLINESS

(Operating a mobile cleaning service)   As much as I hate to say it, you can really clean up if you clean up. You get a van to transport all your cleaning equipment, you get a sign on your van, you get a brochure that you hand to prospects, you do mailings to a carefully targeted audience—and you've got an operating mobile cleaning service. Offer to clean home exteriors, office buildings, storefronts, bridges, billboards, trucks, and you name it. In any urban area there are countless structures that have been discolored by layers and layers of dirt. Air pollution doesn't make it any better. But you can. Then you can smile, knowing you have made the world a wee bit cleaner. Those in this business figure on earning about $100 a day, so a weekend of work can put quite a bit of bread on your table. And with four weekends of work per month, you might not want to work on weekdays at all.

## 272 THE PERFECT POOL

(Maintaining swimming pools)   I mentioned to the gent who maintains my swimming pool that I was writing about his business for my book. Boy, did he give me a dirty look. I guess he didn't like the idea of me creating competition for him. So let me assure you right here and now, Herb, that I will remain loyal as long as my pool remains pure. However, I suggest that all of you who wish to earn the steady income that Herb enjoys should consider maintaining pools for pool owners. Get their business by mailing a brochure to them (their addresses are easy to find). Then, on a regular basis, clean their pools, add the proper chemicals, flush their filters, and collect their money. Herb sends a guy around here twice a week, and the guy spends about fifteen minutes here each time. For that, I get charged $75 per month. If Herb has a hundred customers (and I think he has many more than that), that comes to $7,500 monthly, gross. I've been using Herb's service for ten years now, and I'll bet he'd agree that pool maintenance is a dandy way to earn a steady income. I didn't say easy, but I did say steady.

# 273 TIDY OFFICE

(Running an office cleaning service)  Earn a few extra dollars by starting up an office cleaning service. Don't go after the big offices, for that would eat into your freedom and necessitate the hiring of many employees. Aim for the small offices, the ones not wooed by the big office maintenance companies. You might share this endeavor with someone who will do the actual cleaning while you do the marketing. Do it with direct mailings to the offices themselves, and also with a listing in the Yellow Pages. Because you will keep this business small, your low overhead will enable you to charge very competitive rates ($5.00 to $7.50 per hour). Dirty offices could provide you with income for years and years. No special training is needed—just the ability to clean, dust, empty wastebaskets, mop, and show up reliably.

# 274 SAW MAN

(Sharpening saws and other tools)  Saw Man (who may be of either gender) earns $8 to $10 hourly sharpening saws and other tools for craftspeople. Saw Man works the hours he wants, works out of his own home, and earns the appreciation of skilled workers because of his own skills. Mailings to handymen, carpenters, contractors, and craftspeople will get business for you, along with classified ads and posted bulletins. You can obtain an entire booklet on the art of succeeding as Saw Man by writing to Foley Manufacturing Company, 3747 Foley Building, Minneapolis, Minnesota 55418. The Foley people say no experience is required. Jay Levinson says keep a bunch of Band-Aids around if you're not experienced with sharp tools.

# 275 THE CUTTING EDGE

(Being a mobile sharpening service)  Be a mobile sharpening service. Using only a large sign on your van or truck, offer to sharpen knives, scissors, and the tools that Saw Man doesn't sharpen. Park your van in one shopping center on a Monday, a different shopping center on a Tuesday, and so on. Right off, train someone to do the sharpening for you and to man the van (woman the van?). But since you're providing the van (rented, leased, or owned), the sign, and the sharpening equipment, you're entitled to at least half of the income earned. You can distribute circulars to your customers, offering to make house calls for double your usual sharpening rate. You can also sell new knives, scissors, and tools. Figure your per-item sharpening cost based upon how much you want to earn hourly; $10 per hour doesn't seem outlandish, does it? It is approximately how much our local sharpener earns. For more information, contact the Foley people mentioned in the previous earnway.

# 276 SPEEDY WAX

(Waxing skis)  Provide ski waxing services at ski resorts and cross-country skiing start points. Waxing is important, and most skiers will agree it is a bother to do. Along with waxing, you can offer edge sharpening and overall ski tune-ups. You will probably get the most business if you offer overnight service. Attract that business by placing signs in strategic places or by hooking up with the local ski shop that will help market your service for you. Unless you want to stay up all night waxing skis, find someone who will gladly do it for you. Shouldn't be too hard: many ski bums will take on any kind of work to support their ski habits. Once you've got your service established at one ski area, you can expand to include others. Currently, ski waxing runs for $3.50 to $5.00, and a ski tune-up runs from $15.00 to $20.00. Not outrageous amounts from the standpoint of the skier . . . and adequate from your standpoint, Speedy. Unless you've spent hours and hours waxing your own skis, I suggest you try an apprenticeship to learn the wax biz.

# 277 SPARKLETIME CAR WASH

(Operating a car wash)  You know as well as I do that there are many people who want to earn extra money. A large number of them are high school students. By combining these two pieces of information, you can create a source of income for all of you. Organize a handful of reliable high school students and operate a weekend car wash. Empty space, a water supply, and cleaning materials are all that is necessary. Marketing can take the form of classified ads plus a handsome and easily readable sign at your car washing location. Because your overhead will be low, your washing rates can be competitive—possibly around $2.50 for a first-class wash. Eventually, a leader will emerge from among the students. Put that leader in charge of the others and go take a relaxing drive in the country. Your weekend car wash can become a real institution in your community. Car washes can earn $1,000 per weekend— watch out or you'll be propelled into a higher tax bracket.

## OPERATING/RENTING

## 278 SMALL-TIME OPERATIONS

(Operating specialized equipment)   If you can operate specialized equipment, you can offer to operate it for others— for a fee. It might be a computer, a typesetting machine, a chain saw, a videotape camera, a movie camera, or something else. Many people need to use this equipment and have the means to borrow or rent it, but don't know how to operate it. They need you. They can learn of your services via bulletins posted in retail rental stores, classified ads, even signs near hardware stores or lumber mills or camera shops. The more equipment you can operate, the more opportunities that will open for you. You might even consider renting the equipment yourself and operating it for your customers. Your fee then should reflect your rental costs. If you operate the machines of others, $10 per hour would be pretty reasonable for your skills.

## 279 THE MURAL MACHINE

(Using a machine to paint murals)   Here's some good news for would-be money-earners, art lovers, and those bored by blank walls: the Japanese have recently developed a machine that paints wall-size murals from any color photo. With such a machine in your possession (learn about it by contacting the International Entrepreneurs Association at 2311 Pontius Avenue, Suite 89-1, Los Angeles, California 90064), you can be of valuable service to retailers, parents, decorators, office managers, city planners, and the world at large. Marketing your murals ought to be fairly simple. Do a mailing, inviting prospects to watch your machine in action in some public spot in your community. Since it takes mere minutes for the process to be completed, a demonstration should be a convincing sales tool for you. By leaving your brochure at commercial establishments where you have done your machine murals, you'll probably attract new business. Charge by the mural: $150 on up. And take heart: you can succeed with no prior experience and no artistic talent.

# 280 THE CHAIN MONKEY

(Installing tire chains)  I have lived in two different areas that were near ski slopes. In both, here in California and back in Colorado, the advent of a snowfall would bring out the chain monkeys. These people set up business on the roads leading to the slopes, offering to put on and remove tire chains. The most recent season featured "on" prices of $7 and "off" prices of $5. A good snowfall can net a chain monkey about fifty cars going and fifty more returning, so it does not require a high-priced calculator to see that the chain business is not monkey business. The only marketing tool you need is a sign that says: Chains On and Off. And you need very warm clothes, gloves, a thermos full of something hot, and a sense of humor.

# 281 MY HOUSE IS YOURS

(Renting your vacation home)  Not a lot of people can earn extra money with this endeavor, but if you own a vacation home, you can. Rent it out when you're not using it. Either serve as your own rental agent or work through an existing agent. I notice many ads these days in the classified section of the Sunday paper under "Vacation Rentals." I see the same ads in the classified section of local magazines, all touting glorious vacation lodgings at horribly inflated prices. You can even rent out your main place while you're away on vacation . . . provided your place is in or near a tourist destination. I know of a woman who owns a home near Sun Valley. She leaves her home each December 1, renting it out at $500 per week (that's over $2,000 a month, folks) until May 1, when she returns. While she's away, she earns money as a cleaning lady. Needless to say, her house earns her more money than she earns herself. No experience needed . . . just a place to stay while your home is working for you. Check your Sunday classified section for vacation rentals and consider the possibilities.

# 282 ROOM FOR ONE MORE

(Taking in a roomer)  An obvious way to bring in extra dollars, if you've got an extra room, is to take in a roomer. Earn even more money by providing meals as well. Consider converting a shed, garage, attic, basement, den, or any unused space into a guest room. Be sure you check the local regulations. You can attract your roomer with classified ads under "Rooms for Rent," or with a sign in front of your place. At first, rent the room for one month, or even one week, until you decide whether this earning endeavor is right for you. You might also consider offering free room and board in exchange for the roomer doing your cooking, cleaning, and other household chores. It's worth considering if it would give you more time to devote to earning money in other ways. Charges for a room seem to range from $75 per month to $300 per month depending upon the jazziness of the room and the other accoutrements. Don't forget—food is extra.

# 283 FLOOR BORED

(Installing floor coverings)  If people are bored with their floors, Floor Bored can end their boredom by installing gorgeous linoleum or attractive floor tiles. These days, tiles come in so many designs that almost every domicile has some tiled flooring. Attract business with display ads in the home section of the newspaper, with a listing in the Yellow Pages, with mailings to contractors and decorators, and with free seminars on how to avoid boring flooring. Now that you've done that, find a friendly linoleum and tile store that will grant you a discount for your volume purchases. When we hired someone to tile our floors, we paid $8 per hour. I'm sure prices have gone up since. No special training is required, though it would be a good idea to practice on a few floors before offering your services as a professional.

## 284 KEY TO SUCCESS

(Operating a mobile key-making service) Start a mobile key-making service. The machine that makes keys is certainly transportable, as are the key blanks. Put that fact together with your need to earn extra money, and you can unlock some of your earning power. Advertise your mobile keys with a sign on the vehicle transporting them, with ads in the Yellow Pages, with classified ads, and with signs strategically placed near the key-making machine—wherever it is. Volume ought to be the key here because the unit prices will be low. Still, some people report earning $100 working weekends only. A little bit of training will help, but vast experience is unnecessary.

## 285 COMFY BED, DELICIOUS BREAKFAST

(Providing food and lodging for overnight guests) More and more Americans every day are earning extra money by offering their spare rooms and cooking talents for "bed and breakfast," an overnight accommodation. This has been a common earning method in England for many years. You can offer your spare room to travelers and cook breakfast for them—earning a pretty penny ($15 to $35 a night) in the process. You can attract business with a sign in front of your home, with classified ads, mailings to travel agents, and even signs around town proclaiming your professional hospitality. This is a modest and flexible undertaking—just one-night stands, no month-long commitments. No need to return to college and major in hotel and motel management. Just bone up on changing sheets and scrambling eggs.

# 286 RENT-A-TUB

(Renting time in hot tubs) Many, many people would love to relax and soak in a hot tub, but cannot afford to buy one. Lucky for you. You can have a hot tub rental business, indoors or outdoors. As long as you have a tub, with the water simmering at around 100° to 105°, you can cash in while helping people soak their aching muscles and ease their troubles away. Attract customers to your hot water heaven with signs on bulletin boards, small display ads in local papers, circulars, and a good-looking, attention-grabbing sign near your hot tub or tubs. Charge customers by the half-hour ($3.50 to $5.00 per person)—people can't stay in there too long without melting. One of the nicest fringe benefits of this business is that you can use the hot tub yourself.

# 287 THE VICAR OF VIDEO

(Renting videotape cameras and recorders) Purchase a videotape camera and a VCR (videotape cassette recorder—about $1,700 today for both), then rent them out to others (the current rate is about $40 per hour). There are a multitude of uses for a video camera and VCR: store promotions, sports lessons, videotape therapy, research, insurance record-keeping, to name but a few. Most of the people who need cameras and VCRs for these purposes only need them once in a while, so they're better off if they don't have to buy them. That's why they'll be glad to rent them from you. If a customer doesn't have a TV set—the only other component needed—rent a TV set, too. If you let the world know of your video for rent—via small newspaper display ads in the business section, classified ads (under "Announcements") on Sundays, signs on bulletin boards, and free displays of video at shows and free seminars—you will build a following large enough to pay for the rental of your equipment many times over. In time, you may need several cameras and VCRs, and you may frequently find they're all rented out. I hope so. Market your equipment vigorously during holiday time, and urge people to capture the festivity of their big parties on videotape. All you're required to do is show them how to use the equipment and sell them plenty of tape.

# 288 THE COMMUNITY GARDEN

(Renting space in a large garden)   Rent a good deal of outdoor space, suitable for gardening. Make sure it has rich soil and access to water. Then, rent out space in it, so people can plant their own gardens. Many would-be gardeners don't have enough garden space of their own. So they'll appreciate the opportunity you are giving them to be outside, to garden—to grow food, herbs, and flowers. You don't have to provide the garden tools, the hoses, even the fencing between gardens. Just provide the space, and put the word out properly with circulars distributed in the area around the garden, with signs at the garden, and more signs on bulletin boards. You can tell that this earning endeavor does not require much work on your part, other than marketing. You can also probably tell that it could provide income for a long time. Well, maybe not in the winter, but enough in the spring, summer, and autumn that you won't complain during the winter. The going rental rates run around $15 monthly for a 10-foot-by-10-foot garden.

# 289 YOUR KITCHEN

(Renting kitchen space) Rent a space that can be converted into a kitchen. It must have water, ventilation, electricity, and elbow room. It should have a refrigerator, stove, and shelving. It will be better if it has loads of cooking utensils, too. Then, all you have to do is market your space. As what? As a kitchen for rent. Rent it to private individuals, cooking schools, cooking tutors, caterers—even to restaurants. A well-equipped kitchen is a valuable commodity, as you will see when you advertise it with mailings to cooking schools, classified ads, signs on billboards, and with circulars. The people who rent it should be responsible for keeping it clean, though you should have a kitchen cleaner give it a going over once a week. An unusual business like this is worthy of a free publicity story—try to get one. Rental fees can range from $10 per hour to $25 per hour depending upon the quality of space and materials. No experience whatsoever is required . . . for you. But I hope your kitchen renters know what they're doing.

# 290 RENT-A-CLUNKER

(Renting used cars) A business that is really taking off is that of renting old, used cars. For basic transportation, an old used car, rented at a low price, gets you there just as fast as a sparkling new car rented at a high price. Many economically-minded people have realized this, causing several rent-a-wreck companies to prosper. Now it's your turn to climb aboard the bandwagon, even though it's pulled by a clunker. Market your earnway with classified ads, Yellow Pages ads, with signs on bulletin boards, and with a bright sign near your rental area. If you live in a tourist area, put display ads in the tourist publications. Be sure you look into the legal and insurance regulations. That research will be well worth your time. Such companies, currently operating under names such as Lease-A-Lemon, Rent-A-Heap Cheap, and Ugly Duckling Rent-A-Car seem to be doing very well. First year grosses run from $60,000 to $225,000 depending upon how many wrecks you are renting. Get more information by requesting manual number 108, *Rent A Used Car*, from the ever-helpful International Entrepreneurs Association. Once you get this business moving, you can drive your bank balance ever upward. That doesn't sound like it Hertz, does it?

# 291　MOPED MOMENTS

(Renting mopeds)　Rent out mopeds—you know, those energy-efficient machines that are combination bicycle and motorcycle. Most people may not want to own one, but many would enjoy riding on one for fun. Let them find out about your service with signs on bulletin boards, a large sign near your rental space, Yellow Pages ads, and small display ads in the local newspaper. It is best, for safety's sake, to rent your two-wheelers in a rural rather than an urban environment. Right now, the rental rate is $5.35 per hour with a three-hour minimum. Usually you'll rent mopeds out in groups of two or more. It is not difficult to set up this business, and it can be both fun and lucrative. The number of moped rental firms in my area is increasing, so it appears that the business has a bright future. With the price of gasoline rapidly approaching $2.00 per gallon, it's no wonder moped travel is looking better every day.

# 292 HOLIDAY HABITAT EXCHANGE

(Enabling people to exchange residences) Set up a service that enables foreign visitors to exchange residences with Americans. My wife and I, on several occasions, have traded houses and cars with people, resulting in inexpensive, thoroughly enjoyable holidays for all. You might also offer the exchange to city and farm folk, apartment and home people—even to families who wish to exchange children for the summer. Market this service with classified ads in national travel media and with mailings to travel agents (though they'd rather you stay in an expensive hotel so that they can make more money). Publicity stories in Sunday newspaper travel sections will net even more business for you. You'll have to advertise in the classified section of foreign newspapers to secure foreign residents. But you do get to collect fees from both parties in the exchange. These businesses earn good money for those who run them—and quite a few people are already involved in this line of work. To list your residence with an exchange company runs from $30 to $40 per year, which is quite reasonable. Get more data on this earnway by writing to a company already doing it: Andiamo, Box 3194, Kailua-Kona, Hawaii 96740. As with many other rental operations, experience is not necessary, but a good sense of organization is.

# 293 NEUTRAL TERRITORY

(Renting space for workshops and retreats) If you can gain access to a beautiful space, ideally one with both indoor and outdoor areas, you can make money by renting it out for workshops and retreats. Many groups—business, religious, consciousness-raising, educational, medical, and fraternal—need to get away to a private, neutral place to conduct their activities away from constantly jangling telephones. By providing this territory for them, you can realize a source of income. Attract business with mailings to the groups I've just identified, and to groups that you can imagine enjoying the use of a workshop or retreat in a sylvan setting. Once any group has had a successful meeting at your place, they'll be likely to return each year, maybe even four times a year. Don't laugh—it happens. Incidentally, you make money this way by renting or leasing the space for a small sum, then renting it to the groups for a larger sum. Make additional money by providing refreshments or other assistance to the group members. Rental rates vary, but I know some people who earned $5,700 last year as a result of this earnway.

# 294 OLD SALT SAILBOAT LEASING

(Leasing sailboats)   There is unquestionably a trend toward the renting of sailboats since they cost so darned much to own. Today there are nearly ten million sailboats in the United States. You can be sure there would be more if the prices were lower. But let them stay high. You can cash in by leasing out these wind-borne dreamboats for something like $35 per day or $150 per week. This compares very favorably with the cost of ownership: $10,000 to $20,000. It does not cost much to get into this business due to leveraging, and those in it report annual earnings averaging $45,000 before taxes. The International Entrepreneurs Association can tell you more in their manual number 149. It will help, of course, if you already know all about sailboats and sailing.

# 295 THE PEOPLE'S WORKSHOP

(Leasing workshop space and tools)   Lease workshop space, stock it with tools (either rented, leased, or purchased), then rent time in your workshop to craftspeople. You'll find that your offering will be accepted by many people who have the skills but not the space or tools to exercise them. Advertise your setup with circulars distributed to craftspeople at fairs and exhibits, with ads in the classified section, with signs on bulletin boards, and with large signs outside your workshop. Once established, such a business will continue to prosper as the people working there begin to think of the place as their very own. At $5 to $10 per hour, depending upon the tools they need to use, they'll be helping you earn handsome profits of your very own.

# 296 FARM AND RANCH HOLIDAYS

(Arranging for farm and ranch holiday rentals) This may not be a very creative company name, but it tells the story. The idea is to contract with owners of farms and ranches so that they will rent rooms (or cabins) to vacationers. In return, they get a good chunk of money per vacationer per night. Once you've got a bunch of farms and ranches to offer, prepare a catalog. Mail it to travel agents, and offer it as a free booklet through ads in travel sections of newspapers and in travel magazines. People will contact you, and you'll set everything up. This is another one of those pleasing situations in which everyone wins. The vacationing family has a unique, exciting, and/or relaxing holiday. The farmer or rancher does well because your contributions are almost like "found money." And you really make out well because after you've done all the initial work, your profits will quickly outweigh the work you have to do. If a typical farmer/rancher charges $100 per day for a family of four, and you get to keep 25 percent, and you have ten groups at once, you'll be earning quite a bit of egg money.

# 297 SKI TUNES

(Renting stereopacks to skiers) One of the most euphoric, delicious, ecstatic, transcendental experiences I have had in my life is that of skiing while listening to music through stereo headphones. Listening to music through a personal stereo cassette player has improved my skiing, the weather, and my overall outlook on life. Even waiting in line or riding up lifts is a joy. Personal stereo headphones with radios rarely work in ski areas, so you need cassette players, which many, but not all, skiers own. That's why you can do well by renting them to skiers right at the ski slopes. For a single fee ($10 to $15), the skier gets the stereopack, two or three cassettes, and the headphones. A driver's license or credit card held as collateral assures you that the skier will not ski off into the sunset with your tunes in his or her ears. Signs at ski areas, especially in ski shops (where you might arrange to base your business), will bring in enough customers. You will earn even more money if you allow the renter to apply the rental price to the purchase price of a personal stereo. You can also spend the day skiing after you've rented out your units, while they are making you money. Just be sure you're back in your rental shop by 3:00 to gather in your equipment.

# 298 HOME-MADE

(Operating as a minifactory)  Mail your circular plus a letter to all the factories in your area, offering to do light assembly and product packaging for them. What you will be doing is operating as a minifactory. Your customers won't care that you do it in your own home. They won't care that you do it at whatever hours you feel like doing it. They'll care only that you do it, and that you don't become part of their overhead. In most cases, doing such work won't take up all that much space, and will provide you with welcome income. The longer you're in this line of work, the more tuned in you'll become to the types of businesses that require your services. If you go through the Yellow Pages slowly, you'll discover many, many companies that need

what you have to offer. Because you will probably be paid
by the amount of work you do, it's tough to project an
income for you, but figure that you will earn in excess of
$10 per hour.

# 299    THE LAMINATER

(Operating a lamination machine)    Enter the exciting, fun-
filled world of plastic lamination. Well, maybe it's not all
that exciting or fun-filled, but with your own lamination
machine (not horribly expensive, especially a used one) it
can be steady income from easy work. It seems that people always need things laminated in plastic. If you want
to earn extra money, you may as well set yourself up as
The Laminater. I doubt if you'll earn the "$5,000 my first
year!" claimed in some opportunity magazines, but you'll
earn more than you're earning by not doing it. In case you
wonder what you'll be laminating, the answer is: important documents, memorabilia, licenses, photographs, and
who knows what else. Classified ads plus signs on bulletin
boards should net you some business. Mailings to printers
might net you some more. A listing in the Yellow Pages is
a good idea, but don't bother to take a display ad in the
newspaper.

# 300    SEW WHAT?

(Operating a sewing machine)    If you're looking for a glamorous method of earning money, better go ahead and turn
the page now. This idea suggests that you earn your
money by being a tailor and mender—not with plain needle and thread, but with a serious sewing machine (however ancient). Without question, this will be a consistent
source of a small income, for the skills of sewing and
mending are constantly in demand. Of course, you've got
to be good at it, knowledgeable in the operation of a sew-

ing machine. Let the world know of your talents with mailings to cleaners and clothing stores, along with classified ads and signs on bulletin boards. Do the work in your own home so you won't require much extra overhead. In time you'll find this unglamorous earnway to be a consistent contributor to your coffers. You'll earn about $10 per hour, even if you charge by the rip, tear, or hem.

# 301 RENT-A-PLANT

(Renting plants)   Although most home owners and renters want to own and care for their own plants, most businesses and store owners would be interested in renting theirs. You can provide such a rental service and also offer plant maintenance. But here I'll touch primarily on the rental. (See earnway 333, "The Growing Concern," a plant maintenance business.) Charge a monthly fee, based upon number and type of plants rented, and give the renter complete information on how to keep the plants healthy. Mailings or hand-carried circulars distributed to stores and businesses, along with a Yellow Pages listing, will get your business off and growing. If you give it enough exposure, it will grow like a weed. You may wonder why people would want to rent plants. One reason would be for use on special occasions, but the main reason is just to avoid the hassles of ownership (plant disease and death). If you've got a green thumb, you can earn a lot of green by being the best green-plant renter in town. Fertilize your business with consistent marketing.

# 302 FROZEN RENTAL SERVICE

(Renting space in a freezer)   Although it won't pay your kids' way through college, you can earn extra money by renting space in your freezer. If yours is one of those teeny freezers hidden in your fridge, forget it. But if you

have a large freezer, distribute circulars within your
neighborhood and put up notices offering to rent space in
the freezer. You'll be pleasantly surprised at how many
people will take you up on it. You'll probably have to establish a waiting list. You might even want to invest in a
second freezer. Does it take a lot of brains to succeed at
this business? No. All it takes is a freezer. You might also
consider renting space in your refrigerator or pantry.
Don't laugh. Some people are already making money ($10
monthly) renting space in theirs. You can probably charge
twice that for freezer space—that's $20 a month in cold,
hard cash.

## 303  THE REMAILMAN

(Remailing mail) Sometimes companies or individuals
want mail sent to or from an address other than their
own. You can earn extra money if you offer to provide this
remail service for them. Although individuals will pay you
more on a per-piece basis, the bulk of your remail income
will be from companies since they'll employ your services
consistently. The work is quite simple, and if you get on
with some companies, the income could be quite long-
term. Market your remail service with classified ads in
national magazines and in newspapers in several areas.
Once again, I want to alert you to the fact that consistent
advertising will be crucial to success. Call remail firms in
the classified section of any national newspaper to check
on current rates. You'll find some people in the trade making over $2,500 annually.

## 304  TV TIME

(Renting viewing time on TV sets)  Lease or purchase several TV sets, install coin boxes on them (say, $.25 for
fifteen minutes), and install them in high-traffic areas at

airports, train stations, bus depots, or perhaps even Laundromats. You should frequently retrieve the coins placed in them by TV addicts, and make sure the picture is coming in bright and clear. People seem to dislike waiting, and your TV service takes the sting out of the wait. If you do well with this business, you'll find that it is an easily expandable one. So it can lead to quite a bit of money. But watch out for vandals. The TV sets plus simple signs will be the only marketing tool you'll need. I'd like to tell you more about this business, but first, a word from our sponsor . . .

# 305 VISITOR RESCUE

(Renting items visitors may require) Quite frequently, a family will have several out-of-town visitors. Although the visitors are welcome, the family is in a spot because they are short two beds, four spoons, four knives, three forks, eight dishes, five glasses, six towels, and a TV set. Visitor Rescue to the rescue. You rent these items out. You make your service known with classified ads, signs on bulletin boards, and a listing in the Yellow Pages. Make it clear that you are not a full-range rental service, but merely a service that caters to families with visitors. As such, you will be appreciated, and you will also be the recipient of a consistent, if modest income. Families always seem to be entertaining visitors. Get specifics on this business by looking over a few issues of *Rental Age* at your library.

# 306 FUN FOR RENT

(Renting recreational equipment) Much of today's recreational equipment is fun to use but expensive to own. That's why you can earn extra money by renting recreational equipment. You can even pick your favorite kinds of equipment—kayaks, hang gliders (careful with those two), skis, bikes, canoes, rafts, bows and arrows, roller skates, skateboards, or all of the above. Place big signs at your rental location as a primary marketing tool. To that effort, add display ads in the entertainment section of the Sunday paper, circulars handed out in parks and at beaches, and even radio spots. If there's a cable TV outlet with reasonable rates, look into advertising your service on the tube. I know one man who earns about $1,000 yearly renting kayaks. I know another who earns close to $100,000 renting rafts. Learn more about this business by renting yourself a canoe or bike and talking business with the person who rented it to you.

## 307 SAFE AND SOUND

(Renting storage space) Earn an automatic income by providing storage space. Buy or rent some containers from an oceangoing freighter, then place them on cheap land. Put a fence up around your facility, erect a sign, place an ad in the Yellow Pages—and that's your basic effort. You might need to run classified ads for a while, possibly even a few newspaper display ads, but you'll quickly rent out all of your storage space. And you can either expand, making more space available for rent, or you can be content with the ease with which you've earned this money. The idea of starting a storage business is going around. Now you're in on it. Are you going to do anything about it?

## 308 GAMES PEOPLE PLAY

(Placing video game machines) Install video games in high-traffic locations, either servicing them yourself or taking on a partner who will. You can get your machines placed if you present the powers that be with evidence of the profits these things can produce. If you are a good salesperson, you'll manage to place your machines in several prize locations, and your earnings will be as automatic as your machines. As suggestions for hot locations, I recommend train and bus depots, airports, bars, hotels, motels, bowling alleys, ski resorts, and large drugstores. You might try to place some in furniture store showrooms so that the kids will have something to do while the parents shop around. No marketing is needed, only salesmanship. Get more information about these machines by checking with one of the companies listed in your Yellow Pages under "Vending Machines" and "Amusement Devices." In *The Get Rich Report* (see the appendix), the author claims vending machine companies will give $5,000 to $25,000 cash to people who agree to place vending machines in their stores. That indicates the kind of profits these machines can bring in.

# 309   READY VIDEO

(Videotaping programs for people who missed them) If you've got a video-cassette recorder you can videotape programs for people who missed them, then sell them the tapes or show them the programs at a later date. Classified ads and signs on bulletin boards can be the only marketing tools you use. Your costs of doing business will be very low since you can erase the tapes you don't sell. Since your VCR will probably be programmable, this is about the easiest earnway you'll find—you don't even have to watch the shows. Sell your tapes for the tape cost plus 50 percent; sell your viewings for $5 per person per hour. If you don't think this business has much potential, you don't understand America's addiction to the tube.

# 310   THE BOOKIE

(Renting books) Set up a rental library. Obtain current books and rent them out for a fee—maybe $.50 per day.

You might also rent out records and cassettes. Market this service with signs on bulletin boards and display ads in local newspapers. You'll be competing with the local library, if there is one, but you'll have a shorter waiting list for the best-sellers. The better you are at selecting books that will be in demand, the more money you will make. Just read the best-seller list in your Sunday newspaper and in *Time* magazine to see which books Americans are reading.

# 311 IN SESSION

(Renting classroom space)    Rent out classroom or meeting space. First, rent the kind of building that can be converted to classroom or meeting use. Outfit it with tables, chairs, blackboards, and good lighting. Attract business by mailing to businesses, schools, known teachers (check their classified ads), and people who hold seminars. Naturally, you will make far more money at this if you own the space or can convert a garage or similar space into a classroom. Surprisingly, many schools are short of classroom space and will be prime customers. You won't earn a fortune, but some people take in $500 to $2,500 per classroom per year renting such space.

# 312 COPYCAT

(Placing copying machines)    If I had all the coins I've placed in public copy machines, I could probably buy Xerox Corporation by now. Which leads me to believe that if you place your own copy machines in high traffic areas, you will be one happy earner. No marketing is needed except for a few signs near your machine and in the window of the location. Be sure it stays in good working order (good luck—be sure someone checks it frequently) and has enough paper at all times. With so many people needing to copy so many things, you should find this a good source of income from the first day. If you pick a good location, it will be. Get more information on this business by calling Xerox themselves: (800) 952-5354. They'll be happy to tell how much money you can earn. At $.10 per copy, it adds up.

# 313 RENT-A-DARKROOM

(Renting out time in a darkroom)   It costs money and takes space to have a darkroom at home. For these reasons, photographers will be delighted to rent the fully stocked darkroom that you are going to offer them. Your darkroom should have proper work space and lighting, a good enlarger, and all the necessary chemicals and supplies. Let the photographers provide their own paper. Market your darkroom rental with a Yellow Pages listing, classified ads in the photography section of the newspaper, and signs on bulletin boards. See if the local photo shop will let you place circulars for distribution to their customers (buy your enlarger from a photo shop that will). And you might try a mailing to known camera owners. Nearby camera shops and a mailing list broker can show you where to find the ones in your area. A free seminar on photo processing will net you so much new business that you might have to rent out two darkrooms—it happened to a local chap. Sure hope it happens to you, too, for it will double the extra money you earn. These days a reasonable charge is $5 to $10 per hour.

# 314 RENTING PLACE

(Renting selected items) Read a few recent issues of *Rental Age*, then purchase or lease a few carefully selected items, based upon current rental needs, and start a rental service. Some items currently in demand are power mowers, automatic snow removers, weed cutting machines, chain saws, inflatable rafts, tandem bikes, biofeed-back machines, and home computers. Market your rental items with classified ads, signs on bulletin boards, a small ad in the Yellow Pages, plus free seminars on the merits of the items you rent. If your ads list the items you offer, you will be more successful at renting them. The idea here is not to devote a whole lot of storage space to your rental items, and not to become a full-fledged rental firm, but to become a selective rental firm. You should consider creating an inexpensive brochure that emphasizes the specific merits of renting the equipment you offer. Once a business like this gets established, the public will be hooked on your items, and you'll be hooked on the $3,000 to $10,000 it can provide each year.

## FINDING

## 315 THE TREASURE FINDER

(Finding items lost in sand) Buy or rent a metal detector, then go to the nearest beach (preferably on a Monday morning following a crowded weekend) and look for treasure. Expect no Spanish doubloons, but be prepared for transistor radios, wristwatches, coins of the realm, beer cans, jewelry, and junk of all kinds—some valuable. You can learn of more ways that your metal detector can lead you to treasure by doing some research. You might start by reading *Strike It Rich!* (listed in the appendix). And guess what? You don't have to spend a nickel marketing this earning endeavor. Just turn on your metal detector and dig right in.

## 316 TRACER OF LOST PETS

(Finding lost pets) If you've ever lost a well-loved dog, you know that you would have paid just about anything to find that dog again. A person who specializes in tracing lost pets knows exactly how to go about finding cats, dogs, snakes, and other missing critters. Such a person would win the undying gratitude not only of Fido's owners, but also of Fido (unless he ran away on purpose). If you'd like to bill yourself as Tracer of Lost Pets, and you really can do the job, you'll find that you can get customers with classified ads in the lost and found section, bulletins posted in pet stores, and with a mailing to veterinarians in your area. There's not a lot of money in the business (unless you find Mrs. Higgenbottom's prize Yorkshire terrier and collect her $10,000 reward) but you'll do all right as long as you can follow wandering animals doggedly.

# 317  I FOUND IT!

(Finding things for a fee)   Find things for people. Take out classified ads in newspapers and even national publications and offer your service. Charge about 10 percent of the purchase price of the found object. Old books costing $25.00 net you $2.50. Old Viking ships costing $150,000 net you $15,000. A person I know found one of each as a professional finder (his only source of income). He's the guy who gave me the idea for this cockamamie business. I took him a whole lot more seriously after I heard he had found a Viking ship for a Hollywood studio. Market your services with classified ads and direct mailings to outfits that might be looking for unusual (and expensive) items—like Hollywood studios or antique shops.

# 318  THE STAMP MINE

(Finding rare stamps)   This could also be the Gold Mine— the idea is the same. Get involved in the collecting of stamps or coins for *profit*. If you have fun at the same time, fine, but the idea here is not to amass your own collection. Instead, you ought to sell a collection's worth, one at a time. You'll find customers for both buying and selling with classified ads, ads in stamp and coin journals, and visits to stamp and coin dealers. Direct mail might even be employed. I've even heard of a person who located a good stamp collection, went out and found a person who wanted it, then went back and bought it, selling it immediately at a mind-boggling profit. Good luck in boggling your own mind. Start by perusing *Linn's Stamp News* and/or *Coin Prices*.

## 319  PHIL THE BEACHCOMBER

(Finding items on beaches)  I love writing about Phil because he earns money by doing things that other people do for free. He ambles slowly along gorgeous beaches, keeping his eyes open for things he can sell. What kind of items? Well, driftwood for one. Shells, for another. Rare stones, for a third. And there's more. Of course, Phil already knows where he will sell his driftwood, shells, and stones because he lined up customers before he started combing the beaches. A few in-person calls were all that Phil needed to set up his markets. And now he earns and earns while appearing to stroll aimlessly on the beach. He takes in a "few thousand" a year that way. Good going, Phil. You're one bright beachcomber.

## 320  UNIQUE PROPERTIES

(Claiming abandoned property)  Of the 555 earning endeavors in this book, many will earn you just a bit of money. But some will earn you a ton of money. This is one. Claim abandoned property: buy it for a song and sell it for a fortune. It sounds easy, but it's not. You've got to know who the customers are before you buy abandoned property. If you can line up customers first, then each piece of

abandoned property that you claim will be quickly converted to money in the bank. Market your unique properties (they must be unique or they most likely would not
have been abandoned in the first place) with ads in real
estate magazines and classified sections of metropolitan
newspapers. The key to succeeding in Unique Properties
is being a master of positive perception. If someone else
abandoned property because they could not see its potential, you must discover that potential and convince someone else it's worth money. You can earn a six-figure sum if
you succeed. Begin to learn about this earning endeavor
by reading some back issues of *Rare Earth Report.*

# 321 TO THE RESCUE

(Scavenging buildings that are about to be wrecked) Another way you can really make a lot of money is to know
your stuff and get into the scavenging business. When you
learn of buildings that are about to be demolished (find
out from a city official; it's all a matter of public record),
get permission to enter and scavenge the building for re-
usable or repairable materials or antiques. In some cities
you may have to pay for the right, but it can be worth it.
You can scavenge for and sell banisters, doors, chairs,
bars, windows, doorknobs, decorative molding, and a
whole lot more. Chandeliers, sinks, curtains, stairways—
the list goes on. Next you've got to know where you can
sell what you scavenge. If you do, you can make a fortune.
I know of a Chicago man who purchased old banisters
from an-about-to-be-demolished bank. He paid $2,000 for
them, then sold them for $8,000 to a restaurant. I've read
of similar stories with even more impressive profits. No
marketing is needed, only smarts. You've got to be smart
enough to know in advance where demolishing will take
place, what to look for there, how to get it out and reno-
vate it, and where to sell it for a profit. If you figure that
there's a magazine covering this topic, you're right. And if

you think the magazine is named *Demolition Age*, you're right again. Check out the articles on demolition, salvage, and disposal of contents.

# 322   OBSOLETE ITEMS UNLIMITED

(Finding obsolete items)   There happens to be a big market for obsolete items. The hard part is finding out where to buy them—it will be considerably easier to find a place to sell them (just the opposite of the usual proposition). The types of obsolete items that sell like crazy are wagon wheels, metal advertising signs, park benches, and railroad ties. Talk to antique and junktique dealers to see what sells best, then find it and sell it to them. Or sell direct to the public. You'll probably find that the hardest part is learning what to buy, the next hardest part is learning where to buy it, and the easiest part is selling it. Do the selling with signs, classified ads, mailings to dealers, and exhibits at flea markets and obsolete-item shows. You can learn of the current market and new trends in antiques and collectibles (and of good books on the subject) by reading *American Collector*. Find it in the appendix.

# 323   THE VILLAGE GOLDSMITH

(Reclaiming gold or silver)   If you had gone into the business of reclaiming gold or silver ten years ago, you'd be one rich goldsmith today. But take heart, there is still money to be made reclaiming these precious metals. The idea is to purchase items with gold or silver, then extract the metal for resale. The difficult part is locating useless items of or with gold or silver. It's a bit easier when you get to the extracting and reclaiming part. Selling the reclaimed product is a cinch. So many people will want it that you won't need any marketing at all—except for a few phone calls to eager buyers. Gain some insight into this business by looking through a few copies of *American Metal Market*. With enough insight, you just might earn a ton of extra money.

# 324  THE OLD LOCATER

(Finding items for antique stores)   Send letters to all the antique shops in a given (large) area offering to find exactly what they need. You'll be saving them time and helping them to make money. Certainly some antique and collectibles stores will be delighted to hear from you, especially once they realize that you really can find what they need. Ascertaining the needs of antique stores will be the hardest part. Direct mailings to antique stores will most likely be the only marketing you'll need. You can begin to identify some hard-to-find antiques by reading *The Antiques Journal*. Once you get a line on where to find what local dealers need, you can pull in a steady supply of income—ranging from $100 to $1,000 monthly. You can make even more if you find *really* hard-to-locate items.

# 325  EUREKA!

(Tracing lost items)   *Eureka* means "I found it!" and that's exactly what you'll be expected to shout as a tracer of lost items. A friend of mine recently told me that he figured out the solution to the problem of disposing of nuclear waste. He said we should put it in small suitcases, then check them on flights of a certain airline (name not mentioned here due to compassion and fear of litigation). Without doubt, he told me, the nuclear waste would never be seen again. This person has obviously had problems with lost luggage. Many people have, myself included. We should be able to hire a tracer-of-lost-items . . . especially to recover something irreplaceable, like the ten rolls of film I shot in Italy that were in my missing suitcase. If you're really good at tracking things down, if you have patience and the nose of a bloodhound, you can earn good money as a professional tracer. I've known of a company that paid a tracer $500 to track down missing files (he found them ten days later) and of a private individual who paid a tracer $100 to find a missing $1,000 check (found in two days). Obtain customers with signs and classified ads. You won't be able to live off your earnings, but they'll be welcome additions to your monthly total, I'll bet.

# 326 DAVEY JONES GOLF BALLS

(Retrieving golf balls from water holes)  If you're a golfer, you know well the frustration of hitting a brand new golf ball into a water hole and never seeing it again. If you're a person interested in earning extra money, you may one day know the joy of retrieving a brand new golf ball from a water hole and selling it for a dollar. Eventually, you may know the ecstasy of having retrieved one thousand golf balls from water holes and selling them all for one dollar each. The good news is that there are tens of thousands of golf balls hit into water holes and abandoned each year. Quite a few people are already making money selling reclaimed golf balls. All you need in order to join in is a scuba tank, a face mask, fins, and a good underwater light. Then secure permission from a golf course (or best of all, fifty golf courses) and begin to earn doubloons from retrieving little round treasures lying in Davey Jones's locker. Some caddies claim to earn $1,000 annually doing this. I wonder if Davey Jones was a golfer. Maybe he was Bobby Jones's cousin?

# 327 THE REPLACEMENT PLACE

(Locating and selling replacement parts)  Some people earn money locating rare or hard-to-find books. You can earn money locating and selling hard-to-find replacement parts. For what? For just about anything that needs a replacement part: a toaster, a car, a refrigerator, a TV set—almost anything. The worst that happens is that you don't find the part. If that happens, you don't charge the customer. If you do find the part (and you will get better and better at finding parts), you make out quite well on the sale. Supply and demand. Once you get the hang of knowing where to look, this should be a simple business for you. Market it with classified ads, signs on bulletin boards, distributed circulars, even with mailings to shops that have parts but can't do as well as you with special items. Some people earn their entire living just finding automotive replacement parts. Perhaps you can earn *some* of your living this way. If you do find a part, you can charge double or even triple its cost to you. A good place to do research on this business is your local junkyard or auto graveyard.

# 328 THE GOLD BUG

(Discovering gold)  I recently heard that during California's gold rush of 1849, only ten percent of the available gold was mined. I also know that the price of gold has been rising while the value of the dollar is declining. If this is still true by the time you read this, you might consider panning for gold. With such an economic situation, gold panning can net quite a bit of money for you—the same goes for silver and other precious metals. It isn't too hard to pan for gold, and the equipment isn't costly (until you get into underwater mining). Once you have a claim and figure the best way of mining it (get into underwater mining), you can be assured of income for a long, long time. On a river trip through the California gold country in the mid-1970s, I met a miner who claimed to be taking out $10,000 monthly. Now, I'm not just talking about striking it rich . . . I'm also talking about striking it middle-class. Of several new and good books on this subject, I recommend *Gold Hunter's Field Book* by J. Ellis Ransom.

# 329   OLD STAINED PANES

(Finding old stained glass)   Drive through old towns and keep an eagle eye out for stained glass windows and other old architectural items that might be up for sale. Before you leave on your trip, try to get some customers for your treasures lined up. Such customers may be obtained with mailings to antique dealers, stained glass dealers, contractors, and architects. They'll tell you what to look for. Although you will be combining a holiday with an earnway when you set off on a stained glass journey, even the earning itself will give you joy. When your customers learn that you are a regular source of salable items, you will have a regular source of extra money. A local person earns his entire keep selling the stained glass he finds on his lazy drives through the West. I might add that his keep is quite costly. For further information, consult any detailed road map and stay off the freeways.

# 330   CLIP JOINT

(Finding articles for clipping services)   Go to the library. Get about fifty out-of-town phone directories, Yellow Pages sections. Then, make a list of all the clipping bureaus. This will take at least a day. Big deal. Next, write to all the clipping bureaus, offering to clip articles from the newspapers in your hometown. If they already have a clipping service in your town, you're out of luck. But if they don't (or if the current clipper is a loser), they'll pay you to read the local newspaper and clip articles from it, articles that pertain to specific topics. If you're really lucky, all the clipping bureaus will want your services. You'll be paid about $.50 per clipping, so you'll have to clip hard. You've got to be a good, fast reader, and know how to scan a newspaper efficiently. Learn more about this business by calling either Burrelle's Press Clipping Service, toll-free, at (800) 631-1160, or Luce Press Clippings, also toll-free, at (800) 528-8226.

# 331 IMPORTANT IMPORTS

(Discovering items not available in the United States)  Many items made in Europe and Asia are not available here, though their manufacturers would like them to be. I guess nobody has asked to sell them here. So ask. Select one or two items that seem ideal for the current marketplace and sell them either to retailers or directly to the public. If you have a keen instinct for selecting products, you can take free business trips to Europe. You can be the exclusive distributor for highly desired products. You can also lose a fortune, so be careful—but do check into this possibility. If you find a winning product or two, they might pay your way to finding ten more. Check the publications listed in the appendix under "Product Catalogs" and you'll come across a few that list items available for import. If you can spot an item that fills an existing or new need, you're well on your way to a large income—in excess of $100,000 annually with the right item. Do yourself a favor and put a check mark at earning endeavor number 331.

## NATURE

# 332 THE PLANT DOCTOR

(Keeping plants healthy)  There are more people who love plants than people who know how to keep plants healthy. Too bad for the poor plants. Lucky for you . . . if you're The Plant Doctor. The Plant Doctor knows how to make sick plants healthy, brown plants green, little plants big, bug-ridden plants bug-free, and skinny plants fat. The Plant Doctor performs his or her healing magic professionally. Of course, house calls will be necessary. If you know your way around a wide variety of indoor and/or outdoor plants, you can be The Plant Doctor. You can attract customers by placing your bulletin in all the local plant stores, by distributing circulars in places where plant-owners are likely to be, and even by giving free seminars on plant health. In time, you might have a regular clientele and a group of very grateful philodendrons. Charge on a per hour basis—$5 to $10. And be sure that your expertise matches your ambition. I've asked several experts—real plant doctors—which are the best books. The overall winner (sorry, if you're from east of the Mississippi) is the *Sunset Western Garden Book*.

## **333** THE GROWING CONCERN

(Maintaining plants) The Growing Concern might be the ideal name for a company (person) engaged in the care, feeding, and maintenance of plants. You can rent your services on a regular basis to offices, stores, and homes. You come around regularly and water, fertilize, prune, pinch, sing to, and spray the plants entrusted to your care. This is already a darned big business in my neck of the woods. I suggest checking to see if your service might become an offering of plant stores in your area. I'd do a direct mailing to possible customers first . . . or even better, personal calls. Then, I'd run small display ads in the section of the newspaper that plant owners read. You might have a free seminar on plant maintenance. If you mail to all the businesses in your locale that have plants, you could find that your Growing Concern is a growing concern. Charge clients a monthly fee ($25 to $50) based upon the number of plants for which you might care. Your green thumb might turn out to be green in more ways than one.

# 334  HOW DOES YOUR GARDEN GROW?

(Gardening)  Gardening might be one of the most popular free-lance activities around. All of the local newspapers where I live have quite a few ads for gardeners. Yet when I call these gardeners, they are always busy tending someone else's garden. This makes me realize that gardening is a busy business. When I finally do get a gardener to tend to my disheveled shrubbery, I realize the hard way that gardening is also quite profitable. Gardeners and landscape consultants get to work outdoors with beautiful things and call the shots as far as their work load and hours go. A good thing about this endeavor is that you can rent the equipment you need—no big capital outlay is necessary. You can specialize or generalize. You can specialize in trees if you have that expertise, and you can count on regular work if you're good the first time around. Get your customers with Yellow Pages ads, circulars distributed to homes that have gardens, house-to-house calls at houses that look like they need your services, classified ads, small display ads, and bulletins in plant stores. Television commercials, however glamorous, are not necessary. Gardeners out here are now charging $7.50 to $12.50 per hour, though many charge by the project. They earn additional money selling gardening items as well.

# 335  INTO THE VOID

(Leading backcountry trips)  You can have a great time with your life, meet interesting people, and learn to really love the planet if you decide to earn extra money leading backcountry expeditions. My last holiday was a twenty-day trip in Utah's backcountry—going to some areas very rarely visited by anybody. How did I find such places? My backcountry guide, that's how. For a fee ($1,250), he led me and seven compatriots into some of the most gorgeous, unknown, untamed backcountry in the world. The world? Yep, the world. Psychedelic scenery. He had just as good a time as we did, only he made a wee fortune while he was out there. Market your expeditions with direct mailing to known trekkers, ads in backpacker magazines, exhibits at outdoor trade shows, bulletins in clever locations, and small display ads in the travel sections of Sunday newspapers. This is a part-time earning endeavor that can be quite addicting. Gil, our guide, is an addict. Poor Gil. He knows (as must any pro trip leader) cooking, psychology, geology, singing, botany, zoology, archaeology, ornithology, entomology, history, wilderness survival, rafting, rivers, geography, and medicine. Other than that, he's just a regular guy.

## 336 FISHY BUSINESS

(Fishing professionally) Imagine being able to earn money practicing your favorite pastime. Many fisherpeople do. If you line up your customers first and then do your fishing, you can sell your fish. The end result will be that you get paid for something you'd happily do for free. Direct mail or personal calls to fish retailers and restaurants would be good marketing avenues to explore. Contacting fish wholesalers would also be a good idea: by letter, phone, or personal call. These days, and in the future, more and more people will earn money doing things they'd ordinarily do for free. Pretty nice. Hope you can join them.

## 337 MARINE MANNA

(Catching clams, crabs, and crayfish) Somehow, I don't put the catching of clams, crabs, and crayfish into the same category as fishing. It seems more like work and less like fun. Still, it is a way that people do and can earn extra money. You still have to find your potential customers before you find your clams, crabs, and crayfish. Most likely, you'll find the customers harder to locate than the shellfish. Be careful you don't let the big ones get away. Find them with letters, phone calls, and direct mail. Who are they? Fish stores, grocers, fish wholesalers, and restaurants. Private people, too, will want your delicacies. If you sell to private citizens, you might consider marketing with a sign or two or three. Last time I bought crabs, that's how the crab seller caught my attention. Your earnings will be solely (ha ha) related to the time you spend catching marine creatures . . . and your luck/skill at it. You can earn zilch or you can earn your entire income. Knowing you, you'll probably strike a happy medium.

# 338 FISH FINDER

(Being a professional fishing guide)  The fish finder I have in mind here is a professional fishing guide (or hunting guide—The Game Finder). If that finder is you, you've got to know about the outdoors, about where the fish are, when to catch them, and what bait they're going after. Get customers with ads in fishing magazines, in the recreation section of the classified ads, in the sports pages of your local paper, and with signs in local sports shops. This is almost as much fun as being a backcountry guide. The only problem is that you can always find the backcountry—will you always find the fish? Good guides charge from $50 to $100 (and more) per day. For that, they *do* find the fish. Usually.

# 339 BALCONY LANDSCAPING

(Landscaping balconies for apartment dwellers)  Now more apartments than ever have balconies, and more people than ever are interested in natural things. So what's more natural than offering landscaping services to apartment and condo dwellers? Many of these people know little about gardening, so they'll appreciate your help. It's easy to find them: post bulletins on apartment building bulletin boards, and do mailings to apartment occupants. I'd even try a few small display ads in the Living section of Sunday newspapers. And I'd go for a free story in the same paper. The business is newsworthy enough, and a news report is free publicity. Charge by the balcony, including in that charge your markup for plants and materials plus a design and time charge. You can figure on $100 to $200 per balcony. You'll make out quite well if you can connect up with a big-city plant store, establishing yourself as their in-house balcony landscaping expert.

## 340 HOME ON THE RANGE

(Being a part-time ranch hand)  This earning endeavor, in spite of its name, has nothing to do with cooking. No, instead it has to do with the real thing: being a part-time ranch hand or farmhand. During certain times of the year, part-time people are needed, and if you let ranchers and farmers know of your availability by means of letters, you'll probably earn some extra money while making yourself at home on the range. Last year, certain Arizona ranchers were paying $25 per day for low-level hands, $50 per day for higher level (more experienced) ranch hands. I served as a ranch hand for a brief period while I was in college in Colorado. I earned about $10 a day plus all the horse riding I wanted—which wasn't (ouch) that much.

## 341 KAYAK TOURS

(Leading flat-water kayak tours)  Lead flat-water kayak tours. That means you don't need white-water experience.

That also means you don't need the skill in kayak handling you would need on a river. With a flat-water kayak, you sacrifice excitement for safety. And with a two-person kayak (or two or three or five of them), you can lead tours of shorelines (as long as the waves aren't too big), quietly flowing rivers, marshlands, and swamps. A flat-water kayak gives you (and your passengers) access to scenery and wildlife that would be inaccessible by any other mode of transportation. You'll need insurance, but probably won't need a license (check with a lawyer). You can lead weekend tours (one or two on Saturday; one or two on Sunday) and fill your kayaks with tourists (each paying $15 to $25 for a half-day tour). Advertise with display ads in the sports or travel sections, put up signs on recreation area bulletin boards, and give free seminars or slide shows on the joys of flat-water kayaking. Learn more about kayaks (and rafts and tours) by writing to Outdoor Adventure River Specialists (OARS), Box 76, Angel's Camp, California 95222. They'll take you on a tour or teach you to kayak. Or both.

# 342 PLANTING PERSON

(Starting up plants) Specialize not in gardening, not in landscape architecture, not in weeding, tree removal, balcony plantings, or plant maintenance—but in plant *starting*. If you know plants, you know the importance of a proper beginning. Offer to plant seeds or to germinate seeds and plant the young seedlings. Make your service available for indoor or outdoor plants, trees, bushes, vegetable gardens, and flower gardens. Along with starting, offer tips on keeping plants healthy. Advertise for customers with signs on bulletin boards, classified ads, even circulars distributed to homes with gardens. Shouldn't be too difficult to attract customers if you give seminars (but charge for them—$5 per head). You should probably charge by the hour for your plant-starting smarts—around $5 to $10 per. A local person who is a pro starter says that her entire income comes from plants and that last year 10 percent of her income came from starting plants professionally. On your mark, get set, start!

# 343 PLANT SITTER

(Baby-sitting for plants) People who take extended holidays or business trips often need their plants taken care of. The easiest way is to collect their plants, bring them to a place where they can thrive, and baby-sit for them, making sure all of their needs (light, fresh air, and water) are filled. Find customers by running classified ads, posting signs in plant stores, and putting up as many signs on high-traffic bulletin boards as you can. Then, direct your attention to making the plants healthier than when you first got them. You can also be a plant sitter by just visiting the home where the plants live, rather than bringing them to your place. Charge a daily rate—$5 to $10—for your services. Not a whole lot of experience is required, but you must be tuned in to plants and know by sight or touch when they need more or less water and/or sunlight.

# 344 GREEN GREETINGS

(Creating plant greeting cards) Combine your love of nature with your love of an honest buck by putting together, then selling, greeting cards that grow. Such a greeting card would have a greeting (you knew that part) along with a soil mixture for planting, a packet of seeds, and a mailing carton. It will probably cost no more than $1 to get these items together, and they can sell for $3 to $5. They'll sell year-round, to virtually anyone, and virtually anywhere. Market your blooming earnway with mailings and personal calls to plant stores, hotels, convenience stores, supermarkets, gift shops, stationery stores, and even department stores. Sell your green greetings by the case. A company that already does this, and one that would be delighted to give you more information about it, is FRIA Products, Inc., 23011 Alcalde Drive, Laguna Hills, California 92653.

# 345 THE VEGETARIAN GARDENER

(Setting up vegetable gardens)   You can eat all the filet mignons you like and still make it big as The Vegetarian Gardener. Let it be known that you set up and maintain vegetable gardens. Show people the economics of such a garden and how the food savings pay for your fees many times over. You've got to do your homework so that you can learn how to obtain maximum vegetable production from limited spaces. Once you've learned about intensive gardening—as this science is called—get customers with classified ads, display ads in shoppers, bulletins in prominent locales, even mailings to likely prospects. Put some brochures into your local health food stores. Charge $10 to $20 per hour for your time. You can charge a lot because you'll help people save a lot. Learn a lot by reading *Organic Gardening*.

# 346 JUICY VEGETABLES UNLIMITED

(Growing and selling hydroponically grown produce)   Hydroponic gardening is planting in a container that holds a root support system such as gravel (though lightweight and absorbent vermiculite is preferred) along with water that has been enriched with nutrients. Such a method of agriculture leaves nothing to chance since the nutrient solution is always exactly what the plant requires, and little energy has to be put out by the roots in search of nutrients. Be sure to arrange for enough light, and make certain the water (nutrient solution) is pumped regularly or changed occasionally. The result of hydroponics, or water gardening, as it is known (and used successfully in the Hanging Gardens of Babylon), is 30 percent faster growth and plumper, juicier produce. Some vegetables don't do well hydroponically (corn), while others do fabulously (tomatoes). You can grow and sell the vegetables, plants, herbs, or flowers you grow hydroponically. And you can learn how to grow them by reading *Beginner's Guide to Hydroponics* by James S. Douglas. Sell your produce to stores and private individuals. Market your produce with signs at roadside stands, signs at flea markets (get a stall), and signs at any farmer's market type of food exchange in your area. Make in-person calls to grocers, and don't forget the free samples. A few people I know got so deeply involved in this activity that they now sell not only their tomatoes, but also the hydroponic units they produce. Juicy profits, indeed.

# 347 BUGABOO EXTERMINATING

(Exterminating insects) Right out front you should know that it takes training, knowledge, and time to be a top-rate exterminator. It also takes time to build up a regular clientele. Now that you know the tough side, you should also know that you can make serious sums of money on a regular basis if you market your murder properly and consistently. Marketing is a combination of mailings to homes, phone calls following up the mailings, listing in the Yellow Pages, and regular display ads (small ones) in the Sunday newspaper. Signs around town won't hurt your case, and mailings to developers of housing projects will help it. Once you have people signed up for regular servicing, this business can prove to be quite profitable. As you grow, you'll require specialized equipment and chemicals. But once you have the bug killing down pat you stand a good chance to make a different kind of killing. That's the one that comes when you have a hundred customers signed up at $15 monthly. Check your Yellow Pages under "Exterminating & Fumigating" to see how many competitors you have and how they're putting out the word about themselves. You'll notice that they seem to be out to exterminate the competition.

# 348 KEEP THE HOME FIRES BURNING

(Providing firewood)  Keep the Homes Fires Burning is a cutesy-pie name for a hefty service—the cutting, selling, and stacking of firewood for private residences. Obtain your wood legally, with a truck and chain saw (you can rent the truck and saw or broker that task to someone who already has the equipment). Market your firewood with an ad (or just a listing) in the Yellow Pages along with posted bulletins, and even a test mailing (postcards) to homes within a selected neighborhood. During the early part of winter, a few display ads or classified ads will aid your woody cause. Sell the wood by the cord or the half-cord (a cord is 128 cubic feet of stacked wood—a stack 4 feet by 4 feet by 8 feet), and charge extra to stack it. If your wood is dry and/or aged, charge a bit extra for that. Firewood prices keep going up. Last month, I paid $175 for a half-cord of aged oak, stacked. If you go into this earnway, please accept my thanks for contributing in your small way to solving our energy crisis. Incidentally, if you send letters to chimney sweeps in your area, asking them to recommend your services if you recommend theirs, they probably will.

# 349 CHRISTMAS WOODS

(Growing Christmas trees)  Grow Christmas trees. Ho ho ho! Then cut them down and sell them to professional Christmas tree sellers. Ho ho ho! Make in-person calls to every single place in your area where trees are sold, giving each prospect a circular about your quality, economy, and dependability. Of course, you've also got to arrange for the land and the botanic expertise. If you are more ambitious, you can sell the trees you grow directly to the public yourself. Some people who succeed at growing and selling Christmas trees also grow and sell Halloween pumpkins. In both cases you plant, grow, sell, and earn. Good Christmas tree sellers earn up to $2,500 and even more during the few weeks they are selling. You can't live off tree sales, but you sure can buy some nifty Christmas presents.

# 350 GOOD GOURD

(Raising and selling gourds)   Under the heading of unusual I list the raising and selling of various types of gourds. Don't look at me that way. There are people who are earning money this way right now, and you can do it, too. You've got to figure out who your customers will be (probably people who frequent craft shows and fairs), but once you track down the type of people who love a good gourd, you can grow many varieties and sell all that you grow. The female gourd seller who hawks them at a local flea market won't tell me her gourd-growing income—I doubt if she makes more than $1 per gourd. Still, she sells about fifty on a good day, and she sells at health food stores, too.

# 351 WEEDAWAY

(Removing weeds)   Perhaps you don't love weeds as much as I do. Okay then, start a weed removal service as many people have already done out in these weedy parts. Their classified ads do not bill them as "gardeners," but as "weed removers." They also get business by listing their service in the Yellow Pages (under "Weed Control Services"), by distributing circulars to mailboxes in areas where one is likely to find many weeds, and by putting signs near gardening shops. The main difference between their service and your service is that they are already earning money doing it and you're still reading about it. They succeed with their own or with rented tools. And they charge $7.50 per hour . . . and up, of course. If you do become a deweeder, please leave my weeds alone. A friend once told me that a weed is a flower whose beauty has not yet been discovered. My wife, sneezing as she speaks, says a weed is an ugly, pollen-carrying critter. I say, "Gesundheit."

# 352 GREAT BAIT

(Selling bait)  Position yourself near a place where fishermen fish or depart to fish, and sell bait to them. You'll probably want to sell bait to bait shops, too. You can specialize in one kind of bait or offer several kinds. The only marketing you'll really have to do will be with signs announcing your bait for sale. You might even consider running a classified ad in the fishing section of your paper, maybe even an inexpensive display ad in the sports section. Naturally, the type of bait you offer is dependent upon the types of fish in your area. But you can earn enough from 6:00 A.M. to 10:00 A.M. selling bait to spend the rest of the day fishing. Of the multitude of fishing publications, the most sensible to consider is the current *Field and Stream Fishing Annual.*

# 353 THE BONSAI MART

(Selling bonsai trees)  As any collector of rare, tiny bonsai trees can tell you, they are difficult to find and dig up, but delightful to own. Any bonsai collector will also tell you that bonsais are worth the high prices they fetch. And now, you can be the recipient of those high prices. Once you can spot a concentration of natural bonsais, you can sell them with classified ads, with mailings to plant stores and known collectors, and with signs at flea markets, exhibits, and almost anywhere else you wish to sell your natural beauties. Some people are raking in around $500 per weekend—just selling at flea markets. Although bonsai refers to dwarf trees, the profits are anything but dwarf-sized.

# 354 DOWN ON THE FARM

(Engaging in small-time farming)  Be a small-time farmer, on land that has yet to be farmed. Instead of thinking of the land as a gardener or home owner might, think of the land as a farmer might. That means that you plant food for resale, put up a chicken coop, consider raising sheep, goats, pigs, or cattle on the spread. Small-time farming can be fun, can be delegated, can be profitable. Perhaps you'll specialize in one crop; perhaps you'll specialize in more than one. Market your produce (even before you grow it) by in-person calls to grocers and other outlets where farm offerings are sold. A small mailing to food brokers might net you more customers. If you follow up the mailing with a phone call, it will certainly result in your learning exactly what you should be growing and raising on your farm. At least one of my acquaintances earned over $10,000 in one year engaging in small-time farming, while holding down a full-time job. One friend grew apricots, another grew almonds, a third grew grapes. I can't remember which one earned the $10,000, but all three made out well, and all three delegated most of the work.

# 355 PICKING AND PLANTING

(Picking fruit and planting trees)  Earn extra money by picking fruit during one season, planting trees during another. Work is available doing both of these outdoorsy tasks, and the earnings are lovely, if not lofty. Naturally, you'll have to go where the fruit is for your picking endeavor, and you'll have to go where the trees are needed for your planting. Luckily, both will probably be within a reasonable distance of each other. You'll have to be available to do the work at the time of year when it needs to be done—the picking/planting seasons. A few letters to owners of orchards and vineyards, farms, and lumber companies should be the only marketing you will need. If you enclose a circular that describes your expertise, all the better. An expert on this topic says you should also contact tree-planting or reforestation companies. They'll pay you a by-the-tree-planted rate (it comes to about $.10 per fir and $.13 per redwood) or by the hour—$8.00 to $11.00. My same insider says that you make out better with the by-the-tree arrangement because you get better and better at it. She earned more in two months of tree planting than in six months of teaching.

# 356 THE LAWN RANGER

(Installing and maintaining lawns)  Although Tonto is not there to help him, the Lawn Ranger earns plaudits from people he saves from the ravages of the sun and weeds. By specializing in lawn order, he is able to attract plenty of business. His only experience had been trial and error on his own lawns. Now, he charges $10 per hour plus materials, and he gets all the part-time business he wants. After all, he still wants to keep his job at the bank. Admittedly, the Lawn Ranger does delegate quite a bit of work, but he keeps the lion's share for himself. By running classified ads and a personal letter campaign to local nurseries, the Lawn Ranger is a local hero—he helps keep the county green, including his own bank account. Although he installs and maintains lawns, he tells me that 75 percent of his Lawn Ranger income last year came from installation. A very happy sod story.

# 357 WILD FOOD

(Harvesting food that grows in the wilds)   If you know where
good food grows wild in the countryside, you can turn that
knowledge into income. You might even plant seeds in the
country and see to it that they sprout into money trees.
They will if you can harvest wild fruit, vegetables, and
herbs, then sell them to either food brokers, restaurants,
or grocers. Line up customers with in-person sales calls
and free tastings. Not much marketing is necessary. The
more you know about nutrition, the more money you'll
earn at this endeavor. Begin to learn by reading the
basics in *Thanks, I Needed That: The Beginner's Natural
Food Cookbook* by Judy Goeltz and Patricia Lazenby.

# 358 MUSHROOM MAN

(Raising mushrooms)   When my wife and I attended our
first meeting in England of the club called Mensa—a
group of people with IQs in the upper 2 percentile, the
first person we met was a man who claimed to live in a
barn. He told us he lived there to keep an eye on the
mushrooms he was growing. Although his living conditions sounded, well, interesting, the profits he claimed
were even more interesting. It's not easy, he told us, to
get mushrooms going. But once they start, they are de-
lights to behold—and simple to sell, he explained. Since
that time, I've learned that the world is full of mushroom
freaks and mushroom eaters. You can profit from mushrooms just as our Mensa mushroom man did—he said
mushrooms were his only source of income. Living in a
barn, he didn't require much income, I figured. Sell your
mushrooms directly to grocers or restaurants—with in-
person calls and tastings. They'll want your delicacies on a
regular basis, which means that you can make money on a
regular basis. I hesitate to recommend any mushroom
books knowing the past two presidents of the San Fran-

cisco Mycological Society (read mushroom society) died of mushroom poisoning. So you're on your own, friend. Incidentally, if you are female, you might name your business Mushroom Madam.

# 359   THE WEEKLY BOUQUET

(Selling subscriptions to your flower service)   I once became involved in a company like The Weekly Bouquet. We delivered flowers every Friday to private homes, and every Monday to offices. And all the places to which we made our deliveries were places where someone had *subscribed* to the flowers, just as you might subscribe to a newspaper or magazine. Because of their commitment in advance, they received lower prices along with beautiful flowers and unbeatable convenience. We advertised our service with mailings to residents in targeted areas, with circulars distributed to office workers during their lunch hour, and with the same circulars sent to office managers. We even ran ads (display ads) in the Sunday newspaper. Soon, we began making money—about $400 monthly, split four ways. Then, one fellow worker moved to Central America and another took a job as a hostess for a worldwide travel company, enabling her to visit exotic vacation spots for free. Good for her; bad for the company. I was too involved in my other earning endeavors to fill in for them, or even to find replacements for them. So the business— profits, growth opportunities, and all—withered and died. Had we continued it, I could have enjoyed both flower power and flower profits. We proved it is a viable business. It's already being done in New York City and other places, and I recommend it to you wholeheartedly. I had zero flower experience, yet I profited. Perhaps you can, too.

# 360   THE PLANT EXCHANGE

(Setting up a place where plants may be traded)   Many people are filling their homes with plants and treating the plants with so much loving care that the plants soon get too big for the home. What to do? Exchange the plant for a smaller one, that's what to do. And you can provide the place to do it. Run classified ads and put up signs on bulletin boards. That's about all you'll have to do in the way of marketing. By charging a small fee ($3 to $5) to both the buyer and the seller, you'll make out pretty well. In time, your plant exchange will provide you with steady money. Some plant exchange people sell their larger plants to plant stores. You might also consider taking in plants on consignment, but that calls for more space than just the exchanging does. You should have a lot of plant knowledge so that nobody gets stuck with a lemon (unless, of course, that's what they *asked* for).

## ANIMALS

# 361  ANIMAL WATCH

(Observing animals at a zoo)   Whoever heard of being paid to go the zoo? You have now. Some people are actually paid money ($5 per hour, currently) to observe and note animal behavior at zoos. Serious researchers pay these people. Such researchers work out of the universities or with the zoos. Let them know that you'd like to watch the hippo professionally by writing them and sending your qualifications. Now understand that this is not as popular an earning endeavor as gardening or tutoring, but it sounds to me like a lot of fun. A zoology background will help, but it's not essential. Patience and an honest interest in animals seems all that is really required. You won't get rich, but you will be entertained.

# 362  THE UNIVERSITY OF BOWWOW

(Training pets)  Earn extra money training pets. Train dogs to be housebroken, to heel, to sit, to stay, to roll over, to shake hands, to fetch, to speak, to lie down, to be watch-dogs, to leave postmen alone, to leave cats alone, or to do fancy tricks like catching flying Frisbees. Many otherwise intelligent people are at a loss when it comes to training pets. Consider that a break for you. I wish I could tell you stories of people who have struck it rich training cats, goldfish, or parakeets. No such luck. But The University of Bowwow might net you a neat nest egg. A local animal school charges $300 for the basic obedience course, two to three weeks long. Find your customers by doing direct mailings to vets, kennels, and dog owners. Post bulletins in pet stores, and parade some of your graduates before a local newspaper reporter, hoping for a free story and picture. You might even experiment with classified ads. And let's not forget the Yellow Pages, speaking of housebreaking a dog.

# 363 GROOM WITH A VIEW

(Grooming pets)   Now that your pet is a college graduate, how about eliminating that scruffy look? You can be a pet groomer. It doesn't matter if you do the grooming at the customer's residence or your own—what matters is how well you get along with the animals and how lovely they look after you're done. Little touches like ribbons make the pet owners very happy (and the pets very uncomfortable, I'll bet). Most pet owners will be grateful that you can do your grooming at their homes. Transporting dogs is no problem, but transporting cats is another matter indeed. Moose, my Siamese cat, does not want to ride in autos, ever. And you know how intelligent Moose is otherwise. So some people will be very grateful for a portable pet groomer. You need the right equipment and training to succeed in pet grooming. With these assets, you attract new customers by posting bulletins in pet stores and at vets' offices, by running classified ads in the "Pets" section, and by distributing circulars or doing a direct mailing (postcards) to pet owners in your area. Yellow Pages ads will also help. You can charge $15 to $20 for a dog groomed at your place, $20 to $25 for a doghouse call. That's the price for a miniature breed. It includes nail clipping, ear trimming, bathing, grooming, and cleaning the dog's rear end. I don't know the charge for cats—Moose seems to do all his own work, thank you.

# 364  THE PET BOUTIQUE

(Making clothes and doodads for pets)  Now that all the pets have been found, observed, trained, painted, photographed, and groomed, I have another pet-oriented earning idea for you. Create customized toys and doodads for pets. Make customized pet pillows, blankets, and clothing. Paint customized eating dishes, drinking bowls, or doggie doors. Make customized leashes and collars. You can sell your products directly to pet owners or to pet stores. You can offer your goods with bulletins in pet stores and vets' offices, in display ads in the newspaper (showing a picture of your wares), and in circulars distributed to the good people who own pets. With the population of dogs and cats in the United States so large (80 million), there are loads and loads of potential customers for your creations. I don't know how much you can make, but I do know of a person who sold custom-designed doggie dishes for $25 per, and she sold over a hundred of them her first year. That ought to tell you something.

# 365  ATTACK!

(Training guard dogs)  It's too bad that the guard dog industry is on the rise, but as long as crime is on the rise, maybe it's not so bad after all. So if you can train dogs to be professional and reliable guard dogs (and not all dogs can be trained as such), you will be performing a valuable service for businesses, families, your bank account—for everyone but criminals. This is a different skill than teaching dogs to come or shake hands, and requires that you be a trained trainer. If you are, you'll earn around $1,000 per guard dog trained. And you'll attract business with display ads in business sections of local papers and with mailings of your circular or brochure to businesses and families in high-crime areas. A Yellow Pages listing will put even more bite in your marketing efforts.

# 366   AQUARIUM BEAUTEOUS

(Selling and maintaining aquariums) It is not a simple task to select and decorate the right aquarium for a particular place of business, not a simple decision as to which fish will inhabit the aquarium. That's why Aquarium Beauteous may be just the ticket. This operation would sell aquariums to businesses, recommending the ideal size tank and type of tank denizens and landscaping. It would also maintain the tanks, keeping them beautiful and their fish healthy. Mailings to decorators, office managers, and store owners should begin to bring in the business. Your average sale to businesses should be in the $300 to $650 range, according to people who have done this kind of work, and your maintenance fees will come to about $50 monthly. You might therefore consider concentrating on the sales and delegating the maintenance.

# 367   POOCH WALK

(Providing a dog-walking service) Provide a dog-walking service. Aim for apartment and condo dwellers since they are the ones who have a harder time getting their dogs out. Come around regularly and take pets on nice, long strolls. The pet owner furnishes the leash, the pet, and the monthly fee—$75 to $150. You attract the pet owner with mailings to vets, pet stores, and apartment supers. Bulletins posted in areas with a high concentration of apartments will also net business. Give circulars to doormen and to people walking dogs . . . especially people who look as though they'd rather be doing something else. Be sure you are capable of giving each dog the love, attention, and patience that it receives from its owner. Bill your clients monthly, and give generous Christmas gifts to helpful doormen. Might you walk ten pooches at once? You might and you should. Figure on devoting about thirty minutes per day per pooch. With ten pooches and ten walks, this would take five hours of your time. With ten pooches and one walk, it takes thirty minutes. Please keep your ten pooches off my lawn. I thank you.

# 368  HANDY WITH HORSESHOES

(Shoeing horses)  If you like horses, you'll love earning money as a horseshoer. While my daughter owned her horse, I recall the many times she asked me for a check for $25 for the horseshoer, and I'll bet that 1975 price has gone up a bit. I think horses need new shoes as frequently as kids do. So if you live in an area where there are lots of horses, consider learning the trade. There are courses available. Then you'd post bulletins at stables, do mailings to vets, and, if possible, to horse owners. You might list in the Yellow Pages under "Horseshoeing." Our Yellow Pages, smack dab in the middle of horse country, has but one such shoer. He's busy all the time. You've got to be fond of things equine to make money at this business, but it is a very certain route to extra money.

# 369  LAB ANIMAL FARM

(Raising lab animals)  Skip this earnway if you love animals. I love animals, but I'm writing this down. If you can force yourself to read it, you might forgive me for writing it. I'm suggesting that you earn extra money by raising laboratory animals. That means you'll be raising mice, rats, guinea pigs, and whatever other animals the laboratories want. The laboratories that purchase your animals will use them, in all likelihood, to discover ways of improving the health and well-being of human beings. So if the lab animals die during the experiments, human lives may be extended as a result. Enough moralizing. Back to capitalism. Market your lab animals with mailings and phone calls to labs that use animals. Attempt to develop relationships with labs that use lots of animals (and not with the animals themselves) and breed your animals according to the lab's specifications. When you've got this business going, it can bring in a few thousand per year. Everyone will make out well. Except for the animals.

# 370  PET SLUMBERLAND

(Establishing a pet cemetery)  Owners of pet cemeteries provide an important service for pet owners who have lost a pet they loved very much. Because of the gigantic size of the pet industry, the pet cemetery industry is already a multimillion-dollar endeavor. You need the required permits, fencing, and quite a bit of land. You also need a maintenance person (you?). A listing in the Yellow Pages along with proper signs in pet stores should be all that you need to call your cemetery to the attention of pet owners. If this sounds like a small business, consider this: one pet cemetery made over $300,000 during a recent year, and the very idea of pet cemeteries is just beginning to be accepted. With the trend in the United States away from burial and toward cremation, look for the same trend to hit the pet cemetery business. The Yellow Pages has already anticipated this with their listing of "Pet Cemeteries and Crematories." The ads there offer pet pickup, permanent zoning, personalized service, and private burials. Get more information by checking the International Entrepreneurs Association manual number 138, or write for a free brochure to Pet's Rest Cemetery and Crematory, 1905 Hillside Boulevard, Colma, California 94014.

# 371 ME AND THE BEES

(Keeping bees) A really fascinating hobby is that of beekeeping. Unlike many other hobbies, this one can earn extra money for you. Once you have the science of honey gathering down pat, it might even earn lots of money, and for a long time. Good training is required in the form of book learning and class taking. So why not buzz headlong into this endeavor and make money with honey? You might establish your beehives on someone else's property and let them handle the bees and honey for you. Then, all that's left for you to do is market the honey. Not hard if you try in-person calls on grocers, along with free samples. Try some natural food stores as well. A distant relative claims to earn $1,000 every year with his beekeeping hobby, and he puts in only a couple of hours per week. With more time, perhaps you'll make more money. Meanwhile, read *Beekeeping* by John F. Adams.

# 372 LAND OF LADYBUGS

(Raising ladybugs) As we become more and more aware of environmental, ecologic, and nutritional processes, organic gardening becomes more and more popular. You can get in on this trend by raising ladybugs to sell to organic gardeners. They'll appreciate how the ladybugs will eliminate gardening pests without the danger of chemicals. It should not be hard to obtain a long list of organic gardeners (see any list broker), making it easy to do a direct mailing. You might also advertise in organic gardening publications, and place signs on bulletin boards around town. Once your ladybugs get going they can put you in a position of ease and comfort. Read some back issues of *Organic Gardening* to find out about what's going on. Once you get started you can earn a few hundred to a few thousand dollars annually with your lady and gentleman ladybugs.

# 373 FISH POPULATION EXPLOSION

(Breeding fish)   Breed fish to earn extra money. First, contact local aquarium store owners. Do it with letters or in-person calls. Determine exactly the type of fish they need. Then, do everything in your power to breed those fish and sell them to the store owners. I don't have to tell you that you've got to put in study, research, time, and effort. But with the proper groundwork, the healthy sex lives of the fish you breed will keep you in clover (seaweed?) for years. Eventually you might want someone else to handle the selling, breeding, or delivering. In the meantime, you must admit that the most important work is done by the fish. And I'll bet they don't even consider it work. Gain insight into your marketplace by looking over a few issues of *The Pet Dealer*.

# 374 EARTHY CREATIONS

(Raising earthworms)   For years and years, people have touted the raising of earthworms as a source of income. Well, this year is no different. People still need the squirmy creatures for fishing and organic gardening. The technology is improving to the point that good-sized sums may be earned raising worms. Signs in fishing shops, on fishing piers, at fishing departure points, and in gardening shops can secure some business. Classified ads can secure some more. Mailings to nurseries and bait shops can secure the most. As with ladybugs and fish, the worms will do most of the work. All you've got to do to earn from $100 a year to $100,000 a year (really and truly; a northern California man grossed that a few years ago and probably grosses more now) is handle all the loose ends. Then, watch the profits come wriggling in. Oh yes, read *Organic Gardening*.

# 375 THE PET EXCHANGE

(Setting up a place where people can exchange pets) For the life of me, I couldn't figure why anyone would want to exchange pets. Then I moved to a place where cats were not allowed, but dogs were. Time for an exchange. A friend of mine had a dog that terrorized local sheep. Time for an exchange. Another friend moved from a large house to a small apartment. What to do with his Labrador retriever? Right. Exchange it. With classified ads in the pet section, plus signs on bulletin boards, you'll make some money—not a lot, but some. Charge about $5 to each party in the exchange. You can develop a small but regular source of pocket money. By the way, don't forget to post a sign in a local pet store.

# 376 PET HOTEL

(Furnishing room and board to pets) If you live in an area with enough space so that you can furnish room and board and love to pets while their owners are away, you can earn a fair amount of money. Inflation does not seem to be driving up the daily rates at pet hotels. The current $4 per day for cats and $5 per day for dogs (less for smaller dogs) isn't too much more than we paid five years ago. Offer feeding, brushing, exercising, and enough room for roaming. Signs in pet stores, classified ads, plus a Yellow Pages listing will put the word out, but tender love will result in repeat business. You can't rely on word-of-mouth much because barks and meows aren't all that convincing. But you can provide such good care to the pets that their owners will spread the word for you. Don't get into this earnway unless you have a sincere love for animals, for it is this love that will make you a success.

# 377 AQUARIAN FISH FARMS

(Fish farming)  Fish farming is illegal in some places, legal in others. Where it is legal, it can be profitable. Fish farming seems to be a combination of work and fun, but there is no question that if it is done right, it can be more lucrative than you might think. *Aquaculture Magazine* will prove that to you. Line up the customers for your fish before you even get started in the business. And you've got to learn the intricacies of the science of fish farming in order to succeed. This takes more than a few days at the library—perhaps you should plan a longish visit to a fish farm. *Rare Earth Report* occasionally lists fish farms for sale, should you be interested in living where you earn. With the right preparation, fish farming can be a source of long-term rewards, both financial and spiritual—spiritual because you'll be working hand in hand with nature. You can keep your full-time job, delegate the actual farm work, and still take satisfaction in the knowledge that the fish will be working to make some money for you. Hope they net a lot.

## FOOD AND COOKING

# 378 NOW YOU'RE COOKING PRESS

(Creating cookbooks)  Cookbooks are immensely popular because so many people are eating these days. Also cookbooks don't become dated, which means a good one can sell for years. You can earn quite a sum of money if you can write a unique cookbook. Two friends of mine wrote a cookbook entirely devoted to things to do when you mess up a recipe, and they sold tens of thousands of copies. Other people have cashed in by writing about cooking with woks, or cooking in the wilderness. If you can write a unique cookbook—and unique seems to be the key word—you can make quite a bit of bread. (My friends earned $20,000.) Sell your book by mail order; advertise in food-oriented magazines. Or you can sell it to a publisher who knows how much dough there is in cookbooks. For further information, I direct you to the cookbook section of your local bookstore. The hungrier you are when you visit the section, the more likely you are to come up with ideas for another great cookbook.

## 379  THE TRAVELERS' TABLE

(Serving meals to travelers)   Cook and serve delicious home-cooked meals to travelers—right in your home. Hang out a sign letting them know when you're open (maybe weekends only), and specialize in just a few dishes, so that if you don't sell all you cook you can enjoy the leftovers later. You'll need a goodly supply of travelers, not to mention the proper licenses, cookware, recipes, and ingredients. Many people are offering their homes for bed and breakfast. Here, I'm talking about no bed and no breakfast—dinner only. Signs can do all your marketing. Put one sign at your home, one sign a mile in one direction, and one sign a mile in another direction. You certainly won't be able to live off your earnings, but you may pick up $100 per weekend.

## 380  COOKERY COLLEGE

(Teaching about food)   At your college—actually your home, basement, kitchen, spare room, or attic—teach people the art of canning, preserving, dehydrating, and

smoking. Commonplace as these kitchen tactics once
were, they are becoming lost arts, and it seems appropriate at this time to revive them. There is undoubtedly a
return-to-earth state of mind in this country, and these
skills are very useful. Market your Cookery College with
bulletins in appropriate places, with display ads in local
papers, with radio announcements (free, not paid), and
with a bit of free TV coverage by a local station interested in the grass-roots personality of your college. If you
have any extra grape jam or smoked salmon, drop me a
line—I love grape jam and smoked salmon. But not together. You can learn about the lost arts, about cookery,
about the back-to-the-earth movement, and about books
dealing with these timely topics when you read *Mother
Earth News.*

# 381  THE MIXMASTER

(Being a professional part-time bartender)   Be a professional
bartender at parties. Know all there is to know about the
art of mixing drinks and being cordial. Then advertise in
the classified section, post bulletins in liquor stores or as
near them as possible, give your card and brochure to liquor store employees, and do a mailing to all the catering
companies in your area, informing them of your availability. While you're at it, do a mailing to the clubs and organizations, too. If you're going to be The Mixmaster, you'll
probably have to be the marketing master, too. People
who serve as pro bartenders earn from $25 to $100 per
night, with the emphasis on the latter.

# 382  THE MOVEABLE FEAST

(Preparing first-class meals to go)   One associates fast food
with junk food, but this need not be the case. In London,
one of the fanciest restaurants also runs a carry-out store

where you can get food fast, and I assure you that it is anything but junky. Consider doing the same here. You can prepare and sell the food yourself, or you can arrange to get the food from a fancy restaurant, and merely sell it. The idea is to sell first-class gourmet meals—from soup to salad to dessert—and all "to go." Market your meals with display ads in the newspaper, radio commercials, a grand opening party (with free samples), and with more sampling of your delicacies at fairs and exhibits. You should either know how to prepare the meals or know how to pick the right restaurant to hook up with. You can earn $5 to $15 profit for yourself per meal served. So if you can manage to serve/sell a hundred meals per weekend, you'll come out satiated, with money and probably with food, too. Chow down on your Moveable Feast! If it succeeds, open a branch here, okay? Of several excellent gourmet magazines, *Cuisine* will probably be most helpful to you in this endeavor.

## 383 AN OLD FAMILY RECIPE

(Creating dishes from family recipes)  Make dishes from your own family's best recipes, then sell what you make to restaurants, stores, and the general public. To whom you sell depends upon what you make. Bakery goods may be sold to restaurants and bakeries, of course. They also seem to sell extremely well at flea markets. The basic idea is that you attract customers with mailings, signs, bulletins, and classified ads that offer special foods prepared according to a secret old family recipe. Don't sell the recipe, just the finished fare. At some point, you'll have to reveal the recipe to someone if you're going to delegate the cooking and/or delivering. That's all the easy part. The hard part is turning up new customers (most will become regular customers if you deal with stores or restaurants). And the best part will be depositing checks. If you don't have any old family recipes, try like crazy to discover or borrow somebody else's.

# 384 CAKES FOR OCCASIONS

(Baking special cakes for special occasions) That's right: bake special cakes for special occasions. Let your imagination run rampant when you dream up the varieties of occasions: hirings, firings, promotions, sales, birthdays, anniversaries, confirmations, bar mitzvahs, engagements, plus all the legal holidays—even a few illegal ones. Let your cake decorations, and even the shape of the cake itself, reflect the occasion. Customers may request unique cakes for their friends' special celebrations—you can make a cake in *any* shape. Market your baking abilities with signs on bulletin boards, classified ads, even a small ad in the Yellow Pages. Maybe in your town you can offer to bake for restaurants. It won't be too hard to find enough customers. You can earn a profit of around $10 per cake. I've heard of a woman who bakes special occasion cookies as her only source of income. Maybe she doesn't require much money—or maybe there are more special occasions than I know of. I doubt if you'll be able to earn all you need this way, but if you're a good baker, you sure can earn some money when you turn pro.

# 385 HORS D'OEUVRES WITH VERVE

(Making hors d'oeuvres) You can be pretty sure that it is harder to spell hors d'oeuvres than make them. If you can make them, sell them to restaurants by means of in-person calls (phone for an appointment first), and to people. Use classified ads and a listing in the Yellow Pages. You might even do a mailing to catering services, letting them know you specialize in appetizers and canapés. You can earn $25 to $100 weekly with this business, and you can succeed with it if you keep up on the latest breakthroughs in hors d'oeuvres . . . by reading *Cuisine* or an hors d'oeuvres cookbook. Don't forget that your offerings should look as good as they taste.

# 386 THE DOUGHNUT MASTER

(Making doughnuts) There's dough in doughnuts if you master the art of making them deliciously and selling them while they're hot and fresh. This you can do if you make and sell them at the same place. A mall comes to mind. An amusement park comes to mind. So does a booth at a recreation area, zoo, flea market, or stadium. The best doughnuts I ever tasted were purchased fresh at an amusement park from a free-lance doughnut master. The only necessary marketing tool is a tasteful sign. Hungry buyers happily pay $.25 to $.60 per doughnut. In 1979, $1.5 billion was spent on doughnuts! With gross profit margins of 80 percent, it's no wonder even absentee owners of doughnut shops gross in excess of $150,000 yearly. The International Entrepreneurs Association tells us the average doughnut shop grosses a measly $100,000 yearly. And that's for eight hours work per *week*. Learn more by requesting their manual number 126, *Donut Shop*. They talk about a shop—I'm talking about a part-time stand. Consider both. In either case, be careful you don't eat up all the profits.

# 387 THE PERFECT PICNIC

(Making box lunches) Make box lunches that are ideal for picnics. Perhaps you'll want to include fruit, wine, cheese, or other special touches. Advertise your service with signs at picnic spots (for future business), classified ads, and circulars distributed in picnic areas. Have the lunches picked up at your place—or whatever place they are made (possibly the restaurant to which you broker the making). Don't limit your offering to picnics, either. A box lunch can be good on any type of outing, including auto travel, sporting events, and visits to the beach. You can sell your picnic boxes for $3 to $7 per person, and about 60 percent of that can be pure profit. You don't have to be a great cook, only a great picnicker.

# 388 FOOD MAGIC

(Preserving food for others)   Earn extra money by appealing to other people's taste. Preserve, can, freeze, freeze-dry, dehydrate, and smoke food for people who love this kind of food, but can't (or won't) do it themselves. If you can do any one or more of these food preservation techniques, you can also teach and delegate it to others. To supply your company with enough customers, run small display ads in shoppers, post signs on bulletin boards in shopping centers, and try to arrange to be interviewed on a local radio talk show. This is not a big dollar operation, but it is a steady dollar operation. You can earn around $100 to $300 monthly if you market your preserving skills well. *Mother Earth News* has frequent articles on food preservation.

# 389 NEAT EATS

(Selling food at fairs)   Whether you obtain the food by preparing it yourself, by buying it from others, or just by purchasing it from a store, you should sell it at street fairs and flea markets. A local woman, selling cookies she baked on Friday evenings, arranged for someone else to sell them for her on weekends at a flea market. Result? She earned more during a nonworking weekend than during her entire work week as an office manager. It's all because people have this lovely habit of getting hungry. If you can end their hunger conveniently, you can earn quite a bit of extra cash—up to $500 per weekend. Marketing? Signs will do the trick. Distributing circulars at the fair or flea market helps, too. Wouldn't you know it? The International Entrepreneurs Association has a manual—manual number 83, *Cooking Shop*. In it, they gleefully point out that in a given year, American cookie eaters spend an outrageous $5 billion on cookies. I must plead guilty to contributing a share of that total.

## 390 HOLIDAY FIXIN'S

(Making holiday specialties)   Here's another one for the age of the specialist. Make and sell holiday specialties during the various holidays. That means you should cook up the world's best cranberry sauce for Thanksgiving, bake incredible Christmas cookies during late December, make sexy candies for Valentine's Day (not too sexy; in Maryland, a bluenose tried to have a cookie maker arrested for baking male and female gingerbread cookies), and hardboil and paint Easter eggs. If you can think of any delicacies for the Fourth of July (edible firecrackers?), all the better. Run classified ads prior to the holidays, and post signs on bulletin boards to arouse customers. Then, get an assistant or proxy to take over the creation of the food while you concentrate on the creation of income.

## 391 CAKE ART

(Decorating cakes)   More specialization: turn the decorating of cakes into an art form. Engage in custom decorating. Offer your services in classified ads and in mailings to bakeries and fancy restaurants. Now, I'm not talking about your usual colorful squiggles. I'm talking about framable, edible art and sculpture—performed with love and frosting atop a cake. Unique? Yes. Salable? Just exhibit your work at a fair, show, or art gallery—and see how many people will try to buy your art—up to $100 for a cake. To show how seriously you should take this suggestion, I direct your attention not to *Cuisine* but to *Art in America*. To succeed, your artistic talents should surpass your baking talents. In fact, I was tempted to put this earnway in chapter 2.

# 392   THE CONSUMMATE CATERER

(Catering meals)  If you're going to bill yourself as The Consummate Caterer, you've got to be able to arrange for the creating, cooking, serving, and arranging of memorable meals. Then, you've got to make sure the cleaning up gets done afterwards. By offering wonderful food—all the courses, from appetizers to desserts—and by marketing intelligently, you can partake of some tasty profits. Intelligent marketing entails mailings to party givers, Yellow Pages ads, bulletins where party folk congregate (country clubs, certain bars)—maybe even throwing a party, catering it yourself, and inviting hot prospects. (I know someone who launched a moderately successful catering business that way; she earns $500 per month catering now and she continues to hold down a full-time job as a teacher.) Phoning all of your friends is a great way to start—not only this business, but virtually any business, for contacts will prove to be as important as ability. Got that? *Contacts count.* Okay, now you can consider creating a modular catering organization, developing the recipes, and attracting customers. Then concentrate on graciously accepting compliments. And money.

# 393   CHIEF COOK AND BOTTLE WASHER

(Catering everyday meals)  Instead of catering parties and fancy affairs, position yourself to cater everyday meals, even simple meals for two. Many busy two-career couples appreciate this service. And a catered dinner-for-two can make a good gift or surprise. You can work alone . . . or your delegatee can work alone. All that needs to be done is exactly what is done for large parties—only on a teeny scale. The quality remains the same; only the quantity changes. A simpler business, this, because it involves fewer people: just you and your customers. Try to arrange to clear $15 to $25 per hour, including your food markup. Several such firms (people) are already flourishing in the West.

# 394  MUNCHY HEAVEN

(Serving food to people waiting in lines)  Hardly anyone likes to stand in line. But you can make it more pleasant, whiling away all that time, if you serve (sell) munchies to all those patient folks. They wait outside movies, sporting events, concerts, and at bus stops. Most have no food. Most would buy your munchies out of boredom if not hunger. The munchies served by Munchy Heaven can be just about anything. Marketing is by a sign on your tray of munchies, and maybe on a special T-shirt worn by the vendor. Sampling might be a great way to attract business if your munchies are inexpensive enough to be given away in bite-size quantities. A fellow in London claims to earn the equivalent of $25 daily this way. Delegate the selling and you'll be in earning heaven. Check with your local health department to see if you'll need a license to sell your munchable morsels.

# 395  LUNCHTIME LAD (OR LASS)

(Selling food at offices and factories)  By selling box lunches and sandwiches at offices and factories, you can make a whole lot of steady money, and all it takes to get started is about two months' worth of smart and hard work. First, line up a restaurant that will sell you a large volume of lunches and sandwiches at a discount. Then, after mailings to and phone conversations with office and plant managers, arrange to come by at lunchtime offering your lunches. If the food is good—an absolute necessity—you can offer the workers a variation on the usual cafeteria lunch or brown bag fare. Your signs on bulletin boards, your small ads in factory newspapers, and your charming sign on your nicely decorated lunch truck can extol the virtues of your food. You can start out with free (tiny) samples of the food you are selling. I know a woman who successfully engages in this business in San Francisco. I know a man in Chicago who built a company around this idea and sold it for over $100,000. To learn more about it, just eat in a factory or office cafeteria and you'll instantly see how you can do it better.

# 396 THE RESTAURANT RESTAURANT

(Selling specialty foods to restaurants) Develop a few specialty foods, then sell them on a regular basis to a few deserving restaurants. Your foods might be appetizers, soups, main courses, bread or rolls, desserts, or even side dishes. Whatever your dishes are, they must be superb—up to and beyond the quality of the restaurant. They should be foods that the restaurant itself would find too complex to prepare regularly. Once you have found the right combination of restaurant or restaurants and food or foods, you have the makings of a long-lasting business. Attract restaurants by being very selective, then phoning them for in-person appointments during which they may sample your specialty foods. If your foods are great and the restaurants are popular, you just might become richer—earning $100 to $500 weekly, working part-time. Wouldn't that be delicious? Just be careful you don't put on too much weight. Once again, I call your attention to *Cuisine* magazine, and to *Gourmet* magazine. Both will provide you with recipes worthy of great restaurants.

# 397  THE FLYING DINNER

(Making and delivering hot meals on a regular basis)   A good many people just plain never do their own cooking. Either they eat out, or they buy stuff to go, or they eat frozen foods all the time. Whatever the reason, whether they are too busy or too tired or just unkitcheny, they won't cook. And they need hot meals on a regular basis. All of this is good news for you. What you've got to do now is make and deliver their hot dinners to them on a regular basis. Obtain customers for your tasty earnway by posting signs on bulletin boards (especially in apartment buildings), classified ads in newspapers, a listing in the Yellow Pages, circulars handed out at apartment complexes, even samplings of your cooking at shows or fairs. Because you will be operating from a limited menu, there will be very little waste and very big profits. Someone else can handle the cooking, delivery, billing, and collecting if you'd like—if you're willing to part with some of the profits. (Go ahead, be willing.) If you take this idea and develop it so that you have a regular dinner list, you can make money from this one idea for a gloriously long time. You should understand proper nutrition along with meal preparation to succeed at this. And you can earn about $25 to $50 weekly per regular customer (dinners only). So get yourself a whole lot of customers. And do a whole lot of delegating.

# 398  DOWN WITH FOOD PRICES

(Selling wholesale food at retail prices)   Actually, the idea here is to buy food in bulk at wholesale, then sell it at just under retail. Sounds very clear and straightforward, and it is. If you can service small towns and rural areas, you can enable your customers to realize great savings over the course of time. And even though they are saving, you are profiting because you made such a good deal on your bulk purchases. To hit it big with this basic business, you've got to research your potential markets (check them out in person), determine which foods you will carry, and decide from whom you will do your bulk buying (the closer to the source of the food, the cheaper the price to you). Once you have made these decisions—and be careful you don't buy perishable foods or you might be in trouble—and once you have lined up regular customers (newspaper display ads, signs, stalls at open-air markets, and mailings of brochures to prospective customers), you can devote an ever-decreasing amount of time while earning an ever-increasing amount of money.

# 399 THE WHEELER-MEALER

(Serving food to outdoor exercisers)    Certain areas where I live are absolutely jam-packed with roller skaters, skateboarders, joggers, and bicyclists. If anyone deserves a tasty snack it is these people. But it's not that simple just to roller skate into a restaurant. And frequently, good food is not available where these activities take place. What it adds up to is a chance for you to sell food to these traveling exercisers—an opportunity to earn impressive sums. Just select the kind of goodies you'll be offering (make it a very limited but delicious offering), then market your food with attractive signs on your cart or van or station wagon. You don't need signs on bulletin boards for this one (well, maybe if there's a bulletin board at the cycle or skate rental place). You certainly don't require classified ads. But you do need a permit from the authorities in your town (not all that difficult, even in a place as sophisticated as San Francisco), and absolutely delicious food. You also need a reliable source for the ingredients, a place to prepare your food, and an ability to stick with your own diet. For research, check out your local park and ask a few skaters and bikers what they'd appreciate for a snack. Some people earn $100 per day at this endeavor, and I think that's on the low side compared with the potential.

# 400 THE BROWN BAG

(Selling sandwiches to grocers) Zillions of people carry their lunches to work in brown bags or lunch pails. Not many grocery stores sell sandwiches. You can merge these two phenomena the way my friend Larry did. He made first-rate sandwiches, then sold them to grocers at a fat profit. The grocers then sold them to customers at an even fatter profit. The customers were as happy as clams because they didn't have to go to the trouble of making the sandwiches (bleary-eyed at 6:30 A.M.). It is not all that difficult to get this business going (took Larry about three months). Once it is moving, there is nowhere to go but up, and nothing to get but rich. Larry sure did. (Earning around $.25 profit per sandwich, he sold over a thousand sandwiches daily.)

# 401 COFFEETIME

(Running a coffee route) I have an acquaintance who has a full-time printing shop and a part-time coffee route. The coffee business, which takes only a fraction of his time, is more lucrative than the printing business, which takes a great deal of his time. What he does is provide coffee-making equipment (and the coffee, cream, sugar, and tea) to stores, showrooms, and offices. Because his coffee is good to begin with and his coffee-making equipment does not kill the delicious flavor, his business continues to grow and grow and prosper and prosper. My friend loves the money so much that he does all the coffee servicing himself. You, on the other hand, love life more than money, so you'd be likely to let somebody else do all the servicing once you got the customers. Get them with mailings, radio commercials, Yellow Pages ads, and free samples wherever possible. For more data on this service, look up ARA in your Yellow Pages; they're listed under "Coffee Break Svce. & Supls.," and they're about the largest such company in America. That being the case, you'll find them in most large cities.

# 402 JUICE TOWN

(Selling juices)   Rent, buy, or trade for a first-rate juicer, then offer fresh fruit and vegetable juices for sale. Sell them from pushcarts in high-traffic locations, at fairs, at flea markets, beaches, parks, malls, and anywhere else that fresh juice will be gratefully purchased. Signs can serve as your only marketing tool. Quality will be the single factor that will keep you in business, though convenience will help a lot. You can see how some juice vendors earn up to $100 daily selling juice. If nobody is already slaking thirst this way in your area, you're in for some juicy profits.

# 403 YUMBOX

(Selling gift boxes of food)   When I was a kid at camp, I'd write home bemoaning the food and the lack of between-meal treats. My loving parents would respond with a gift box filled with food: cookies, a salami, fruit, brownies, even an occasional cake. A real potpourri of goodies, those boxes, and very much appreciated. You can save parents the trouble by prepacking boxes of goodies. Naturally, they will be sent to more than just kids and to more places than just camps. Almost anyone is happy with a gift box of delicious food. Makes no difference where they are. Market your boxes directly to retailers at gift shops, department stores, and grocery stores—with in-person calls. But also market your Yumbox endeavor with classified ads in the food section of the newspaper—especially around holiday periods when these boxes will make smashing gifts for deserving snackers. In time, you can establish yourself as a prime source of prepacked gift boxes of food, endearing yourself to eaters everywhere (and probably to your banker). Getting this business started requires selecting the right kinds of nonperishable foods, the right packaging, the right way of mailing, and the right marketing. Once you've got these, you can offer your Yumboxes in national ads. At that point, my friend, you've got it made.

# 404 DR. DIET

(Preparing nutritionally intelligent foods)  I don't know how the human race has made it this far knowing so little about nutrition for such a long time. It seems that some very basic nutritional facts have come to light only recently. We seem to be on the brink of understanding things we should have understood a century ago. It's up to you to make money with these new nutritional findings. One way is to prepare a line of diet foods and sell them to grocers, restaurants, and private individuals. It is possible to prepare foods that are both delicious and contribute to intelligent nutrition—even to specific problems like weight loss, depression, and even alcoholism. You'll have to read some books on the topic—*Laurel's Kitchen* by Laurel Robertson comes to mind—and you'll have to keep current on the subject—*Better Nutrition* magazine can do that for you. Once you have the topic down pat, market your diet foods with mailings, phone calls, and in-person visits to grocers, restaurants, and food brokers. You might run a few display ads to see if you can attract individual orders in enough quantity to cover the cost of your ads. And you certainly ought to be able to get a newspaper food editor to write a story. If there's a local TV show about cooking, see if your diet foods are deemed newsworthy enough for a free spot for you. This is not a simple business to start properly. But if you do it, you can make a healthy sum of money.

# 405 HEALTHY VICTUALS

(Preparing health foods) The breakthroughs in nutrition information are as applicable to health nuts as they are to alcoholics and fatsos. And these days, health nuts abound. You'll find them in health stores paying fancy prices for what are frequently not-so-healthy health foods. When I saw potato chips in a health food store I wrote that store off. Oh well, maybe the placebo effect keeps people fit. You can help them far more with honest-to-goodness health foods, prepared after you have done your homework, reading up on how to prepare them and what to put into them (and read *Better Nutrition* on a regular basis among other things). Check with a lawyer to see if you'll require a special permit. Market your finished natural foods or health foods (natural isn't always healthy you know) directly to health food stores—with in-person calls and free samples. Put them on exhibit (and out for tastes) at fairs and shows. If they are not perishable, advertise them in the classified section of health magazines. Without too much difficulty, you should be able to make health food stores a lot healthier than they already are. And your bank balance will reap healthy benefits as well. Some acquaintances from Boulder, Colorado, earn six-figure incomes with this business, so remove any artificial limitations to your earning. Oh yes, the word victuals is pronounced "vittles." But you probably knew that all along.

# 406 GOOD ROAD FOOD

(Marketing food from a roadside stand)   You can prepare the honey, sandwiches, coffee, juice, assorted yummies, diet food, health food, and bakery items—along with fresh fruits, veggies, herbs, and more—and market it all directly to a hungry public from your roadside food stand. Now I'm not talking about a restaurant. And I'm not talking about a fresh fruit stand. I'm talking about a comprehensive and wonderful roadside food market—possibly located in a makeshift building, maybe even an ornate cart, yurt, or teepee, perhaps even a truck. Marketing can take the form of well-designed and clearly-worded signs near your stand and all over and around it. You might hand out brochures to all of your customers to help them spread (and remember) the word. Of course, you have to do quite a bit of out-front work yourself: selecting the foods, finding sources, preparing the foods that require preparation, picking the right location, choosing and preparing the stand, securing any necessary licenses, deciding how to market the food. Once all that is handled with grace and hard work, you can delegate the selling and just partake of the sweet profits. One has only to drive through farmland near large cities to see several thriving roadside stands. Hope yours is one of them. Hope it's not too far from here.

# 407 HOT POTATO HAVEN

(Selling hot potatoes to go)   Among the many foods that may be successfully vended from their own stands, from flea market stalls, from roving vendors in public places, and from either sit-down or take-out restaurants is the potato. Served hot and stuffed with cheese or tomatoes or bacon or veal or hamburger or caviar or some other goody, a hot stuffed potato is an appetite pleaser as well as a money-maker. The profit potential is quite attractive—hot potato stand owners claim $500 to $1,000 weekly in profits. And the business is easy once you have it established in a very-high-traffic (how else can you clear $1,000 with potatoes?) location. Marketing need come only from appetizing signs and free samples (spoonfuls, really) at fairs, shows, and gatherings. You might write the local arenas and ball parks in your area to see if they're interested in a hot potato concession. If you'd like to learn all the good qualities of potatoes, I hereby invite you to go to Idaho and ask any farmer.

# 408 FABULOUS FLOATING FARE

(Setting up a floating snack bar for boaters)   Start up a floating snack bar for boaters and fisherpeople. Use only a bright sign to herald your delectable fare, and travel the lakes, rivers, and bays of your area, fattening the boaters and your wallet at the same time. Not a very tedious business to run (floating on the water is work?), and it can bring a steady stream of income into your life. Investing a few months in getting this going can provide a long-term source of profits as well as an interesting opportunity for expansion. To make money in this endeavor, naturally, you've got to live near an area frequented by boaters, and you've just got to ignore the time-honored advice of "don't go near the water."

# 409 VEHICLE VALET

(Setting up valet parking for a restaurant)   This earnway barely qualifies for a section on food and cooking, but if you can earn a bundle establishing valet parking for a fancy restaurant, I doubt you'll complain. I recommend the fancy type of eatery since you can earn more due to the high tips. (One valet parker here says he earns $300 "on a good night.") Market this service with letters and phone calls to restaurants. You've got to be able to drive (and park) any type of car, regardless of size. And you should have the proper insurance coverage. You'll be paid a fee by the restaurant, a parking fee by the car owner ($1 to $3 these days), plus a big, juicy tip. How much of this should be delegated? Well, I'd delegate all of it, allowing my delegatee to keep all the tips himself along with 50 percent of the parking fees. That still leaves you with plenty. With this easily obtained income, you might be tempted to open valet parking outlets at other restaurants. And you know something? I wouldn't blame you.

# 410 MAIN COURSES

(Raising game as food) Raise rabbits, pheasants, and ducks and sell them as food. That's right: as food. This ain't the animal-lover's section, Charlie. Sell what you raise as fresh main courses by means of mailings to restaurants and small grocers, along with classified ads to the general public. You might expand your offerings by raising other critters that people like to eat. But you can get the thing going with the small selection suggested here. If you want, you can get a farm to raise these main courses for you, and handle the marketing and selling yourself. Or, you can handle the entire show. Once you have a list of regular satisfied customers, you'll find that the marketing will almost take care of itself. But there's still the care of the rabbits, the pheasants, the ducks, and the frogs. The *frogs?*

# 411 THE RECIPE EXCHANGE

(Setting up a place where recipes may be exchanged) This exchange isn't too different in concept from a plant exchange, only it can be run on a national basis. You'll make less money with recipes (maybe only $2 to $5 per recipe), but you'll have a far larger roster of exchange members. Place classified ads in food magazines (*Gourmet* and *Cusine* to start) and in a few Sunday newspapers in major cities. You'll be helping people to exchange recipes, and you'll collect a small fee from each party to the exchange. By consistently advertising, you will be known as a recipe exchange to those who exchange recipes, and that will lead to a small but steady supply of checks, which in turn will lead to peace of mind.

# 412 HEIRLOOM RECIPES

(Selling old family recipes by mail)   If you come from a family that has guarded its old family recipes, it may be time to turn them into a family fortune. You can sell old family recipes. Offer them by mail to restaurants. Offer them by advertising in the classified section of food magazines. I know a woman who has sold her family recipe for English shortbread to over one thousand people. At $3 to $5 per sale (she increased her price), it's too bad she didn't have more recipes to sell. If you do, you're in luck. The more recipes you have and the more places you advertise them, the larger the size of your extra income bank deposits. To see how others do it, I call your attention to the classified section of food magazines. Yep, *Gourmet* and *Cuisine*.

# 413 THE GREAT AMERICAN COOKOFF

(Establishing cooking contests)   Everybody loves a good cookoff, right? Well, some people do. For those who do, establish recipe contests and cookoffs. Get your business going by a mailing to stores that are connected with cooking, and to manufacturers of cooking products. Offer to set up the contest, arrange for the judging, and establish criteria for winners. Naturally, the sponsor of the cookoff stands to gain the most, but the entrants also have fun, especially the winners. And since cookoffs seem to be annual events, you can have a regular source of income from this venture. Figure to earn from $100 to $1,000. Get it by collecting the entry fees and a cut of the sales of whatever products are sold by the sponsor. Here where I live, a cookware store sponsors cookoffs. If you earned 10 per cent of their gross sales during the cookoff events (entering, judging, prize-awarding), you'd exceed the $1,000 figure. You might want to drop a line to the Pillsbury people in Minneapolis to see how they run their bakeoff.

# 414  GOURMET COOKWARE

(Selling gourmet cookware)   Speaking of cookware, there's a whole lot of money in cooking even if you don't ever touch food. Sell gourmet cookware. In 1980, Americans spent over $400 million on specialized cooking items, including kitchen gadgets and serving items. That's why some cookware sellers reported incomes—that means profits, folks—as high as $125,000 in one year. It doesn't take all that much to get involved in this earnway, and your enthusiasm may make up for your lack of cooking experience. As luck would have it, the good old International Entrepreneurs Association offers manual number 142, *Gourmet Cookware Shop*. It should come in very handy for this venture.

If you weren't oriented to things before, perhaps you are now that you realize how you can earn money with things. I hope you will not only have made a number of check marks in this chapter, but will also have realized that it is possible to create a source of income that never ceases, never dries up, never withers away. Many of these earnways require furious start-up efforts, then later provide you with long-term low-effort incomes. All you've got to do is get your business started, work out all the details, get it going smoothly (get the bugs out), then enjoy constant and certain income. You will have created a stream of money that results in regular checks, week in and week out, month in and month out, for years and years.

I'm not talking about tons of money, although I won't say obscene wealth is impossible. But you can have automatic income. You don't get rich, but you don't get ulcers either, and you do get money regularly. As you can plainly see, the methods of obtaining extra money consistently do not entail deep, dark secrets, magic formulas, carefully guarded earning ideas, or intimidation. They do call for research, library time, planning, smart work, hard work, an open mind, and optimism. Many of the methods just revealed have been proven through the years to be producers of cash. Most require no special investment, no mastery of difficult skills. Many can be accomplished by anyone, providing the proper planning is done and detail attended to. Anybody, everybody—including you—could earn money using at least ten or twenty of the earning avenues set down in this chapter. Some people could make a go of two hundred avenues.

If you really want to, you could make many of these methods the main source of your income. But you'll probably find that most do a fine job of supplementing your current income. Many of these earnways are totally compatible with other earnways already listed or about to be listed.

Up to this point, we've concentrated on earning ventures that are for those who are artistic or oriented to people or oriented to things. Certainly, all of us fall into at least one of those categories. But in case you feel uncomfortable in all three, there's another chapter coming up that is directed to those who are oriented to *ideas*. Before delving into that, I want to make clear that nearly every earnway mentioned thus far requires further study and research on your part. I'm sure you already realize that. You can use the recommended publications listed within the earnways as well as the suggested reading at the end of the book for some of that research. But you'll probably have to go to the library, the bookstore, and to people who are already earning money in these ways for the hard information you'll need. The visits will be painless if you realize that they are small but necessary steps toward earning extra money.

Now that we've got all that straightened out, let's examine ways you can earn money because you're fascinated with ideas.

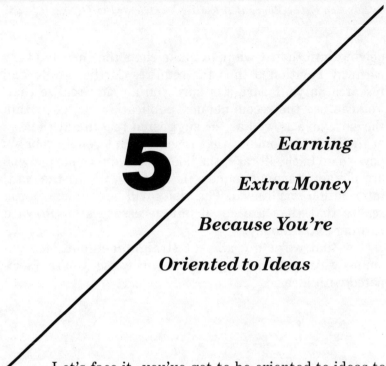

# 5

## Earning
## Extra Money
## Because You're
## Oriented to Ideas

Let's face it, you've got to be oriented to ideas to earn money in the first place, and in that sense every single earnway thus far is centered around an idea.

But there are ideas focused on people, ideas focused on things, and ideas focused on abstract things that are in themselves other ideas. In this chapter, I've divided these other ideas into four sections: business, unique services, printing/publishing, and problem-solving. All four are very idea-oriented, just as you are.

The first section deals with items that most people would automatically put into the category of business. Now of course all 555 earnways in this book are about business. An earnway is a business by its very nature. In fact, the word business is defined as "a profit-seeking enterprise or concern." So if I wanted, I could have called this book *555 Businesses*.

But many people, me included, are put off by the concept of business. "Oh, I don't know anything about business," says the woman who earns $2,000 a month baking cookies. "I'd never go into business; I hate business," says the guy who trains guard dogs at $1,000 per pup. Well, if that's the way they want to perceive life, that's okay with me. But between us, if you earn money on your own, you're in business. Still, the businesses up to this point have been centered around something other than ideas. In this chapter the businesses are idea-oriented, and business itself is one of the ideas.

As with all of the other earnways, those in the next section require you to seek out more information than you'll read in these pages. They require intelligent and well-planned marketing. And they should be combined with other earnways to create your own system of patchwork economics.

Take a moment here to sharpen your pencil, or even your ballpoint if that's what it takes to get you to put check marks next to the earnways that you think look potentially rewarding. Come on—be an active participant in your earning process.

Okay. Now, let's get on with the earning information.

## BUSINESS

# 415 DEDUCTING DAN

(Preparing income tax returns for others)   If you're up on all the income tax laws, and experienced at preparing your own tax forms, you might consider offering an income tax preparation service. Mind, you've got to be at least as good as H&R anyone. But you don't have to be as big. Lots of money-oriented people perform this work and earn their entire year's income during January, February, March, and half of April. Others add enormously to their overall income, for the fact is that you can charge from $50 to $1,000 doing someone else's income tax. The fee depends upon the complexity of the return. Figure on charging $25 to $75 per hour. How to attract customers? A five-media approach might result in all the business you need: notices on bulletin boards, classified ads, Yellow Pages listings, newspaper ads (in February, March, and the first week in April), plus free seminars. Be honest. Be accurate. Be careful. And be informed about the latest IRS guidelines. I sincerely hope that the preparation of tax forms for others propels you into a higher income tax bracket.

# 416 COMPUTER WIZARD

(Writing programs for home and small-business computers)  A very intelligent man once told me that the world is situated in a rather small room these days. He said that connected to this rather small room is a gigantic room. But the only people, he told me, who can gain admittance to that gigantic room are the people who have the key to the door. The key, my friend pointed out, is knowledge of computers. Now I am not trying to tell you that you should go into the computer business. But if you do know about computers, your knowledge can help you do business with virtually any business . . . as well as with a lot of private individuals. More and more people today are purchasing home computers, but they benefit from only a fraction of the potential rewards of computer ownership. That's where you come in. You perform a dazzling array of computer-related services for both individuals and small businesses, computer owners and noncomputer owners. You can use your computer modem to collect information from huge data banks, then sell that information to anyone who needs or wants it. Doesn't matter if they own a computer. You can launch a service that matches parents or students with college scholarship loans, a service that serves as an electronic clipping service, a source of foreign news summaries, specific industry reports, inside sports stories. Computer Wizard *also* publishes newsletters, personalized documents, business presentations, directories—well, you get the idea. You can write programs and application packages for both home and business. Reach prospective customers with direct mail, consistent display ads, and/or classified ads in the "computer" section of your newspaper, with tiny ads in big computer magazines, and with letters to stores that sell computers. List in the Yellow Pages. Do what you can to offer *all* these services, then focus on the two, three, or five that give you the best balance of financial ecstasy and precious freedom.

I hope you earn so much money at this endeavor that you require a state-of-the-moment computer to compute your assets. Charge hourly fees, project fees, or a monthly retainer—ideally, all three—depending on how you use your computer. To become involved in the world beyond the world, start reading five computer magazines and the newspapers in your own town. You'll learn who's offering what, how they're doing it, and a way you can fit right in.

# 417 THE ORGANIZATION ORGANIZATION

(Organizing the time and files of others) Many people are loaded with talent, energy, and brains. The only thing that keeps them separated from success is lack of organization. You can connect them up with success if you handle their organization for them. Show them how to organize their time, their files, and thereby—their lives. Get them into the discipline of working with a daily calendar, with a carefully planned filing system, with advance planning. You can offer your services to individuals, to companies, and to groups. You can attract these customers with local

newspaper ads, even classified ads, with bulletins, and
with informative circulars. People will truly appreciate the contribution you can make to their lives if you
can help them "get organized once and for all." Charge
$25 an hour for your own well-organized time. Lots
of good books on the subject can be found—four of them
right in the appendix, under the listing "Books about Efficiency."

# 418 PAY OR ELSE

(Becoming a collection agency)   Becoming a collection agency
is a method by which you can: (1) earn extra money for
yourself; (2) earn gratitude from your customers; (3)
earn wrath and hatred from those from whom you are
collecting money; (4) earn a guilty conscience for earning
money by such a nasty method. The collecting of money
is not fun, but it is necessary. Because businesses know
it is no fun, they'll gladly turn their collections over
to you—if you can demonstrate that you are good at
collecting. Being good requires persistence, meanness,
clarity of communication, sensitivity, staying within the
bounds of the law (meaning you cannot harass dead-
beats, unless they owe the money directly to *you*), fear-
lessness on the phone, and an unwillingness to take no
for an answer. Given those attributes, you can market
your meanness by direct mail to companies, listing in the
Yellow Pages, a few small display ads in business sections of newspapers, and by offering free seminars on bill
collecting. You might be more of a success at this earning endeavor if you try sweetness rather than toughness.
Expect to earn anywhere from 10 percent to 50 percent
of the money you collect. Bill collecting is ugly, necessary, profitable, and a reasonable earning-from-home-in-
your-spare-time method. Please do not practice on my
account.

# 419 KEEPER OF THE BOOKS

(Free-lance bookkeeping)  Earning extra dollars by doing bookkeeping for small businesses is a far nicer method of survival than bill collecting. Just as necessary and profitable, too. Of course, you require more training to be a bookkeeper than to be a bill collector. Bookkeeping on a part-time basis usually means regular work. It is also a popular earning endeavor in these days of patchwork economics, so expect competition. Attract customers in a myriad of ways: personal contacts to start, also direct mailings of brochures, display ads in business sections of local papers, listing in the Yellow Pages, holding free bookkeeping seminars, even advertising in regional editions of national magazines (then using reprints of the ad in future mailings in which you'll be able to say things like "as advertised in *Time*"). You can market your services with individual letters—in fact, that may be all you need if your skills are high and your prices are low. Charge an hourly fee—$7.50 to $75, depending upon the difficulty of the bookkeeping chore and the value of your input. I know of one bookkeeper who charged $500 for an afternoon and was worth every cent. Although the books listed in this appendix under "Accounting" will help you, practical experience will help even more. On balance, free-lance bookkeeping can do wonders for your profit and loss statement. You do know what a profit and loss statement is, don't you?

# 420 THE PENSION DEPARTMENT

(Setting up pension plans for small businesses)  These days, small businesses are finding it difficult to attract the same quality of employee that signs up to work for large businesses. Why? Because small businesses rarely offer the lush pension plans and profit-sharing plans provided by large businesses. You can change that by offering to serve as the part-time, modular, pension and profit-sharing department for small companies. While many people are beginning to earn impressive sums by this method, the field remains wide open. Get your customers with phone calls, personal letters, direct mailing of brochures, a listing in the Yellow Pages, and by running small display ads in the business sections of local newspapers. Some companies already offer franchises in this field, the most notable being Hicks Corporation, 2416 West Shaw Avenue, Fresno, California 93711. A note to them will obtain for you both the literature and the leads you need to learn more about how you might set up a company in this industry—even working part-time at it. Charge your clients a monthly fee based upon how much of your time is required. If you can set up pension and profit-sharing plans, you might do better than the people who collect the pensions and share in the profits.

# 421 LEAVE YOU A LOAN

(Counseling others on how to obtain business loans)   Some people are able to counsel others on how to get a loan. It's not that hard, though there is a certain mystique surrounding the process. Hence the old joke that if you can prove you don't need a loan, you'll probably get your loan application accepted. The basic trick is preparing a proposal and business plan that impresses the pants off the bank's loan committee. Some people know exactly how to put together such plans, and can counsel you on getting started in this business. They charge a small percentage of the total loan (1 percent to 3 percent), depending upon the size of the loan. So if the loan doesn't come through, they collect zilch. If you're able to make loans come through for others, you can probably obtain appreciative customers with classified ads, display ads in business sections, and direct mailings to banks, asking that they recommend you as a person who can help more people qualify for the loans upon which they thrive. *Guerrilla Financing* by Bruce Blechman and Jay Levinson tells how to obtain money, where to find it, what to say, and what to write, then identifies a treasure trove of alternative funding sources—far beyond banks and rich relatives.

# 422 FILLAFORM

(Filling out forms for others)   If you're looking for a big bucks earnway, skip on down to the next one, for it can bring in a few thou with one good customer. This earnway won't bring in a few thou in a lifetime. But it can and should earn some money for you. Now it's pretty simple to fill out a form for your driver's license. But have you ever tried filling out a form for a grant? For recognition as a nonprofit corporation? No joy, I can assure you. And franchise offering forms are unwieldy as all get-out. Many other types of forms plague many other people. If you can help people fill out complex forms, you can earn a bit of extra money. Market your skills with classified ads, bulletins posted in strategic locations (colleges, banks), and circulars distributed in likely neighborhoods. Charge by the hour ($10 to $50), or get a small percentage of the money at the other end of the forms. Many lawyers earn a good chunk of their incomes as glorified form-fillers. Fillaform won't make you wealthy, only fulfilled.

# 423 BOAT BROKER

(Selecting boats for others)   Offer to find boats for people who are looking for them. It can be difficult and rather time-consuming to shop for boats. And it requires quite a bit of expertise. Some people might be quite happy to hire you and let you do the shopping, looking, surveying, question-asking, and recommending. You'd better be good at all of those aspects of buying a boat before you offer to do it professionally, but for your services you'll be entitled to a portion of the purchase price, possibly payable by both the buyer and the seller. I've heard more than a few stories of boat brokers earning well over $1,000 for finding just the right boat for a delighted customer. Find potential customers, both buyers and sellers, with bulletins posted at local yacht and sailing clubs, classified ads in the boat section of the Sunday paper, those same ads in boating magazines, and even circulars placed on the windshields of cars parked in boat club parking lots. If you're going to make out well in this endeavor, you're probably already familiar with *Boat Owners' Buying Guide.*

# 424   JAY LEVINSON & PARTNERS

(Operating a consulting company) That's the honest-to-goodness name of a real consulting organization made up of one person: me. The partners are the large number of outside suppliers with whom I work when their talents are needed. I consult on the topics of advertising and marketing, career alternatives, and even on the subject of individual enterprise—setting up a business and getting it going. Friends of mine consult on all kinds of topics. These days, seminars, books, and cassettes tell you how to succeed as a consultant. And let me not turn away from my own *Secrets of Successful Free-lancing.* Consulting seems to be a trend for the future as more and more corporations find themselves unable to pay expert staffs on a full-time basis. If you are an expert in any particular field, consider offering your services to business or government in that field, as a consultant. I find it fun, rewarding, profitable, fulfilling, and challenging. I do it from my own home, and I do it only three days a week—hardworking days. That ability to set my own working conditions, hours, and income is a wondrous side benefit of consulting. Almost everyone is an expert on something. Does that mean that almost anyone can be a consultant and earn from $15 to $500 an hour? Beats me. You'll have to check with a consultant consultant.

# 425 WANNA TRADE?

(Establishing a barter exchange) Coordinate a barter exchange in your area and charge a nominal fee ($10 to $25) to both barterers. You'll make out well at both ends. During rough economic times, more and more people are tuning in to the intelligence of bartering. A good barter exchange should provide a good income—if you can line up enough people who have valuable products or services to trade. By offering this barter service to businesses (charge a percentage of the total dollar amount of goods bartered) as well as to the general public, you ought to do twice as well. Line them up with classified and display ads (experiment to find out which is best), along with posted bulletins, and seminars on bartering. A San Francisco man recently earned nearly $150,000 setting up bartering deals for businesses. So if you think you have a good sense of organization and know enough about bartering, this can be a big one.

# 426 FUND FINDER

(Organizing fund-raising benefits) Earn extra money organizing fund-raising benefits for nonprofit organizations. It takes talent, knowledge, energy, and personality. But if you have these attributes, you can collect a fee based upon the funds you raise . . . and that can be a hefty fee—sometimes up in the five-figure range, though more usually it will be two digits less. Many nonprofit organizations are very worthy groups deserving of your talent, knowledge, energy, and personality—not to mention perseverance. And if you can enrich their assets, you deserve all you earn. Direct mail is the best way to approach these nonprofit organizations. Come to think of it, personal letters may be better, and with the current state of word processing technology, your direct mail can look exactly like a personal letter. Any charity work you've done in the past will help you in the future, should you put a check mark by this earnway. Hope you find a lot of funds for yourself while you're the Fund Finder.

# 427 THE BUSINESS MART

(Being a business broker)   Be a business broker. If you check a large metropolitan Sunday classified section under "Business Opportunities," you'll find that you won't be the only one. Business brokers find buyers for businesses that are for sale; they also find businesses for people interested in buying them. This kind of matchmaking earns quite a bit of money for the enterprising broker. You can succeed at this business if you understand the true nature of businesses—what makes them tick or not tick. And you can attract customers with a Yellow Pages listing, small display ads, classified ads, ads in business publications and opportunity magazines, even with occasional commercials on business-oriented radio stations such as all-talk or all-news shows. Truth is, you never know where you'll find a customer. Just call any business broker to inquire what he or she has for sale, and you'll quickly understand what this business is about. I have found it relatively easy to sell even a medium business in a great city to a citizen residing in an ungreat city. No names mentioned, but you know which are the great cities and which are the ungreat ones, don't you? As with other brokerages, you get a teeny portion of the overall selling price. In this case, however, that overall selling price may be anything but teeny. If you help sell a business for $250,000 (not unreasonable for many enterprises), and require a mere 1 percent fee, your cut is $2,500. You don't have to sell many businesses to make a financial success of this baby.

# 428 THE INFORMATION ORGANIZATION

(Conducting market surveys)  You can be The Information Organization if you can conduct market survey interviews. To get started, all you need do is write letters to all the companies that engage in market surveys (get their names by writing to the American Marketing Association, 420 Lexington Avenue, Suite 1733, New York, New York 10170) offering to obtain answers to the questions they are asking. Then, ask the questions either in person or by telephone, whichever is required. You may be able to find all of your respondents in shopping centers, or you may have to go from door to door asking questions. By conscientiously compiling the answers the askers seek, you can earn extra money—not much, but from $25 to $100 weekly, once you connect up with a dynamic research organization. So you won't get rich—unless you combine this earning endeavor with several others. Any questions?

# 429 BLOCK PARTY PEOPLE

(Throwing block parties for retailers)  Next to actual profits and sales, what retailers like best is lots of "traffic." That means loads and loads of people will come into their establishments. How to attract this traffic? Well, advertising to be sure. But also block parties. If you can organize block parties for groups of retailers (not terribly difficult; advertise the parties with newspaper ads and signs in retail store windows), you can earn money and gratitude from local merchants. If you organize four such parties a year, and if you sign up ten retailer groups, that will make forty times a year you'll earn your well-deserved fee ($10 to $50 per retailer per party). You can get retailers to sign up if you contact them with in-person calls, direct mail, and follow-up phone calls. Each retailer pays a rate that covers advertising, party festivities (mime, music, clown, balloons, refreshments, decorations), plus your fee. Learn about promotions that attract traffic by reading *Advertising Age*.

# 430 PARTY PARTIES

(Organizing parties for political purposes)   If you'd rather deal with politicians than retailers, organize parties in support of political people and issues. The purpose of these parties is to raise enough money to garner enough votes for your politician or political issue. Again, you earn a fee for your service—normally a very high fee (in Chicago, a man was paid $5,000 to organize such a party, a minor one at that, for a recent mayor). Get known for your party-giving ability by writing letters to influential members of political parties in your region, or better yet, by making in-person calls. Throwing your first party for no fee might be the best way to get started . . . a marketing technique called sampling. You've got to know the insides and outsides of the political scene in your area—not always an easy or pleasant task—but armed with such awareness you can become known for your prowess in attracting dollars to candidates and can, thereby, become the life of the (political) party.

# 431 LET'S CELEBRATE

(Coordinating events for retailer groups) This company coordinates grand openings and open houses for stores, offices, shopping centers, movies, and more. The work entails enlisting the cooperation of the store, office, or shopping center moguls, handling all decorations, entertainment, hoopla, and refreshments, and publicizing the event to the skies. If this is for you, you'll get a fee—a goodly fee (up to $100 per retailer) if you truly are good, for you'll be earning far more than your fee in sales for your clients. Get the word on yourself out with direct mailings to prospects, enclosing a brochure that describes all of your capabilities. These should be in the areas of organization, publicity knowledge, community awareness, patience, connections, imagination, and unflappability. If you have all of those characteristics, you have good reason to celebrate.

# 432 COMPUTERS TO LET

(Renting time on a computer) Rent time on a computer. Of course, you first have to know how to use a computer, and have one at your disposal, either your own or rented. Then, you can in turn rent time to small firms that cannot afford computers. You can also rent time to enlightened individuals. Advertise your computer usage with small display ads in business sections of newspapers, and mail your brochures (describing the benefits of computer technology along with the benefits of dealing with you) to likely customers. You might even exhibit your computer at a fair and show people the miracles of the computer age. Of course, you should bone up and keep up on the technology by subscribing to one of the many computer magazines. How much you charge will depend upon the sophistication of the machine you rent to your clients and your level of involvement. But this business can provide

the total income for several individuals, so there's got to
be something in it for you.

# 433 AT FINE STORES EVERYWHERE

(Serving as an invention broker)  Maybe you possess both
marketing talent and the knack of tinkering—putting
things together. That may qualify you as an invention
broker. As such, you will help bring inventions to market. Inventors will come to you. After evaluating an invention and your ability to produce and/or market it, you
help get it patented (if it isn't already), then you either
produce it or cause it to be produced by others. Next, you
market it—either directly to the public or through a company or store. You can get the attention of inventors with
ads in scientific magazines and in the Sunday paper. Ordinarily, you earn a portion of what the invention earns—a
royalty (3 percent to 10 percent). Some companies in this
field charge a fee ($300 to $1,000) to inventors. If you do,
be sure you give them their money's worth, and make no
empty promises.

# 434 NOTABLE NOTARY

(Being a notary)  No way you're going to live high off the hog
if your only income is that of a notary, but you will pull in a
few dollars now and then ($3 to $10 per notarization). And
the work sure isn't strenuous. As a notary you will attest
to signatures, and make certain that all papers are in
order. You will then affix your stamp, and everything will
be official—thanks to you. To become a notary, you've
got to fill out forms, pass a test, and be a generally good
person. Then, you can market your notary skills with
Yellow Pages ads and letters to banks and insurance companies, even to lawyers and accountants, offering your
modular notary services.

# 435 READY RENTALS

(Selling lists of apartments and houses for rent)    Because nearly one-third of all the people who rent apartments and houses will move this year, Ready Rentals can put you in possession of some ready money. Contact all the landlords you can (by direct mail), and let them know you'll list their rentals at no cost. They'll probably be delighted because it costs them from $50 on up to list with a real estate agent. Then, with classified ads in the "Rentals" section, let renters know that you have an ever-changing list of rentals, and that they can check your lists for up to one year for a mere $25 or $35. A good deal for the renters since they can save hours of telephoning and driving and inspecting. A good deal for the landlord since he'll have a no-cost vehicle for listing rentals. And a good deal for you since you: (1) won't need a real estate license (in most states), (2) won't require any special schooling; (3) won't have a large overhead—just update your lists weekly, then mail them to people registered with you who request them. With a hundred customers per year, you earn $2,500 to $3,500. With a thousand customers, you earn $25,000 to $35,000. Between us, I'd recommend a thousand customers. The International Entrepreneurs Association offers their manual *Rental List Publishing* to help you.

# 436 TAPE TYPER

(Transcribing dictated tapes)    Specialize in transcribing dictated tapes, that is, turning them into typewritten papers. Many executives like the convenience of machine dictation. Many secretaries hate to take dictation from tape. That's one reason why your service will be valuable. Another is the increasing use of microcassette tape recorders by people other than business executives. To succeed, you've got to be a good listener, good typist, good speller, and good punctuator. If you are, you'll make good money—$10 to $15 per hour, and rising. Market yourself with letters to companies, classified ads under "Services," and ads in writers' magazines. For further enlightenment, I call your attention to *How to Start and Run a Successful Home Typing Business* by Peggy Glenn. She also wrote *Word Processing Profits at Home.*

# 437 HOME GROUND

(Selling vials of earth)  If you're planning to travel abroad extensively, particularly through Europe, consider selling vials of earth from the countries you visit. My inspiration for this earnway is a certain man who has really hit pay dirt with it. He has collected vials of dirt from Poland, England, Germany, Israel, and eight other countries, and he sells them to department stores in the Midwest. The vials are billed as "a piece of home," which indeed they are, and they *sell out* during holiday seasons. Currently he operates his business only in the Midwest, so that leaves the rest of the country to you. Market your vials at gift shows and with mailings direct to stores in your region. Print up affidavits attesting to the authenticity of your soil. And package your vials attractively. You can earn about $2 clear profit per vial and sell thousands of vials, maybe tens of thousands. And that's on top of some enjoyable travel.

# 438 PAID IN FULL

(Operating a bill-paying service)  Even when people have the money to pay their bills, it's a time-consuming, unfun chore. That's why you can earn money with a bill-paying service. You can charge on the basis of how many checks you prepare for your customers, or on an hourly basis. A rate of $5 to $10 an hour seems fair, based on the $7.50 a local check-writer charges. However you charge, you should be prepared to handle the whole process of bill-paying: preparing checks, addressing envelopes, and affixing stamps . . . everything except signing the checks. That part is handled by your clients, before you take care of the mailing. Get those clients with posted bulletins, classified ads, even small display ads in local papers. Just be sure they pay your bill as soon as you've paid theirs.

# 439 THE POLL STAR

(Being a pollster)   The more sophisticated a market or industry, the more likely it is to require research. Research, however, is expensive. That's good for you, because you can earn money from marketing organizations as a pollster—either for your own polling company or someone else's. You can accomplish your polling by phone or mail, in person from a fixed location, or in person while moving about. This earning endeavor includes taking the census (once every ten years, so don't expect steady bucks), polling for a private company (retailer, wholesaler, manufacturer, service organization), or supplementary polling for a professional marketing organization that already conducts polls and may need someone in your area. The real money lies in setting up your own company. Customers for it can be found with well-targeted direct mailings (a good research company can tell you exactly to whom you should send your mailings) and ads in business sections of newspapers or business magazines. Because the money can be so high in this field (a friend of mine in Chicago earns a six-figure annual income doing just this), it might prove worthwhile to visit your local library and lean on the reference librarian. He or she is there to help everyone in the community, not just scholars, so feel free to ask for books on this specific topic, then stand by and watch the resourcefulness of your reference librarian. You'll be impressed, I'll bet. Once you get a business such as this going, you just might find it to be the perfect way to strike a happy balance between money and freedom. Read more about it in the *Journal of Marketing Research* and the *Journal of Marketing*.

# 440 STICK 'EM ON

(Making custom bumper stickers)   An inexpensive printing machine (find several advertised in the opportunity magazines) can put you into the custom bumper sticker business. You can run this business on a local and a national basis—locally by posting signs and running classified ads in the local papers, nationally by running classified ads in carefully selected publications. In the ads, give a few examples of custom bumper stickers, being careful not to include "Help Stamp Out Bumper Stickers." Personal letters to a few stores and businesses might result in volume orders. You can even offer your service to advertising specialty companies and to tourist shops that sell bumper stickers. You can sell individual bumper stickers for $.50 apiece, $.05 in large quantities. Since you'll be able to sell more than ten times as many stickers in bulk as through individual sales, go for the big volume orders. If you're clear on all this, you're ready to consider just what to say on all those bumper stickers for all those bumper sticker lovers.

# 441 LICENSE TO FRAME

(Making custom license frames)   Every motorist has a license to frame, so the market can be enormous, indeed, if you make custom license plate frames. These frames have weird, funny, sex-jokey, religious, political, or chauvinistic sayings such as "Bankers Make Better Lovers" and worse. As with bumper stickers, discover ads for frame-making machines in some of the opportunity magazines listed in the appendix. As with bumper stickers, you can get volume orders from specific businesses or individual orders. Mailings to businesses should accomplish the former; small ads in car buff publications should accomplish the latter. Hit upon some winning frame slogans, then sit back and indulge your license to relax while you're earning. You can clear about $3 per frame.

# 442 THE BED AND BREAKFAST BROKER

(Running a brokerage of bed and breakfast places)   Run newspaper display ads and do a mailing to owners of large houses, apartments, and condos offering to rent out their spare rooms if they provide breakfast for the party doing the renting. Market the rooms as alternatives to hotel rooms, not as alternatives to apartments. For renting out the room and providing breakfast, each cooperating home owner gets a flat (and fat) fee per guest per night. You get a cut of that fee. In my area, a company that started in this business a couple of years ago now has over three hundred rooms for rent, with a virtual sellout during the peak tourist season. Great for everyone: the tourists, the people who rent out their rooms, and especially the company that got the whole thing going. This is a relatively smooth-running business once you've done the initial groundwork. After soliciting, inspecting, and contracting for your rooms, you can obtain customers for your bed and breakfast establishments by mailing your offerings (circulars or brochures, good-looking ones to inspire confidence) to travel agents, by posting signs at tourist attractions, and by running small ads in tourist publications. Just think: if you had 300 rooms for rent at $40 (a reasonable and going rate) per night, and if you rented them all, charging only a 10 percent fee, you'd make $1,200 per *day*. Now, you won't rent all your rooms, but even if you rented half of them, $600 per day ain't hay . . . especially considering that once you get it going, the business pretty much perpetuates itself. To pull this baby off, you should be wonderfully organized, an impeccable host or hostess (so that you know how tourists should be treated), and an expert on your corner of the world.

# 443  HOT NEWS

(Making logs from rolled newspapers)   After taking in $1,200 per day with your bed and breakfast brokerage, it may seem like a comedown to make and sell logs created from rolled newspapers. But such logs are ecologically responsible, burn well, and compare favorably with logs of wood. A simple machine (selling for under $5) makes the logs, and it ought to be relatively easy to get all the old newspapers you want. Sell your newspaper logs with classified ads, at flea markets, with posted bulletins, and with circulars delivered to homes with fireplaces (just note the chimneys around). Since you'll earn only about $.50 to $.75 per log, you'll probably want to have several machines and thereby be able to delegate the rolling and selling chores to others. This is an earning endeavor that fills in the cracks in one's income but rarely, if ever, provides it all.

# 444  FLYING FINGERS

(Being a free-lance typist or word processor operator)   As a further application of earnway number 436, you can earn money as a free-lance typist or word processor operator. Many entrepreneurs, in their attempt to avoid unnecessary overhead, require free-lance typing. Where do they find a free-lance typist? From the mailings you send to

them, from your classified ad in the local newspaper, from
your classified ad in a national writers' magazine, from
your listing in the Yellow Pages, from your posted bulletins, even from your circulars left in stationery stores,
typewriter stores, computer stores, and college stores.
And you can do a mailing to all the businesses in your
area, offering your services on an as-needed basis. Be
sure to read Peggy Glenn's *How to Start and Run a Successful Home Typing Business* and her *Word Processing
Profits at Home*. Charge by the page ($1 to $2) or by the
hour ($6 to $12). With proper marketing, your Flying
Fingers enterprise will get off to a flying start.

# 445 ABSENTEE MANAGEMENT

(Running a business without being there)   Pay close attention
now because this particular earning endeavor is quite different from the others. It calls for you to buy or create a
real business, one that can easily be run in your absence
with its management delegated to someone else. No, I'm
not talking about a business that requires a whole lot of
brains or energy or original thinking. Instead, I'm referring to more mundane businesses such as Laundromats,
dry cleaners, and newsstands. In new communities, businesses such as these are almost certain income producers.
You've got to get them going and keep them going, but
once the doors are open, most of the work can be delegated. Start as small as possible, and lease your equipment to keep your initial expenses down. If they're high,
consider an SBA loan. Location will probably be more
important than marketing (technically, location *is* part of
the marketing process). So concentrate at first on finding
a winning location; don't even think about standard marketing. When the time comes—location located, inventory secured—you can think marketing, especially via
the Yellow Pages and attractive window signs. Bet you

can earn more money doing this than using the same
money for a regular investment. Bet you have more fun,
and more aggravation, too. Bet you can earn up to
$10,000 per year and more if you do it right.

# 446  A.T.&T-SHIRT

(Running a T-shirt enterprise)   With a small heat-transfer machine and a wide and outrageous selection of decals, you can
be in the T-shirt business. This need not be a full-time
operation, and you don't need a store. All you'll require is
space to display your wares (the open cargo space of a
station wagon serves nicely) and a good supply of customers. Get your customers with the right signs, and
maybe even a few small display ads. Park your station
wagon in areas with high foot-traffic. Mailings to businesses might net you some volume customers. It's not
a tough business to start, and the profits are surprisingly high. People who sell T-shirts at rock concerts often
make $500 profit in one night. The International Entre-
preneurs Association (ubiquitous, aren't they?), in their
manual *T-Shirt Shop*, says that the lowest volume shop
they've discovered was doing an average of $823 weekly.
They also will be glad to point out how to gain the
maximum-size sale, and how most T-shirt shops average
about $6,000 per month. If you don't have a shop, but still
earn half that amount, my hat . . . and T-shirt . . . are off
to you.

# 447  CALIFORNIA IMPORTS

(Importing unavailable products to your state)   Offer to sell in
California any type of item or service not yet available in
California. You can do the same in Hawaii, Vermont,
Virginia, Florida, Kansas, and the rest of the United
States, not to mention the rest of the world. If a product

is not available where you live but is available elsewhere, and you feel that your own home-staters might want it, you can gain distribution rights and import it into your state. If you've done a good job of sizing up your state's consumer appetites, the demand may be well in excess of the supply. You'll have to let the actual product or service that you import dictate the methods by which you market it. Once, I imported smoked salmon from the Columbia River via Chicago (for that great Midwest smoking process) to California. I needed no marketing other than inperson sales calls, and the profits were even more delicious than the fish. What could you import?

# 448 LISTS OF LISTS

(Compiling mailing lists)    Earn a whale of a lot of money compiling mailing lists of people in your community. You can learn exactly what types of lists are needed by contacting list brokers in your area (listed under "Mailing Lists" in your Yellow Pages). Since you'll later be selling lists to those same list brokers, be nice to them. They may ask merely for a general list of people in your particular community—that you can get from the phone book, and it won't make you all that much money. For more dollars, you might get the chance to compile lists of house owners, lawyers, owners of Mercedes-Benzes, and homes with school-age children. Such lists can be obtained from established sources such as school records or other records readily available from your local chamber of commerce. To make still larger dollars, walk down streets and make lists of homes that require new roofing, houses in need of exterior paint jobs, unkempt gardens, and homes with old cars parked in front. Sell these names (for $.50 to $1.00 per) to local roofing companies, painting contractors, gardeners, and new-car dealerships. Very valuable, these lists, because they contain the names of prospective customers. And they can be updated regularly (each month, if you want). Plus, they can be extended to include other nearby communities. There is more than a little money in list making. One man reports earning $90,000 in one year doing just what I have described. So I hope list making is on your list of money earners.

# 449 THE PEARL DIVE

(Operating a pearl-diving shop or stand) A small shop or stand, open weekends only or whenever you want to open it, can allow customers to dive for a pearl (actually, reach into an aquarium for an oyster), charging $3.75 to $5.00 per "dive" and guaranteeing a pearl each time. The real money comes when the customer buys a setting for the pearl—at $15.00 to $200.00 a shot. Such an operation can be started for a few thousand dollars, and some stores well engaged in the business report an average gross of $110,000 per year. The marketing should come in the form of newspaper display ads, Yellow Pages ads, publicity stories, even radio and television spots—since the offering is unusual. If you think the International Entrepreneurs Association has a manual on this off-the-wall business, you're right.

# 450 GOOD ECONOMICS

(Interstate buying) Ever notice how the prices of certain items drop drastically as soon as you cross a state line? Well, even if you hadn't noticed, it's true for many items (such as cactus, trucks, wire, crafts, videotape, bricks, candy, and lots more). If you can learn which items are drastically lower-priced in your own state or in the states that are near you, you can establish a business that engages in interstate buying and/or selling. Such businesses can provide tremendous benefits to their customers with virtually no risk to themselves. Market with direct mailings targeted to the people who would most benefit from the lower prices. As soon as you learn which items are available to you at lower prices, their audience will be apparent. For instance, if you learn that you can buy sand at rock-bottom prices in your state, then sell it at considerably higher prices in a neighboring state (making sure your prices are still competitive), you can direct your mailing to all outlets that sell sand. It's a straightforward method of marketing. And a straightforward method of earning money. Just be sure you don't get caught bootlegging to avoid a state's sales tax. I'm happy to say that although the International Entrepreneurs Association has nary a word to say about it, I know of one Arizona man who earns his entire living this way. Earned over $50,000 last year. The harder you look, the more you can earn.

# 451 THE ANTIQUES DEPARTMENT
(Setting up an antiques department in an existing store)
Convince an existing store in your community—furniture store, department store, gift store—that it would greatly benefit from its own antiques department. Explain that if the store allocates some space, you will fill that space with wonderful antiques—and provide the information necessary to sell them. Offer the store a tantalizingly large chunk of the profits. (When the store hears the profit margin in antiques compared with the profit margin at which the store probably operates, it will likely accept your offer with glee.) Let the store owner know that you will even advertise his "antiques department." Then begin running regular Sunday ads in the classified section under "Antiques." Pass out brochures at antiques fairs and flea markets. Place a tiny ad in the Yellow Pages. Even offer to hold a free antiques seminar at the store.

This kind of marketing, if pursued on a continuous basis, will: (1) attract many customers; (2) make the store owner deliriously happy; (3) establish the store as a viable place at which to purchase antiques; (4) provide you with something you've always wanted (lots of money for a long time). It's quite a bit of work at first. But if you play it all right, it'll be well worth the effort. It is worth your while to read a lot about antiques if you pursue this earnway. And you should if you're an antiques buff. Or a money buff: antiques can be purchased by go-getters like you for one-twentieth of their retail value.

# 452 BUCKINGHAM GALLERIES

(Setting up an art gallery in an existing business)    Before you read on about this earnway, understand that I suggest the name Buckingham Galleries only if the store, restaurant, or theater at which you market your art is called the Buckingham Store, Restaurant, or Theater. If it's Sam's Store, then I suggest your business be called Sam's Galleries. (The idea is quite a bit like the preceding one about establishing an antiques department in an existing store.) On the ordinarily dull (not profit-producing) walls of a store, restaurant, or theater, offer to hang stunning and salable art—being especially careful to offer the owner stunning profits. With such an offer, it shouldn't take long until you get an affirmative answer from a retailer, restaurateur, or theater owner with vision (and/or greed). Then, market your art with brochures and signs at the point of purchase, classified ads in the Yellow Pages under "Art Galleries," signs on bulletin boards, brochures handed out to people coming out of art museums, and small display ads in the art section of your Sunday newspaper. In time, the establishment at which your art is displayed will develop a reputation as a good place to purchase art, and all of your hard work will be rewarded.

See *Art in America* to get in on the current art scene, and be very aware of the tastes within your community. You can earn a few hundred dollars a month this laid-back, artistic way. Maybe you can earn even more.

# 453 ON CONSIGNMENT

(Taking goods in on consignment)    Take the concept of setting up an antiques department in an existing store. Mull it over. Then, consider the idea of establishing an art gallery in an existing business. Combine the two and you've got this next business almost all figured out. The store sets aside a small area for you. You fill it with goods you have been given on consignment (meaning: free, until you sell them). They can be records, books, antiques, clocks, or whatever. Then, three things happen: (1) you market the goods with classified ads, signs, circulars, even seminars; (2) customers purchase the goods; (3) the store owner and you profit handsomely and consistently. Some people in this business report profits of $8,000 monthly. To be sure, that's for selling cars on consignment, but who's to stop you from doing that?

# 454 THE PERMANENT GARAGE SALE

(Having a garage sale every weekend)    You can have an every-single-weekend garage sale. No law against it (not here at least; better check in your own community). You can advertise it with signs on trees (just like the usual garage sales), classified ads, signs on bulletin boards, even display ads in newspapers. Naturally, you'd want to pass out brochures to people at flea markets and other garage sales. And the goods you'd sell would be goods taken in on consignment. Now consider this: you can set up your garage sale in space that you rent or in an existing store. Understand that existing stores care how much money per square foot they earn. If you can prove to a store that you can offer a greater dollar volume per foot than it realizes at present, you will have that store owner for a friend. The concept of a permanent garage sale is the powerful idea here—if it is marketed to enough people. There are tales of people earning $1,000 per weekend with their lingering garage sales. Now it's your turn. Where the sale takes place is not as important as the overall idea, for it's fairly easy to see that once this kind of enterprise takes hold, it has the potential of staying around for some time. Read *American Collector* just to keep abreast of the market. And carefully study *Garage Sale Manual* by Jean and Jim Young. You can never tell when a Ming vase will be mingled with a Sears chair.

# 455 THE PROFITEER

(Setting up a new department in an existing store)   Many retail stores do almost everything in their power to maximize profits. However, most of these stores just cannot find the time or talent to establish a new department and maximize its profits. This is where you come in. If you can set up a mail-order department, repair department, delivery and/or installation department, maybe even a rental department—you and the appropriate store could realize exceptional mutual profits. You'll have to get your department running smoothly and oversee it on a regular basis, but then, before long, it can support you and the store in the style to which it would be a joy to become accustomed. How to market your service? Easily, with personal letters and follow-up phone calls to prospective stores. This is not so much a specific earning idea as it is a broad earning concept. But as such, it has the capability of earning a fortune for you. The nature of your own skills and resources should dictate the nature of the department you'll be setting up.

# 456 METER MADE

(Marketing a device that converts U.S. measurements to the metric system)  Like it or not, the United States is converting to the metric system, and you can endear yourself to Americans if you develop and produce a simple metric conversion device such as a slide rule or a cardboard computer (with one "window" showing U.S. measures and the other showing metric measures). Market your device with mailings to sellers of advertising specialties, hoping they will purchase millions of your metric converters. If you don't get what you hope for from the manufacturers, consider marketing the devices yourself with mailings to stores where they might be sold, or even with classified ads—direct to the public. Ideally, you will find someone else (an advertising specialty salesperson) who can sell your device for you while you profit from it for the next one hundred years. Check *Opportunity* magazine and *Specialty Salesman and Entrepreneur* as places to advertise your converter or as places to find salespeople for it.

# 457 PRODUCT SAMPLE INSTITUTE

(Matching sample-giving companies with sample-wanting consumers)  Many companies market their products with free samples. Many consumers love to receive free samples. Your job? Match up the companies with the sample-loving consumers. With small display or classified ads in the local newspaper, you should be able to come up with a sizable list of people who want free samples. You might even charge each person a few dollars per year ($10 to $25) for the privilege of receiving all the free merchandise. Then, sell the list to companies that wish to distribute free samples. They'll be more than happy to learn that you will target their samples to interested people only. So you will make out well at both ends. It will take some time to get your list of sample-lovers, and it will take even more time to line up interested companies (via letters to them). But once you've made the match-up, you ought to profit from it mightily and lengthily. The profits will come from renewing customers, new customers, and companies purchasing the names of the new customers. Done properly, this can be a six-figure-per-year earnway. *Advertising Age* will probably be your best source of sample-giving companies.

# 458 SHOWPLACE ENTERPRISES

(Establishing trade shows) When the water bed business was about four years old, some bright person had the brilliant idea of starting a water bed trade show. He charged manufacturers of all products that might be sold in a water bed store (mattresses, heaters, frames, massage units, pillows, bedding, wall decor, bedroom furniture) a hefty fee (graded according to the number of applicable retailers attending, $250 minimum) for a booth, then invited all the water bed retailers in the United States to attend the show. Because so many retailers accepted their invitations, many manufacturers set up booths and paid through the nose to display their wares. Who won? Everybody: the retailers learned of new products; the manufacturers sold many products; the man who created the show earned so much money that there has now been at least one water bed show every year since. But it needn't just be water beds. These days, new trade shows are being established for new industries: solar energy, wind energy, hang gliding, skiing, and a lot more. Almost all marketing for trade shows is done through direct mailings and ads in trade magazines, though I'm sure a fair amount of inperson calling is necessary, too. From the looks of things, it takes a ton of energy to get the first trade show going, but once it starts it seems to keep going forever. And you can then usually clear in excess of $10,000 in profits per show. You should have an intimate knowledge of a specific industry, as many contacts as possible in that industry, a terrific sense of organization, and the ability to delegate small tasks to many people. You work about two or three months per year setting up a show, so it is necessary to have that amount of time available. To learn more about trade shows, you have only to look in the many trade magazines listed in the appendix. Start with *Tradeshow/Convention Guide*. And consider attending any and all trade shows in your area.

# 459 INSTANT SOUVENIRS

(Marketing timely souvenirs) If you have an eagle eye for noteworthy events, you can make a small fortune as a marketer of souvenirs commemorating those events. When Mt. St. Helens spewed its volcanic effluvia across the Pacific Northwest, many eager earners earned loads of money selling souvenir containers of volcanic ash. When the San Francisco Forty-Niners won their second Super Bowl in a row, some creative earner spotted the possibilities of hitting it big with T-shirts saying "ThreePeat," and because so many Niner fans loved the very idea of a third consecutive victory, zillions (okay, maybe only trillions) of T-shirts and sweatshirts were sold. You can do the same if you are quick to recognize the opportunity and to put your ideas into production. Market them with in-person calls to stores, through reps who make sales calls for you, or through ads in the classified section of the local newspaper. Or you can sell your brainstorm by mail, with display ads in newspapers and magazines. Once you establish momentum in this type of endeavor, it will be easier with each new item. Soon, all you may have to do is make a phone call to start the wheels rolling and the money rolling in. By far your best source of inspiration is your daily newspaper on the day of a dramatic event.

# 460 PETALPUSHER

(Selling roses to men in the company of women) Let roses make money for you. Let pretty young women sell them for you, one at a time, $1 each, in nightclubs and restaurants. Each of your rosepushers will call on about ten locations per night, offering to sell the roses to men who are escorting women. Naturally, most men will accept, knowing full well that a single red rose carries with it a message of love. An energetic rosepusher ought to be able to sell about two hundred roses per night. With a sales force of five, that comes to $1,000 per night. If you pay $.25 for each rose and $.25 commission per rose, you still make a healthy $500 per night. And if your rosepushers hawk their roses five nights a week, you will be the happy recipient of $2,500 weekly. Naturally, the International Entrepreneurs Association publishes a manual, *Flower Vending*, which tells you more. It won't necessarily be as rosy as earning $2,500 every week, but if you play your cards right (market your roses with attractive signs and attractive women), you can reap a large amount of green as a red petalpusher.

# 461 THE TRAVELING DEPARTMENT STORE

(Selling from a van in rural areas) Check out several rural areas to learn what commodities residents are unable to purchase in their local stores. Then, stock a truck or van with the very items they are lacking, and travel through the selected areas offering your goodies for sale. You'll be very much appreciated, even though, or even because, you show up only a few times a month. Advertise your service with ads in the local rural papers, commercials on their radio stations (delightfully inexpensive), and a clear, confidence-inspiring sign on your vehicle. Expand your inventory as you learn the needs of each community, and keep making regular runs—once a week, or once every two weeks, or even once a month. You should be attuned not only to the needs and lacks of rural communities, but also to retailing in general. Once you have a good idea of the merchandise you should be selling, the costs to run your operation, and the maximum profits you can realize, you might even delegate the traveling to some other willing earner, limiting your own travel to going to and from the bank. My rural spies tell me you can earn about $250 profit per town per sales call. So if you call on four towns in one day, you're doing all right—to say the least.

## 462  PLEASURE PALACE

(A place where people can enjoy the pleasures of life)   Provide a place where people can partake of pleasure. Such a place might offer massages, to be sure, but there are many other pleasurable offerings to consider: hot tubs, saunas and steam rooms, water beds for resting, biofeedback machines, videodisc players, stereo headphones with a wide selection of music. For nongambling gaming you could provide video games, pinball machines, pool tables, and Ping-Pong tables. Think of anything that's pleasurable. And legal. Lease as many items as possible, and recognize that many game machine companies will give you good hard cash ($5,000 to $15,000) for agreeing to install their machines. Got it all going? Okay, advertise it with display ads in the entertainment section of the Sunday paper. See if you can interest a local TV station in doing a free segment on your pleasure palace (they might; it sure would be newsworthy enough). And, of course, have a pleasing sign out front. You've got to use your imagination and inherent sense of hedonism to apply yourself to this unique earnway, for although all of these pleasurable offerings are to be found elsewhere, with information available on each, nowhere are they all under one roof. Put them there and you can earn big money making other people's pleasure your business.

# 463 THE HAPPY MEDIUM

(Developing a new advertising medium)   Invent a new advertising medium for your area and sell advertising space on it. Such a new vehicle might be ads on benches, ads on a car or van that travels through high-population areas, sandwich-board ads worn by willing walkers, even ads in a local TV-listing publication that you have created. Or you could develop a local entertainment newsletter and sell space to advertisers. There are loads of possibilities. Once you have your medium, give it a message with which to advertise it *on itself* (such as a bench billing itself as an effective advertising medium), and do mailings to businesses and advertising agencies. New media seem to be springing up all over the place (especially TV listings and entertainment guides). With enough bright thinking you ought to be able to develop an advertising medium that can earn money for you ($10,000 per year in profits is not unusual) for years and years.

# 464 LEASE ART

(Leasing art to corporations)   Lease Art mails a letter to a large selection of talented artists, explaining that Lease Art is an art rental business and offering to rent the paintings of these artists. Once you have a decent collection, prepare a brochure and mail it to large and medium-sized corporations. Offer to set up an entire art collection for them on a rental basis. Tell them that you'll not only provide the framed artwork, but will also hang it for them if they'd like (at an extra charge). Then, let them have the collection for, say, two months. You get paid a lump sum for the two-month rental. From that sum, you must pay each artist a rental fee, handle your overhead, and be sure money is left over for you. A woman who runs an art rental business says that each month with three collections on show (about fifteen paintings per collection), more than $1,000 is left over for her, and she's aiming to increase the size of the leftovers. Once you've got the kinks ironed out for one collection, establish a second, third, and fourth collection, and try to keep them all rented out simultaneously, even on a rotating basis. Along the way you'll be earning enough capital to expand and to live well during the expansion process. Eventually you should be able to provide companies with year-round rotating art collections on a rental basis, providing you in turn with the assurance of being paid twelve months a year, not just two months a year, for a long-term source of money. It won't hurt you to check out a few copies of *Rental Age*.

# 465 RUBBER STAMP HEADQUARTERS

(Making rubber stamps)   After straining your brain to make a success of Lease Art, here's an opportunity to rest it with a real no-brainer. Go into the business of making rubber stamps. A rubber stamp–making machine is about all you'll need. Market your service with a Yellow Pages listing, a regular classified ad, and a circular distributed to everyone in your area who may need a rubber stamp. According to the Rubber Stamp Division of Warner Electric Company (1512 Jarvis, Chicago, Illinois 60626), beginners can earn up to $22.50 an hour at this endeavor, and Warner Electric will be glad to send you a 104-page book showing how to do it. You may not make the cover of *Fortune*, but you will find that many businesses need rubber stamps. And if yours are competitively priced, companies will buy them from you. Joyous? Nope. Easy? Yep.

# 466 PET TAG

(Selling I.D. tags for pets)   Help keep Rover from getting lost and Tabby from disappearing by selling I.D. tags for pets. Sell them directly to pet stores with in-person calls, or persuade the stores to let you post your signs with them. Sell them to pet owners with signs on bulletin boards and circulars distributed directly to them. Place classified ads in the pet section of the Sunday newspaper. You'll need an engraving machine to imprint the name and address of the pet, along with the name and phone number of the pet owner. Again, not a very imaginative business, but one for which you will be appreciated. By pet owners, by pets, and by the dog pound. Don't expect big bucks, but do expect repeat orders from pet stores. This is a rather commonplace earning endeavor, I'm told.

# 467 TAILOR MAID (OR TAILOR MAN)

(Being a tailor and mender)   If you're looking for a glamorous method of earning extra money, better hurry ahead—this idea suggests that you earn your money simply by being a tailor and mender. Naturally, a sewing machine will help, as will good sewing and mending skills. Without question, this is an almost automatic source of income, for those skills are fundamental, continually required, and necessary almost everywhere. Let the world know of your talents with mailings to cleaning establishments and clothing stores, along with classified ads and signs on bulletin boards. Even if your modular services are engaged by local cleaning establishments, you can do the work from your own home, so you won't require much in the way of overhead. According to people who already do this, you charge by the project ($7.50 per hem, for example), which can work out to about $15.00 to $20.00 per hour. And the work comes in regularly. In time, you'll find this unglamorous earnway to be a consistent contributor to your coffers.

# 468 TELERIDE

(Providing rides and passengers by telephone)  Teleride is a phone switchboard service that provides both rides for passengers and passengers for drivers to long-distance destinations. Teleride attracts business with signs on bulletin boards, especially near college campuses, and gets even more business with regular classified ads in the Sunday paper in the rides or transportation section. Teleride charges a fee ($15 to $25) to both the passenger and the rider, but refunds the fee if a ride cannot be worked out. Recently, my daughter and a friend were about to embark on a two-thousand-mile drive. They called a company such as Teleride (found in the Sunday classified section), paid the fee requested ($15 in this case), and soon were furnished with two passengers who shared driving and gas expenses. Who came out best on the deal? You know the answer: Everyone did. Bet you can be a winner with Teleride.

# 469 KIDS TO GO

(Creating a pickup and delivery service focused on children)  Create a pickup and delivery service that concentrates strictly on children. If you figure the demand for such a service to be sufficient in your area, you might contract with an existing van/bus service for their van and driver.

Then, obtain customers by mailings to schools, nurseries, and day care centers. Let them know that you will be a reliable service for picking kids up at their homes or wherever. In addition, parents can arrange to have their kids picked up at school or wherever and dropped off back at home. Most school kids are transported very well by their own two feet and by school buses, but many of them cannot be transported as easily to or from the many other places they might want or need to get to, much to the anguish and inconvenience of their parents. That's why your service will be appreciated and employed for years to come. After you've got the whole thing running smoothly, you can figure on clearing about $15 per kid per week—and that's after you delegate the hard work (the driving). Don't forget, it's not going to be as simple as I've made it sound in these few sentences. You'll have to deal with a lawyer to learn of all legal and insurance implications; you'll have to deal with an accountant to learn how best to set up your service and handle the finances; you'll have to get along well with owners of the bus service, bus drivers, school officials, parents, and kids; and you'll *always* have to be reliable. But you know all that, don't you?

# 470 BUSYWORK

(Addressing and stuffing envelopes)   If enough people know that you will always be available for addressing and stuffing envelopes, enough people will sign up for your services so that you'll end up with a small but appreciable income from this busy work. The way to spread the word is to mail circulars to printing firms, direct-mail houses, and businesses in your community that engage in direct mailings. Because direct mail is a marketing tool that is best when used regularly, you can count on regular income if you let it be known that you provide these services regularly. The work can be done from your home, requires little concentration, and is something hardly anyone likes to do. That's why you'll be an appreciated member of your community while earning your appreciable income. Beware of those ads that promise big money stuffing envelopes at home. Those are usually mail-order schemes that provide big money for the people offering them, and not for you. But by charging, say, $.03 per envelope addressed and stuffed, the 2,500 envelopes you'll work on will net you a real $75.00.

# 471 OMNI STENOGRAPHY

(Offering a full range of stenographic services) If you name your business Omni Stenography, you ought to offer a complete range of steno services: dictation in person, dictation by phone, dictation by cassette tape. This goes beyond the normal typing service. Offering it should net you quite a bit of stenographic business, if you put out the word the right way. That would be with mailings to offices and with classified ads. A Yellow Pages listing is also in order. Figure on earning $10 per hour or so. With such a broad offering and consistent marketing, and if you're good, you'll turn your talents into instant income.

# 472 FLEA WITH FLAIR

(Starting a flea market) Start a flea market. It's not as hard as you might think—just read *Garage Sale Manual* and the International Entrepreneurs Association's manual, *Flea Market and Swap Meet Promoting*. But such a business is not easy, either. First, you arrange for the weekend rental of a lot of land within an hour's drive of a major population area. (It's an advantage, of course, to start your flea market where no regular one exists.) Then, you run classified ads, and direct a mailing to people known for selling at flea markets, informing them of your new market-to-be. You charge each stallholder a flat fee ($25 to $100) and, one hopes, attract a large crowd with publicity, display ads in the newspaper, and radio commercials. After a while, you won't have to do any advertising, for the word will spread. Because you can charge a stallholder fee *plus* a percentage of sales, it's said you can work two days a week and earn $220,000 a year. Some flea markets earn money for their promoters by charging admission fees, too. In fact, $1.5 million in income has been reported by some flea market operators. Considering it costs just a few hundred to get into the business, it may be worth looking into. Once again, you need a strong organizational ability and a knack for selecting the right location.

# 473 THE FLOWER HOUR

(Selling flowers to homebound motorists)   During the evening commuting hours you can earn extra money by means of pretty girls in long dresses (maybe that can be you; sure can't be me) selling flowers to homebound motorists. Stationed at corners where there are stoplights—or at least stop signs—they can offer inexpensive ($2.00 to $5.00) bouquets to weary commuters. The pretty girls and their long dresses will be just about the only marketing tool you will require, though signs will help, too. If you sell your bouquets at $2.00, and give each salesgirl $1.00, you can still clear $.50 per. And it's not uncommon to sell a hundred bouquets per location. So you'll earn $50 per day per location. You can be sure of gaining steady customers if your flowers are always fresh, beautiful, and attractively wrapped. By varying the flowers, you can help commuters surprise their spouses each day. Not a difficult business to start. Not much experience required. So go do it.

# 474 FRANCHISE ANGEL

(Sharing in the cost of a franchise)   If you happen to have a healthy savings account, stocks, bonds, Treasury bills, money under your mattress, or any type of investment, you should examine the possibility of using that money to share the cost of a franchise. Get a line on which one by studying the *Franchise Opportunities Handbook* published by the Department of Commerce and the *Inc.* magazine annual directory of franchises. Many franchises earn their owners far more than do standard investments. If you can get in on such a franchise, you can use your imagination and energy to make the operation even more profitable than it would normally be, and you can have the fun of contributing to its growth, all without the day-to-day responsibilities of running it. A lot of today's franchises are owned by investment groups, and I know from firsthand experience that many of the group members laugh at the folks whose money remains invested in savings accounts, stocks, bonds, or Treasury bills. Some of these groupies earn a full 100 percent return on their investments (that's doubling it, folks) with hardly any drain on their time. They fully understand why over 90 percent of franchises will still be in business after five years. Select a franchise that matches your own line of expertise. Marketing? Don't worry about it. The franchise manager will take care of it for you.

# 475 SILENCE IS GOLDEN

(Being a silent partner)   Of all 555 ways to earn extra money, perhaps the biggest no-brainer of all is to become a silent partner. To become one, you need three things: (1) enough money to become a partner in the first place; (2) enough judgment to select a business that will turn your investment into income; (3) enough savvy to make sure that a bright, effective, honest person is the unsilent partner. But if you have that money, judgment, and savvy, you can rest assured that gaining your income will not tax your brainpower in any way. Okay now, shhhhh!

# 476 AT YOUR SERVICE

(Being a service broker)  Be a service broker. Using your telephone plus classified ads in the newspaper, line up as many independent contractors as possible. Check them out carefully. Then, run display ads in the newspaper offering their services. Charge your customers a flat fee ($10 to $35) for access to a service contractor (always having ascertained the competence of that contractor). In time, you will have satisfied customers who know they can trust your recommendations, satisfied contractors who are grateful that you handled the marketing for them, and a steady and good-sized income. That ought to satisfy you. A company such as I've just described started up in my area a couple of years ago. Called themselves Whim. They are now so successful that they have expanded to several other U.S. cities. There are no books on this concept as yet, so you're on your own. You'll succeed if you are organized, informed as to the needs and resources of your community, and a person who is honest, customer-oriented, and pleasant. Whim is all of these things.

# 477 ON COURSE

(Offering courses comprised of existing materials)  Notable experts in many fields have published books and papers, written workbooks, and made cassette recordings of their teachings. If you coordinate their materials, you can offer topflight courses. And you won't have to do any of the teaching yourself. A man in the furniture industry earns in excess of $100,000 yearly doing just this—part-time. With enough research out front, you can combine the teachings of several authorities into the best course ever offered on the subject. Market your courses with classified ads in national magazines and newspapers, signs on bulletin boards, and with display ads in selected regional editions of national magazines, along with trade magazines. Mailings to people who take correspondence courses would also be in order. If you play your cards right on this one, you can have an entire school comprised of your preexisting books and tapes. And you can have a pretty large part-time income as a result.

# 478 THE SUCCESS INSTITUTE

(Copying successful mail-order offerings)   If ever there was a sure way to earn a part-time income, this is it. Go to your library. Get current copies of a couple of opportunity magazines (see the appendix of this book for the names of a few). Get year-old copies of the same magazines. Then, carefully go through the magazines, noting which ads appeared in both the year-old copy and the current copy. You can be fairly sure that any ads thus repeated were winners. People will not repeat unsuccessful ads over the course of a year, but they will repeat successful ads. Copy their offerings. Copy the merchandise they offer, the medium in which they advertise, and their basic advertisement. Don't copy them to a point where you can be sued for plagiarism, but copy the basics. If someone else is making money selling address labels, get a slice of that pie for yourself. It's a large pie. If another person is earning extra money selling aerosol alarms, go into the aerosol alarm business yourself. Not a lot of brains are required to earn income in this way, but common sense should tell you that this is as certain a money-maker as you'll find. I think *surefire* is the word. Market your items the same way your competition markets them—with small display or classified ads in opportunity magazines, maybe even in consumer or trade publications, perhaps even in newspapers. Check as many opportunity magazines as possible so you can get a fix on which ones are working for the person you are copying . . . or rather, are inspired by. I think you will be both gladdened and amazed at how many earning endeavors are copyable. So go to it. But whatever you do, *don't* write a book about 555 ways to earn extra money.

# 479 BILLING UNLIMITED

(Operating a billing service)   Provide a billing service for the businesses (and professionals) in your community, including people such as yourself who are earning extra money on their own. Most any billing for services rendered is somewhat of a bother, and by eliminating the bother for others, you can create extra income for yourself. Once you get the billing procedures down pat, you will find this a relatively easy way to earn. Market your billing service with a mailing to the business community, with small display ads in the business section of the newspaper, and with circulars distributed to any business that may be a prospect. Charge by how many bills you must type and mail, typically $.50 to $1.00 per bill, with a $25.00 monthly minimum. I'm sure you will be reliable, and if you are, you will succeed.

# 480 CASH FOR SALE

(Marketing shredded money)   Looking for an unusual way to earn extra money? Market shredded money. The law states that banks must shred their old money, but the law does not tell them where to dispose of it. By coming up with gift items that use shredded money, you can earn quite a bit of unshredded money. Examples: one company sells paperweights filled with shredded cash; another sells plastic see-through writing pens with shredded currency inside; some companies market plastic eggs and nests with shredded money as the nesting material. Your local bank will ordinarily give you the shredded money or sell you large amounts of it for tiny sums. Market your items either through the mail, with ads in national magazines and newspapers, or directly to retailers. Some department stores already offer such items. The government does demand that you comply with certain regulations if you are going to go into the shredded cash biz: You must seal the cash permanently in glass or plastic, and you must not use the shreds to manufacture paper suitable for commercial printing. To be able to buy or receive shredded currency and go into this money-minded business, you must first write to the U.S. Treasury Department in Washington, DC, submitting your product idea. The great majority of those ideas (95 percent) are approved. And of course the more ideas you have, the greater can be the size of your extra income, for once you have the idea and the processes for manufacturing and marketing that product, the income it brings you will be as steady as it is appreciated.

# 481 THE POSTAL STORE

(Operating a small mail-order business) Probably the single most common source of extra income for individual entrepreneurs is the mail-order business. I believe that anyone who is interested in earning extra money should have a small mail-order business going. I'm not talking about making millions in mail order, just thousands, even hundreds. I earn several hundred dollars a month with a piddling mail-order business, and I spend no more than half an hour a month keeping it going. Yet it's been going and growing for seven years now. In order to succeed at mail order, you've got to have four things. First, you need the right product or service. Second, you need the right message with which to advertise your product or service. Third, you need the right place in which to put your advertisement. And fourth, you need the information contained in some of the mail-order books, most specifically, *How You Too Can Make At Least $1 Million (But Probably Much More) in the Mail-Order Business* by Gerardo Joffe, or better still, *How to Build a Great Fortune in Mail Order* by the same Mr. Joffe (the latter consisting of seven volumes of solid information and examples). Mr. Joffe's book and seven-volume course are easily the best works on the topic of mail-order that I have ever read, and I've read a lot. For all the other good books on the subject, Mr. Joffe's writings spell out the details in the most realistic fashion. But you needn't emulate Mr. Joffe—who did earn millions in the mail-order business, though working at it full-time (starting in his forties). I'm suggesting that you work at it just part of the time. Set it up so that you have a formula for selecting products, writing ads, and either placing ads or selecting lists for direct mail. Ordinarily, a successful mail-order company starts with small display or classified ads, then it compiles its own list of customers and makes them offers via direct mail, and finally it publishes a catalog and goes after the megabucks. I'm happy to report that the stories of people who get started from their kitchen tables are true; you do not need a whole lot of equipment or space to begin. But I will not try to delude you into thinking this is a very simple business. Proof of that is before you in my inability to do the business justice with just a few pages. I do, however, call your attention to my book, *Earning Money Without a Job*, wherein half a chapter is devoted to the intriguing mail-order business, with lots of juicy details. To be sure, mail order is a business that can earn you a consistent income. I suggest that you mail-order only categories of items that appeal to you personally. That means if you're into fishing, go into the fishing equipment mail-order business. In sum, mail-order marketing is gigantic and getting bigger, so it is worth your examination if you seriously wish to earn extra money. Profit margins run as high as 700 percent; the energy crisis and increasing sophistication of mail-order companies make it one of the fastest-growing industries; and the convenience of mail order cannot be overstated. In 1990, over $100 billion of America's retail business went into the mail rather than over the counter. Listen, take out a subscription to *Direct Marketing* and see for yourself.

## UNIQUE SERVICES

# 482 TRAVELING TERRY'S TRIP SERVICE

(Helping plan trips to places you know)   You should not consider earning money along these lines if you don't have detailed knowledge about one or more exciting places. But if you have spent time in places that many people visit, you might be able to offer more valuable information than a travel agency. You need not make reservations for prospective travelers, only provide them with inside tips about eating, places to stay, spots off the beaten track, and locales not found in the usual guidebooks. People offering this type of service charge from $50 to $75 per hour, figuring that's a mere pittance compared with the overall cost of the vacation. How to reach customers? Classified ads, small regional magazine ads, circulars, even direct mail if you can target your audience. The nicest thing about this earning endeavor is its rather glorious fringe benefit: the more you travel, the better you become at your job. The fact remains that the best source of information about this earnway is another visit to the place or places about which you will be consulting.

# 483 RENT-A-SPOUSE

(Providing homemaking services and then some) Rent-A-Spouse, modeled after a similar company in my parts, might offer to greet guests, beat carpets, shop for food, fix a table, decorate a room, paint a wall, pay bills, take relatives on a tour, meet people at the airport, and maybe even more. All for $15 to $20 per hour. If you can and want to do these things, you'll find people who need these things done. Advertise in local newspapers, on local radio stations, in the classified ads under services, and with posted bulletins. The answer to the question that may have entered your mind by now is no.

# 484 DISPLAYS ON WHEELS

(Organizing traveling displays) Organize traveling displays or exhibitions for companies, and take them to public places such as libraries, airports, hotels, and other spots where a lot of people are to be found indoors. You can make your displays a kind of advertising medium for companies to show their wares. Get to those companies with direct mailings and ads in business sections of newspapers. You'll be surprised at how many will want you to take their products to public places. And you'll be delighted at how much they'll pay. Charge them a fee based on the complexity of the display itself, the number of people who will see it, and how long the display will be displayed. It can range from $250 to $1,500. *Advertising Age* can shed more light on this.

# 485 STARGAZINGS

(Preparing astrological charts)   Prepare complex astrological charts for a stiff fee ($25 to $100). Since the astrology section is the most widely read section in the newspaper, find your customers with ads placed as near to that section as possible. Direct mailings to astrologically attuned folks (get their names from mailing list companies) will also net customers. If you can get behind this idea, you might also consider phrenology (reading the bumps on heads) and palm reading. I see loads of palm reading and other psychic-type ads in the classified section of my local newspaper, under the heading of "Announcements." It seems that astrologers, phrenologists, and palm readers flourish at fairs, so you might follow their marketing example. If you don't really believe in these pseudosciences (don't shoot!), try earning your money elsewhere, but if you're convinced that your horoscope is right on target daily, you'll find that there are lots of other people just like you. Learn a bit more (a lot more) by reading *The Coffee Table Book of Astrology*. And keep in mind that this is the age of Aquarius. (That's me.)

# 486 TAN YOUR HIDE

(Running a suntanning center)   As evidenced by all the suntanning centers that have sprung up in the United States since 1978, you can tan other people's hides in your spare time. All you need are ultraviolet bulbs plus tanning booths. Maybe you can put the booths in your basement, garage, or spare room. Maybe you'll want to rent space. All year long, people can come to you for Florida (or Hawaii) tans. You can attract them with small display ads in the main news section of your newspaper, and with posted bulletins, classified ads, and radio commercials run on local stations. The usual charge is $5 for ten minutes of "sun," so the profits, you can see, can become as brilliant as your tanning lights. If you're figuring that the International Entrepreneurs Association has checked this one out, you're right. *Suntanning Centers* covers the business in great detail. It sure doesn't take much work or talent on your part. Just be careful you don't burn any of your clientele.

# 487 CAREER HEADQUARTERS

(Serving as a career counselor)    One of the most difficult decisions a human must make is the choice of a career. Often, that human has very little data upon which to base his or her decision, other than a gut feeling and a general education. Worse still, the average American now faces the prospect of three separate and distinct careers, so thrice the career aid is required these days. That's why your services as a career counselor will be so valuable. But first, you've got to know about people and work, be able to administer the proper aptitude tests, and have the ability to interpret the tests and make intelligent recommendations. There's a group now that trains career counselors—the National Career Development Project. You'll find their address in the appendix; they'll be happy (for $1) to supply you with people in your area who have completed their 120 hours of training. Once you have that training, through them or anyone else, market your talents with Yellow Pages ads, in bulletins for educational institutions, with display ads in college and metropolitan newspapers, and via direct mail to educational counselors. In my opinion, this necessary profession is bound to grow during the 1990s and beyond as increasingly enlightened people give more thought to their career selection. If you become a career counselor you will deserve the $20 to $50 hourly charge you can levy. Yours will be a necessary profession, and you'll be a valued addition to your community if not your planet.

# 488 THE SHOPPING CONSULTANT

(Consulting with others on their shopping) Yep, this earning endeavor is exactly what you think it is. You consult with others for clothes shopping, furniture shopping, car shopping, anything shopping. Charge a small percentage of the amount they spend (with a minimum charge) or set a flat hourly fee—in the area of $10 per hour. Attract customers with classified ads in the newspapers and, if you live in a tourist-frequented town, with ads in tourist publications. You'll be pleasantly surprised at how many people require your services. You've got to know your way around your town and its stores, and be up on the current prices. In addition, you should know where to find the best selections, the hard-to-locate items, and the best bargains. Plus, you should be a pleasant person. With those attributes, you've got what it takes to succeed. But I must ask you to make me a promise: that you will never consult with my wife or daughter. They both know all they have to know about shopping, thank you.

# 489 LEGAL EAGLE

(Serving as a legal investigator) You don't need a law degree to serve as a legal investigator. Many practicing professionals with law degrees are just too busy to conduct their own investigations, so they'll be pleased to hire you. A friend of mine worked as a legal investigator while he was getting his own law degree. He was paid $7.50 per hour in the early seventies, and I've been informed that the fee has more than doubled since. Moreover, it's something you can do part-time, virtually anywhere that lots of lawyers may be found. Get your business started by

running classified ads in legal journals and by mailing
your credentials (in a brochure) to lawyers around town.
It's fun, and it's rarely dangerous. In fact, legal investi-
gating is often more boring than dangerous. Not that Sam
Spade would agree.

# 490 IN BRIEF

(Speed-reading and outlining books)    When I was at the University of Colorado, skiing and matriculating simul-
taneously, a certain book digest publication got me
through some boring literature classes and boring
authors. I would have been a good customer for this
earnway. If you know how to speed-read or can learn
how, you can speed-read assigned books in colleges and
sell outlines of those books to students. You can also
speed-read and outline the many new business books
that astute businesspeople should be reading. The *Wall
Street Journal* recently reported that many executives
are turning to digests and consultants to help them cope
with a flood of reading matter. One 216-page book was
turned into a nifty 4-page outline, outraging the author. Soundview Books of Darien, Connecticut, rewrites
business books condensing them into 4- to 8-page summaries, selling thirty of them per year for a $50 subscrip-
tion fee. At this writing, five thousand subscribers are
reported. And that's just one of several such services.
You might charge as much as $5 per outline copy for your
own such service, considering how much time you'll be
saving your customers. Market your outlines with ads in
student and business newspapers, also bulletins in
dorms, clubs, and school cafeterias. And for the executive
trade, get hold of one or more industry directories and try
a direct-mail campaign to your own selected list of company officers.

# 491 TAKEN FOR GRANTED

(Being a grant consultant)   Become a grant consultant. Learn how to wade through those complicated grant forms. Talk to foundations to see exactly what they base their granting on. Research the many organizations with grant money. You'll learn a lot by studying the *Annual Register of Grant Support*, listed in this appendix and to be found in your local library. More information comes from *Foundation 500*, published by the Foundation Research Service, 39 East 51st Street, New York, New York 10022. And there are other books on the subject, too. You'll earn a percentage of the total grant—a goodly sum since most grants are for large amounts of money. Attract business by placing ads in scholarly and scientific magazines (classified if possible), sending letters to granting organizations letting them know you're a grant consultant, and distributing your card to any other people who might vaguely connect up with people seeking grants (find them in universities, hospitals, law offices, cultural groups). Your service will be much appreciated by those people who deserve grants but can't make their way through the paperwork or untangle the red tape.

# 492 TOP MANAGEMENT

(Managing an apartment building)   While you may not earn much money managing an apartment building, you should at least earn your entire rent. And that sure counts for something in a system of patchwork economics, leaving you free, as it does, to pursue lots of other earnways. Most likely, you'll put in only a few hours a week for your free rent, and most of the work will be troubleshooting. You'll have to be able to show apartments for rent, handle tenant problems, and collect rents on time. You won't have to fix the furnace, though you will have to locate the

janitor so he can fix the furnace. Not a very difficult job.
Not hard to obtain in a big city. Not a bad idea. Check the
classifieds under "Help Wanted" any Sunday and you may
find yourself in top management quicker than you think.
My mother-in-law, while in her seventies, handled this
job with aplomb.

# 493 PARTY PLANNER

(Planning parties for others)   If you've been complimented on
your parties, you might be good enough to be a professional
party planner. Many people throwing parties desperately
need your services. So let them know that you can handle
everything from the invitations to the catering, from the
entertainment to cleaning up afterward, from the liquor
shopping to the decorations. Best places to herald your
services would be the Yellow Pages, the classified section
under "Entertainment," and through the mail with brochures to clubs and organizations that throw parties.
Give each of your clients several business cards so that
they may pass them on to people who said they loved the
party. Generally, this work goes for a flat fee, depending
upon the size of the party. From $100 to $1,000 is the
common range. Whoopee!

# 494 GUINEA PIG LIMITED

(Being a professional experimental subject)   Not a very glamorous name for an earning endeavor, this one. Small
wonder—being a professional experimental subject for
scientific studies is not the world's most glamorous work.
But interesting, yes. At least sometimes. Letters to universities and laboratories, plus scanning of classified sections (especially under "Announcements") for ads
requesting experimental subjects will put you in touch
with the experiment grapevine. Some of the studies in

which you may become involved will be boring boring boring. Others may be so fascinating that you may wish they were a bit more boring. In today's newspaper I noticed a NASA ad requesting women fifty-five to sixty-five for a "vital space study." Hmmm, wonder what they have in mind? Other ads have requested volunteers for studies involving sleep, marijuana, loneliness, and stress. Most such projects involve a single chunk of time—one to four weeks, or even more. Even though the NASA experiment will have been completed, you might contact Management Systems Associates, Inc. at (415) 964-0702 to see what's doing the day you read this page. The pay usually isn't enough to make you rich, but you're too busy being a guinea pig to spend what you do earn. As one who earned a few dollars and a few credits in college as an experimental subject, I can assure you that I was both bored and overstimulated as a guinea pig. Suggestion: Be more anxious to become a subject for a psychological study than for a drug study.

# 495 THE INVESTIGATION ORGANIZATION

(Doing insurance and retail credit investigations) You can call yourself The Investigation Organization if you serve as a part-time insurance and/or retail credit investigator. As such, you'll ask questions about applicants for certain types of insurance or credit, filling out forms as you do. You'll ask the questions right in the applicant's neighborhood. And you'll secure employment by writing to the insurance and retail credit companies in your area (try looking up Equifax in your directory). The work is usually available and the pay comes to around $5 to $10 per hour, though some companies pay by the report. When I served as an insurance investigator while attending college, I considered it a good part-time earning endeavor—

glad to have it temporarily, glad not to do it on a full-time basis. All that the insurance or retail credit companies want is the answers to their questions. So the hours and days you work are up to you.

# 496 PRIME MOVER

(Being a moving consultant)  Of the 35,000 ways to earn money listed by the U.S. government and the 555 ways listed by this U.S. citizen, one of the more unusual but useful ways is to be a moving consultant. You can do your consulting on both sides of the move. For people about to leave, you can help with selecting a moving company, packing, planning, and being there on the day of the moving out. For people about to arrive, you can help with being there on the day of moving in, acquainting them with the community, and unpacking and putting things away. My wife and I have moved more times than I care to recollect. But I do recollect that your services were needed every time. Where were you when we needed you, Prime Mover? Had you advertised in the Yellow Pages, the classified section under "Moving," or even with circulars, we would have heard of you. Had you engaged in a mailing to large companies whose employees move frequently, we would have heard of you. Had you mailed your brochure to our moving companies, we would have heard of you. And we'd have ever-so-gladly paid the $10 to $20 you'd justifiably have charged as your per hour fee. Oh well, maybe you'll be around next move. Next move? No way.

# 497 PUT IT IN WRITING

(Engaging in handwriting analysis)  There seems to be quite a bit of substance to the findings of handwriting analysts, or graphology experts, as they're called. You may want to study this science, then earn extra money analyzing the handwriting of others. You can offer your services with mailings to police departments and large corporations. You can also use classified ads in national magazines to offer to analyze handwriting. Because there is a lot of science in this endeavor, so much so that computers now aid in handwriting analysis, please don't embark upon it unless you really know your stuff on other people's handwriting, or are prepared to learn it. But if you do, you can charge from $10 for an analysis at a fairground to $25 for an analysis by mail to $100 for an analysis for a professional group such as a corporation or law enforcement agency. Once you do know your business, you'll have the pleasure of analyzing the handwriting on many a check made out to you. And when the police aren't asking you to solve a major case, don't forget you can ply your trade at a fair.

# 498  I AUTO BUY

(Consulting on the purchase of automobiles)   Maybe you know a lot about cars. That knowledge can be turned into income if you offer to select cars, especially used cars, for others. Most people are at a loss in a used-car lot, unable to tell a clunker from a classic. But you can. So you should (and can) be paid a fee for selecting the exact car your clients need. By saving them a lot of money and aggravation, you can make yourself quite a bit of money. Some car-buying consultants charge a percentage of the purchase price; others charge an hourly rate starting at $10, with a minimum fee of $60. Get customers with ads in the used-car section of the classifieds, plus posted signs on bulletin boards. This business is already going on in several U.S. cities, and you can be sure the people engaged in it do a lot more than kick tires.

# 499 OUNCE OF PREVENTION

(Serving as a disaster consultant)   I hope nobody ever has to appreciate the work you do in this earnway, but advising people as a disaster consultant can be important work. That's right—a disaster consultant—one who prepares people's homes, pantries, water supplies, water heaters, light sources, communications sources, foundations, and lives for the possibilities of earthquakes, blizzards, fires, volcanic eruptions, floods, nuclear wars, hurricanes, typhoons, seiches, tidal waves, and disease epidemics. Not pleasant subjects. So most people know little about preparing for them. That leads to loss of life and property. So your input can save life and property. But only if you're proficient, only if you know what you're consulting about. You will notice a number of ads for these people in Miami following a hurricane, in Portland following a volcanic eruption, and in San Francisco and/or Los Angeles following an earthquake. Obtain business, as these existing disaster consultants do, with small display newspaper ads, classified ads, brochures distributed in public places, and with free publicity stories. Almost every area of the country is subject to one form of disaster or another. Here in California, earthquake counseling costs $25 per hour for information only, or a flat $150 for information plus emergency supplies. Such supplies include a safe store of food and water, a transistor radio, a fire extinguisher, an escape ladder, smoke alarms, flashlights, and a list of evacuation procedures. In flood-prone areas, it also helps to know where high ground is. And in the beautiful San Francisco Bay area, earthquake-proofing the hot-water heater and the foundation is serious business, too.

# 500 THE SETTLER

(Mediating) The judicial system is clogged with pending cases, most of which never need to be brought to court. That's why the field of arbitration is growing. And that's exactly what you might consider being—a professional mediator. In Robert Heinlein's fine novel *Stranger in a Strange Land*, he writes of a future day when such people are known as fair witnesses. Well, fair witnesses already exist, and with the support of several legal professionals, you could be one. You should have some legal experience to engage in this pursuit, and as with many of the other 554 ways to earn extra money, this earnway is more complex than it seems on paper. Still, it might be simpler than you suppose. A growing number of people avoid litigation through arbitration. You can attract business with a Yellow Pages listing under "Arbitrators & Mediators," and with mailings to lawyers, advising them to put the concept of arbitration in contracts and noting that you offer such a service. The current pay for an arbitrator runs in the area of $150 for a half-day.

# 501 RELIABLE RINGING

(Running a wake-up and reminder service) Establish a wake-up and reminder service. Offer to phone people at agreed-upon times so that they can get up on time, remember an anniversary, not be late for the ballet, pay that bill, collect that money, or do any one of a host of tasks for which you will be paid to remind them. Charge a per-call rate with a monthly minimum. The minimum should be around $15.00 to $25.00 with $.25 to $.50 per call as the standard rate. Just be sure your calls are always on time. Advertise your reliable ringing with small display or classified ads in the newspaper, signs on bulletin boards, even a distribution of circulars. In addition to phoning, you'll have to handle your own billing. Other than that, this is a simple and effective business. I know a woman with ten regular clients; she spends about ten minutes per day awakening them by phone. In return, she receives $250 per month. She claims the only drawback to this earnway is an inability to sleep late. Quite true.

# 502 GO NATIVE TOURS

(Running a touring service)   The big tour buses can go only where big buses fit and only to places where many people don't create a crowded feeling. That's why your own touring service, operating with a mere van or car, with its ability to reach those hard-to-get-to places and its lack of capacity for crowded loads, might be a real small-crowd-pleaser—taking a few people at a time (no more than you can fit into your van or car) to off-the-beaten-track points of interest. Leave the tourist attractions to the tourists using the big buses. You can show your customers aspects of the area reserved only for its native inhabitants. That's why it will be worth the $50 per day you charge each customer. Almost any city or area is worth touring if the person conducting the tour is a positive perceiver, knows the history of the area, is enthusiastic, and can offer true insights to a visitor. Lay out several tours, and attract customers by means of mailings to travel agents, distribution of circulars, placing of signs in high-tourist-traffic locales, and running ads in tourist magazines. Naturally, you'll want to put a captivating sign on your touring vehicle. Good luck. I'll bet you prosper as the tourists go native.

# 503 INVENTORY AID

(Helping others take inventory)   If you've ever worked in a retail store, you know it is one big drag to take inventory. But that inventory must be done. You can help do it by offering your services to retail stores via mailings, delivered circulars, and ads in the Yellow Pages under "Inventory Svce." Just let them know you'll be available (at $10 to $15 per hour) when it's time to take inventory. Boy, will they love you! As prosaic as this earnway may sound, it is an almost surefire money-earner. So if you want to find a need and fill it, taking inventory is the need, and your willingness to help take inventory fills it.

# 504 ENERGY ECONOMICS

(Consulting on energy conservation)   There are more energy-saving devices available now than ever before. Some are very simple to install, others are computerized and quite complex; almost all of them result in a real saving of energy. With the right devices, a substantial saving of energy (and money) can be achieved. This new technology is not understood by many people who would otherwise own the contraptions. Enter you. You consult with families about energy conservation, then possibly sell and definitely install energy-saving devices. Display and/or classified ads tell of your service. But mailings to home owners will most likely result in the most business for you. New thermal cameras pinpoint heat loss right on the spot, and with heating and air conditioning bills up 200 percent to 600 percent (and even more) since the mid-seventies, heat loss is money loss. Some states share with home owners the cost of an energy survey, with 10 percent of the cost paid by the home owners and 90 percent by a combination of federal funds and utility company funds. You might check your state's policy to see if they can furnish some help for you here. Some contractors in this business are grossing $500,000 per year, with the average around $150,000. The International Entrepreneurs Association publishes *Energy Loss Prevention* to shed further light on this earnway. If you know its contents, your customers will benefit, you will benefit, and so will America's energy situation.

# 505 SCENE SCOUT

(Scouting locations for film scenes)    If films are made where you live, you can earn extra money by scouting locations for the producers. Having used such a service when producing TV commercials, I've been very impressed with the expertise of the scouts we've used. By writing to film production companies, you might find yourself with some well-heeled customers willing to pay the $100 per day you demand (and get, because that's a competitive price). Offer to scout for movies, TV commercials, or TV shows. You, or at least the person to whom you delegate the scouting, must have a detailed knowledge of your region. In truth, the work is so much fun (once I accompanied a scout on his day, and it was one gigantic joy), you probably won't delegate. If that's the case, up and at 'em, scout.

# 506 WINTER WAYS

(Providing a winter sight-seeing service)    If you can get your thermal-mittened hands on a snowmobile, jeep, or sleigh, consider earning money by providing a winter sight-seeing service. Many absolutely gorgeous places are inaccessible during winter—except to snowmobiles, jeeps, and sleighs. Of course, all of these places are also accessible to people with cross-country skis. But however you get around, the concept of winter sight-seeing will be pleasing to many people. They'll pay around $10 to $20 for a two- or three-hour tour, and they'll find out about your service by means of your posted signs, ads in tourist publications, classified ads, and signs at your point of origin. And let's not forget the sign on your snowmobile, jeep, or sleigh, eh?

# 507 THE BOARD OF BULLETINS

(Posting bulletins professionally)  When I suggest that you advertise an earnway by posting signs on bulletin boards, who do you suppose actually posts all those signs? Sometimes it's you, but often it's a professional bulletin-poster. Such a person maintains bulletin boards in countless locations: supermarkets, Laundromats, schools, bookstores, depots, clubs, churches, and the like. Such a person could be you if you inaugurate a bulletin board posting service. This is a new and effective job in the media, and it can be yours at a handsome profit. Charge by how long the message will stay up and upon how many boards it will appear. Example: $10 per month per board will net you $100 if you have ten boards. And that's for just one client. Suppose you have one hundred clients . . . you can see how it adds up. Advertise your service with letters to frequent advertisers, with bulletins on your own bulletin boards, with mailings to the media departments of local ad agencies, with classified ads, and even with a listing in the Yellow Pages under "Bulletin & Directory Boards." You can enter this business from the standpoint of maintaining the boards, posting the bulletins, or both.

# 508 BIGFOOT TOURING SERVICE

(Conducting walking tours)  The best way to see most cities is on foot. That's why walking tours are so popular in London and Paris. But for some reason, you don't find walking tours in many American cities. Certainly our cities could be viewed by tourists on foot just as nicely as the cities of Europe, and with the energy situation what it is, it sure makes sense to tour a city by walking around. An ideal situation for a practitioner of patchwork economics, right? Right. Place display ads in tourist publications.

Place classified ads in local newspapers. Put up signs at tourist attractions. Then, get set to give slow, leisurely, fact-filled walking tours lasting from two to six hours—charging each tourist $10 to $20 for the tour. You've got to know your locale, its history, and several colorful tales. During the heart of the tourist season, you might have as many as four tour departures per Saturday and four more per Sunday. So have several people on foot—er, on hand—to lead your tours for you. To learn how a walking tour might be set up, read *The Bay Area at Your Feet* by Margot Patterson Doss.

# 509 UPSTANDING UPHOLSTERY

(Reupholstering furniture)   Let's get this straight right out front: it is not easy to reupholster furniture, nor is it easy to repair damaged upholstered furniture. There. Now that you know the facts, you should realize that you will need training and information to start a business of reupholstering and repairing upholstered furniture. Armed with this training—best obtained at a school or in an apprenticeship—you ought to make out quite well with display ads, classified ads, circulars distributed to home and condo owners, and signs on the right bulletin boards. Ads in the Yellow Pages will help, too. Set up your fees so that you end up clearing between $15 and $25 per hour for your newly acquired skills. I know a person who learned the craft, made quite a bit of money at it, then quit because it was so darn hard. So perhaps the greatest help you can give yourself will come at that moment when your brilliant marketing efforts will enable you to delegate the actual work to a pro upholsterer.

# 510 THE SHOP HOPPER

(Shopping for others)   Some people love to shop (my wife).

Some people hate to shop (me). If you're more like me than my wife, you'll understand why people will gladly pay someone else to do their shopping for them. Such a Shop Hopper will advertise in the classified section, post signs, and even distribute circulars outside shopping plazas. Then, that person will, for a fee, handle all the food, clothes, and any other shopping that the client desires. Ideally, a person like me would run this business, then delegate all the shopping to a person like my wife. Figure that you can charge from $10 to $15 per hour for this unique service.

# 511 STAND-IN

(Standing in line for others)   All set for an off-the-wall earn-way? Here goes. Because so many people just detest standing in line, you can make money by standing in line for them. That's right. Charge someone a fee ($5 to $10 per hour) for standing in line for him or her. Among the famous lines that need stand-ins are lines to buy World Series tickets, Super Bowl tickets, and a few other kinds of tickets. People would pay (and have paid) fancy sums to have someone spend several hours standing in the hot sun or cold wind for them. Marketing need be accomplished only by distributing circulars to people already lined up, or by walking along the line holding a sign saying that you'll stand in line for anyone for a price. Bet you'll get takers from virtually every long line. Zero experience needed. But a folding chair will help immensely. Say, you might consider renting folding chairs!

# 512 SNUG, SAFE, AND SECURE

(Acting as a security guard)   Be a part-time security guard and keep things snug, safe, and secure. It takes minimal training and experience to succeed at this endeavor. The company hiring you will provide all the information and security education. And the work can be handled on a part-time basis. Advertise your availability to guard with letters to all businesses and buildings that might need your services. Figure on earning from $7.50 to $12.50 per hour. And then, by putting several people together into a security network, you might find yourself as the owner of a snug, safe, and secure business. Just be careful you never fall asleep on the job.

# 513 BOUNTEOUS BASKETS

(Compiling personalized gift baskets)  A wonderfully unique and appreciated service is that of creating gift baskets. What kind of gifts? Any kind. The woman who runs this service in Chicago fills some gift baskets with food, others with wine, others with clothing, others with books, and others with, well, other things. (She even once created an erotic gift basket, but I don't know what was in it. Hmmm . . .) The idea is to offer your basket-compiling services to others by means of classified and display newspaper ads, then charging either an hourly rate ($10 to $15) or a straight percentage of the total price. Depending upon the basket, the total price can run as high as $500 (even more for a jewelry gift basket I guess). The Chicago entrepreneur gained quite a bit of free publicity by giving free baskets to visiting celebrities who in turn told the local radio, TV, and newspaper people about them. By offering personalized gift baskets you provide a memorable gift for the gift-giver, a delightful gift for the gift-receiver, and a gift of extra income for yourself.

# 514 FOLLOW-UPPER

(Following up on the projects of others)  Many people begin projects and then lose interest. They may start on a needlepoint pillow or a brick barbecue or a furniture refinishing job or whatever, but then fail to complete the project. You can earn money as a professional follow-upper, simply by offering to complete their projects for them. Make your offering with classified ads in local newspapers, with signs on bulletin boards, and with a free publicity story explaining your unique service. You'll certainly earn whatever your hourly charge happens to be, because if you can be the same person who completes a needlepoint pillow one day and finishes off a brick barbecue the next, you are entitled to rich rewards.

## 515 PERFECT ATTENDANCE

(Attending events for others)    Attend classes or lectures for others who cannot attend. Offer this service with ads in school newspapers and with postings on bulletin boards. Ideally, word-of-mouth advertising will cause further growth, as it does in just about any business. Keep good notes for the person hiring you, and make a copy of the notes so that you can show prospective customers what a conscientious class-attender you are. Charge about $10 per hour, depending upon the current economic situation at the time. And you'll even learn as you earn.

## 516 ALL-AMERICAN HOUSE-SITTING

(House-sitting)    You may not earn much money, but you certainly can save on your housing costs if you're a professional house-sitter. When people go away on their holidays, they usually need a person to tend their plants, feed and let out their pets, and generally keep an eye on their homes. Where do they find such a person? Through your classified ads, Yellow Pages listing, posted signs on bulletin boards in affluent neighborhoods, and circulars distributed in shopping centers of wealthy suburbs. Naturally, it would be just wonderful if your service required a fee in addition to the free housing, and indeed many people will pay a nominal fee such as $10 per day.

# 517 HARD-TO-GET NEWS

(Selling and delivering hard-to-get newspapers)  Provide a service that sells and/or delivers desirable out-of-town newspapers. Such newspapers usually include *The New York Times*, *The Times* (*London*), the *Wall Street Journal*, plus a wide assortment of other big-city dailies away from those big cities. Market your ability to offer this service with classified ads run once a week, plus display ads run once a month in the main news section of your Sunday paper. Accompany this propaganda with signs on bulletin boards, a tiny listing in the Yellow Pages under "Newspapers," and a mailing to a targeted audience. Naturally, the farther you are from the city from which you offer the paper, the more attractive your offering. Perhaps that's why a 400 percent markup is not unusual. So let your geography dictate your selection.

# 518 OFF THE BEATEN TRACK

(Arranging tours)  Be a tour arranger. You've got to have some training in the travel business, plus instincts for the people business. And you've got to have an intimate knowledge of the areas to which you will arrange tours. Then, you've got to make arrangements with transportation companies, hotels, tour guides, restaurants, and possibly more unusual contributors such as local celebrities. That accomplished, you've got to attract people to take your tours. Do it with unique ads in the travel section of the Sunday paper, with signs on bulletin boards, with brochures (unique brochures, mind you) handed out at shows, even with mailings to known tour-takers. If your tours are unusual enough, you might be able to fill each one with grateful travelers while filling your bank account with warmly received (and well-deserved) profits. As you can easily see, this one asks that you put forth a Herculean effort at the outset—but after that, it's Easy Street. At the very worst, you'll get a free vacation or two. At best, you'll earn tens of thousands of dollars per year. A twenty-four-year-old tour arranger last year earned $30,000 doing exactly what I have outlined here. And that was for all of four months of work.

# 519 MAGIC CARPET TRANSIT
(Transporting the elderly) Establish a transportation service that is devoted to the elderly. As with a similar service for kids (number 469), contract with a bus or van service for a vehicle and driver. Then market your service with mailings to senior citizens' homes, bulletins in senior citizens' buildings, and ads in senior citizen newspapers. Such a service would benefit the customers, the bus service contractor, and you. Charge enough so that the bus owner, the driver, and you make out well. And don't forget, for you, personally, the hardest work will be at the beginning. Once you get this going, you can be almost certain it will continue moving.

# 520 MONEY FOR SALE
(Compiling packets of foreign currency) From the time I lived in Europe, I remember well the confusion of dealing with foreign currency. I was not alone in my confusion. You can end that confusion for many fledgling world travelers by compiling foreign currency packets with clear explanations of currency equivalents and informative data re-

garding items such as tipping and taxes. It is not expensive, the compiling of such packets, yet you can sell them at wonderfully high (55 percent) profit margins. Truth is, your profits will be well earned, for you'll be providing a worthwhile and necessary service. Market your services with signs in international airports, circulars distributed to travelers in these airports, small display or classified ads in national travel publications, and mailings to travel agencies. A mailing to airport shops would be a good idea, for then, ideally, you could get someone else to sell the packets you compile. If that should happen, you'd be making a lot more money than you'd be selling.

# 521 THE GENIAL GENEALOGIST

(Tracing family trees)   Ever since the astounding success of "Roots" on TV, many American families have tried to trace their family trees. *Tried* is the key word, because genealogy is easier imagined than actually traced. Still, with effort and patience, with study and research, you can be a successful genealogist and offer to trace the roots of many American families. Market your services with ads in national magazine classified sections, ads in local classified sections under "Announcements," publicity stories (this is a natural for free coverage), and exhibits at fairs and shows of family trees you have traced. Be sure you train a budding genealogist to follow in your footsteps, because if you're good, you'll have quite a few trees to trace. I'm told (by one who wrote a check for the service) that tree-tracing can run up to $1,000 per family. Read *Trace Your Own Roots Workbook* to get in on the fun and profits. You might want to look under "Genealogists" in your Yellow Pages (there are three in my directory) and pay them their consulting fee for consulting about their field with you. If they're really *genial*, they'll gladly tell all.

# 522 THE RECYCLIST

(Recycling virtually anything) Improve the planet and your bank account by providing bottle, can, paper, and plastic recycling. Classified ads, signs on bulletin boards, free publicity stories, and a sign at your recycling center (the place where items to be recycled are brought) can net the customers for you. Be sure you know ahead of time exactly what you will do with the bottles, cans, paper, and plastic products you will be recycling. That means you should have customers (usually companies) all lined up wanting them. Companies pay $50 per ton for used newsprint, $75 for used cardboard, $110 for used high-grade office paper. In time, your venture will be appreciated by the community, by the people getting rid of their "garbage," and by future populations of the earth. As a side benefit, you'll profit ($100 to $300 per month once you get started, since you'll be selling by weight). You might also consider recycling organic waste—known during these energy-shortage days as biomass. Get a lead on this business with the International Entrepreneurs Association's manual on *Paper Recycling*. Or talk to the managers of the recycling centers listed in your Yellow Pages (twelve are listed in the San Francisco directory).

# 523 THE TOY EXCHANGE

(Setting up a toy exchange) By the time you finish this book, you may get the idea (and rightly so) that income can be earned quite easily by those who set up exchanges. Good thinking. A toy exchange may be advertised with classified ads, mailings to nursery schools, circulars handed to parents in playgrounds, and signs on bulletin boards. Although it is kind to give used toys to charity, tight economic conditions make it more practical to exchange them. To a kid, a new toy is exciting whether it is really new or merely new to the kid. Again, you charge fees ($2 or $3) to both exchangers.

# 524 THE BABY-SITTING EXCHANGE

(Setting up a baby-sitting exchange)   My wife and I were once members of a baby-sitting exchange that arranged for free sitters in return for an annual fee. We would call the exchange to get a free sitter, and sometimes the exchange would call us requesting that we provide free sitting services. Everyone who was a member of the exchange had to exchange free baby-sitting time, and as I recall, all members paid a yearly fee ($25, and that was back in the sixties) to the person who set up the exchange. That person can now be you. Obtain customers with signs on bulletin boards (that's how we learned of the exchange), and mailings to nursery schools. Get 300 customers; earn $7,500. Raise your fee to $50; earn $15,000. Bet your community appreciates it if you get this baby going.

# 525 PEN PALS INTERNATIONAL

(Establishing a correspondence club)   The human need for friendship is satisfied, partially, by having a pen pal. But where does one find a pen pal? Through your organization, if you'd like to set one up. You'd probably have to run classified ads in national newspapers (plus international newspapers), along with a few selected national magazines. You'd charge a fee ($10 to $25) to each member. This would be an annual fee, for which you'd furnish each prospective pen pal with the particulars of several other prospective pen pals. Consistent advertising, the key to most business successes, will turn this venture into a source of happiness to others and a source of income to you. Sincerely yours, Jay.

# 526 THE TRAVELERS' EXCHANGE

(Setting up an exchange for travelers)   Traveling is fun, but more fun with a partner. Guess what? The Travelers' Exchange provides partners. Register them when they send you their fees ($30 to $50) with their travel dates and destinations. They'll then be sent a list of companions from whom they may choose. These companions will have much in common: they're going to the same (or nearby) place; they're going at the same time; they don't want to travel alone. The Travelers' Exchange attracts customers with mailings to travel agencies, signs on bulletin boards, and classified ads. Probably you can run those same classified ads in travel magazines and, as display ads, in the travel sections of the Sunday paper.

# 527 THE ROOMIE EXCHANGE

(Setting up an exchange for roommates)   With rentals soaring, it's not too easy to afford a rented house or apartment without a roommate. But where do you find a roommate? Right, you establish a roommate exchange service by running classified ads in the Sunday paper and by posting signs on bulletin boards. Charge a fee ($25 to $50) for registration, and that's about all you've got to do to earn money at this endeavor. Oh, you've also got to match roommates together. But that's not too difficult or time-consuming. Like setting up any other exchange, it requires a good sense of organization, especially in your filing system, and more work in the beginning than at any other time. And, of course, regular advertising will make the business work. The International Entrepreneurs Association writes about a woman who made $60,000 in one year at this business, and they predict it will be as big as the employment agency business by 1990. To learn more, you might want to look over their manual, *Roommate-Finding Service.*

# 528 BOOK AND RECORD EXCHANGE

(Setting up an exchange for books and records)   I certainly don't have to tell you that zillions of people would be willing to exchange books that they've read or records they've played hundreds of times for books that they haven't read or records they want. You can earn extra money if you can facilitate such an exchange. Do it with the inevitable signs on bulletin boards and with classified ads. Do it also by distributing circulars at flea markets. Each party to the exchange pays you a small ($1) fee. But as you become known as a source of good books and records, albeit used, you will become known at your bank as a regular depositor.

# 529 THE RIGHT ANSWER

(Running an answering service)   Earn extra money by starting up an answering service. You can handle the answering yourself and do it from home. Or you can delegate the answering to someone else and do your earning away from home. Attract business by listing your service in the Yellow Pages, by running small classified ads, and by phoning businesses and individuals that ought to employ your answering service. Although telephone answering devices are increasingly popular, many people will have nothing to do with them. That's why your answering service can prove to be a success for years to come. The best way to make this business work is to sign up customers at extremely low introductory rates, then keep them as you raise your rates (because your service is so friendly, accurate, and on the ball). The International Entrepreneurs Association tells us that a typical one-office operation grosses about $200,000 annually and takes home 35 percent net profits. They tell even more in their manual *Telephone Answering Service.* As you may have heard, the majority of lost business is lost because of apathy after the initial sale. So, especially on this earnway, be sure you do not fall into that trap. Always maintain enthusiasm and friendliness, and you'll earn real money as an answering service.

# 530 IN OTHER WORDS
(Operating a translating service)   Do you speak a foreign language? Do you have friends or family who speak other foreign languages? You do? Great! You can start a translating service. List it in the Yellow Pages. Put up signs on bulletin boards. Place display ads in the business section of the newspaper. You might even place classified ads in national newspapers and magazines, since this business can be handled easily by mail. As with virtually every other business listed, time will be your ally. And with enough time, the word will spread. Charge either by the hour or the project. One way or the other, you should arrange to clear $15 or so per hour. Eventually, find people who speak other languages so you can broaden your offerings. *Comprende?*

# 531 AQUARIUS
(Delivering water on a regular basis)   The zodiac sign Aquarius is the sign of the Water Bearer. If you become Aquarius, that's what you'll be doing to earn extra money. Allow people to *subscribe* to your water. Deliver fresh spring water to your people once a week, collecting their empty bottles with each delivery. You can market this business with mailings to residents of a community. If the mailing brochure shows a highly magnified view of a single drop

of the water that comes from their taps, you should have little trouble attracting business. Abet your marketing with newspaper display ads and signs on bulletin boards. As long as you keep your water pure, your prices competitive, and your deliveries regular, you can be assured of a continuing income—$.25 to $.50 per gallon bottle.

## 532 LIGHT UP THE SKY

(Leasing out a searchlight)   Please don't do this in my neighborhood, but you might consider earning extra money by purchasing or leasing a searchlight, then renting it out for store or showroom promotions. These attention-getting devices are used during sales, grand openings, special events, and slow periods because they do generate a feeling of excitement. You have the choice of operating the light yourself or turning that part over to another person. A listing in the Yellow Pages and a mailing to prospective retailers are the main marketing tools you'll need. And once your searchlight offering becomes part of your business community's awareness, it can be a brilliant source of income. Currently, it costs $50 per hour, with a four-hour minimum, to rent a searchlight.

## 533 TELEVISION MONITOR

(Monitoring TV commercials)   What happens when an advertiser pays a bundle for a TV commercial and then the commercial gets bungled in transmission? What happens is that the advertiser loses out . . . unless a TV monitoring service was employed to check up and see that the commercial ran as planned. You can earn extra money just by watching TV if you pay close attention to the commercials and keep a written record of when they run. Mailings to media-buying services will put you on the track of the existing monitoring companies who may wish to take advantage of your kind offer and pay you for your services. You can even establish your own monitoring service if you limit it to your own locality and have a video-cassette recorder to pick up the stations you're not watching.

## PRINTING/PUBLISHING

## 534 HOW-TO-DO-IT PUBLISHING COMPANY

(Publishing how-to or problem-solving books) Many people need to be told exactly how to do things, and if you can tell them in writing, they'll gladly buy your books. The most reasonable topics to consider are those dealing with solutions to problems. Such problems include how to: quit smoking, lose weight, keep a marriage solid, find a mate, make money, get promoted, make household repairs, keep cars in shipshape, invest money wisely, protect money already saved, and achieve a blissful sex life. By writing such how-to books, or even by finding someone else to write them for you, you can become a well-compensated member of the publishing world. Book publishing requires knowledge of writing, typesetting, book design, printing, binding, distributing, and selling. *The Rogue of Publishers' Row* by Edward Uhlan shows how one person succeeded in this endeavor. You can either publish and promote the books yourself—a good idea if you can zero in on your audience—or you can find a willing publisher. I did.

## 535 GO-FOR-BROKE PRINTING BROKERS

(Acting as a printing broker) A printing broker is a person who arranges for things to be printed, using any of a large number of printers rather than through prearrangement with any one printer. Such a person works on a markup basis. So if he or she brokers a printing job that costs $10,000—not an unusually high cost—and works at a 10 percent commission—considered very reasonable—that person (you?) earns $1,000. By becoming familiar with the work, quality, prices, and reliability of various printers in your area—and away from your area, too— you can become a printing broker. Begin to learn about the subject by leafing through *American Printer and Lithographer.* People who need printing—companies, advertisers, publishers, individuals, all categories of humanity—will be better off calling you than calling a printer directly. The reason is that you can get competitive bids and samples for them, and you can oversee the job. That's easily worth the commission you are charging. Printing brokers can earn a lot of money, as I hope you will find out. They get customers by joining the right organizations and attending meetings, by direct mailings to users of printing, by advertising in the Yellow Pages, and by placing small ads in business publications. If you already know anything about printing, you'll know this is a lucrative field.

# 536   WHO'S WHO PUBLICATIONS

(Publishing Who's Who directories)   Are people vain? If they weren't, other people wouldn't be cashing in by compiling and selling Who's Who directories. Once you have enough names and biographies, you can publish your directory, making certain it has a handsome cover. And you can sell copies for as high as $35. Statistics show that you can sell 1.05 times the number of people listed. So if you have a thousand listings you'll gross $36,750. And even after expenses, your net will be almost 70 percent of that:

$25,000 plus. Direct mail is the way to get started. Look through any of the many Who's Who directories in your library. You can publish them by field (advertising, aviation, law, and so on) or location. Some publishers even charge the people they list! Vanity, thy name is Who's Who.

# 537 PROOF POSITIVE

(Proofreading professionally)   Be a professional proofreader. Authors will hire you. Newspapers will hire you. Magazines will hire you. Publishers will hire you. Many businesses will hire you. It is not the mere act of reading that makes one a professional proofreader; it is the act of *meticulous* reading. That's why local readers charge up to $2 per page. You have to know proofreader's marks, how words break syllabically, and standards of copy editing. You also need an eagle eye to catch inconsistencies and typographic errors. Attract customers by running classified ads in national writers' magazines, in daily newspapers, and by mailing brief brochures (with absolutely no misprints) to authors, newspapers, magazines, publishers, and businesses that print enough material to warrant a part-time proofreader.

# 538 PASTE-UP PERSON

(Doing paste-ups of material about to be printed)   The usual process of making advertisements for print media involves the setting of type and creation of art or printed photography, then the pasting up of these elements into a carefully designed layout. For the latter crucial step, special paste-up people are required. And to be sure, many graphics firms and departments have full-time paste-up people. But other smaller entities need paste-up services, too, and may not have a full-time paster. Free-lance paste-up people can offer their services to publishers, newspapers, artists, ad agencies, and graphics firms. It takes quite a bit of training to be a paste-up person, but if you are one, you can earn from $12.50 to $25.00 per hour. Put out propaganda about your pasting with direct mailings of brochures (pasted up by you, I hope) to the target markets I just indicated. Canvassing, personal letters, and phone calls won't hurt either. And keep up with the state of the art by checking the publications recommended by *Advertising Age*.

# 539 TERRIFIC TYPESETTING

(Setting type)   Publishers, newspapers, artists, ad agencies, and graphics firms all need typesetters. Typesetting (or composition, as it's also called) requires specialized training. If you have the training or experience, you can find work as a part-time typesetter for a host of people. I find ads in the classified section quite frequently that offer typesetting services (and request them, too). Other ways to offer the setting of type include the Yellow Pages, mailings to print users, and display ads in the business sections of newspapers. If you're interested in earning extra money ($10 to $20 per hour this way), it might be a good idea to take a course or two in typesetting. Check your local community college. And while you're at it, try to get an apprentice job in a print shop. There are many types of typesetting machines around these days, and if you become proficient in the use of any one, you can easily earn your tuition and then some.

# 540 NEWSLETTER PUBLICATIONS

(Publishing newsletters)   There are more and more newsletters being published these days. That piece of information presents you with two possibilities: write your own newsletter, or offer to publish the newsletters of others. The former course dictates that you be skilled in gathering data, then writing intelligently about it. The latter course suggests that you be adept at newsletter design, typesetting, and printing. Even if you do not perform those functions yourself, as long as you can coordinate them you can go into the business of publishing newsletters for others. Most newsletters run from four to twelve pages, and subscribers willingly pay from $12 to $250 (and even $500) for a year's subscription. If you know of a business that has no newsletter yet, consider publishing one for that business. In 1974, there were 1,300 newsletters being published; today that number exceeds 5,000. Attract subscribers with mail-order ads in publications where the newsletters are pertinent, such as a food newsletter advertised in *Cuisine*. Or, write to newsletter publishers and printing firms, offering to sub-publish their newsletters for them.

# 541 THE OTHER YELLOW PAGES

(Publishing an alternative Yellow Pages directory)   Where I live, there are two types of Yellow Pages—the standard directory, and a kind of underground directory called *The People's Yellow Pages*. The latter type of directory, which is what I suggest you compile for your community, lists business categories not found in the normal Yellow Pages: draft counseling, parent counseling, drug-abuse centers, secondhand stores, encounter groups, free legal help, meditation instruction, and more. Once you put together your pages of yellow (they don't have to be yellow), you can market them with in-person calls at bookstores and any other stores where publications are sold. You don't have to publish a new directory each year, but you do have to know the publishing business in order

to make this work, and you do have to be a good re-
searcher. Booksellers will find it hard to turn down a local
directory with the comprehensiveness and good looks
yours will have. For more information, see the Yellow
Pages.

# 542 MAPMAN

(Making and publishing maps)   Once when I was on a vacation
in Utah, I explored a little-known area called The Maze.
Someday, I hope to return there for an extended visit.
Recently, I tried to get a map of The Maze only to learn
that no map exists. Aha, thought I, this may be my big
opportunity at cartography (mapmaking). That thought
was as far as I went with the notion, but you can be more
venturesome. If you're a good mapmaker, cartography
can be an income producer for you. Many natural areas
either have not been mapped or have inferior maps. By
publishing maps of special points of interest, you can have
a decent stream of income. Sell your maps with display
ads in travel journals, at bookstores, and with small ads
in newspapers near the area you are mapping. The making of an accurate map requires a lot of skill, even though
each final printed map sells in the $1 to $5 range. You can
learn more about maps by contacting Gousha/Chek-
Chart, 2001 The Alameda, San Jose, California 95150.
Call me if you ever map The Maze.

# 543 HOW ABOUT A DATE?

(Publishing calendars)   How About a Date would create and
publish the kind of calendars that can successfully be sold
(for about $5 to $10 each) in greeting card stores, supermarkets, gift shops, and by mail order. Today, the art
and business of creating calendars is at an all-time high.
It's going to get better as people become more calendar-

conscious and aware of calendars as an art form, and it can make you many dollars (5,000 calendars times $5, for instance) each year you produce and sell your calendars. Usually, great photography or illustration is required, along with the days of the year. Display your calendars at trade shows and with ads in selected magazines. In July and August, when the new calendars come out (to the trade), look over the selection and compare it with the selection when you were a kid. Maybe you'll get an idea. And How About a Date will be born.

# 544 STAMP ME

(Creating a line of postcards) If you're a talented photographer or artist (or even know one), and you live in an area visited by tourists, you can create a new line of postcards and sell them directly to all the places where postcards are available. This endeavor entails the photographing or illustrating of, say, twelve scenes, then the production of a quantity of postcards featuring your creations. To play things safe, produce only prototypes at first. Go into serious production after orders have been placed. They will be placed if you can visit enough outlets in person, or hire a salesperson to do so for you. And you need not limit your line to local scenes. If you can interest a national distributor in your postcards, all the better. You'll have to go to a trade show to find the best distributors. Ask your local postcard store which trade show. I know someone who earned $12,000 his first year at this business; he went to the New York Stationery Show.

# 545 PRESTO PRESS

(Quick-printing the works of others) Establish yourself as a quick printer of the works of others: poems, books, newsletters, recipes, almost anything that wants publishing.

Lease or rent the equipment as you need it. List your press in the Yellow Pages. Run classified ads in local newspapers as well as national publications. Do direct mailings to companies that have their own house organs. If you're conscientious, you might get regular business— especially from those companies that require that their house organs be printed in a hurry. You've got to know the ins and outs of printing before you begin. Your earnings can run from meager to enormous ($50,000 yearly with only one simple press) depending upon the quality and reliability of your work, and your tenacity in marketing. You might even want to hook up with Go-For-Broke Printing Brokers—starring in earnway number 535.

# 546 THE CUSTOM MATCHMAKER

(Making customized matchbooks)  The Custom Matchmaker is not a dating bureau. It's a human who makes personalized matchbooks: for restaurants, hotels, private parties, cruise ships, and more. My wife and I were really impressed when we were seated at a restaurant table upon which were an ashtray and an elegant black book of matches. On the matchbook, in gold lettering, was spelled "The Levinsons." Little did I realize then that someone was earning extra money as a custom matchmaker, doing quick work off the restaurant's reservations list. Since then, I've received personalized matches on only two other occasions—making me recognize that there is a lot of opportunity in this business. Do a direct mailing to restaurants (fancy ones), hotels, cruise lines, caterers, and party planners. The engraving machine you require to run your earnway won't set you back too much, and it could prove a matchless source of earning for you. With enough restaurants ordering regularly, you could earn in excess of $300 weekly with this ego-inflating earnway. (Not your ego, but your customer's.) My ego was obviously stroked because even as a nonsmoker, I felt good about the matches.

# 547 THE DESIGNING PRINTER

(Printing and designing)  A lot of people earn extra money printing, and a lot of people earn extra money designing. You can earn more than both groups if you print *and* design. Let it be known that you print business cards, stationery, and advertising fliers. Let it be known also that you design these items at no extra cost. Then, tell your community. Tell them with Yellow Pages ads, with mailings to the business community, with follow-up phone calls. If you consistently market your printing/designing ways, you will eventually develop a regular flow of customers. You may even have to delegate either the printing or designing. The main idea here is to offer both for the price of one. You've got to rent (or buy) the right printing machine and locate the right space to put it in. But once you've set up your printing palace, you can expect it to be a place that nearly prints money for you. Not a lot of money, but you can earn your entire keep this way. Even if it helps just a bit, the money will be a welcome contribution to your bank account and your services will be a welcome contribution to your community.

# 548 THE AUTHOR'S FRIEND

(Compiling indexes)  One of life's most painstaking tasks is the compiling of an index. Because it takes time, attention, energy, effort, and a clear head, most fuzzy-headed authors shrink from the task. Thank heavens, they must figure, for The Author's Friend. The Author's Friend compiles indexes, and does a darn good job of it. The Author's Friend attracts business by doing mailings to nonfiction authors, to authors' agents, and to publishers.

If The Author's Friend is smart (and I'll wager he or she is a flaming genius), each author will be charged about $15 per hour, and will pay it gladly. Classified ads in magazines directed to writers (*Writer's Digest, The Writer*) should also attract index-avoiding authors.

# 549 CONSUMER DEFENSE

(Publishing evaluations of new products)   Defend consumers against shoddy merchandise. Set up a service that tries, tests, and evaluates new products. Publish your findings in a newsletter, written by you or someone else. Then advertise the newsletter with signs on bulletin boards, classified ads, small display ads in national publications, and even a free sample mailing of your newsletter to likely subscribers. You've got to set up unbiased testing conditions. And you've got to be certain your newsletter inspires confidence. America currently has at least two publications that evaluate new products, and both are greatly appreciated. But there's room for yours, too. Charge anywhere from $1 to $5 per issue of your privately produced newsletter. And be happy in the knowledge that you will be getting paid for shooting off your big mouth in public.

# 550 CLASSY ADS

(Publishing a free classified ads newspaper)   Okay, here's an earning endeavor that should appeal to everyone who has been groaning over my constant recommendations of the classified ads as a fruitful marketing medium. Start up your own classified advertisement newspaper. Allow people to run their ads for free, paying only if they sell what they advertised. Similarly, distribute the paper for free. Everyone is a winner with this kind of business—a big winner. The advertisers (usually private parties) get to spread the word about their offerings with no risk. The readers get to scan the newspaper at no risk. And while you may not collect from all your advertisers, you will collect from plenty of them. Our local paper, *The Classified Gazette*, estimates 50 percent of their advertisers pay honestly. By making yours a national paper, you can run up to five thousand ads per issue, more if you really go at it. Even if only half the advertisers sell and pay the low percentage you require (5 percent for expensive items, up to 25 percent for inexpensive items), the profits are really impressive. One such paper reported over $200,000 in profits in one year, which proves that many advertisers honorably pay their percentage. The only marketing tools you'll need will be signs near the places where your paper is distributed, plus small signs on bulletin boards all over the place. And of course, you'll advertise like crazy in your own paper. You can be sure almost everyone will be attracted by your free offer. Once you have a smooth-running operation, including layout, printing, distribution, and continued marketing, you can be as involved in the operation as you wish. So many homes in the United States have items for sale, there is room for many papers such as yours. So stop knocking the classified ads I keep suggesting.

## 551 THE EXTRA MONEY NEWSLETTER

(Publishing a newsletter for people interested in part-time work)
Write to the retail, industrial, and service businesses in your region. Tell them that you're publishing a newsletter for people interested in part-time and temporary work, and that you publish twice a month. Tell in your letter how many newsletters you will be distributing, and mention that you will distribute them for free. If you distribute, for instance, ten thousand newsletters (not difficult when they're free), you can charge about $10 for

a business to list a part-time or temporary vacancy. In time, you might have about two hundred listings per newsletter. That comes to $4,000 income per month, and even if your newsletters cost $.10 each to print, their cost of $2,000 monthly (for publishing two a month) leaves you with $2,000 monthly profit. Add more listings, and you make more money. Distribute your newsletters by placing them in stores and in public places. In time, you might also list full-time opportunities.

---

## PROBLEM-SOLVING

## 552 AND THE WINNER IS . . .

(Winning contests and sweepstakes) Enter contests and sweepstakes. As many as you can. As often as you can. Be fast, original, and neat. Enclose whatever box top or coupon they want you to enclose. Follow the rules. Believe it or not, there are a number of people who earn a fair-sized chunk of cash year in and year out just entering contests and sweepstakes. You may not ever win that two-week vacation in Hawaii with the $10,000 spending money, but in time you'll get the hang of winning *something* . . . and on a regular basis. Look through the magazines at your local magazine shop to see how many contests are going on. If you ever win the Irish Sweepstakes, don't forget who put you onto this gambit in the first place.

## 553 THE RIGHT ANSWER

(Appearing on quiz shows) Just as it is possible to earn extra money entering and winning contests, it is also possible (and practiced by quite a few people) to earn extra money appearing on quiz shows. One day spent staring back at the TV tube will show you that TV uses up bunches of contestants. So, if you live near where the game shows are taped, consider becoming a professional contestant. You've got to be charming, enthusiastic, sincere, bright, and pleasant to look at. That gets you on the show in the first place. Then, if you're brilliant under pressure, you might win large prizes. But it's not one large prize I'm getting at here. It's lots of smaller prizes, lots of times. Not too long ago, I read about a woman who said she had won over $10,000 in prizes during the past five years, and never a first prize. Letters to all the game shows will be your best way of starting, but also check the classifieds under announcements; sometimes there will be an ad seeking contestants. Good luck, and don't cheat.

# 554 CROSSWORD CREATIONS

(Creating crossword puzzles)   Most newspapers have crossword puzzles. And there are loads of books of crossword puzzles. Well, who do you think dreams up all those puzzles? I don't know who does either. But I know that some people *can*. I did once. If you can, and if it's not as hard for you as it was for me, you can earn extra money creating crossword puzzles for newspapers, syndicates, or crossword puzzle companies. Letters to these concerns enclosing puzzle samples may be the best way to start. As with a syndicated column, you can go through an existing syndicate or you can self-syndicate. You can even create special-interest puzzles (à la *TV Guide*'s TV crossword puzzle) and sell them to special interest publications.

# 555 PROBLEM-SOLVER

(Solving problems for companies in your field of interest) Perhaps the most fulfilling way of earning extra money is to decide what field excites you the most—out of a combination of your own interest in it and your aptitude for it—then select the company or companies in that field that seem to be most in need of your services. Arrange for an appointment with a high executive in one of your selected companies (the president, you hope) and talk about his company with him. You can be sure it's his favorite subject. If you know of a problem within that company or an as yet unexploited opportunity, offer to solve the problem or capitalize on the opportunity. According to Richard Nelson Bolles's *What Color Is Your Parachute?*, there's a great chance your offer will be accepted. After all, you will have proven your interest in the field, searched out the company because of that interest, and identified the problem or opportunity. The sky is the limit with regard to how much you can earn—your idea might be a million-dollar idea, or, who knows, you might just come up with a billion-dollar solution. A great many people have obtained jobs this way (the "creative minority," as Mr. Bolles calls them), but all you are after is some extra money. One of the key chapters in Mr. Bolles's book is entitled: "You must identify the man or woman who has the power to hire you and show them how your skills can help them with their problems." So the moment you become recognized as a problem-solver may be the moment you begin to earn extra money in the most fulfilling way of all.

There you have them: 555 ways to earn extra money. I fervently hope that you have already made at least fifty check marks in this book indicating the fifty earning endeavors out of the 555 which are most promising and appealing to you, that would fit most comfortably with your current job, and that would enable you to be of maximum service to your community (and vice versa).

When talking to any person or company that can provide work for you, be sure you talk to them in *their* terms . . . perceive their company through *their* eyes . . . orient your offerings to *their* needs. Pretty basic, this advice. But you'd be amazed (and a bit depressed) at how many people don't do it.

Once you've got your earnway going, don't let yourself be deluded by any initial flashes of success. Of all new businesses, 51 percent fail during the first five years. So if you've made fifty check marks, you have a lot of second chances lined up.

The amounts of money you can earn pursuing the ventures of which I've written were based on facts that were true in 1991. But you know about inflation. To see what these earnways pay the day that you are reading about them (if that happens to be well beyond 1991), you might check into a monthly government publication called *Employment and Earnings*—usually available in most libraries. You won't find all these earning endeavors listed, but you can expect to find some.

# 6 / *Marketing Your Earning Endeavors*

Unless you learn how to market your product or service, your chances of succeeding at earning extra money are just about nil. Marketing includes advertising, public relations, packaging, selling, sampling—100 different weapons in all, and more developed every month. Marketing is everything that concerns your product or service. Everything? Yep.

The first thing you need to do is develop a marketing plan. In developing that plan you should have in mind a clearly defined purpose. One way to define your purpose clearly is to put it in writing. If you wanted to earn extra money setting up a window washing business, the first sentence of your one-page marketing strategy might be: "The purpose of Distant Vista Window Washing marketing is to convince the maximum number of Omaha retail store owners that they will benefit by using my service on a weekly basis."

That's basic and clear. Not a whole lot of business

babble. The rest of your marketing strategy should tell how you intend to accomplish your purpose. Distant Vista might put its second sentence like this: "This will be accomplished by offering the most economical, reliable, and spotless window washing in Omaha."

Devote a line in your strategy toward focusing on the niche you want to occupy—exactly what you want to stand for. Distant Vista could say, "Distant Vista will be known for reliability and quality."

One more sentence should detail your target audience. Distant Vista might put it like this: "Our target audience is retail store owners throughout Omaha; our secondary audience is mall owners."

Next, your strategy ought to state the identity you wish for your business. I say "identity" instead of "image" because I'm not talking about what your business *appears* to be but what it *is*. You might say: "Distant Vista Window Washing will be a solid member of the business community, a professional service in every way, and an excellent value for its customers."

Then, you should examine all the marketing tools and specify which ones you intend to use—in-person calls, personal letters, phone calls, circulars and brochures, signs on bulletin boards, classified ads, posted signs, Yellow Pages advertising, newspaper advertising, direct mail, radio advertising, television advertising, billboard advertising, public relations, advertising specialties, sponsored events, seminars and demonstrations, sampling, trade shows and fairs, magazine advertising, paid word-of-mouth advertising, searchlights, parade floats, skywriting, dirigible and airplane advertising, bowling and Little League sponsorships, and any more you can discover or invent. For instance: "Distant Vista Window Washing will achieve its marketing goals by employing in-person sales calls, brochures, a Yellow Pages listing in the Omaha directory, small weekly newspaper ads, business cards with discount offers, weekly sales training or sales learning, tie-ins with five local service businesses, greeting my customers by name at each visit, speed of service, testimonial letters from satisfied customers, and free demonstrations for qualified prospects. The guiding force behind all marketing efforts will be professionalism and consistency."

The final sentence of your marketing plan should state in writing how much money you plan to invest in marketing. Feeling aggressive and wanting to generate maximum profits, Distant Vista might say, "We will invest 10% of projected total gross income in marketing."

Your marketing strategy can go on from there and outline your plans for growth and your design for expansion, but such information need not be part of a basic strategy. This basic marketing strategy is the first portion of a three-part marketing plan.

Part two is equally simple and equally important: the advertising strategy. It lists the purpose of the advertising (in this case, your sales talk, your brochure, and your Yellow Pages listing), the prime information that will be included in it, and its mood and tone.

Part three of the basic marketing plan elaborates on the media strategy. It lists the specific media that will be used—naming, for instance, particular newspapers and radio stations, and giving the locations of billboards. It goes into detail about the size, placement, and frequency of the ads, stating "the ads will be 5 columns by 18 inches and run twice per month in the Sunday supplement" or "they will be 2 columns by 3 inches and run four times a week in the main news section." This part of the marketing plan need be no more than four or five sentences long.

Armed with a three-part marketing plan, you have specific objectives, and know how you will seek to attain them.

Advertising is the most common, most complicated, and most misused marketing tool. About 90 percent of advertising falls short. The advertising profession is still in its infancy—it's not much more than a century old. But more and more is being learned about this combination of art, science, and business. If you truly follow the advice I am going to give you now you will never create lackluster advertising that fails to communicate and motivate.

Please understand that you can earn extra money *only* if you promote your earning endeavor actively and consistently. All the skill and talent you put into setting up your earnway, all the brains and energy you devote to training yourself to be good—all that will be totally wasted in the vacuum you will be operating in if you have no promotion and no advertising. If you ignore this fact, your earnway will remain a dream and never become a reality.

If there is one word to memorize before embarking upon any advertising, that word is *commitment.* An advertising program has little chance of success unless you are committed to it. You must stick with it, expect no miracles of it, and realize that it is nothing more than a conservative investment.

Because you want people to get to know you better so they can trust you more, be consistent in your marketing. Don't keep changing your ads, your message, your media, your format, your logo, your theme line, or your identity.

The reason is that people tend to patronize businesses in which they are confident. In fact, a national research survey proved that confidence in the seller ranks ahead of both quality and service. There's little question that your commitment, consideration of your marketing funds as an investment, and marketing that is consistent will make your prospects and customers confident.

To accomplish this, you must be patient, not impetuous. It's interesting to see that five of the keys to marketing success end in the letters "ent." The keys are *commitment, investment, consistent, confident,* and *patient.*

But those aren't the only keys. There are three more. And they, too, end with the letters "ent."

The marketing that you do *subsequent* to the sale will prove more profitable in the long run than the original sale. So practice follow-up. All good guerrilla marketers do. And in these times when people cherish their time above all else, make Herculean efforts to be *convenient*—make it easy to buy from you. Your small size encourages this flexibility. Finally, remember that marketing is not advertising, it's a wide *assortment* of marketing weapons. The more the merrier. Take a closer look at these weapons in my *Guerrilla Marketing Weapons*, he said, in his earnest earning fashion.

Advertising is important, but it's only 1 percent of marketing. Still, because I want you to excel 100 percent, let's investigate this particular marketing weapon.

The only times advertising works dramatically or instantly are when you have a major sale, give something away free, announce a fabulous new product, or launch a trillion-dollar ad campaign.

Basically, advertising should say what you do, why you're good, and what the benefits are of dealing with you. It should also tell people what you want them to do. We'll get into that in a moment.

Keep in mind that your newspaper ad is competing for reader attention with the ads for banks, airlines, supermarkets, department stores, deodorants, furniture, and the rest. Your ad must do something special to create a desire for your service or product, whatever it is. It must get attention. It must get your message across. It must motivate people. Direct your ad to a single person, a single reader, not to the "people." More specifically, direct it to the person "inside the ego."

People have built-in BS-detectors when it comes to advertising. Any word, any picture in your ad that rings of BS will turn off your readers. Thanks in part to consumer watchdog groups, advertising may be entering an age of honesty. That's good. Enter the age with it.

Do whatever you can to get people to agree with *all* that you say in your advertising. Get people to nod yes. I know a woman who sells water beds. In the Yellow Pages, under the heading of "Water Beds," her ad is headlined, "Looking for a water bed?" Brilliant. Automatically, she gets a yes from her readers simply because they've turned to the water-bed section and the probability is that they *are* looking for a water bed. She hasn't made the sale yet, but she sure is on her way.

*The Great Soviet Encyclopedia* recently redefined advertising as "the popularization of goods with the aim of selling them, the creation of demand for these goods, the acquaintance of consumers with their quality, particular features and the location of their sales, and explanation of the methods of their use." Earlier editions defined advertising as "hullabaloo, a means of swindling the people and foisting upon them goods frequently useless or of dubious quality." Either advertising has improved or the Soviet Union has become more capitalistic. I think it's a combination of both.

I can understand the earlier misunderstanding of advertising. Many people who do their own advertising believe it should be jazzy or hip or clever or funny. Not so. Advertising should be centered around an idea, solid and meaningful. Advertising should be interesting and clear. Most advertising misses on both marks.

Advertising should be directed to a potential prospect, an individual person and not the world in general. When creating advertising, don't worry about the advertising itself. Concentrate instead on the product or service being advertised—that's what must be the most fascinating part of any ad.

Let me spend a short time explaining exactly how to create or recognize great advertising. I taught advertising on the college level. I took a full year explaining this. Now I'm going to condense the information into a few pages, so you will get only the cream of the data. Pay close attention. This information will be applicable to all kinds of advertising, whether on a large or small scale. It is comprised of many advertising rules. It's more important that you know these rules than that you follow them. At least if you know them you'll know when to break them creatively. Breaking rules can often result in superb advertisements and commercials. But don't break them unless you have a powerful reason.

People do not deliberately read ads or listen to commercials. Instead, they read what interests them and listen to what interests them. Sometimes, it's an ad or commercial that interests them. So your primary obligation is to interest people. Interest them in your offering, not your ad.

Once you have your ads created, plan to run them consistently. If you don't, you'll be setting yourself up to lose the time and money you've invested. Experts tell us it takes approximately nine impressions of an advertising message to bring a customer to the point of purchase readiness.

The following six questions should help you in formulating and assessing your advertisements.

### Is the ad centered around the inherent drama of your offering?

Every product or service has some inherently dramatic quality. It is this inherent drama that makes the product or service salable in the first place, that caused you to conceive of the business at all. There are no exceptions to this. Find the drama in your offering, and make that the focal point for your advertising campaign.

***Does the ad emphasize the benefits of your offering?***
Women do not buy shampoo, they buy beautiful hair. Men
do not buy cars, they buy style, power, status, and value.
Determine the most appealing benefits of your offering,
then state them clearly. Many products or services have
multiple benefits. Pick the most important, but mention
the rest. Emphasizing the benefits is called "selling the
sizzle and not the steak."

***Is your ad believable?***
The built-in BS-detector that I mentioned was developed
by consumers to protect them from the many unbeliev-
able ads that assault their senses. There is a difference
between honesty and believability. You can state facts
that are completely honest and still not be believed. So
you must do what my advertising idol, the late Leo Burnett (founder of one of the world's great advertising agencies), suggested: talk to people in "shirt-sleeve English."
Don't be too highfalutin, don't be too lowbrow, don't be
too fancy. Talk with warm, realistic language if you want
a warm, realistic response. It's not all that easy to sound
completely believable in an ad. If one word hints of undue
exaggeration, the entire ad will probably be unbeliev-
able. So try like mad to be believed, and be sure you are
telling the truth. No BS.

***Does your ad or commercial attract
attention to the product?***
Leo Burnett once said that it's easy to get attention. Just
come down the stairs with your socks in your mouth.
What is important is to draw attention to your product, so
make it as interesting, compelling, and fascinating as possible. Let that allure come shining through in every ad,
sign, commercial, letter, and brochure. It's not easy to
do. That's why a pro usually does a better job than an
amateur.

### *Is your message motivating?*

If you create an ad that has inherent drama, features important benefits, is stated believably, and draws attention to the product, it still may fail if you don't tell people what you want them to do. It might be to make a phone call, write a letter, go to a store, ask for a product, fill out a coupon, or test-drive a car. State it clearly. Say: "Call 555-3565 today." That's proper motivation—it says precisely what you want the consumer to do. It seems very elementary, this point, but it's important. Even many professional ad makers strike out on this one.

### *Is your ad unique?*

Do what no others are doing. Be unique, even astonishing. Don't do it in a manner that detracts from your message. But do it. If you fulfill the five points already listed, but someone else fulfills them in a more interesting way, your ad will probably be ignored. If your ad is unique, it will almost automatically attract attention.

I have mentioned only a few points on the complex subject of advertising. Advertising is a combination of writing, art, music, drama, and psychology. It is also selling. Just because you can write clearly doesn't mean you can advertise intelligently. Some of the worst ads I've seen were written by brilliant writers.

Production is also important. If you don't produce your ad or commercial well, you may as well not run it at all. Shoddy production gives your earnway a shoddy identity, regardless of the quality of the service itself. In the world of printed advertising, production includes design, layout, photography, illustration, typography, paste-up, photostats, and printing. Types of print media include newspapers, magazines, signs, circulars, brochures, letters, Yellow Pages ads, and direct-mail materials. In the world of electronic advertising (radio, television, sales films, slide shows, telephone marketing), production includes casting, voicing, music, acting, directing, filming, taping, mixing, and editing. As a rule, plan to spend 10 percent of your advertising budget on production. Saving money by skimping on production will cost you more in other ways.

When choosing your advertising think first about your prime customers. Who are they? What do they read, watch, listen to? Maybe they watch TV, but if 95 percent of the other people watching TV are not in the market for your offering, you will waste a good deal of your effort on TV. Try to target your prime customers and get to them with as little waste as possible. Professional media-buying services can help you with this.

Try to coordinate your oral presentations and sales visits with your printed or other ads. The more cohesion in your various approaches, the more confidence people will have in you.

Word-of-mouth advertising is extremely effective, and you can help inspire it. Create a good-looking brochure about your company and give it to every customer *after* the sale. Because people like to rationalize and talk about their purchases, they will read your words and pass them along when talking to friends. You are putting words into their mouths, and the result is word-of-mouth advertising.

You will make your advertising far more effective if you operate with a marketing calendar. Try to plan all of your marketing efforts for one year in advance, deciding on the dates of every ad, every commercial, every mailing, every sign posting, and every direct selling push. This gives you a perspective on your efforts that will aid strategic planning and help prevent errors.

How much should you spend on advertising? A tough question. You should spend a predetermined percentage of your total anticipated sales volume. A good, aggressive figure to start with is 10 percent. So if you will sell $50,000 worth of products or services, plan to spend $5,000 on advertising. Out of that, spend $500 on production. Giant advertisers spend as little as 2 percent of gross sales on advertising (in the case of large industrial corporations) or as much as 33 percent (in the case of the big cosmetics companies). A healthy figure you could live with would be 5 percent. But to rise above the normal businessperson (your competition) who hasn't a clue about marketing, I'd go with 10 percent, maybe even more at the very beginning, maybe less later on. If you have made no sales yet, you've got to project your advertising budget as a percentage of anticipated sales. Try to make realistic projections. I find it best to look at the whole thing on a monthly basis, to keep in touch with the real world and not get too tangled up in detail.

As you become an advertiser, begin to be acutely aware of all other advertising in all other media, especially that of your competition. You should do research to get information. You can do valuable research for free, just by asking your customers questions. Do it with questionnaires. (How did you hear of us? From whom did you buy before? What is your sex? Your age group? Your income group? Your educational level? Did you shop around prior to purchasing?) The list of questions goes on and on, and they can get quite personal, so be sure you do not ask your customers' names when obtaining this information.

Separately, you should be sure to get the names of all your customers. These will be valuable for future mailings and promotional activities. Plus, they are salable to other businesses.

There are probably seven million kinds of advertising, but let's look at two: institutional and promotional. Institutional advertising focuses on your business's identity and merits. Promotional advertising offers something for sale, something for free, something to do or buy *now*.

Great advertising ordinarily employs both institutional and promotional techniques, but the less promotional advertising you do, the better off you'll be in the long run. Often, an advertiser will run a promotion or sale and be overwhelmed by the positive results. That advertiser will repeat the sale, and run another promotion. The results will be down, but still impressive. Eventually, the advertiser runs so many promotions that people cease to believe that a real savings is involved. The net result is that people just wait for promotions from this advertiser, and otherwise stay away. Institutional advertising will then be useless to change the impression, and eventually the sales or promotions that do run will lose their effectiveness. The advertiser promotes himself into a corner. Sales and promotions are superb marketing tools—if they are used with caution and restraint. Are there exceptions to this? Of course.

To succeed in advertising, you need a combination of creativity, judgment, and patience. Without creativity, you can still succeed by allowing others to be creative for you. You can also delegate judgment to a person who might be better at advertising than you. But you can't delegate patience. After three months, even if sales are going up, the first person to get tired of your advertising will be you. Next, your friends and family will get tired of it, followed shortly by your salespeople (if you have some). Finally, your ad maker will get tired of your advertising. But if sales are up, at least you can be sure your accountant will not get bored or put off. So I've found it to be a good idea to put the accountant in charge of deciding when to change an advertising campaign.

Some great advertising has run, almost unchanged, for over ten years. Throughout that time sales have climbed. Just think what would have happened if the Marlboro cigarette people had become bored with their "Marlboro Man" campaign after five months.

There seems to be a myth that people do not read long copy ads. Utter nonsense. Most people don't read all the ads, but your prospects will read every single word if they see you are addressing their needs. They expect the ad to give them information. They want information. Don't get obsessed with having lots of "white space" or only a few words in your ad—you'll shortchange yourself. Interested people like to read if the reading is good and the facts are plentiful.

A word about the Yellow Pages. This is the only medium that enables you to stand on an equal footing with your biggest and most established competitor. Most Yellow Pages directories will run no larger than a quarter-page ad, so if you run one, and if your ad looks and "feels" as good as that of your competitor, you will have put yourself in his league. You can't do this with newspaper ads because big companies can run really big ads frequently. Little companies just can't cut that particular kind of mustard.

There are four exceptionally motivating words that are used in advertising. If you don't abuse them, you will be delighted with the results when you use them. Those words are: *free, new, sale,* and *you.* People love things for free, are excited by new items, take notice of sales, and absolutely love to hear about themselves. Enough said.

Before embarking upon the creation of your marketing/advertising/media plan, decide what you stand for. Find your niche. A simple niche. It may be quality or economy or convenience or innovation or expertise or something else. Don't be too ambitious and try to personify quality, economy, value, style, and service. Pick one niche and occupy it. Intentional overreaching is unintentional underreaching.

Having spent twenty-two years of my life as a professional ad maker, I must admit I know far more than the average person about advertising. But I know far less than there is to know. Be that as it is, I want to close this chapter with several things that I know I *do* know.

I *do* know ten very common mistakes made by advertisers, and I *do* know ten very esoteric secrets that help advertisers. Here they are:

*Mistake* 1: Doing your advertising yourself without the help or advice of a pro.

*Mistake* 2: Making a marketing plan as you go along rather than ahead of time.

*Mistake* 3: Switching from one advertising medium to another.

*Mistake* 4: Being impatient with your advertising and changing it often.

*Mistake* 5: Expecting miracles of advertising—instant results and huge sales.

*Mistake* 6: Being cute and clever in your advertising. Being funny just to be funny.

*Mistake* 7: Letting the radio station or TV station write your copy and plan your commercial.

*Mistake* 8: Letting the newspaper or magazine write and design your advertisements.

*Mistake* 9: Stopping advertising in order to save money.

*Mistake* 10: Skimping on advertising production so that you'll have money to run more ads.


*Secret* 1: Be prepared to invest properly in this conservative investment.

*Secret* 2: Pinpoint your audience and direct your ads right to them, and to no one else.

*Secret* 3: Involve your audience by gaining access to their unconscious mind.

*Secret* 4: Consider using a pro to make your ads.

*Secret* 5: Stick with the niche you have selected for yourself. Be constant.

*Secret* 6: Newspapers are best for newsy ads; TV is best for ads that demonstrate; radio is best for intimate copy; magazines are best for personally-involving and longer-copy ads.

*Secret* 7: If you run an ad once in a regional edition of a nationally respected magazine, you can use reprints of that ad for years and gain the same credibility for your business the original ad brought.

*Secret* 8: Consistency will be your greatest advertising ally: consistency in exposure, media, message, look, sound, identity, and format.

*Secret* 9: Judge your advertising against your strategy to be sure all points are covered. Then judge it by how interesting and desirable it makes your product or service.

*Secret* 10: Advertising is a fancy name for selling.

In the first chapter of this book, I asked that you read, then reread chapter 6. I suggest that you read it again after you choose your earnways—before preparing your marketing plan. Be sure that the person who will be masterminding your marketing also reads this chapter so that both of you are on the same wavelength.

If you've been serious about earning extra money, you've made check marks next to the most appealing of the 555 earning endeavors. Now may be a good time to look them over, to check up on the check marks. Don't actually do anything about them yet, but before you read the next chapter, look over the earning methods you've checked so you will have them in mind as you read on.

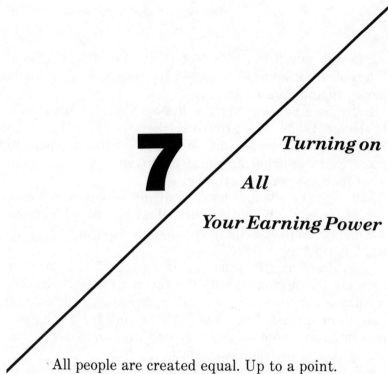

# 7 / Turning on All Your Earning Power

All people are created equal. Up to a point.

That point is the ability to tap into the staggering power of our unconscious minds, the place where the majority of our mental abilities reside. Scientists estimate that we employ only 10 percent to 30 percent of our minds. By gaining access to our unconscious, we tap into a source of pure, shimmering earning power.

You can tap your own unconscious. And by combining the pursuit of multiple earnways with this new access, you will be able to turn on all of your earning power. You will then feel as though magic has been performed.

Before getting to the real meat of the magic, there are a few important points for you to consider. First, I want you to know something of my experience. I was working for an advertising agency, making a fat and sassy salary in excess of $50,000 per year. Hot stuff, I figured. Then, it was revealed that my work for one particular client earned approximately $1,500,000 for my employer!

Suddenly, I realized that my $50,000 wasn't hot stuff at

all. It was only 3.33 percent of the money I had *earned.* Who got the other 96.67 percent? My employer. That made me sit up and take notice.

I also became aware of the inherent human resistance to change. Companies are worse than individuals . . . the larger, the more resistant. We know that fortunes are made by those who recognize new trends and act upon what they see before anyone else.

But, most people and most companies seem to follow a rule that states: When confronted with a new idea, you are more certain of being right if you vote against it. This went against my nature.

As a practicing futurist (meaning that I have always been utterly fascinated with the future), I was constantly reading about new products, new concepts, new trends, new opportunities. I realized that working for a company prevented me from diving headlong into any new opportunity that really caught my interest.

In short, I was being denied the opportunity to take risks.

This book gives you an opportunity. And with that opportunity, you can move up toward a loftier income. You can minimize the risk by weaning yourself away from your current employment instead of making a clean and instant break. Or, you can eliminate risk entirely by sticking with your job and aiming only to supplement your wages.

To provide you with the ability to succeed regardless of which option you select, you should have access to your unconscious mind. The three methods that have worked for me, that are working for others, that have worked well enough to the point that they may be considered *proven* avenues to the unconscious are:

Stimulation
Affirmation
Visualization

The three overlap a little, yet they are distinct. Rather than selecting which one of these methods works best for you, I strongly suggest you use all three.

### Stimulation

Stimulation is a simple three-part process that most people, without realizing it, frequently use.

Here's how to do it. Use it on any problem or puzzling decision you are faced with. Get out a pencil and a piece of paper and try to solve your problem using *direct* thinking. Spend about ten or fifteen minutes really giving it serious effort. That's part one.

Next, using the same paper, think of ideas that are not direct solutions, but which have some relation to it. This is called *lateral* thinking. You might list areas that interest you, areas of expertise, areas that fall into your realm of experience, or trends that interest you. That's part two.

Part three is the easiest part of all. *Forget the whole thing.* Take your mind off it and relax. Don't think about it. You've activated your unconscious, and it will come up with the solution. When you least expect it, it will pop into your head. It may be one that you considered earlier, then discarded. It may be one that never even entered your mind. It may be obvious or obscure. But one thing's for sure: it will be a correct solution, a real dandy. And you'll know it.

### Affirmation

Stimulation, is mere child's play when compared with affirmation. Stimulation may be used to solve problems and create ideas. With affirmation you can program yourself for prosperity, then *force* your unconscious mind to achieve it.

To begin with, you will again need a pencil and paper.

Now write a list comprised of the things you *need* to solve certain problems and the things you *want* just because you want them. For example, I might list a paid-in-full Visa bill to solve the problem of the $3,500 on my unpaid balance, comfortable, extended-wear contact lenses to solve the problem of my requiring glasses, a brand new red Jeep Cherokee to solve the problem of my daughter's old, beat-up Volvo.

That takes care of the things I *need*. For the things I *want* I might list a five-foot-screen TV set, an extra bathroom, a weight lower than 160 pounds, five books with healthy sales. Make your own list.

A few pointers:

List only things you *really* need or *really* want.
List only things that are realistically *possible*.
List only things that would harm *no one* else.
List only things that are *specific* and *positive*.
Be sure you list *enough*—don't limit yourself.

Finally, list two more things: the income you earned last year, and the income that you really want. If the income you really want isn't at least twice the income you earned last year, you may be aiming too low.

Now that you've got your list in front of you, you're ready to turn each desire into an affirmation.

*An affirmation is a sentence stating a specific fact about yourself as though that fact were already true.* For example, I might list my first affirmation like this:

"I, Jay, have paid off my entire $3,500 Visa bill." Notice that I stated it positively and specifically. Notice that I stated it as though it already happened.

Here's why: the unconscious mind takes *everything* literally. By stating my affirmation as though it was reality, my unconscious forms an image of my Visa bill having been paid in full, all $3,500 of it. The unconscious mind is so very powerful that it not only *believes* the affirmation, but it actually *rearranges reality* to make it true.

In a moment, I'm going to ask that you list your affirmations in writing. Most people seem to do best when they deal with anywhere from three to twenty affirmations. Here are what mine might be:

I, Jay, have paid off my entire $3,500 Visa bill.

I, Jay, have extended-wear contact lenses that give me near and far vision so I can see perfectly without standard glasses.

I, Jay, have given my daughter, Amy, a red Jeep with four-wheel drive.

I, Jay, have a fiberglass hot tub with bubbly jets in my backyard.

I, Jay, have three healthy new evergreen trees growing on my property.

I, Jay, have a five-foot-screen TV set with remote control.

I, Jay, have a third bathroom with a ceiling fan and stained glass window.

I, Jay, weigh less than 160 pounds.

I, Jay, have fifteen books enjoying healthy sales.

I, Jay, have met all of my writing deadlines for this year.

Okay. Now write your own affirmations. Look them over, mull them over. To bring them to life, you must take three simple steps.

Number one: Immediately upon awakening each morning, say your affirmations out loud. Say them loud and clear. Listen to the sound of your voice.

Number two: Each day, select one affirmation and repeatedly write it. Write it a minimum of twenty times, no less. But use only one affirmation per day. When you write it, state it three ways:

I, Jay, have a five-foot-screen TV set with remote control.

You, Jay, have a five-foot-screen TV set with remote
    control.
He, Jay, has a five-foot-screen TV set with remote
    control.

Writing your affirmations should take no longer than
five minutes a day. Write legibly and smaller than usual
to increase the clarity of thought directed to your unconscious and to improve your concentration.

Number three: Just before going to sleep each night,
say your affirmations out loud, and see the image of each
one as though it has happened and you can feel it.

That's it. There is nothing more for you to do. The
reason why you state your affirmations aloud each morning and night just after and just before sleep is because
that is when your unconscious mind is most receptive,
most sensitive to suggestion. The reason why you write
an affirmation a minimum of twenty times a day is because the unconscious is extremely susceptible to repetition.

To be certain that your affirmations work for you, be
sure you repeat them every day. Don't miss a day. And
don't tell anyone about your affirmations until they come
true. If you don't keep them entirely to yourself—they
just will not happen.

Each month, reevaluate your affirmations and write
them down. Periodically you'll be ready to add new ones.

At first, I can guarantee you that you'll feel like a class-
A moron while you are saying your affirmations aloud.
Not to worry. Your unconscious mind is in charge.

How long will it take for your affirmations to come
true? In my case, some of them materialized before the
end of the first month. By the end of the first full year,
seven of my fifteen original affirmations came to pass, two
more were in the process of coming true, and the other six
had started to take shape in the distance. Of the nine

listed here, all nine have come true. This took over one year, but I surpassed my goal in some cases.

By planting affirmations like seeds, you will be able to reap a harvest of your goals. Without the seeds, there will be no harvest time. Your unconscious mind has the ability to restructure reality and to make real the images that become planted within it. If you want to get into the concept a little more, I highly recommend *The Silent Pulse* by George Leonard.

### Visualization

*Visualization, also known as imaging, is the forming of a clear mental image of each goal as though it had come true for you.* The image must be detailed and distinct, complete and actually "seen."

You can utilize visualization to achieve your goals either by itself or in combination with affirmation.

Combined with your affirmations, each visualization should take only ten or twenty seconds.

To visualize the results of my extended-wear contact lenses, I would imagine myself reading a newspaper by candlelight, without glasses, without straining. I'd visualize my daughter grinning in her gleaming station wagon, with "Subaru" and "4-wheel drive" clearly emblazoned on the vehicle.

Such specific visualization of my affirmations energizes my unconscious, which seems to take great pleasure in "seeing the picture," and is thus given direction, guidance, and momentum.

Visualization works best immediately upon awakening and just prior to retiring—as does affirmation.

The important thing is that you have a clear picture of your goals having been attained, that you focus on your goals frequently and consistently, and that you possess desire, belief, and a positive attitude. Your unconscious will do the rest.

The results will be like magic.

Now that you know 555 ways to earn extra money, and how your unconscious can help you attain that extra money, there is one more suggestion that can increase the flow of money into your life—"outflowing." Outflowing is called "tithing" by some people, "charity" and "glad-giving" by still others. They all mean the same thing.

To increase the flow of money into your life, you should make the conduits as wide and clear as possible. This happens with outflowing. Outflowing is the act of regularly giving a set percentage of money to others. Whether it be 5 percent or 10 percent is not important. To which group or individual you give it is not important. That you give it regularly is very important.

You should decide to give, say, 10 percent of all the money you earn by virtue of reading this book, and give it happily. Since I started outflowing, I have given more money away than ever before. By the same token, I have made more money than ever before. Is there a connection?

You bet. The Bible speaks of the connection between reaping and sowing. The concept of karma deals with getting from life exactly what you are willing to give. People who have tithed regularly can tell you that it does work.

I am not just talking about donating to a religious group, though I do not exclude it. My outflowing has benefited the U.S. Olympic Committee, the Multiple Sclerosis Society, the American Cancer Society, American Heart Association, Friends of the River, Greenpeace, World Future Society, United Way, American Aging Association, U.S. Ski Association, and Common Cause, to name but a few. Along with giving money to organizations, I have given money to needy friends and relatives. That, too, counts as outflowing . . . just as long as it is a gift and not a loan.

Now it may strike you as strange that here I am telling you, who bought this book to earn extra money, to give money away. But that is exactly what I am telling you. Give money away. Let it flow out so it can flow in. You'll enjoy it.

Naturally, you can claim your donations to legitimate charities as tax-deductible contributions.

When I first heard of the concept of tithing, I was puzzled, put off. But now that I have practiced it, I am impressed, and convinced that it works. The hardest part, as with so many endeavors, is the first part— getting started. It becomes easier after you have made outflowing a habit and can see some positive results.

Now that you have the methods of earning money, the secrets of manipulating your unconscious power, and the way to open the flow of money into your life, you're just about set.

All that remains is to activate the entire process.

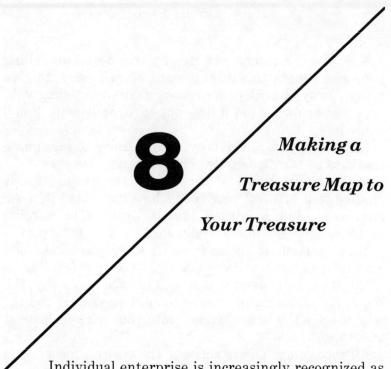

# 8

## *Making a Treasure Map to Your Treasure*

Individual enterprise is increasingly recognized as a reliable hedge against inflation, a solid safeguard against recession, a source of security and inner fulfillment, and a method of creating a profitable and salable business.

If you feel that your life can be more of an art than a drag, consider taking over ownership of yourself. If you believe that you are in a rut, try to equate the sound of these pages turning with the sound of opportunity knocking.

As you begin, be careful you don't get carried away with money. I've seen people succeed so easily, so rapidly that they went hog-wild in their individual enterprises, earning much money, relinquishing much freedom. I don't recommend that degree of earning fervor.

If your earning endeavor becomes too big it will eat into the rest of your life, destroying the collateral values of individual enterprise. If you hire employees you may get embroiled in the problems of being an employer, imprisoned by your own success. I'm trying to emphasize your ability to break the shackles of employment, not just give you a chance to create new ones.

The more earning endeavors you develop, the better protected you will be against the inevitable loss of some sources of income. From multiplicity comes the security that is one of the best by-products of entrepreneurship.

Now is the time to plot the map to your treasure trove. The steps to take are simple. The more of them you take, the more certain your success.

### List your goals

Write down the monthly income you wish from individual enterprise. Write also the amount of time you are willing to devote to it. Make two sets of goals: one for the end of your first year, another set for the first three years. In my case, I set $4,000 monthly working four days a week as my original goal for the end of one year, then $5,000 monthly working three days a week as my goal for the end of three years.

### List your obstacles

If you know about any barriers ahead of time, you'll be able to deal with them when they confront you. Typical ones might be that you've never tried working for yourself before, that your friends advise you against it, that your family will feel insecure if you leave the corporate womb, that you might lack the self-discipline, that the economy is suffering, that you would be forced to give up too many fringe benefits, that you just don't have the time, that you lack imagination, that you will receive no emotional support from anyone, that you are honestly fearful of going it alone, that your fellow workers are laughing at your plans, that you know nothing about being in business, that you cannot afford to risk time or money with a mortgage hanging over your head, and that you're not very good with details.

All of these obstacles were suggested to me by people who have *succeeded* at earning extra money, who have *succeeded* at individual enterprise. If your obstacles match their obstacles, you're in good company.

### List the things you like to do

Make this a long list. Put on it not only things that are related to earning, but also things that seem unconnected with earning. List things that you do now, that you've done in the past, even things that you've longed to do.

These lists will help you draw your treasure map. The items on the lists can be likened to landmarks on a map. The more landmarks there are, the easier it will be to guide yourself to the treasure.

### List the things you're good at

Be immodest. Have a ball patting yourself on the back by listing your skills, talents, abilities, strengths, and good points. Include on this list everything for which you have been complimented. Include, too, awards, life experiences, secretly-held beliefs about yourself, capabilities that date back to grammar school, high school, college, military service, summer jobs, volunteer work, past employment and organizational activities. Be sure to remember your aptitude at chores around the home.

### List the earning tools you have

If you're not sure that you have any earning tools, consider that a person can earn extra money if he or she has a camera, home, condominium, extra room, basement, yard, adding machine, calculator, typewriter, video cassette recorder, tape recorder, telephone, kitchen, recipes, sewing machine, car, truck, van, bicycle, garden tools, boat, standard tools, home computer, piano, drafting table, painting equipment, or a garden. Most of these items are fairly common. Your list may include some of these items along with others not included here. Take a few moments to give this one some real thought—you may remember an important earning tool that you already have.

### List the earnways you've checked in this book
If you haven't made those check marks yet, make them now. Then list all of the checked earnways on a separate sheet of paper. I hope (for your sake) the list is a long one.

When you've made the list, circle the ten earning methods that feel best to you. Read the last three lists you've made: things you like to do, things you're good at, tools you have. Those three lists should direct you to the ten earning methods most likely to succeed. For now we will consider those ten. Later, you can add others.

### Pick one earnway for a model
From your list of ten earnways, select your favorite, and let's submit it to the kind of scrutiny that all ten deserve—give it what I call a "brain search," as outlined in the next ten steps. Naturally, the earnway you now pick should be one that you are most ready to activate now. So apply careful thought, then write it down in large capital letters. Underline it. Stare at it a moment and say it out loud so as to prime your unconscious mind to make it succeed for you.

### Brain-Search: Pick a name for your business
Your ability to earn extra money will somehow seem much more real the moment you give your selected business a name. So name it here and now. Use a name you can live with for a long time, a descriptive name, a memorable name.

### Brain-Search: List the modules to which your business can connect
Ask yourself: What kind of related businesses can my business connect with as part of a modular system? List all that come to mind. Remember, the more businesses

that are part of your modular system, the more customers you will attract.

### Brain-Search: List your prime customers
Make a short list of your prime customers. They may be housewives or fishermen or teenagers or churches or small businesses or retailers or just about anyone.

### Brain-Search: List the media you'll need
Refer back to chapter 1 for the various types of marketing media. Look over the media that I suggested for the particular earnway you are considering. If I suggested classified ads, now is the time to list the newspapers in which the ads will appear. If I suggested posting signs on bulletin boards, now is the time to list the locations of those bulletin boards. It ought to be easy for you to make this list because you have a clear idea of your prime customers.

### Brain-Search: List the services you'll need
Depending on the complexity of the earnway, you may or may not need some services to get your business going. If you do, list them now. Perhaps you'll need the advice of a good lawyer. Most likely you'll want to talk with an accountant. You may need to develop a relationship with a banker or an insurance person. You may need an advertising agent, an artist, a printer, a person to distribute your circulars or pin up your signs. This is the time to determine the exact services required to make your business professional in every way.

### Brain-Search: List the training you'll need
To succeed in your chosen earnway, perhaps you'll have to read a few books. Maybe you'll have to take a course, attend a seminar, put in time as an apprentice, talk to someone who is already succeeding doing what you wish to do.

It's amazing, but people will usually be more than happy to tell you exactly how to succeed in their businesses. They're usually pleased that you recognize them as experts.

### Brain-Search: List the tools you'll need

Be sure you're armed with the proper earning tools. You can buy them, rent them, find them, lease them, borrow them, trade for them, or finance them handling the payments with the earnings you realize using them. There's a very good chance you already have many or all of the tools you need.

### Brain-search: List the costs that are involved

It is possible to get involved in earning endeavors without investing one cent, but chances are you will have to put out some cash. This will probably go to your lawyer, accountant, ad makers, printer, Yellow Pages listing, stationery, training costs, tools, business phone (if required), and advertising. Of course, your earnway may not require those costs.

You may need to include the cost of renting an office, work space, or warehouse, the cost of a free-lance typist, postal costs, office equipment costs, or licensing fees. Typically, your total cash outlay will not be very high, but be prepared to pay a little now to earn a lot later.

### Brain-Search: Write your marketing plan

Once you've written your marketing plan, your earning gun is loaded and aimed. So take the time to write a great plan, rereading chapter 6 before you do, even seeking the advice of a marketing consultant if necessary (but it probably won't be necessary since you have most of the data you require in chapter 6). By now you should be prepared to write a very effective marketing plan.

### *Brain-Search: List the steps you must take and when you'll take them*

List the exact steps that must be taken to get your earnway going. Such steps might include calling a lawyer for an appointment, selecting an accountant, ordering stationery and business cards, actually placing an ad in the Yellow Pages, putting a sign up on a bulletin board, telling some prospects that you are in business, writing a circular for your business, enlisting the aid of a fellow earner, creating a classified ad.

As you list each step, write down exactly *when* you will do it. By giving yourself the timing and then keeping to the deadlines you make for yourself, you will bring your earnway to life.

As you actually do the things you have scheduled yourself to do, you'll be pulling the trigger of your carefully loaded and aimed gun. Your target will be extra money. By following the route that you mapped out in this chapter, you cannot help but score a bull's-eye.

### *Complete a brain-search for your nine other earnways*

This has been a relatively long book, especially compared to my first book on earning, which was only forty-three pages long. I'm taking no chances. I want you to succeed in a big way. Now I'm telling you to complete a brain-search for each of your nine other earnways—as comprehensive a brain-search as you have just completed for your first earnway. Do these things and I am certain that you absolutely will earn extra money, quite a bit of it.

### *Write your affirmations*

Turn your selected earnways into affirmations. Look over chapter 7 again and plug into your unconscious power. Make your earnways into affirmations, and your unconscious will make them into money.

I have been assuming that you sincerely want to earn extra money. Although patchwork economics can be fun, it is not a game. It is basically a survival system, and I honestly want it to work for you, either as a supplement to your current one-main-job life-style or as a fully developed alternate system.

You began this book because you wanted to earn extra money. Now you've learned 555 ways to earn it. You have the magic to ignite your mind. You know the exact route from dream to reality.

As the book reaches its end, you have reached a beginning.

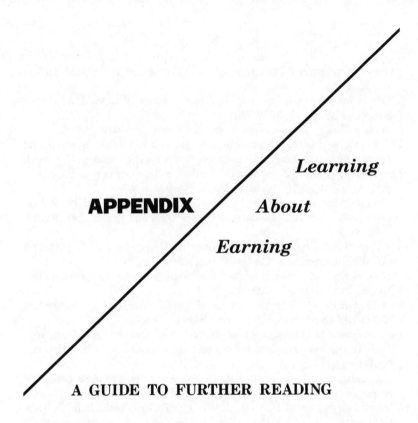

APPENDIX

*Learning*

*About*

*Earning*

## A GUIDE TO FURTHER READING

*Reference Information*

*Annual Register of Grant Support*, Marquis Academic Media, 200 East Ohio St., Chicago, IL 60611.

*The Bradford Book of Collector's Plates*, The Bradford Exchange, Niles, Chicago, IL 60648.

Brand, Stewart, ed. *The Next Whole Earth Catalog*. New York: Random House/Sausalito, CA: Point (PO Box 428, Sausalito, CA 94966), 1980.

Cole, Katherine W., ed. *Minority Organizations: A National Directory*. Garrett Park, MD: Garrett Park Press, 1967.

Daniells, Lorna M. *Business Information Sources*. Berkeley, CA: University of California Press, 1976.

*Dictionary of Occupational Titles*, Superintendent of Documents, U.S. Government Printing Office, Washington, DC 20402.

*Employment and Earnings*, U.S. Department of Labor, Bureau of Labor Statistics, U.S. Government Printing Office, Washington, DC 20402.

*Franchise Opportunities Handbook*, U.S. Department of Commerce,

Superintendent of Documents, U.S. Government Printing Office, Washington, DC 20402.

*Guide to Summer Camps and Summer Schools*. Boston, MA: Porter Sargent Publishers, 1979–80.

*Lovejoy's College Guide*. New York: Simon and Schuster, 1979.

*The Magazine Index*, Information Design, Ltd (an index machine that helps you locate magazine articles; you'll find it in most libraries).

*The National Career Development Project* (a list of career counselors in your area), Box 379, Walnut Creek, CA 94596.

*Reader's Guide to Periodical Literature*. Bronx. NY: The H.W. Wilson Company. (This is a standard reference book and is available in most libraries.)

*Small Business Reporter*, Bank of America, Department 3120, P.O. Box 37000, San Francisco, CA 94137 (periodical).

*Standard Rate & Data Business Publication Rates and Data*, MacMillan, Inc., Skokie, IL 60077.

*Standard Rate & Data Consumer Magazine and Farm Publication Rates and Data*, MacMillan, Inc., Skokie, IL 60077.

*Subject Guide to Books in Print*. New York: R.R. Bowker Company. (This is another standard reference that is available in libraries and bookstores.)

Todd, Alden. *Finding Facts Fast: How to Find Out What You Want to Know Immediately*. Berkeley, CA: Ten Speed Press, 1979.

*Ulrich's International Periodicals Directory*. New York: R.R. Bowker Company.

*The World Almanac and Book of Facts*. New York: Newspaper Enterprise Association (annual).

### Books About Living

Alpert, Dr. Richard. *Be Here Now*. New York: Crown Publishing, 1971.

*America's Centenarians*. 14 vols. Washington, DC: Social Security Administration.

Bach, Richard. *Illusions*. New York: Delacorte Press/Eleanor Friede, 1978.

Bateson, Gregory. *Mind and Nature*. New York: E. P. Dutton, 1979.

Bettmann, Otto L. *The Good Old Days—They Were Terrible!* New York: Random House, 1974.

Charland, William A., Jr. *Decide to Live*. Philadelphia: Westminster Press, 1979.

Emerson, Ralph Waldo. *Self-Reliance* (essays). New York: Peter Popper, 1967.

Fromm, Erich. *To Have or To Be?* New York: Harper and Row, 1976.

Gussow, Joan. *The Feeding Web*. Palo Alto, CA: Bull Publishing, 1978.

Hecht, Miriam, and Traub, Lillian. *Alternatives to College*. New York: Macmillan, 1974.

Johnson, Warren. *Muddling Toward Frugality*. San Francisco: Sierra, 1978.

Leonard, George. *The Silent Pulse*. New York: E. P. Dutton, 1978.

Linden, Eugene. *Affluence and Discontent: The Anatomy of Consumer Societies*. New York: Viking, 1979.

Miller, Arthur F., and Mattson, Ralph T. *The Truth About You: Discover What You Should Be Doing With Your Life*. Tappan, NJ: Fleming H. Revell Company, 1977.

Nelson, Richard C. *Choosing: A Better Way to Live*. Lake Park, FL: Guidelines Press, 1978.

Perls, Frederick. *In and Out of the Garbage Pail*. New York: Bantam Books, 1972.

Sale, Kirkpatrick. *Human Scale*. New York: Coward-McCann and Geoghegan, 1980.

Schumacher, E. F. *Guide for the Perplexed*. New York: Harper and Row, 1979.

Schumacher, E. F. *Small Is Beautiful*. New York: Harper and Row, 1976.

Valaskakis, Kimon, et al. *The Conserver Society*. New York: Harper Colophon, 1979.

Wagschal, Peter H., and Kahn, Robert D., eds. *R. Buckminster Fuller on Education*. Amherst, MA: The University of Massachusetts Press, 1979.

### Books About Working

Bart, Joe. *The Ten Dollar Book That Can Make You Rich*. Secaucus, NJ: Lyle Stuart, 1976.

Baty, Gordon. *Entrepreneurship: Playing to Win*. Reston, VA: Reston Publishing, 1974.

Bolles, Richard Nelson. *What Color Is Your Parachute? A Practical Manual for Job Hunters and Career Changers*. Berkeley, CA: Ten Speed Press, 1980.

Burns, Scott. *The Household Economy*. Boston: Beacon Press, 1977.

Caple, John. *The Right Work: Finding It and Making It Right*. New York: Dodd, Mead, 1987.

Caple, John. *The Ultimate Interview: How To Get It, Get Ready, and Get The Job You Want*. New York: Doubleday, 1990.

Channing, Peter. *Scratching Your Entrepreneurial Itch*. New York: Hawthorn Books.

Daly, Herman. *Steady-State Economics*. San Francisco: Freeman, 1977.

Dible, Donald M. *The Pure Joy of Making More Money*. Santa Clara, CA: The Entrepreneur Press, 1968.

Dible, Donald M. *Up Your OWN Organization: A Handbook for the Employed, the Unemployed, and the Self-Employed on How to Start and Finance a New Business*. Santa Clara, CA: The Entrepreneur Press, 1974.

Elkstrom, Ruth; Harris, Abigail; and Lockheed, Marlaine. *How to Get College Credit for What You Have Learned as a Homemaker and Volunteer*. Princeton, NJ: Educational Testing Service.

Gilchrist, Glenn. *How To Make Money With Your Home Computer*. West Islip, N.Y.: Information Sources Unlimited, 1989.

Goldberg, Herb, and Lewis, Robert T. *Money Madness: The Psychology of Saving, Spending, Loving and Hating Money*. New York: New American Library, 1979.

Greer, Rebecca. *How to Live Rich When You're Not*. New York: Ballantine, 1977.

Hill, Napoleon. *Think and Grow Rich*. New York: Fawcett Books, 1979.

Hirsch, Fred; Doyle, Michael; and Morse, Edward L. *Alternatives to Monetary Disorder*. New York: McGraw-Hill, 1977.

Kamaroff, Bernard. *Small-Time Operator*. Laytonville, CA: Bell Springs, 1981.

Kroll, Kenneth. *The Freelancer's Bible*. West Orange, NJ: Kroll Enterprises, 1974.

Levinson, Jay Conrad. *Quit Your Job!* New York: Dodd, Mead, 1987.

Linder, Staffan B. *The Harried Leisure Class*. New York: Columbia University Press, 1970.

Lutz, Mark, and Lux, Kenneth. *Humanistic Economics: Fundamentals and Applications*. Menlo Park, CA: Benjamin-Cummings, 1979.

Matthews, Kathy. *On Your Own*. New York: Vintage Books, 1977.

Medley, Anthony H. *Sweaty Palms: The Neglected Art of Being Interviewed*. Belmont, CA: Lifetime Learning Publications, 1978.

Meier, Gretl. *Job-Sharing: A New Pattern for Quality of Work and Life*. Kalamazoo, MI: W. E. Upjohn Institute for Employment Research, 1979.

Orr, Leonard. *The Money Seminar*. San Francisco: Prosperity International.

Phillips, Michael, et al. *The Seven Laws of Money*. New York: Random House, 1974.

Rivers, Patrick. *The Survivalists*. New York: Universe, 1976.

Schwimmer, Lawrence. *How to Ask for a Raise Without Getting Fired*. New York: Harper and Row, 1980.

Scitovsky, Tibor. *The Joyless Economy*. New York: Oxford University Press, 1976.

Weaver, Peter. *YOU, INC., A Detailed Escape Route to Being Your Own Boss*. Garden City, NY: Doubleday, 1975.

### Finance

Blechman, Bruce, and Levinson, Jay Conrad. *Guerrilla Financing: Alternative Techniques To Finance*. Boston: Houghton Mifflin, 1991.

Edwards, James D. and Black, Homer A., eds. *The Modern Accountant's Handbooks*. New York: Dow Jones-Irwin, 1976.

Myer, John N. *Accounting for Non-Accountants*. New York: E. P. Dutton, 1980.

Picchione, Nicholas, CPA. *Dome Simplified Bookkeeping Record #612*. Providence, RI: Dome Publishing Company, 1981.

### Law

Last, Jack. *Everyday Law Made Simple*. Garden City, NY: Doubleday, 1978.

Nicholas, Ted. *How to Form Your Own Corporation Without a Lawyer for Under Fifty Dollars*. Wilmington, DE: Enterprise Publishing, 1980.

Ross, Martin J., and Ross, Jeffrey S. *Handbook of Everyday Law*. New York: Harper and Row, 1981.

### Marketing

Lant, Jeffrey L. *The Unabashed Self-Promoter's Guide*. Jeffrey Lant Association, 1983.

Levinson, Jay Conrad. *Guerrilla Marketing: Secrets for Making Big Profits from Your Small Business*. Boston: Houghton Mifflin, 1984.

Levinson, Jay Conrad. *Guerrilla Marketing Attack: New Strategies, Tactics and Weapons for Winning Big Profits from Your Small Business*. Boston: Houghton Mifflin, 1989.

Levinson, Jay Conrad. *Guerrilla Marketing Weapons: 100 Affordable Marketing Methods for Maximizing Profits from Your Small Business*. New York: Plume, 1990.

Ogilvy, David. *Ogilvy on Advertising*. New York: Crown, 1983.

Phillips, Michael, and Rasberry, Salli. *Marketing Without Advertising*. Berkeley: Ten-Speed Press, 1986.

Ross, Tom and Marilyn. *Big Marketing Ideas for Small Service Businesses*. Cincinnati: Writer's Digest Books, 1990.

Slutsky, Jeff. *Streetfighting: Low-Cost Advertising Promotion Strategies for Your Small Business*. Englewood Cliffs: Prentice-Hall, 1984.

## Salesmanship

Bach, Karl. *Selling Is Simple . . . If You Don't Make It Complicated.* San Francisco: Advance Books, 1979.

Bender, James. *How to Sell Well.* New York: McGraw-Hill, 1971.

Bettger, Frank. *How I Raised Myself from Failure to Success in Selling.* Englewood Cliffs, NJ: Prentice-Hall, 1958.

Buzzota, V. R. et al. *Effective Selling Through Psychology.* New York: Ballinger Publishing, 1968.

Evetts, Jonathan. *Seven Pillars of Sales Success.* New York: Sterling Publishing, 1990.

Gallagher, Bill, with Wilson, Orvel Ray and Levinson, Jay Conrad. *Guerrilla Selling.* New York: Houghton Mifflin, 1992.

## Mail Order

*Direct Marketing*, Hoke Publications, 224 7th Street, Garden City, NY 11535 (periodical).

Hodgson, Richard. *Direct Mail and Mail Order Handbook.* Chicago: Dartnell Corp., 1974.

Joffe, Gerardo. *How to Build a Great Fortune in Mail Order* (7 vols). San Francisco: Advance Books, 1980.

Joffe, Gerardo. *How You Too Can Make at Least One Million Dollars (But Probably Much More) in the Mail-Order Business.* San Francisco: Advance Books, 1979.

## Product Catalogs

*Asian Sources*, c/o Trade Media Ltd., PO Box K-1786, Kowloon Central, Hong Kong.

*Hong Kong Enterprise*, 3rd floor, Connaught Centre, Central Hong Kong.

*The Importer*, c/o East Asia Publishing Company, 2-11 Jingumae, 1-Chome, Shibuya-ku, Tokyo 150, Japan.

*Made in Europe*, PO Box 174027, C-6, Frankfurt/Main, 17, West Germany.

*The Next Whole Earth Catalog*, Point/Random House, Point, PO Box 428, Sausalito, CA 94966.

## Books About Efficiency

Cooper, Joseph. *How to Get More Done in Less Time.* Berkeley, CA: Whatever Publishing.

Drucker, Peter. *The Effective Executive.* New York: Harper and Row, 1967.

Laken, Alan. *How to Get Control of Your Time and Your Life.* New York: Peter H. Wyden, 1973.

LeBoeuf, Michael. *Working Smart.* New York: Warner Books, 1979.

Levinson, Jay Conrad. *The Ninety-Minute Hour.* New York: Dutton, 1989.

### Books About the Mind

Alexander, Joe. *A Winner's Workbook.* Los Angeles: Price/Stern/Sloan, 1978.

Bylinsky, Gene. *Mood Control.* New York: Scribner's, 1978.

Ehrenberg, Otto and Miriam. *The Psychotherapy Maze: A Consumer's Guide to the Ins and Outs of Therapy.* New York: Holt, Rinehart and Winston, 1977.

Erickson, Milton H. *Advanced Techniques of Hypnosis and Therapy.* New York: Grune and Stratton, 1967.

Erickson, Milton. *Hypnotic Realities.* New York: Irvington Publishers, 1976.

Gawain, Shakti. *Creative Visualization.* Berkeley, CA: Whatever Publishing, 1978.

Hanks, Kurt; Belliston, Larry; and Edwards, Dave. *Design Yourself.* Los Altos, CA: William Kaufmann, 1977.

Keyes, Ken, Jr. *Handbook to Higher Consciousness.* St. Mary, KY: Living Love Publishing, 1975.

Lester, John. *How to Solve All Your Money Problems Forever.* Los Gatos, CA: Vorco Publications, 1979.

Maltz, Maxwell. *Psycho-Cybernetics.* North Hollywood, CA: Wilshire Book Company, 1963.

Morris, Freda. *Self-Hypnosis in Two Days.* New York: E. P. Dutton, 1975.

*Patterns of Hypnotic Techniques of Milton H. Erickson, M.D.* Cupertino, CA: META, 1975.

Roberts, Jane. *The Nature of Personal Reality: A Seth Book.* Englewood Cliffs, NJ: Prentice-Hall, 1974.

Silva, Jose, and Miele, Philip. *The Silva Mind Control Method.* New York: Simon and Schuster, 1977.

### Books About the Future

Best, Fred. *The Future of Work.* Englewood Cliffs, NJ: Prentice-Hall, 1973.

Bundy, Robert. *Images of the Future: The Twenty-first Century and Beyond.* Buffalo, NY: Prometheus, 1976.

Gershuny, J. *After Industrial Society? The Emerging Self-Service Economy*. Atlantic Highlands, NJ: Humanities Press, 1978.

Harman, Willis. *An Incomplete Guide to the Future*. San Francisco: San Francisco Book Co., 1976.

Henderson, Hazel. *Creating Alternative Futures*. New York: Berkley Publishing, 1978.

Hiltz, Starr Roxanne, and Turoff, Murray. *The Network Nation: Human Communication via Computer*. Reading, MA: Addison-Wesley, 1978.

Kent, Saul. *The Life-Extension Revolution*. New York: William Morrow, 1980.

Kerr, Clark, and Rosow, Jerome M., eds. *Work in America: The Decade Ahead*. Work in America Series. New York: Van Nostrand Reinhold, 1979.

Mueller, Robert Kirk. *Metadevelopment: Beyond the Bottom Line*. Lexington, MA: Lexington Books, 1977.

Panati, Charles, *Breakthroughs: Astonishing Advances in Your Lifetime in Medicine, Science, and Technology*. Boston: Houghton Mifflin, 1980.

Sheppard, C. Stewart, ed. *Working in the Twenty-First Century*. New York: Wiley-Interscience, 1980.

Toffler, Alvin. *The Third Wave*. New York: William Morrow, 1981.

## Books About Earning Endeavors

Adams, John F. *Beekeeping*. New York: Avon, 1974.

Anderson, Jack. *The Plum Book: The Official United States Guide to Leading Positions in the Government, Presidential and Executive Appointments, Salaries, Requirements, and Other Vital Statistics for Job Seekers*. New York: Bolder Books, 1977.

Brown, Norman. *Trace Your Own Roots Workbook*. New York: Grosset and Dunlap, 1978.

Casey, Betty. *The Complete Book of Square Dancing*. Garden City, NY: Doubleday, 1976.

Cole, Nancy H. *Puppet Theater in Performance: Everything You Need to Know About Putting on Puppet Plays*. New York: William Morrow, 1978.

Crookston, Stephanie. *Creative Cakes*. New York: Random House, 1978.

Doss, Margot Patterson. *The Bay Area at Your Feet*. San Francisco: Presidio Press, 1981.

Douglas, James. *Beginner's Guide to Hydroponics*. New York: Sterling Publishing Co., 1979.

Downing, George. *The Massage Book*. New York: Random House, 1972.

Fox, Carl. *The Doll.* New York: Harry N. Abrams, 1973.

*The Foxfire Book* (and *Foxfire,* 2, 3, and 4). Garden City, NY: Anchor Press/Doubleday, 1972.

Fridell, Squire. *Acting in Television Commercials for Fun and Profit.* Greenport, NY: Harmony Books, 1980.

Glenn, Peggy. *How to Start and Run a Successful Home Typing Business.* Huntington Beach, CA: Pigi Publishing, 1980.

Glenn, Peggy. *Word Processing Profits At Home.* Huntington Beach, CA: Aames-Allen, 1983.

Goeltz, Judy, and Lazenby, Patricia. *Thanks, I Needed That: The Beginner's Natural Food Cookbook.* Salt Lake City: Hawkes Publishing, 1975.

Hardigree, Peggy. *Strike It Rich!* Greenport, NY: Harmony Books, 1980 (a good book on metal detecting).

Hoffman, George. *How to Inspect a House.* New York: Delacorte, 1979.

Inkeles, Gordon, and Todris, Murray. *The Art of Sensual Massage.* New York: Simon and Schuster, 1974.

Johnstad, Jack and Lois. *Attaining Financial Peace of Mind.* San Rafael, CA: Bright Spirit Press, 1980.

Kahm, H. S. *101 Businesses You Can Start and Run with Less Than $1,000.* Garden City, NY: Doubleday, 1973.

Kloss, Jethro. *Back to Eden.* Santa Barbara, CA: Lifeline Books, 1976.

Kraus, Richard. *Square Dances of Today and How to Teach and Call Them.* New York: Ronald Press, 1950.

Kuroff, Barbara. *Songwriter's Market 1981.* Cincinnati: Writers Digest Books, 1980.

Lapin, Lynne. *Artist's Market 1981.* Cincinnati: Writers Digest Books, 1980.

Lapin, Lynne. *Craftworker's Market 1981.* Cincinnati: Writers Digest Books, 1980.

Lembeck, Ruth. *One Thousand One Job Ideas for Today's Woman.* New York: Doubleday, 1975.

Levinson, Jay Conrad. *Earning Money Without a Job.* New York: Henry Holt, 1991.

Levinson, Jay Conrad. *Secrets of Successful Free-Lancing.* San Rafael, CA: Prosper Press, 1981.

Lynch, John, ed. *The Coffee Table Book of Astrology.* New York: Viking Press, 1967.

Ransom, J. Ellis. *Gold Hunter's Field Book.* New York: Harper and Row, 1980.

Robertson, Laurel, et al. *Laurel's Kitchen.* Petaluma, CA: Nilgiri Press, 1976.

Rogovin, Mark; Burton, Marie; and Highfall, Holly. *Mural Manual: How to Paint Murals for the Classroom, Community Center, and Street Corner.* Boston: Beacon Press, 1973.

Schemenauer, Peggy. *Writer's Market 1981.* Cincinnati: Writers Digest Books, 1980.

Seltz, David. *A Treasury of Business Opportunities.* Rockville Centre, NY: Farnsworth Publishing, 1976.

Shenson, Howard. *How to Establish and Operate Your Own Consulting Practice.* Englewood Cliffs, NJ: Prentice-Hall Spectrum, 1979.

Shindler, Robert E. *The Get Rich Report.* Herndon, VA: NVP Publishing, 1979.

Siposs, George G. *Cash In on Your Bright Ideas.* Costa Mesa, CA: Universal Developments, 1980.

*Sunset Western Garden Book.* Menlo Park, CA: Lane Publishing, 1981.

Uhlan, Edward. *The Rogue of Publishers' Row.* New York: Exposition Press, 1956.

Young, Jean and Jim. *Garage Sale Manual.* New York: Praeger Publishers, 1973.

### Earning Periodicals

*Advertising Age*, 740 N. Rush St., Chicago, IL 60611.

*American Collector*, Crain Consumer Group, 13920 Mt. McClennan Ave., Reno, NV 89506.

*American Film*, The American Film Institute, John F. Kennedy Center for the Performing Arts, Washington, DC 20566.

*American Metal Market*, Fairchild Publications, 7 East 12th St., New York, NY 10003.

*American Printer and Lithographer*, 300 West Adams St., Chicago, IL 60606.

*The Antiques Journal*, Babka Publications, 100 Bryant St., Dubuque, IA 52001.

*Aquaculture Magazine*, Briggs Associates, Box 2451, Little Rock, AR 72203.

*Art in America*, Whitney Publications, 850 Third Ave., New York, NY 10022.

*The Be-Your-Own-Boss Catalog. Entrepreneur* magazine, 2392 Morse Avenue, P.O. Box 19787, Irvine, CA 92713, 1-800-421-2300.

*Better Nutrition*, Syndicate Magazines, 6 East 43rd St., New York, NY 10017.

*Bicycling*, Rodale Press, 33 E. Minor St., Emmaus, PA 18049.

*Boat Owners' Buyers Guide*, Yachting Publishing, 1 Park Ave., New York, NY 10016.

*Business Intelligence Digest,* 1501 Broadway, New York, NY 10036.

*Coin Prices,* Krause Publications, 700 E. State St., Iola, WI 54945.

*Computerworld,* CW Communications, 375 Cochituate Rd., Framingham, MA 01701.

*Cuisine,* 420 Lexington Ave., New York, NY 10017.

*Demolition Age,* Bracker Communications, 940 Pine St., Glenview, IL 60025.

*Direct Marketing,* Hoke Publications, 224 7th St., Garden City, NY 11535.

*Editor and Publisher,* 575 Lexington Ave., New York, NY 10022.

*Entrepreneur Business Manual Catalog,* International Entrepreneurs Association, 2392 Morse Ave., P.O. Box 19787, Irvine, CA 92713, 1-800-421-2300.

*Entrepreneur* magazine, 2392 Morse Ave., P.O. Box 19787, Irvine, CA 92713, 1-800-421-2300.

*Entrepreneurial Manager's Newsletter,* The Center for Entrepreneurial Management, Inc., 180 Varick St., New York, NY 10014, 1-800-247-7642.

*Field and Stream Fishing Annual,* CBS Publications, 1515 Broadway, New York, NY 10036.

*Fins and Feathers,* 318 W. Franklin St., Minneapolis, MN 55404.

*Fishing Facts,* Northwoods Publishing Co., Inc., U.S. Highway 41-45, PO Box 609, Menomonee Falls, WI 53051.

*Fishing World,* Allsport Publishing Corp., 51 Atlantic Ave., Floral Park, NY 11001.

*Fly Fisherman Magazine,* Dorset, VT 05251.

*Free Enterprise,* 800 Second Ave., New York, NY 10017.

*The Futurist,* World Future Society, PO Box 30369, Bethesda Branch, Washington, DC 20014 (a periodical with many earning-oriented articles and ideas).

*Gourmet,* 777 Third Ave., New York, NY 10017.

*Greetings Magazine,* MacKay Publishing Corporation, 95 Madison Ave., New York, NY 10016.

*The Guerrilla Marketing Newsletter,* 260 Cascade Drive, P.O. Box 1336, Mill Valley, CA 94942, 1-800-748-6444.

*In Business,* The JG Press, 625 Third St., San Francisco, CA 94107.

*Inc.,* United Marine Publishing, 38 Commercial Wharf, Boston, MA 02110.

*Income Opportunities,* Davis Publications, 380 Lexington Ave., New York, NY 10017.

*Insiders Magazine,* PO Box 879, New Hyde Park, NY 11040.

*Journal of Marketing,* American Marketing Association, 222 S. Riverside Plaza, Chicago, IL 60606.

*Journal of Marketing Research*, American Marketing Association, 222 S. Riverside Plaza, Chicago, IL 60606.

*Linn's Stamp News*, Amos Press, 911 Vandemark Rd., Sidney, OH 45367.

*Money Making Magic*, Leo Minton, LeTono Publishing, 622 NE Paloma Ave., Gresham, OR 97030.

*Money-Making Opportunities*. Success Publishing Company, 13263 Ventura Blvd., Studio City, CA 91604.

*Moneysworth*, 251 W. 57th St., New York, NY 10019.

*Mother Earth News*, 105 Stoney Mountain Rd., Hendersonville, NC 28739.

*New Ventures*, 9003 Reseda Blvd., Northridge, CA 91324.

*Opportunity* magazine, 6N Michigan, Chicago, IL 60611.

*Organic Gardening*, Rodale Press, 33 E. Minor St., Emmaus, PA 18049.

*The Pet Dealer*, Howmark Publishing, 225 W. 34th St., New York, NY 10001.

*Popular Mechanics*, 224 West 57th St., New York, NY 10019.

*Popular Science Monthly*, 380 Madison Ave., New York, NY 10017.

*Specialty Salesman and Business Opportunities*, Communications Channels, 307 N. Michigan Ave., Chicago, IL 60601.

*Tradeshow/Convention Guide*, Budd Publications, PO Box 7, New York, NY 10004.

*Vending Times*, 211 E. 43rd St., New York, NY 10017.

*Venture: The Magazine for Entrepreneurs*, 35 W. 45th St., New York, NY 10036.

*The Writer*, 8 Arlington St., Boston, MA 02116.

*Writer's Digest*, 2 East 12th St., Cincinnati, OH 45210.


# HOT LINES

| | |
|---|---|
| Department of Agriculture | (202) 447-5551 |
| Bureau of the Census | (202) 568-1200 |
| Department of Commerce | (202) 377-3263 |
| Department of Commerce: Economic News | (202) 393-4100 |
| Department of Commerce: News Highlights | (202) 393-1847 |
| Department of Commerce: Weekend Feature | (202) 393-4120 |
| Congress: | |
|    HOUSE OF REPRESENTATIVES | |
|      Floor Activity Democratic | (202) 225-7400 |
|      Floor Activity, Republican | (202) 225-7430 |
|      Democratic Legislative Program | (202) 225-1600 |

| Republican Legislative Program | (202) 225-2020 |
|---|---|
| SENATE | |
| Floor Activity, Democratic | (202) 224-8541 |
| Floor Activity, Republican | (202) 224-8601 |
| Bureau of Economic Analysis | (202) 523-0777 |
| Consumer Product Safety Commission News | (800) 638-8329 |
| Economic Development Administration | (202) 377-5113 |
| Economic News Highlights, Joint Economic | |
| Committee of U.S. Congress | (202) 224-3081 |
| Department of Energy News | (800) 424-9128 |
| Federal Reserve System | (202) 452-3204 |
| Federal Trade Commission | (202) 523-3598 |
| General Services Administration | (202) 566-1231 |
| Health and Human Services | (202) 245-1850 |
| Housing and Urban Development | (202) 755-6980 |
| Department of Interior | (202) 343-3171 |
| International Trade Administration | (202) 377-3808 |
| Interstate Commerce Commission | (202) 275-7252 |
| Department of Justice | (202) 633-2007 |
| Department of Labor | (202) 523-7316 |
| Department of Labor News | (202) 523-8756 |
| Department of Labor News Features | (202) 523-6899 |
| Bureau of Labor Statistics | (202) 523-1913 |
| Minority Business Development Agency | (202) 377-1936 |
| U.S. Patent & Trademark Office | (703) 557-3428 |
| U.S. Postal Service | (202) 245-4144 |
| Small Business Administration | (202) 653-6822 |
| Small Business Administration | |
| Business Publications | (800) 433-7212 |
| Department of State | (202) 632-9606 |
| Treasury Department | (202) 566-2041 |

## COURSES AND SEMINARS

Career Workshops, Inc., 1801 East Franklin St., Chapel Hill, NC 27514.

Cross, Wilbur. *The Weekend Education Source Book.* New York: Harper and Row, 1976.

The John C. Crystal Center, Inc., 894 Plandome Rd., Manhasset, NY, 11030 (lectures, workshops, courses on career development).

*Directory of Approved Counseling Agencies*, prepared by the International Association of Counseling Services, Inc., 1607 New Hampshire Ave. NW, Washington, DC 20009.

*Guerrilla Marketing International*, Box 1336, 260 Cascade Dr., Mill Valley, CA 94942, 1-800-748-6444.

Job Forums–run in various cities by the local chamber of commerce (also run by service organizations, sales executive clubs, advertising clubs).

Marketing Professional Services, New York University, School of Continuing Education, 360 Lexington Ave., New York, NY 10017 (this course offered nationally–call (800) 223-7450 for a free brochure).

New Ways to Work, a nonprofit resource center, 457 Kingsley Ave., Palo Alto, CA 94301.

Referrals, National Career Development Project, Box 379, Walnut Creek, CA 94596.

Right Livelihood Associates, 1152 Sanchez St., San Francisco, CA 94114.

The Small Business Administration (SBA), U.S. Department of Labor, Washington, DC 20416; free workshops at least once a month in ninety U.S. cities.